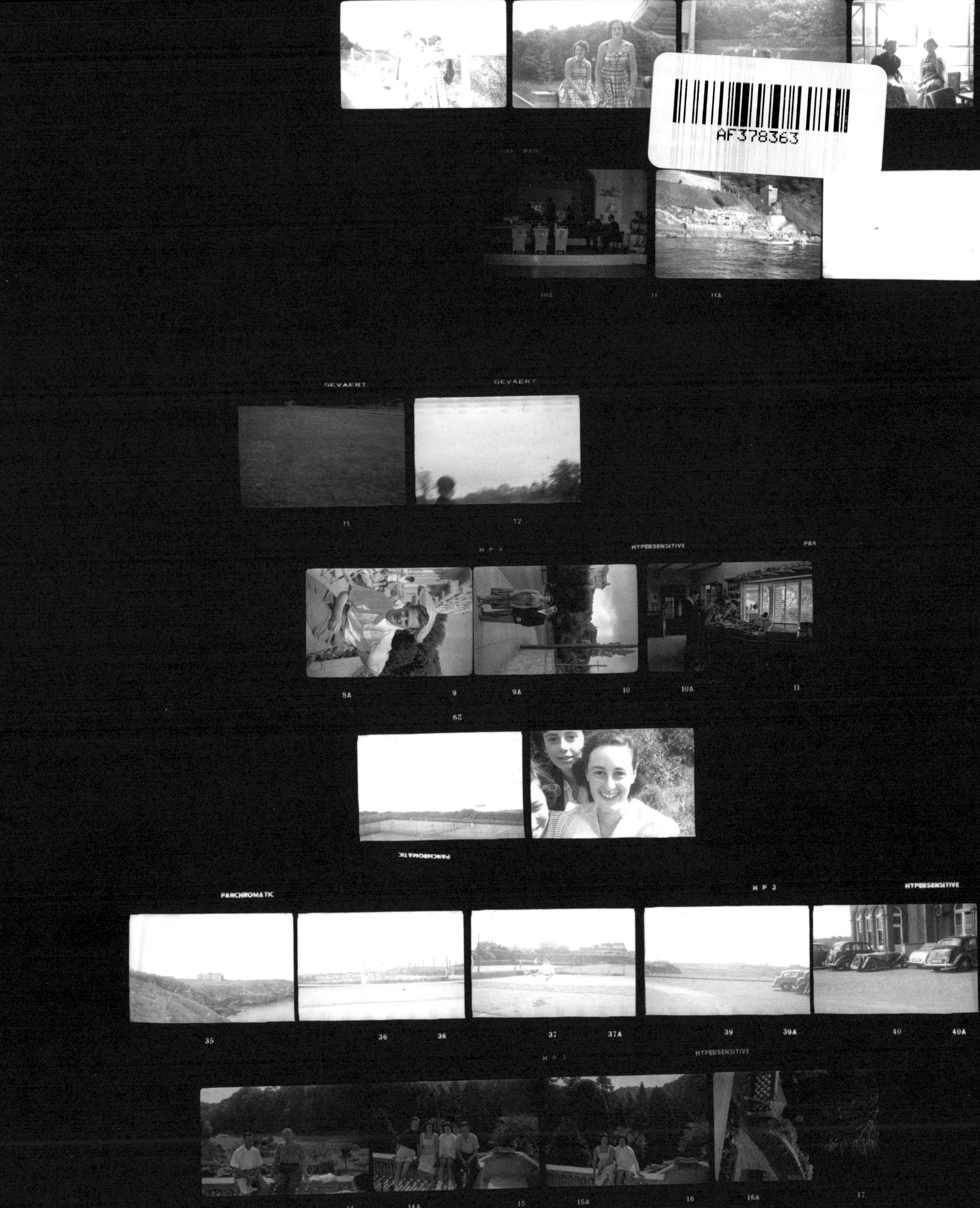

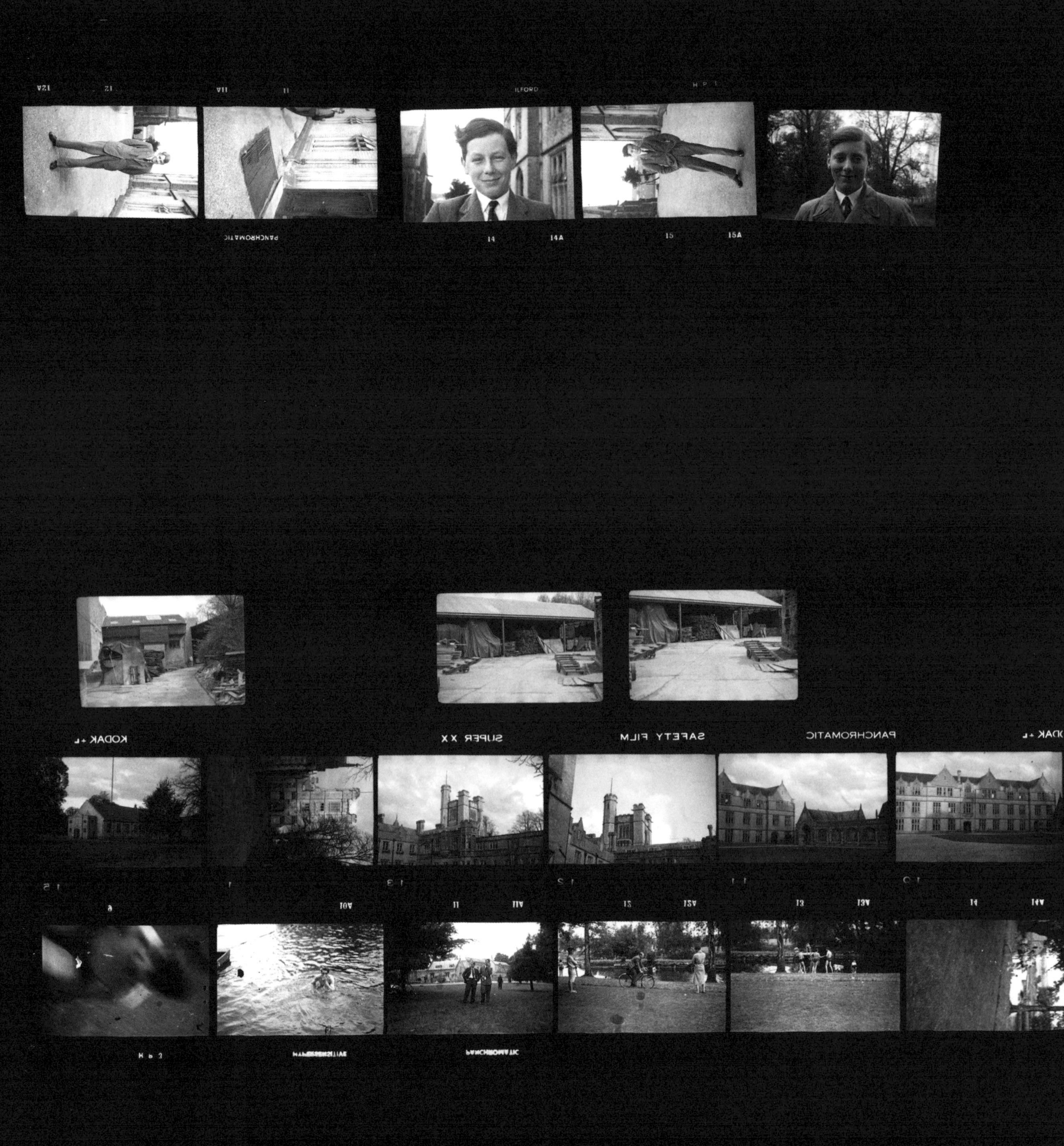

Photographs Found

by Basil Hyman

Booth-Clibborn Editions

Original concept by Value & Service and ARPA
Designed by ARPA (A Research Projects Agency)
Edited by Anna Bennett
Additional material co-ordinated by Binny Hudson
Photographic assistance Julia Campagna
Text © Basil Hyman and Anna Bennett

All photography by Basil Hyman with the exception
of pages 11, 16, 26, 28–29, 53, 58, 60–61
© Basil Hyman's family archive

First published in 2012 by Booth-Clibborn Editions
in the United Kingdom, www.booth-clibborn.com

© Booth-Clibborn Editions 2012
Printed and bound in China

The information in this book is based on material
supplied to Booth-Clibborn Editions by the author.
While every effort has been made to ensure accuracy,
Booth-Clibborn Editions does not under any
circumstances accept responsibility for any errors
or omissions.

A Cataloguing-in-Publication record for this book
is available from the Publisher.

ISBN 978-1-86154-332-5

Also by Basil Hyman, *Collecting Photography*, *The Lost
Album* and, with Steven Braggs, *The G-Plan Revolution*.

Photographs Found

A Personal Memoir of 1960s Britain

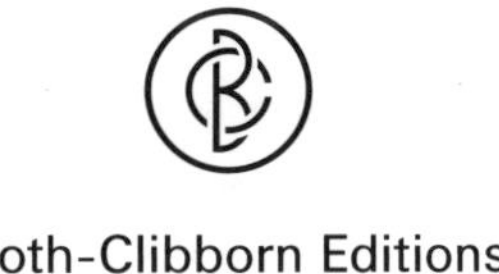

Booth-Clibborn Editions

Preface

Following the gift of a camera on my ninth birthday, I began to take photographs
of unusual or special events or people, quite unaware that these pictures might
one day be a historical record of everyday life in Britain.

I took photographs throughout the 1950s and 1960s, after I purchased
a dream Leica camera (second-hand) and these shots, which I have recently
unearthed, in some way sum up Britain during those days for me. What a time
it was. As the fifties gave way to the sixties, everyday life and indeed life on
a wider, more international level changed. The innocence of the fifties was lost
forever, as people, with the advent of the sixties, grew to know and expect a
lot more. Characterised by change and social revolution, the crazy, hedonistic
sixties are wedged between the post-war austerity of the fifties and the drabness
of the seventies. Much happened on the international stage during the sixties.
The American invasion of the Bay of Pigs in Cuba took place in 1961 and the
Cuban missile crisis followed in 1962. It was a decade during which the Cold
War – very much in the foreground in the fifties – still raged, and the Vietnam
War (which had begun in 1955) continued, in the face of mounting opposition,
mainly in the form of protest marches. There were high-profile assassinations,
of President John F. Kennedy and, later, his brother Robert, and of civil rights
activist Dr Martin Luther King. The Berlin Wall was erected in 1961, the actress
Marilyn Monroe was found dead in 1962, Nelson Mandela was imprisoned in
1964 and Dr Christian Barnaard performed the world's first heart transplant
operation in South Africa in 1967. The Six-Day War in the Middle East took
place in 1967, and the Prague uprising occurred in 1968, the same year which
saw the student riots in Paris. The decade ended with Neil Armstrong taking
his first steps on the Moon in 1969. By the end of the sixties we had come
a long way since the fifties.

Britain, too, saw its fair share of momentous historical events during the
sixties. The decade began with Princess Margaret marrying Antony Armstrong-
Jones, a commoner and, in true sixties fashion, a photographer. Also in 1960
British yachtsman Francis Chichester sailed solo across the Atlantic. Abortion
became legal during these years, as did homosexuality between consenting
adults, and the contraceptive Pill paved the way for the sexual revolution that
was to change society in Britain irrevocably. The Profumo scandal took the
country by storm in 1963, when the MP John Profumo lied to the House of
Commons about his relationship with call-girl Christine Keeler and was forced to
resign. It was the time of Beatlemania and the untimely death of their manager,
my cousin and friend Brian Epstein. I took photographs of Brian at this time.
Never did I imagine the fame and excitement that lay ahead for Brian and his
protégés, but also the imminent tragedy that was to befall him.

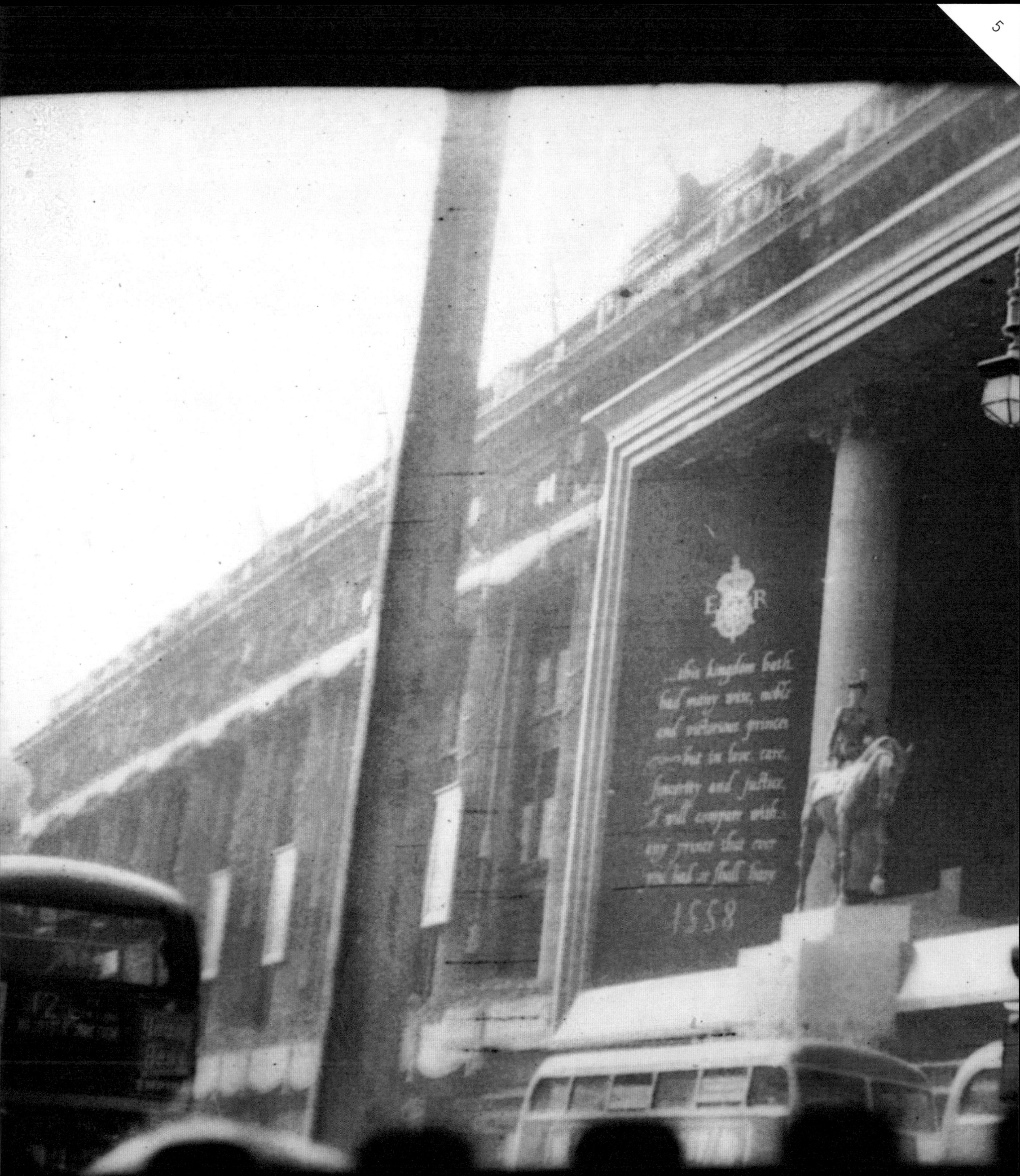
E R
...this kingdom hath
had many wise, noble
and virtuous princes
but in love, care,
sincerity and justice,
I will compare with
any prince that ever
you had or shall have
1558

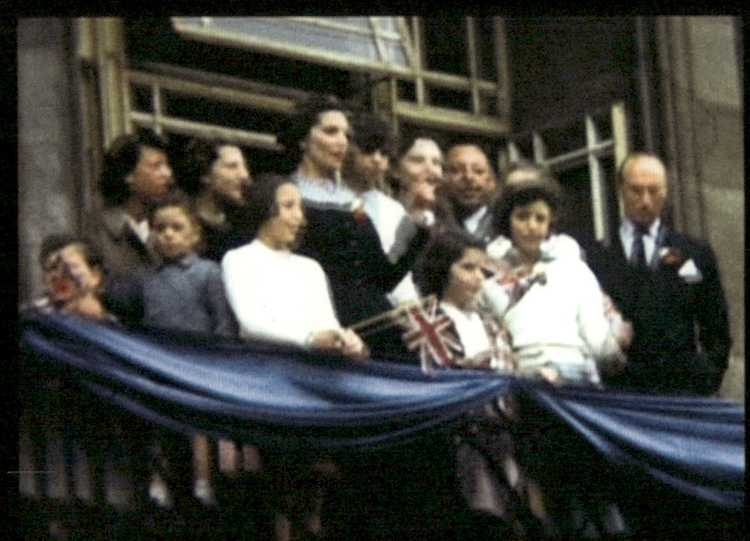
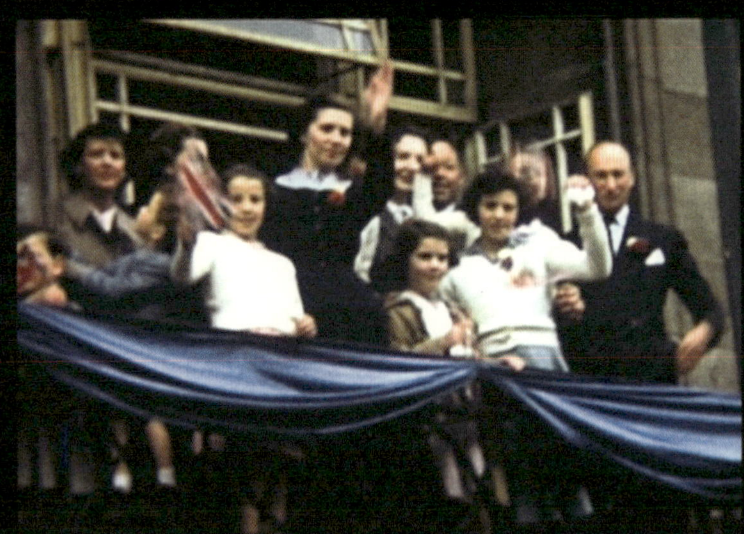
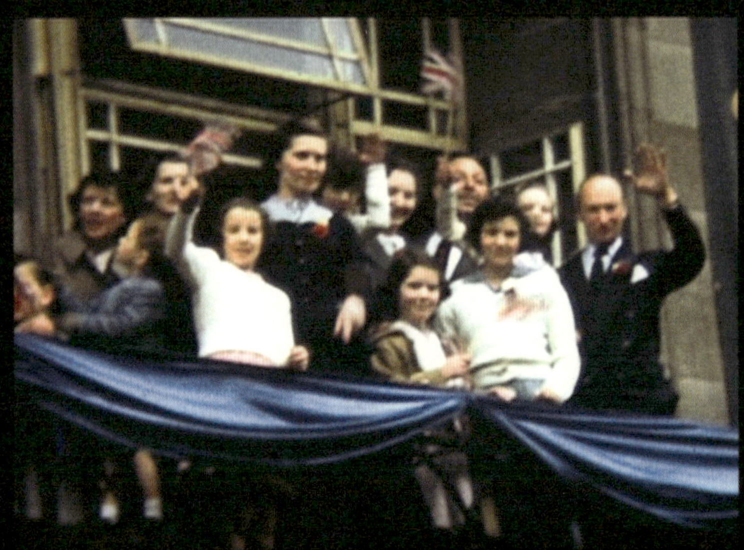
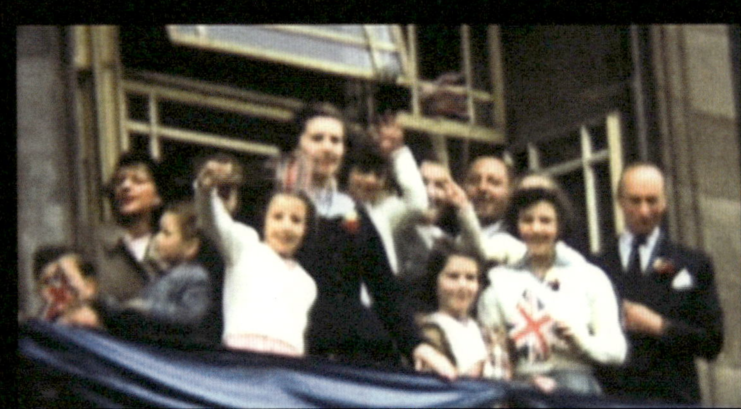
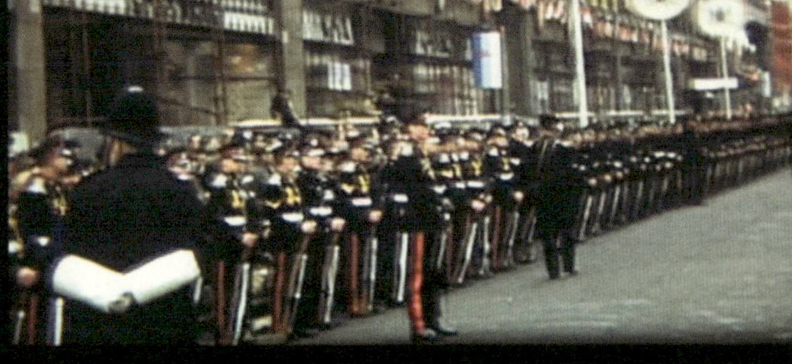
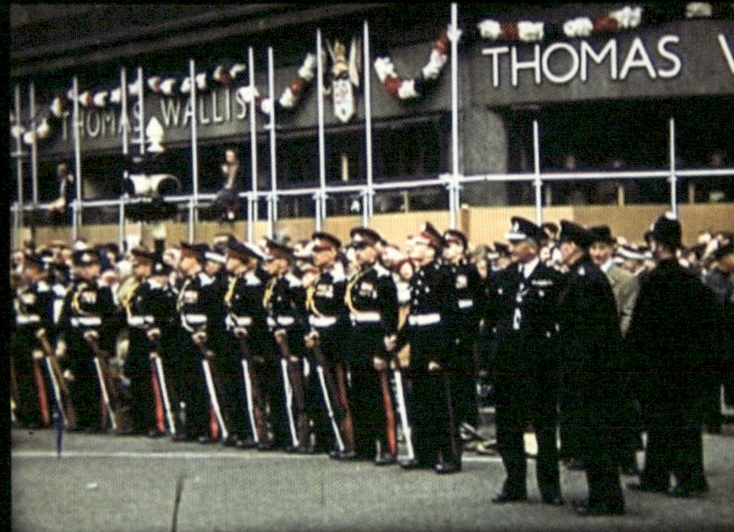
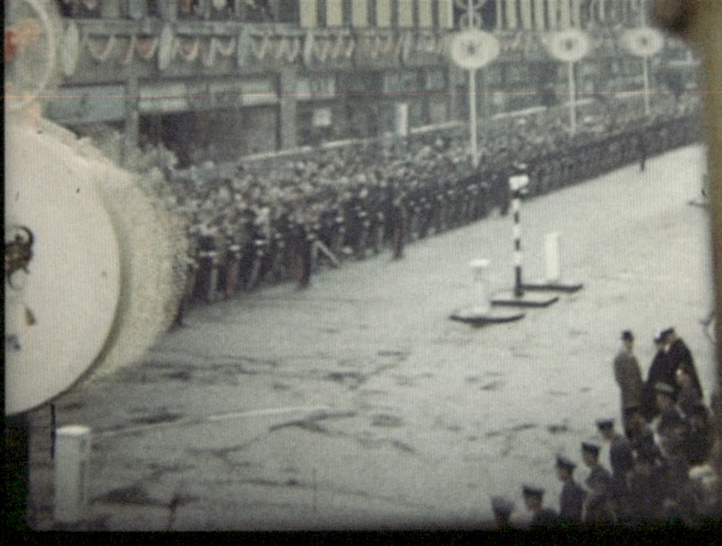
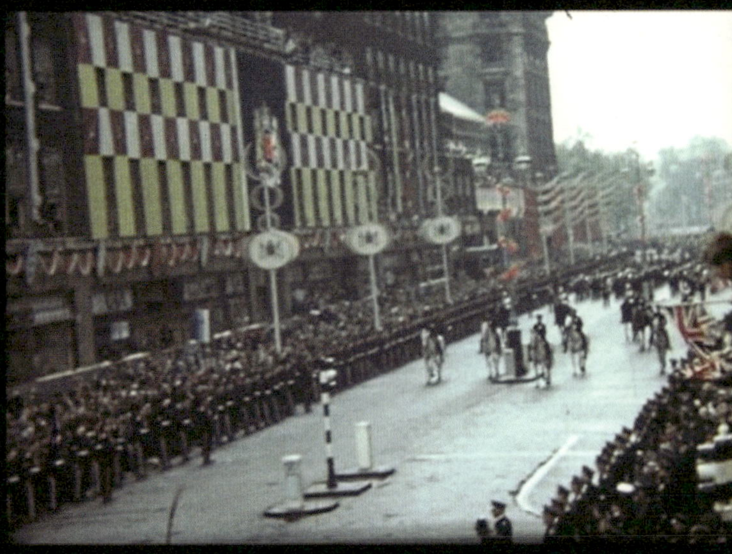

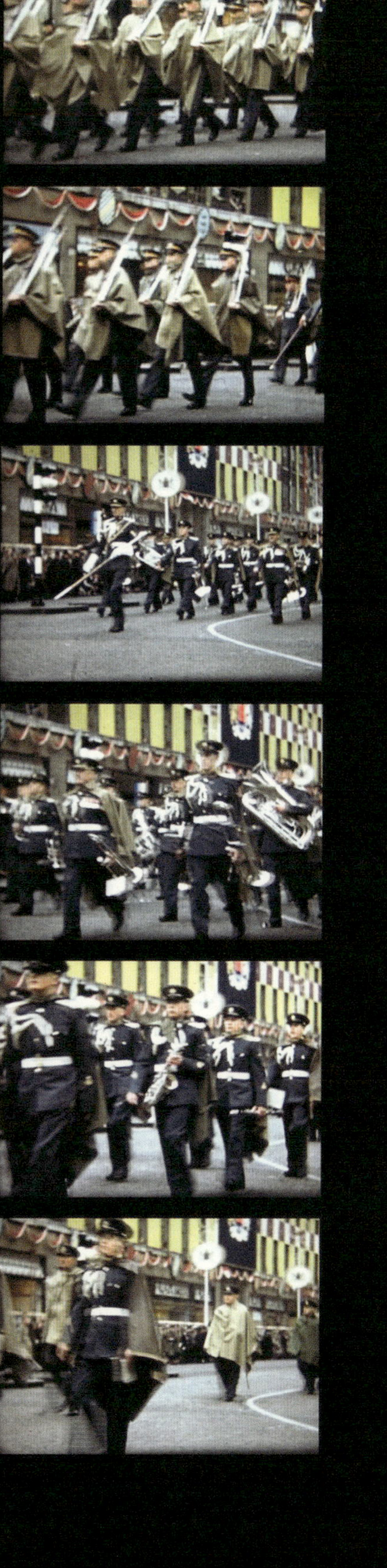
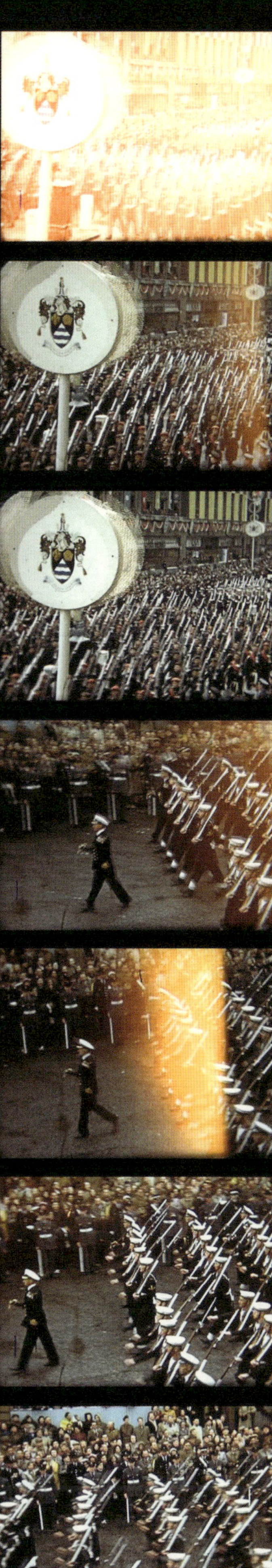
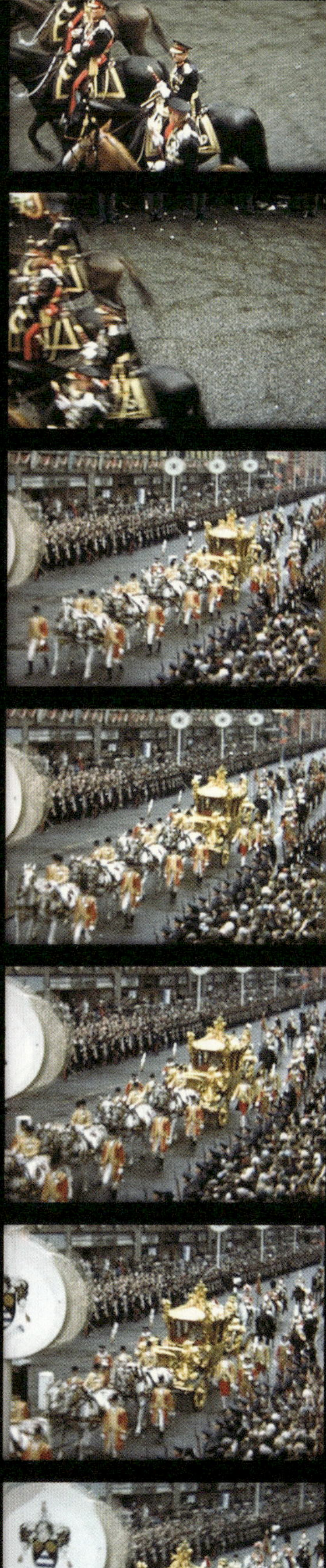

Alongside Mary Quant, the mini-skirt (my wife, in common with many other young women at the time, wore a mini-skirt during the sixties, much to her parents' horror), Twiggy, David Bailey and Jean Shrimpton, Biba and Carnaby Street, Flower Power, the Summer of Love and the wild psychedelia of the 1960s, however, ordinary life in Britain still went on, much as it had during the fifties, albeit with certain dramatic changes. There was a total change of dress, for example, and ladies' hair was piled high on their heads in the traditional 'beehive' style; many saved up to have their hair cut and styled by Vidal Sassoon, who sadly passed away recently, one of the innovative hairdressers of the decade.

The sixties were undoubtedly very colourful years which, in a sense, picked up where the fifties had left off. They were years during which an on-going rebellion against the establishment, an aspired-for classlessness, the rise of consumerism and an overall mood of change prevailed, but it was also in many respects an age of innocence and naivety, and a time when the pace of life was slower. Avocadoes, as well as other foods, hit the supermarkets for the first time during the sixties, an unheard of luxury in the UK at the time, and strawberries were merely 1/6d a punnet. Restaurants were making their mark with the introduction of new dishes: La Popote in Walton Street was very popular (they constantly played music by Ray Conniff), as was Ronnie Scott's. This was the start of new clubs: the Saddle Room instigated a new type of night club where people would twist the night away. Furniture became ever sleeker, a trend which had begun in the fifties, and house design as a whole changed. Package holidays enjoyed a heyday at this time, with many people taking night flights. There may have been a set limit on the amount of currency you could take out of Britain, but people nevertheless travelled further afield in search of new adventures. And if you preferred to stay in Britain, it was the era in which the popularity of Butlins holiday camps soared; activities presided over by the ever-present Redcoats (staff in red blazers) guaranteed an action-packed holiday. It was also the age of the cine camera: whereas in the 50s photographs (typically, in black and white) were the record of choice of important events, so in the 60s colour film prevailed instead. The old order was superseded by a buzzing cult of the new.

These photographs try to capture everyday life in Britain at this time, and pay tribute to the transition between the 1950s and the 1960s. There was now no going back.

Basil Hyman

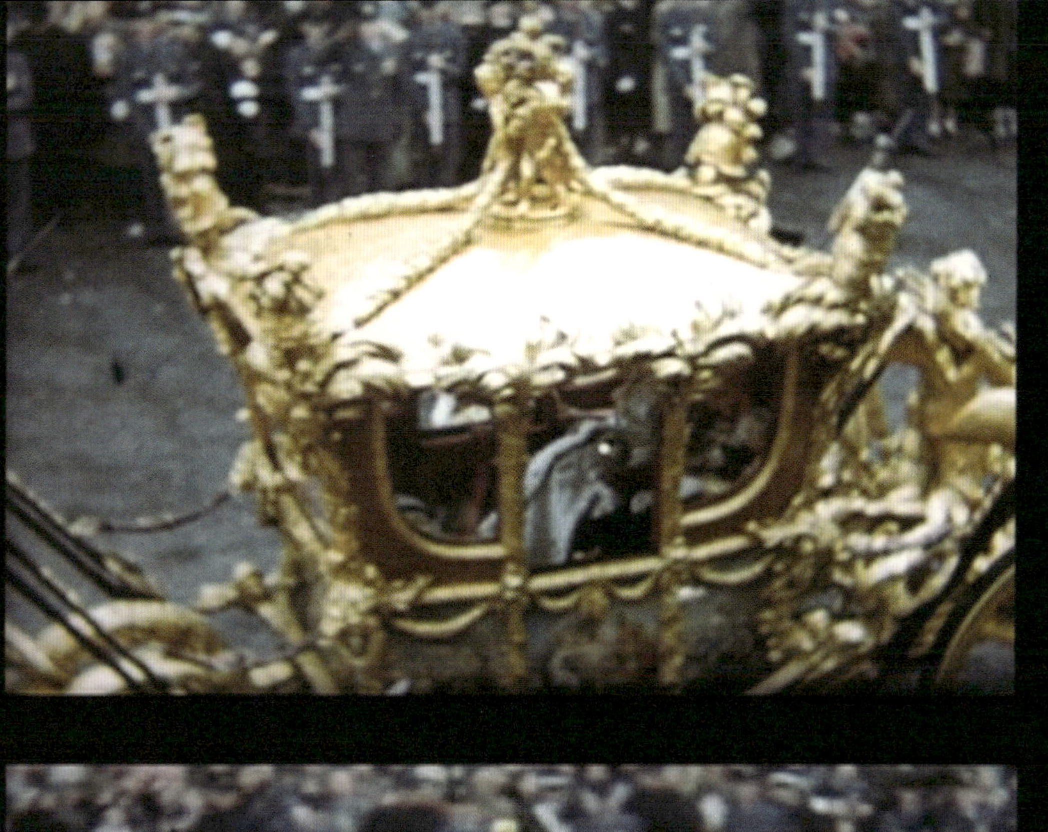
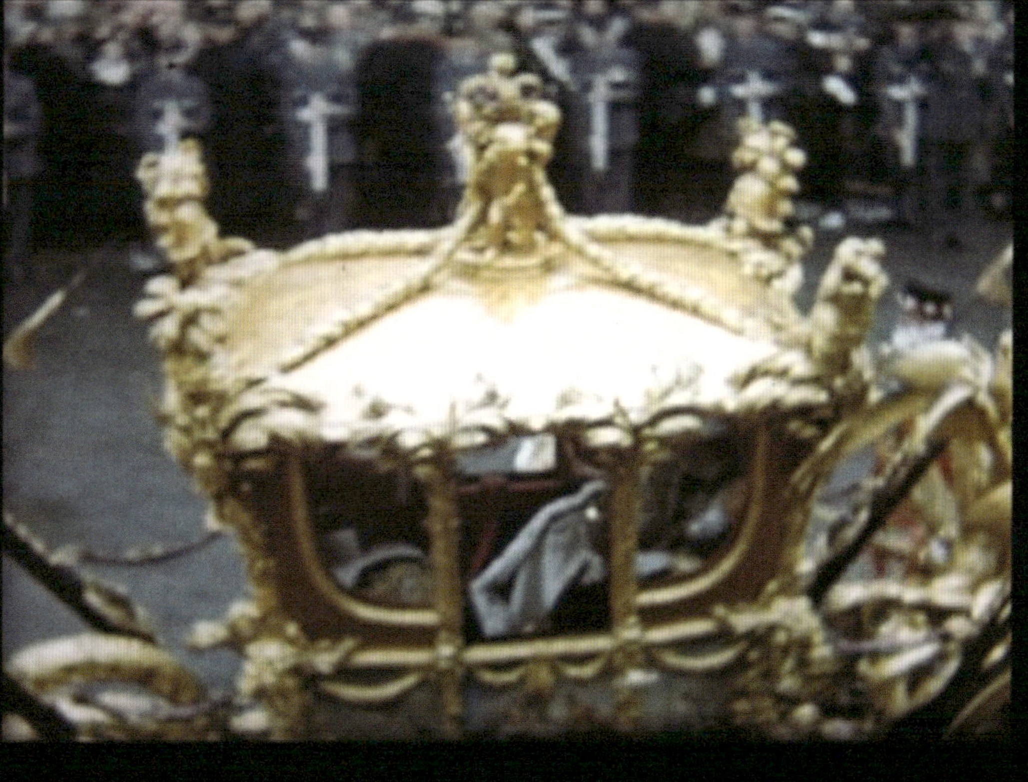
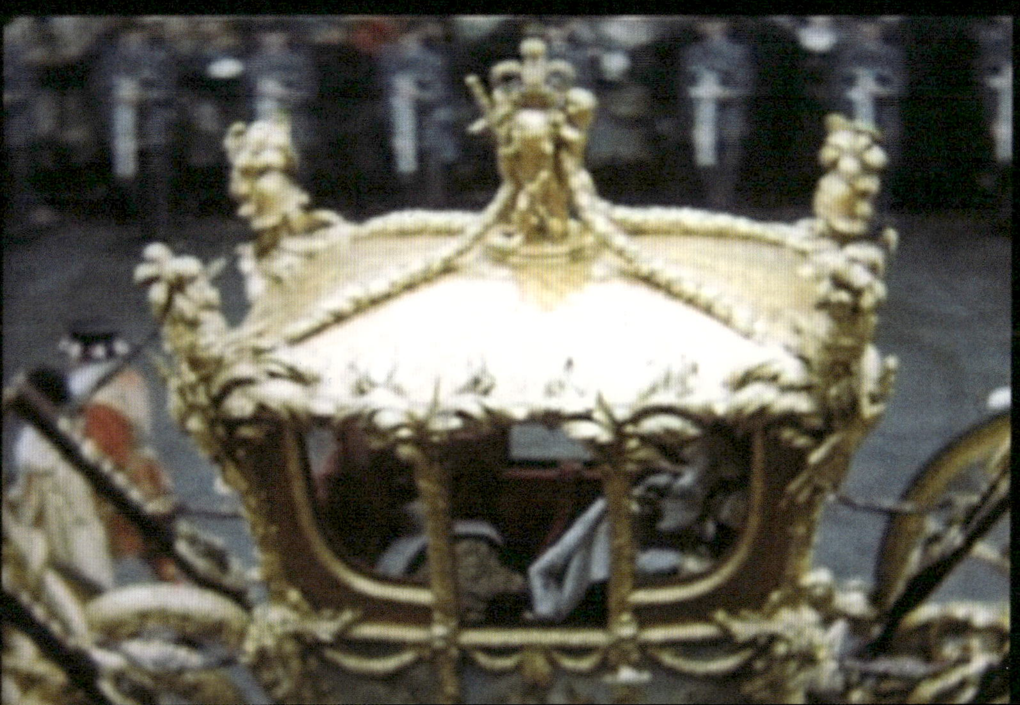

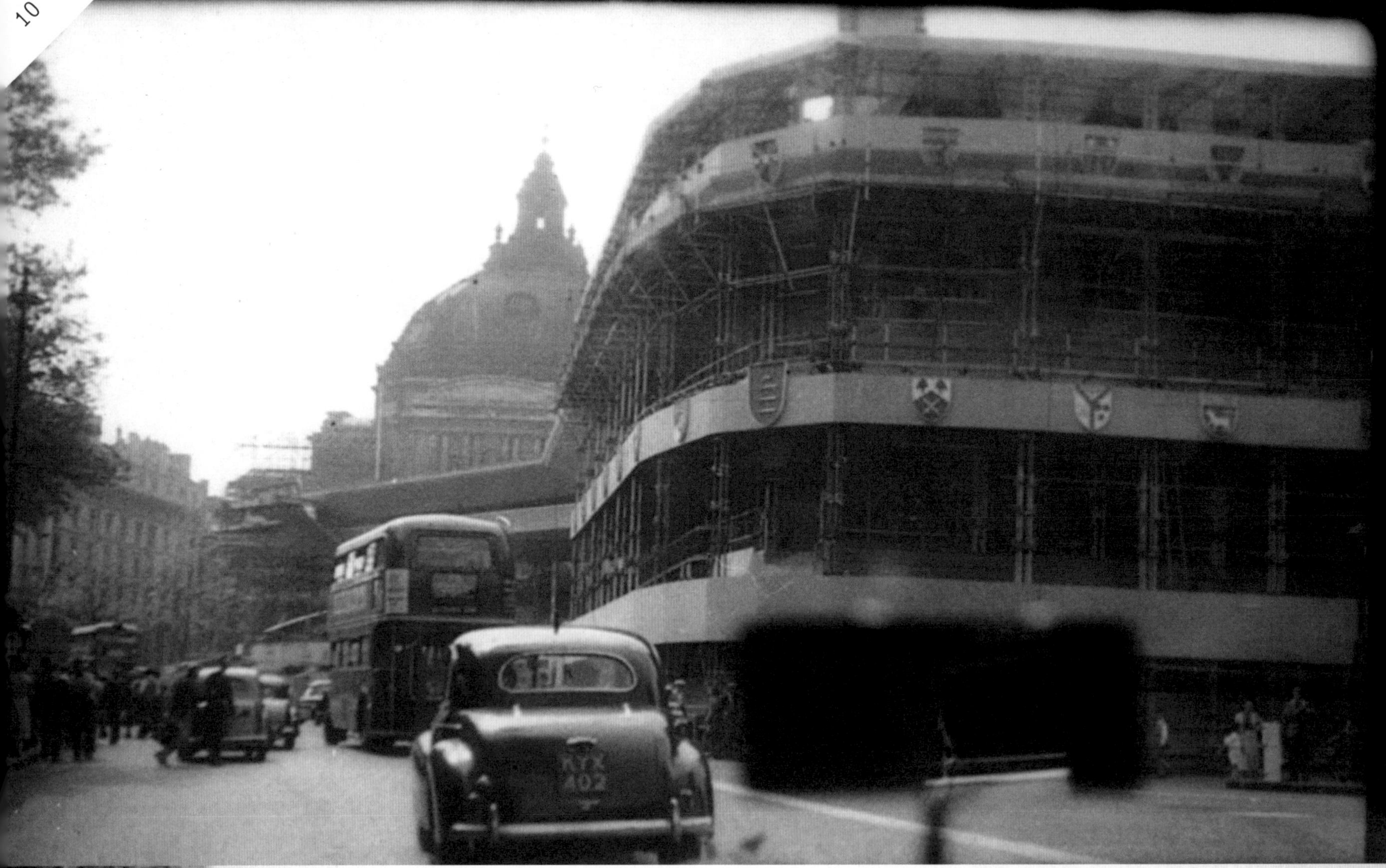

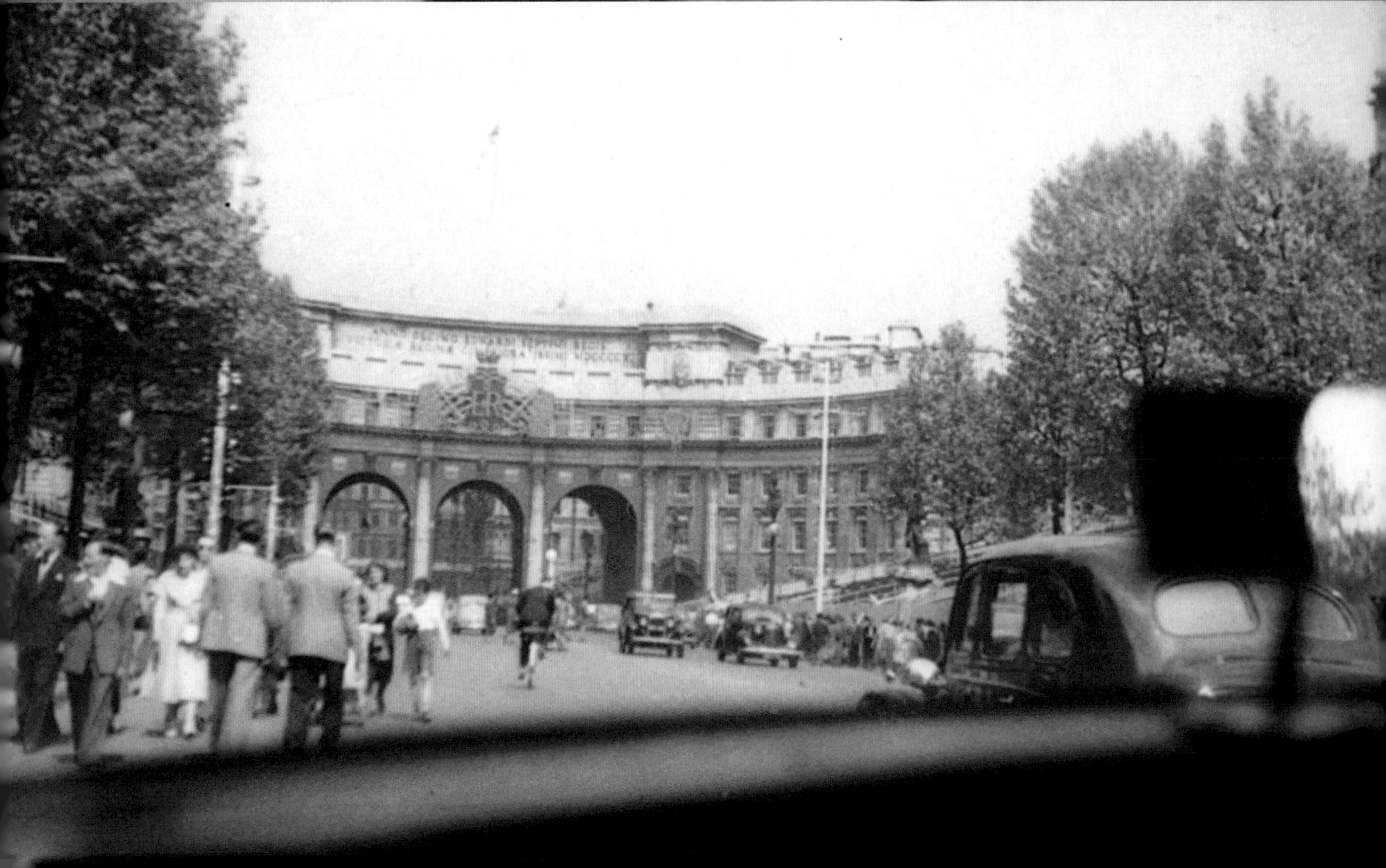

FOLLOW THE QUEEN

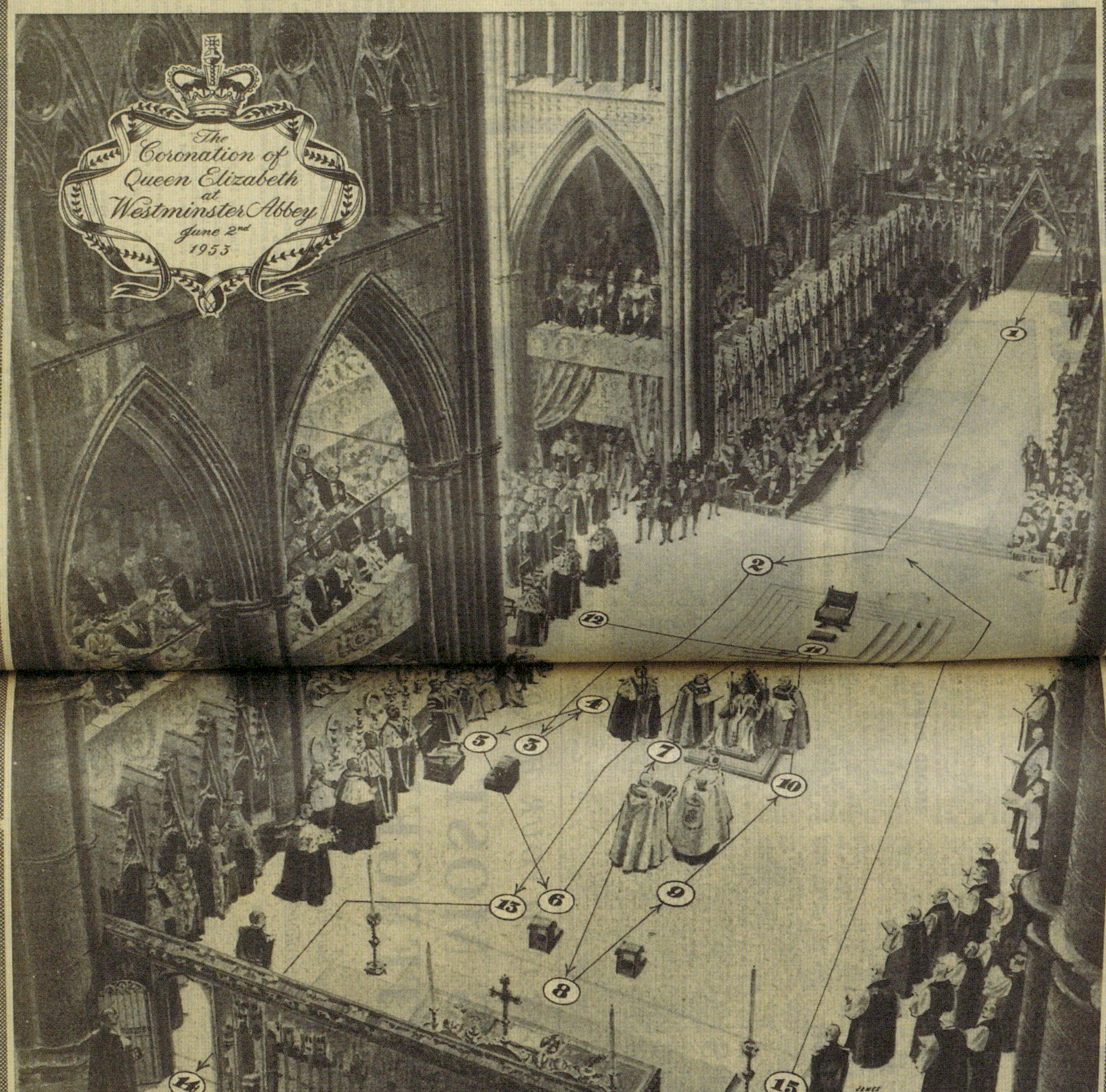

PRESENTATION GUIDE TO THE ABBEY CROWNING

Specially drawn for 'Pic' readers by James Gardner

1 *The Queen* wearing a robe of crimson velvet held by seven ladies of high degree and on her head a jewelled diadem, passes up the Nave. As the Queen passes under the choir screen into the Sacrarium the Queen's Scholars of Westminster School shout, "Vivat Regina Elizabetha."

2 *Ascending* the steps of the Theatre before the Altar the Queen is met by the Archbishop of Canterbury.

3 *Proceeding* to the Chair of Estate, passing on her right the Royal Dukes behind whom stand the Peers, the Queen first kneels in private prayer. She seats herself, the ladies-in-waiting standing on either side. Behind her are the Queen Mother and members of the Royal Family. From here Prince Charles will view part of the ceremony.

4 *The Archbishop* moving along the Theatre, cries out so that all may hear: "Sirs, I here present unto you Queen Elizabeth your undoubted Queen." The Queen steps forward for the recognition by her people, who cry loudly: "God Save Queen Elizabeth."

5 *The Archbishop* stands before the Queen, who is now seated in the Chair of Estate, and asks her: "Will you solemnly promise to govern your peoples according to their respective laws and customs ?..." This she promises.

6 *The Queen* then passes to the Altar and, kneeling, lays her hand on the Great Bible and completes the Oath. The Archbishop begins the Communion service.

7 *The Choir* then sings the anthem, "Zadok the Priest," the Queen is divested of her crimson velvet and, dressed in simple white, sits down in King Edward's Chair. The Dean of Westminster comes down from the Altar with the Ampulla and pours the Holy Oil into the Spoon of Anointing. Four Knights support a canopy of cloth of gold over the Queen, who sits bowed and still. The Archbishop anoints her, then she is clothed in Cloth of Gold by the Dean, and receives the gold Spurs of Chivalry and the Bracelets—the latter a gift from the Commonwealth of Australia.

8 *The Queen* then takes the Jewelled Sword, rises and offers it on the Altar.

9 *Her Majesty* is then invested with the Robe Royal, a sheath of gold, in token of Imperial Dominion.

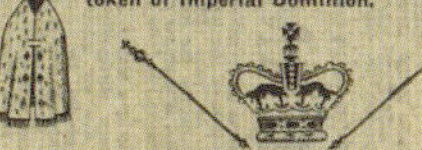

10 *Seated* again in King Edward's Chair, the Queen takes in her hand The Orb, which represents the world under the Cross of Christ the Redeemer. The Ring is placed on the Queen's finger, wedding her to her people. She then receives the chief symbols of authority: a Sceptre with a Cross for Power and Justice, and a Rod with a Dove for Equity and Mercy, and sits holding one in either hand. The Archbishop then lifts the Crown from its velvet cushion and lowers it on the Queen's head. The Peers and Peeresses put on their coronets. Then all present shout "God Save The Queen."

11 *The Queen* rises and, surrounded by dignitaries, proceeds to the Throne, where she is lifted to her seat by dignitaries of the Church and State. The Archbishop of Canterbury kneels before her, surrounded by the Bishops, who pledge allegiance through the Church.

12 *The Duke of Edinburgh* attended by a Page, then kneels before the Queen, places his hands between hers. He rises, kisses the Queen's cheek and touches the Crown. He is followed by the Royal Dukes and the senior Peers.

13 *Queen Elizabeth* then puts off her Crown and, with her husband, kneels to make her Communion as a simple Christian, before the Altar.

14 *She* then proceeds to St. Edward's Chapel for the Recess, to be robed in purple velvet and don the Imperial State Crown.

15 *So* robed and crowned, with the Sceptre in her right hand and the Orb in her left, the Queen passes down the Nave, followed by Lords and Ladies, to pass forth among her people, where she will ride crowned Queen in the Coronation Coach.

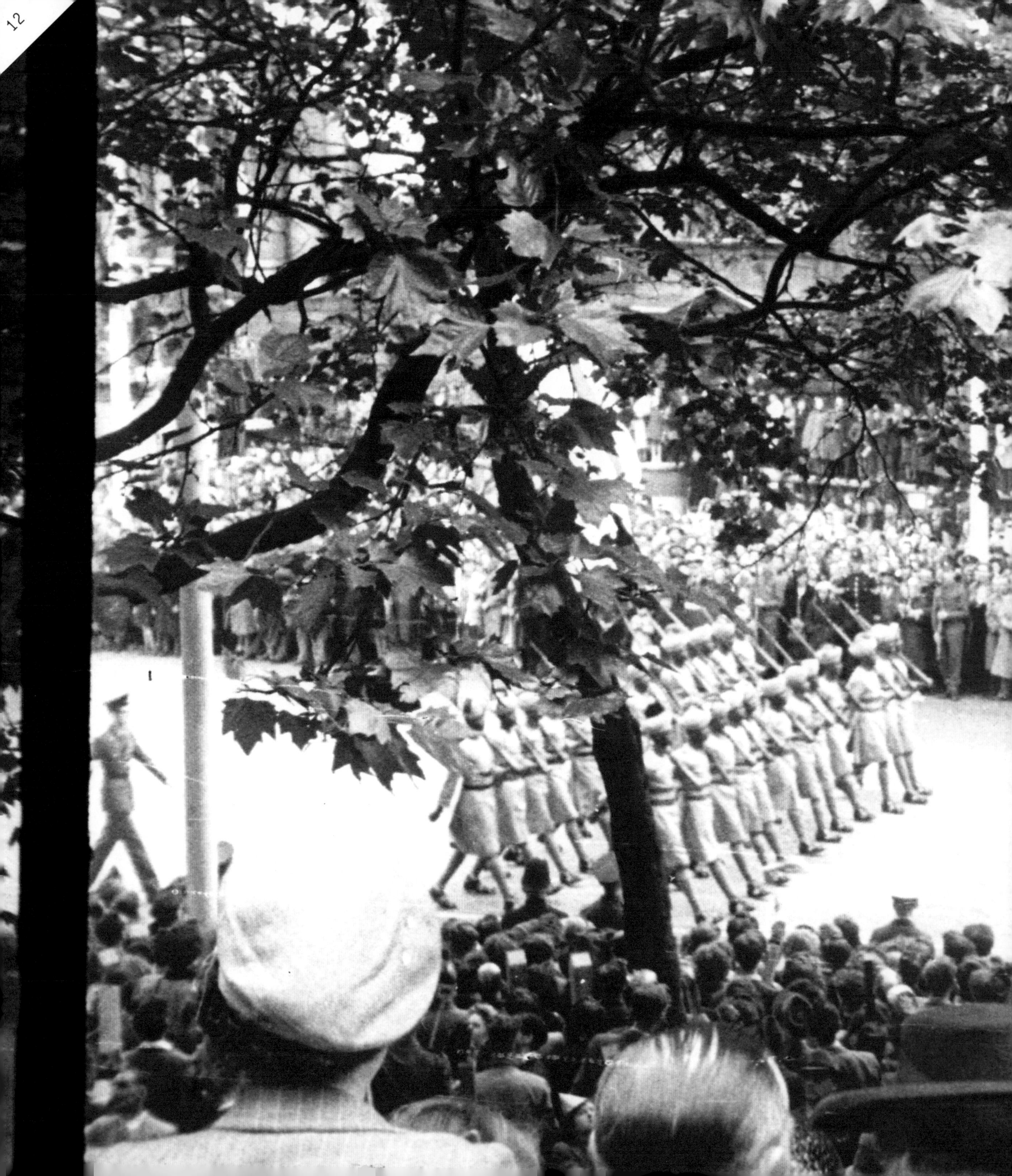

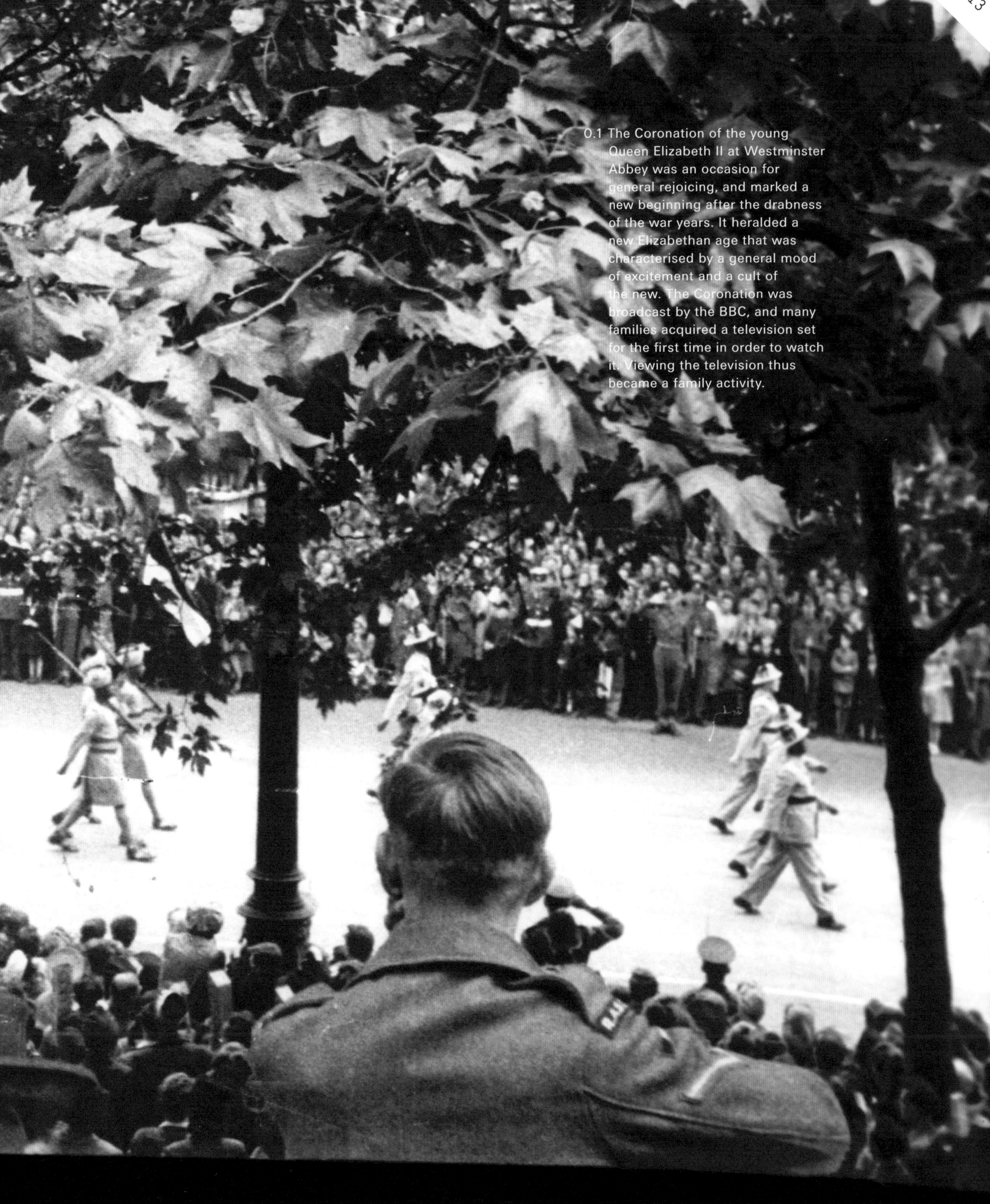

0.1 The Coronation of the young Queen Elizabeth II at Westminster Abbey was an occasion for general rejoicing, and marked a new beginning after the drabness of the war years. It heralded a new Elizabethan age that was characterised by a general mood of excitement and a cult of the new. The Coronation was broadcast by the BBC, and many families acquired a television set for the first time in order to watch it. Viewing the television thus became a family activity.

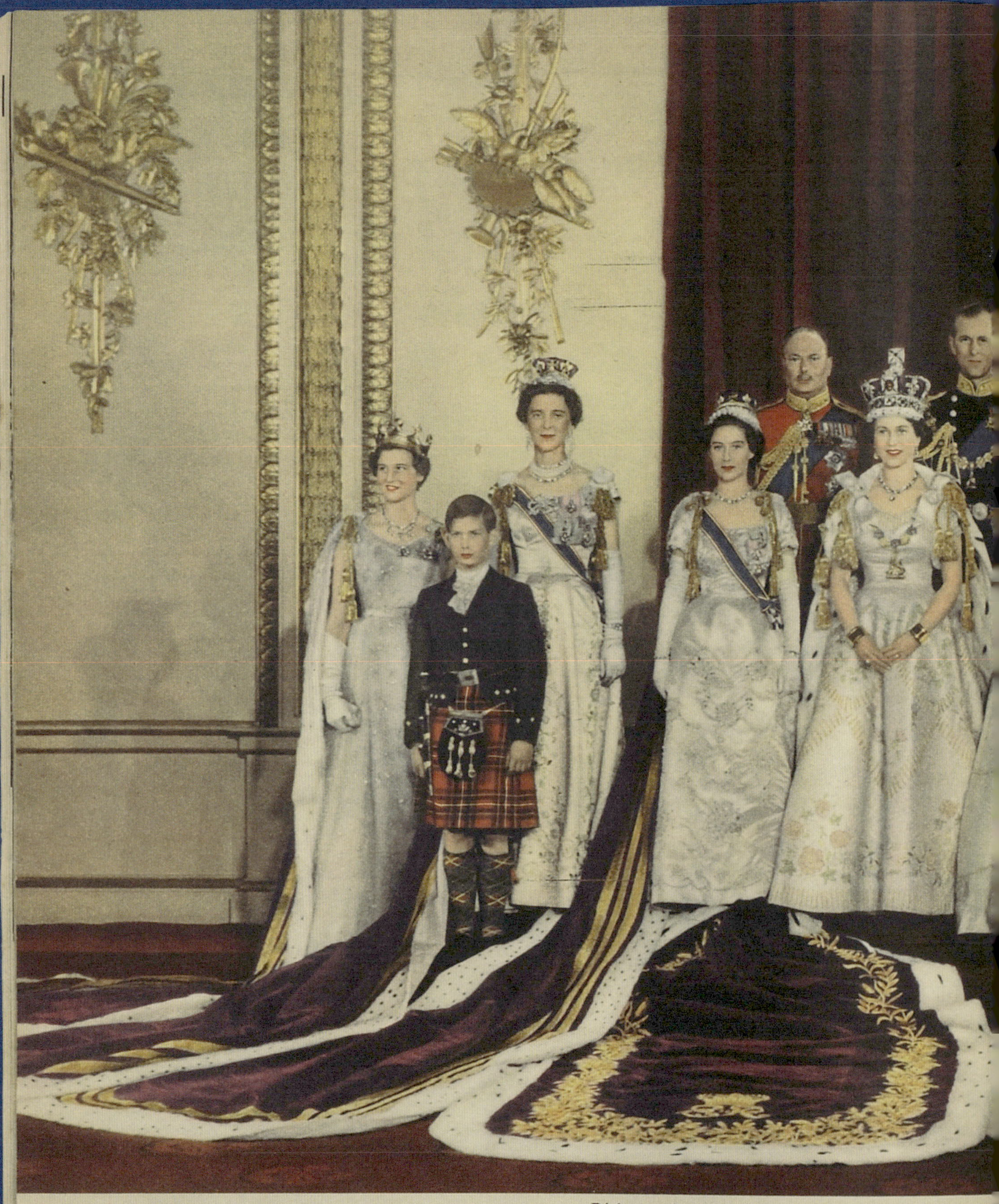

SOUVENIR OF A GREAT DAY

Rich curtains, and the magnificently decorated wall of the Throne Room at Buckingham Palace, form the background to this picture of the Royal Family in Coronation dress. Left to right are: Princess Alexandra, her younger brother, Prince Michael, their mother, the Duchess of Kent, Princess Margaret, the

ILLUSTRATE

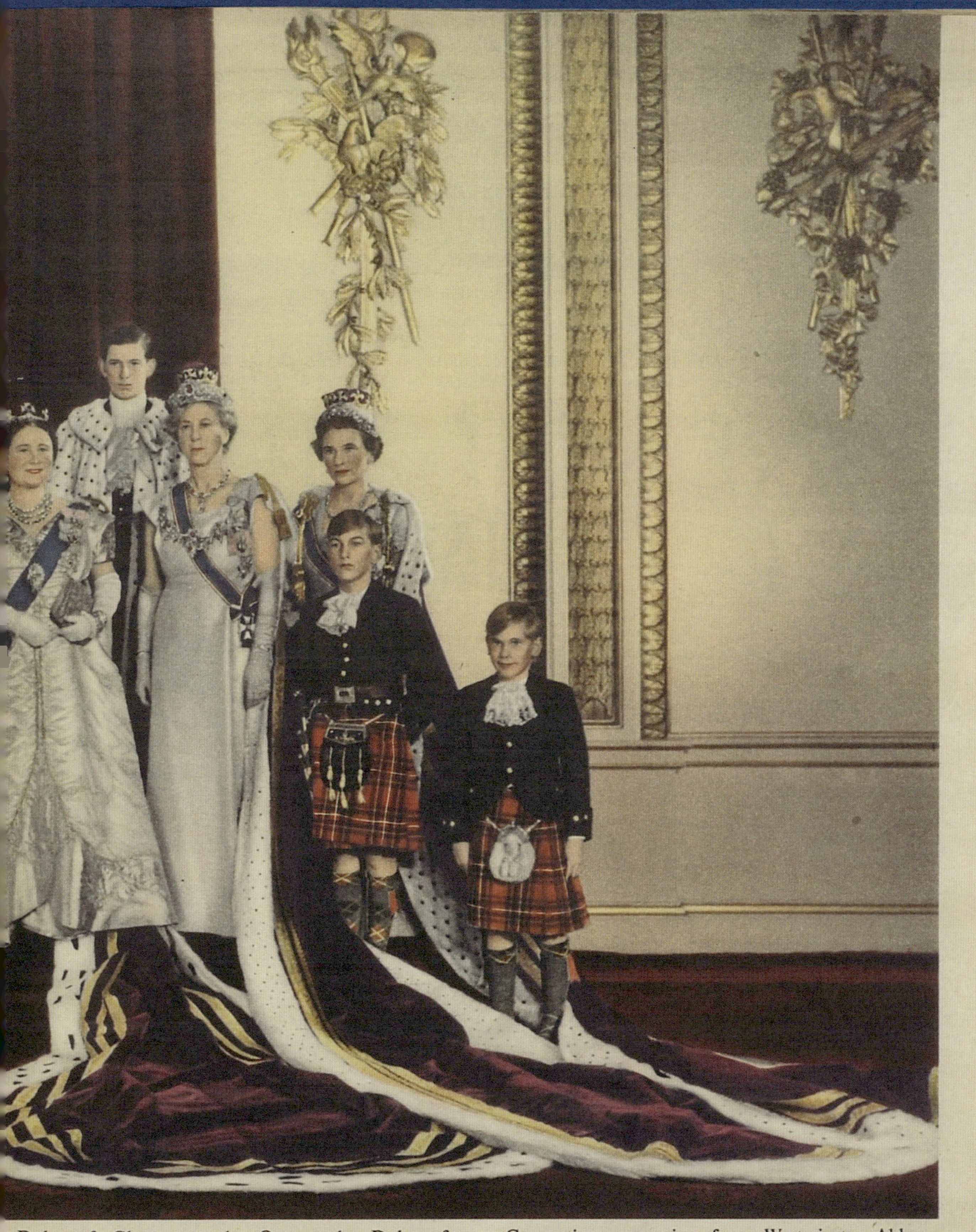

Duke of Gloucester, the Queen, the Duke of Edinburgh, the Queen Mother, the Duke of Kent, the Princess Royal, the Duchess of Gloucester and her sons, Prince William and Prince Richard. The photograph was taken on the return of the Queen and the Duke of Edinburgh to the Palace after the Coronation procession from Westminster Abbey. The Queen is wearing the Imperial State Crown and the gold Armills, or bracelets, which were presented to her by the nations of the Commonwealth. On the fourth finger of her right hand she wears a gold ring, often called the Wedding Ring of England

—JULY 4, 1953

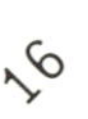

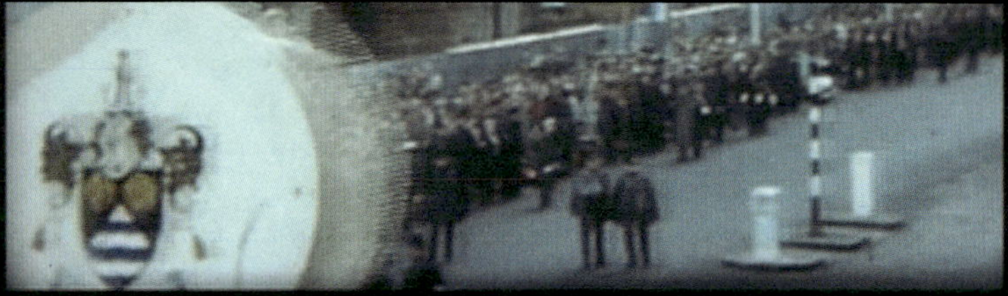

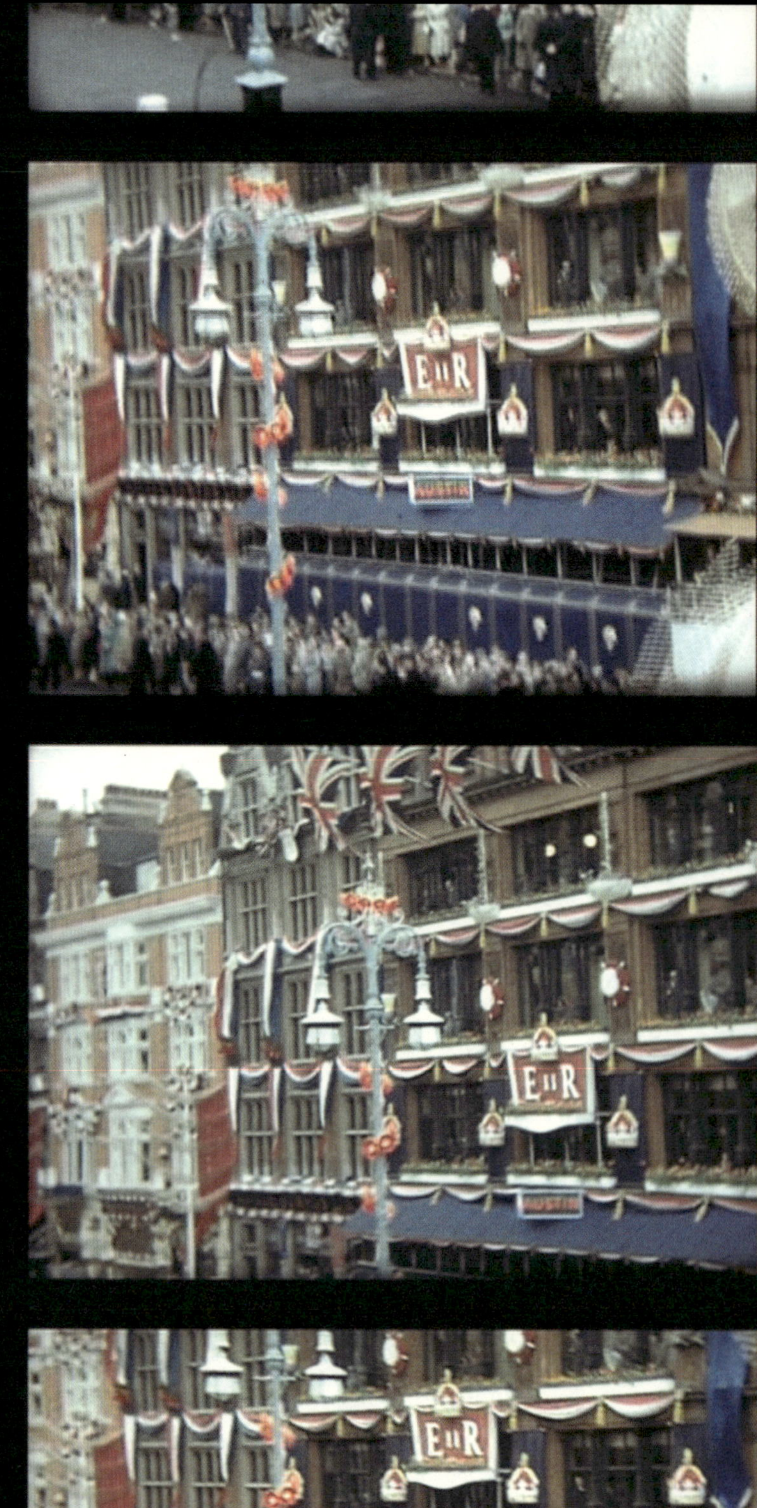

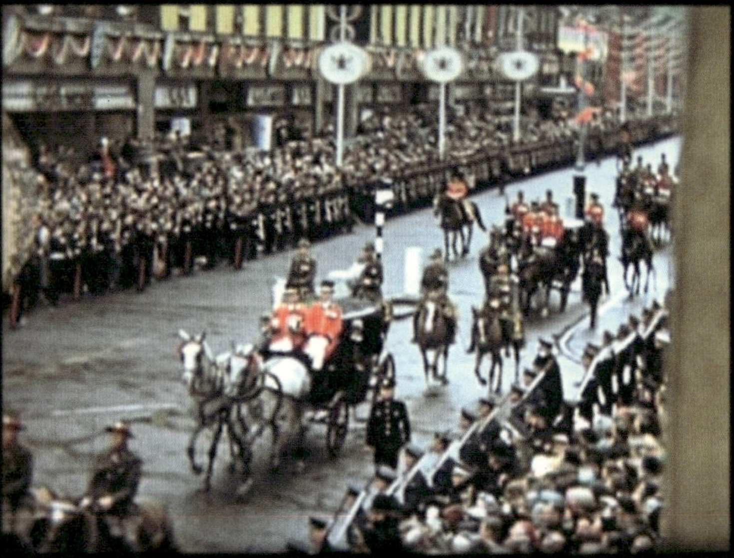

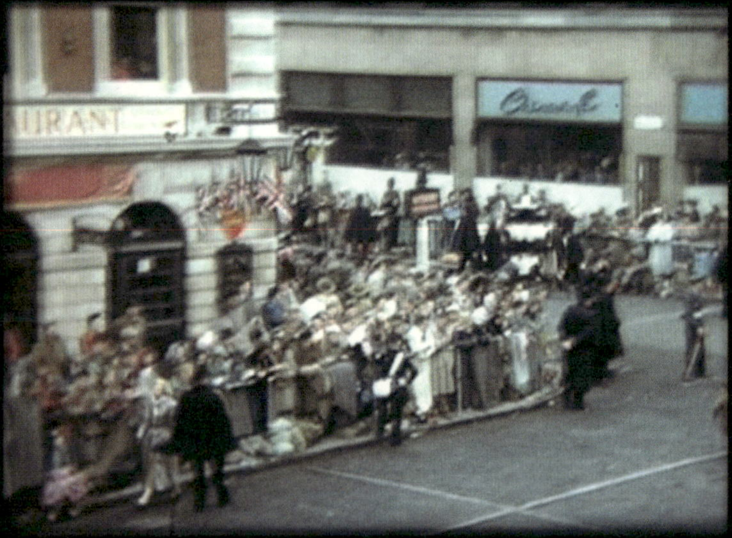

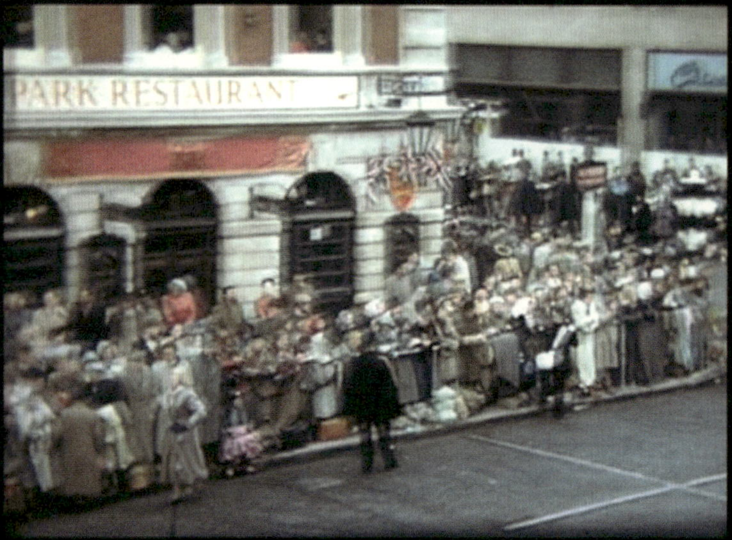

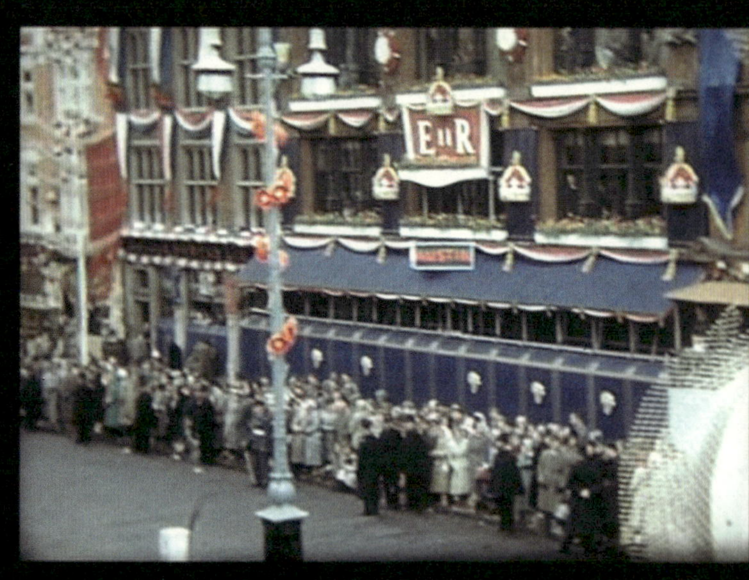

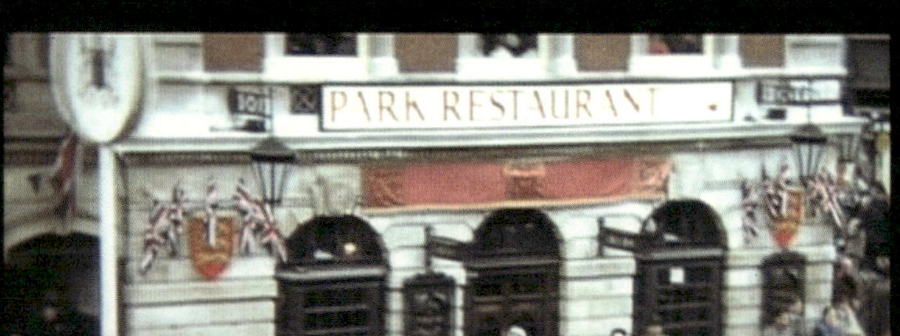

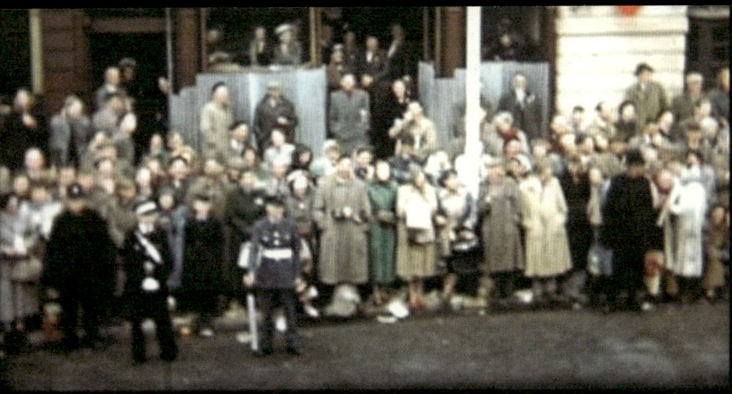

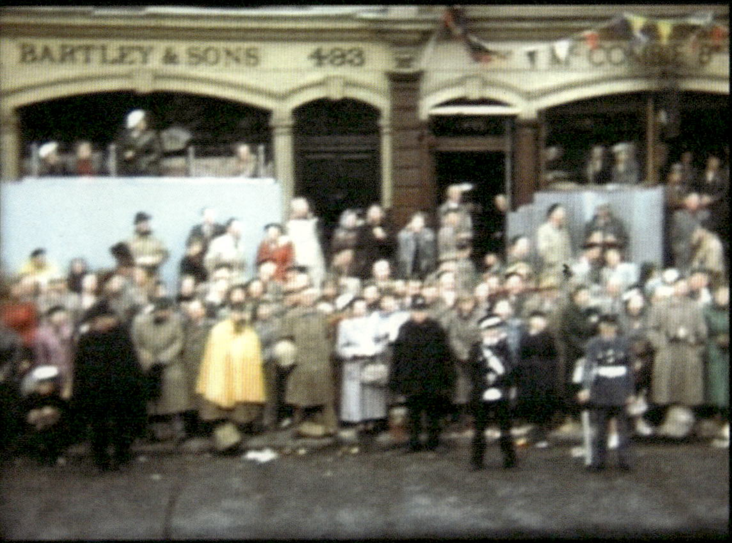

BARTLEY & SONS 483

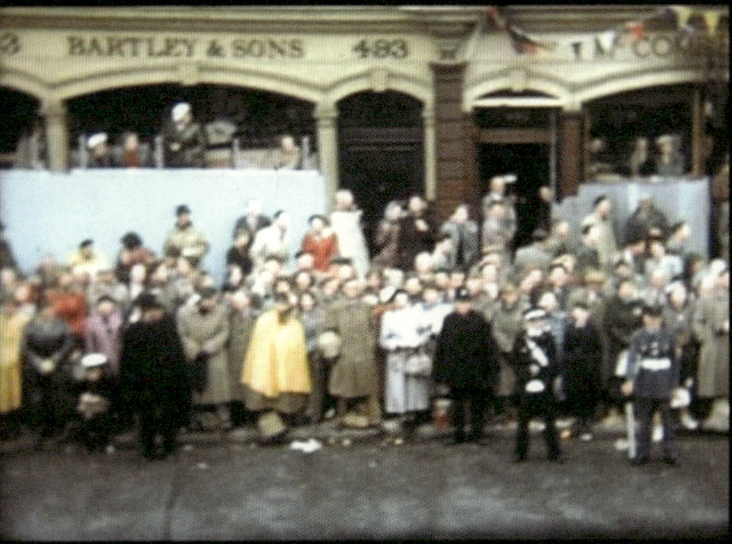

BARTLEY & SONS 483

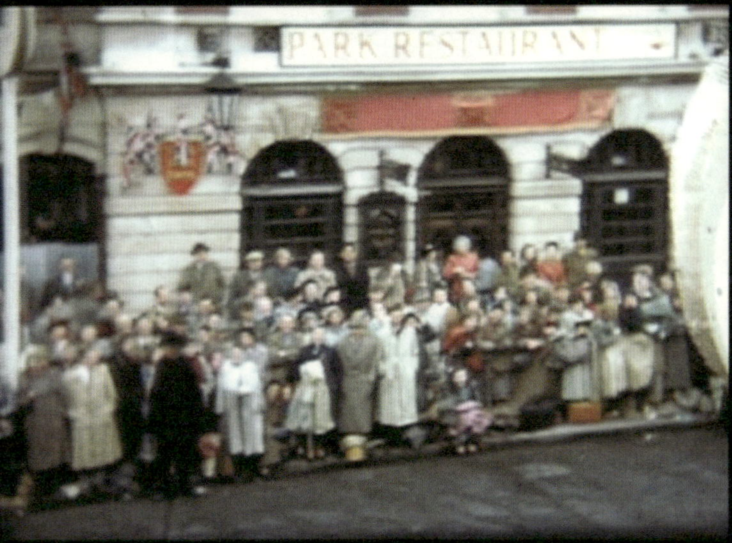

PARK RESTAURANT

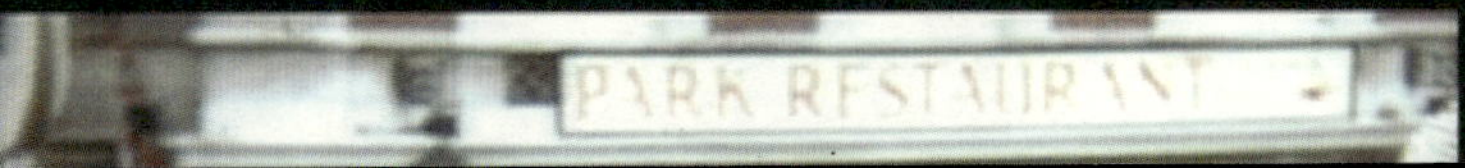

PARK RESTAURANT

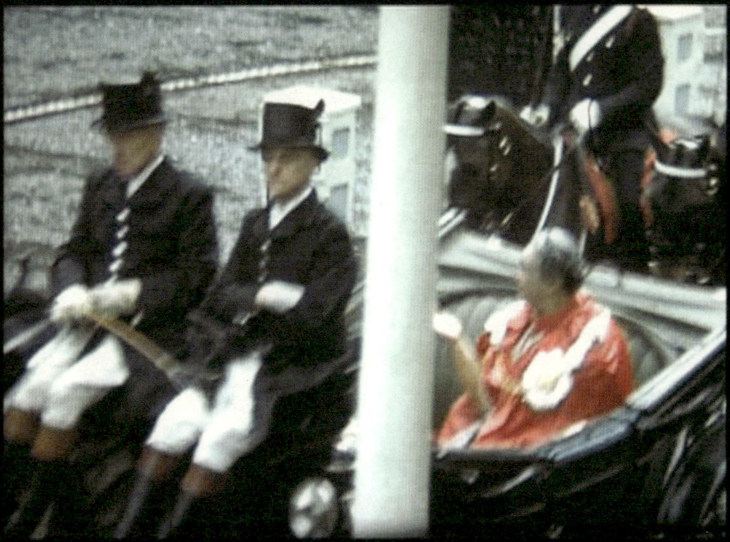

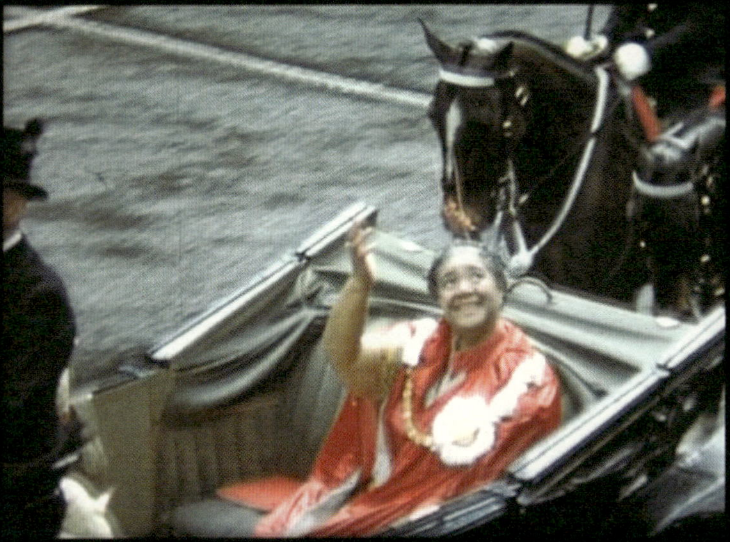

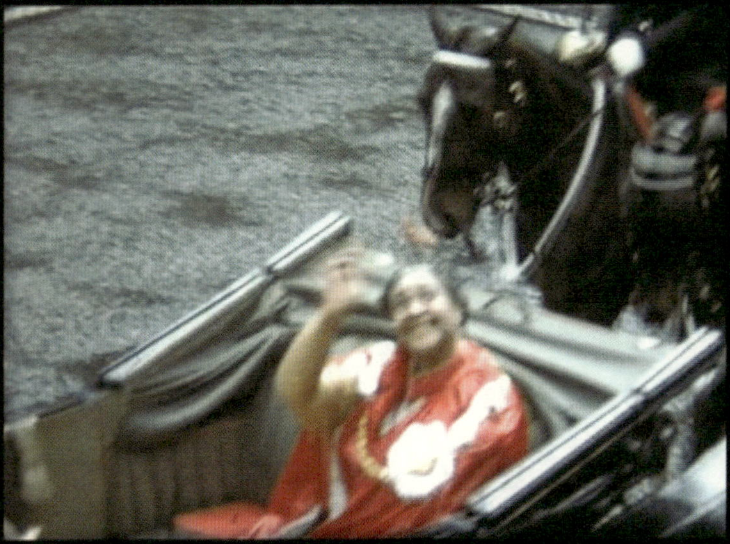

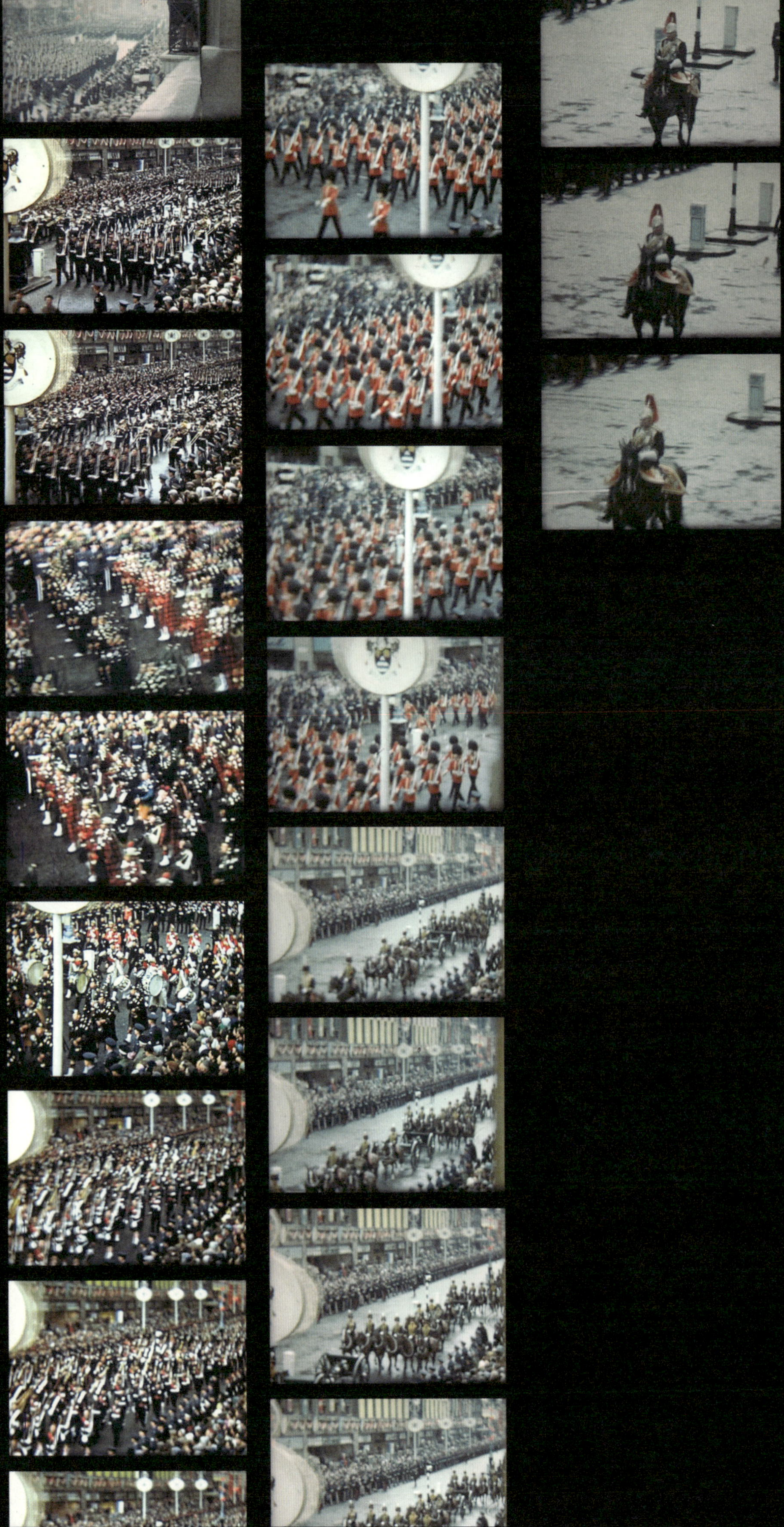

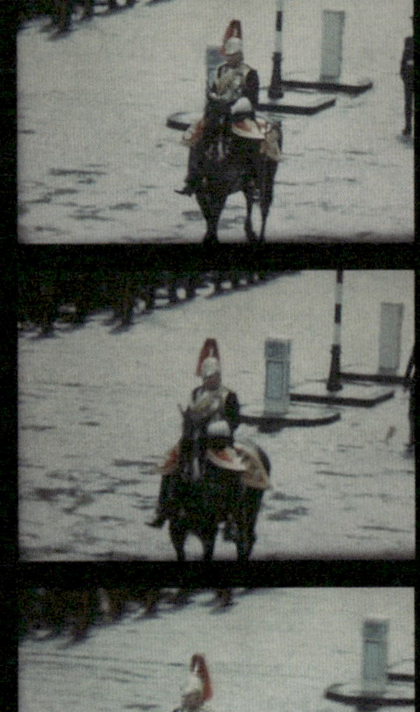

THE ROYAL LINE OF ACCESSION

QUEEN ELIZABETH II

KING GEORGE VI — LADY ELIZABETH BOWES-LYON
KING GEORGE V — PRINCESS MARY of Teck
KING EDWARD VII — PRINCESS ALEXANDRA of Denmark
QUEEN VICTORIA — PRINCE ALBERT of Saxe-Coburg and Gotha (Prince Consort)
EDWARD, Duke of Kent — VICTORIA of Saxe-Coburg-Saalfeld
KING GEORGE III — CHARLOTTE of Mecklenburg-Strelitz
FREDERICK LEWIS, Prince of Wales — AUGUSTA of Saxe-Gotha
KING GEORGE II — CAROLINE of Brandenburg-Anspach
KING GEORGE I — SOPHIA Dorothea of Celle
ERNEST AUGUSTUS, Elector of Hanover — SOPHIA
FREDERICK, King of Bohemia — ELIZABETH
KING JAMES I — ANNE of Denmark
MARY, Queen of Scots — HENRY STUART, Lord Darnley (2nd husband)
KING JAMES V of Scotland — MARY of Lorraine
KING JAMES IV of Scotland — MARGARET Tudor
KING HENRY VII — ELIZABETH of York
EDMUND, Earl of Richmond — MARGARET   KING EDWARD IV — ELIZABETH Woodville
JOHN BEAUFORT, Duke of Somerset — MARGARET Beauchamp   RICHARD — CECILY Neville
JOHN, Marquess of Dorset — MARGARET Holland   RICHARD — ANNE Mortimer
JOHN of Gaunt — KATHARINE Swynford   EDMUND — ISABEL of Castile
Duke of Lancaster   (3rd wife)   Duke of York   (1st wife)
KING EDWARD III — PHILIPPA of Hainault
KING EDWARD II — ISABELLA of France
KING EDWARD I — ELEANOR of Castile (1st wife)
KING HENRY III — ELEANOR of Provence
KING JOHN — ISABELLA of Angouleme (2nd wife)
KING HENRY II — ELEANOR of Aquitaine
GEOFFREY, Count of Anjou — MATILDA
KING HENRY I — MATILDA (1st wife)
KING WILLIAM I — MATILDA   ST. MARGARET — KING MALCOLM III
(the Conqueror)   of Scotland
EDWARD ATHELING THE EXILE — AGATHA
KING EDMUND II IRONSIDE — EALDGYTH
KING ETHELRED II THE UNREADY — ELFLEDA (1st wife)
KING EDGAR — ELFRIDA (2nd wife)
KING EDMUND I — ELGIVA (1st wife)
KING EDWARD — EDGIVA (3rd wife)
KING ALFRED — EALHSWITH
KING ETHELWULF — OSBURH (1st wife)
KING EGBERT — REDBURH

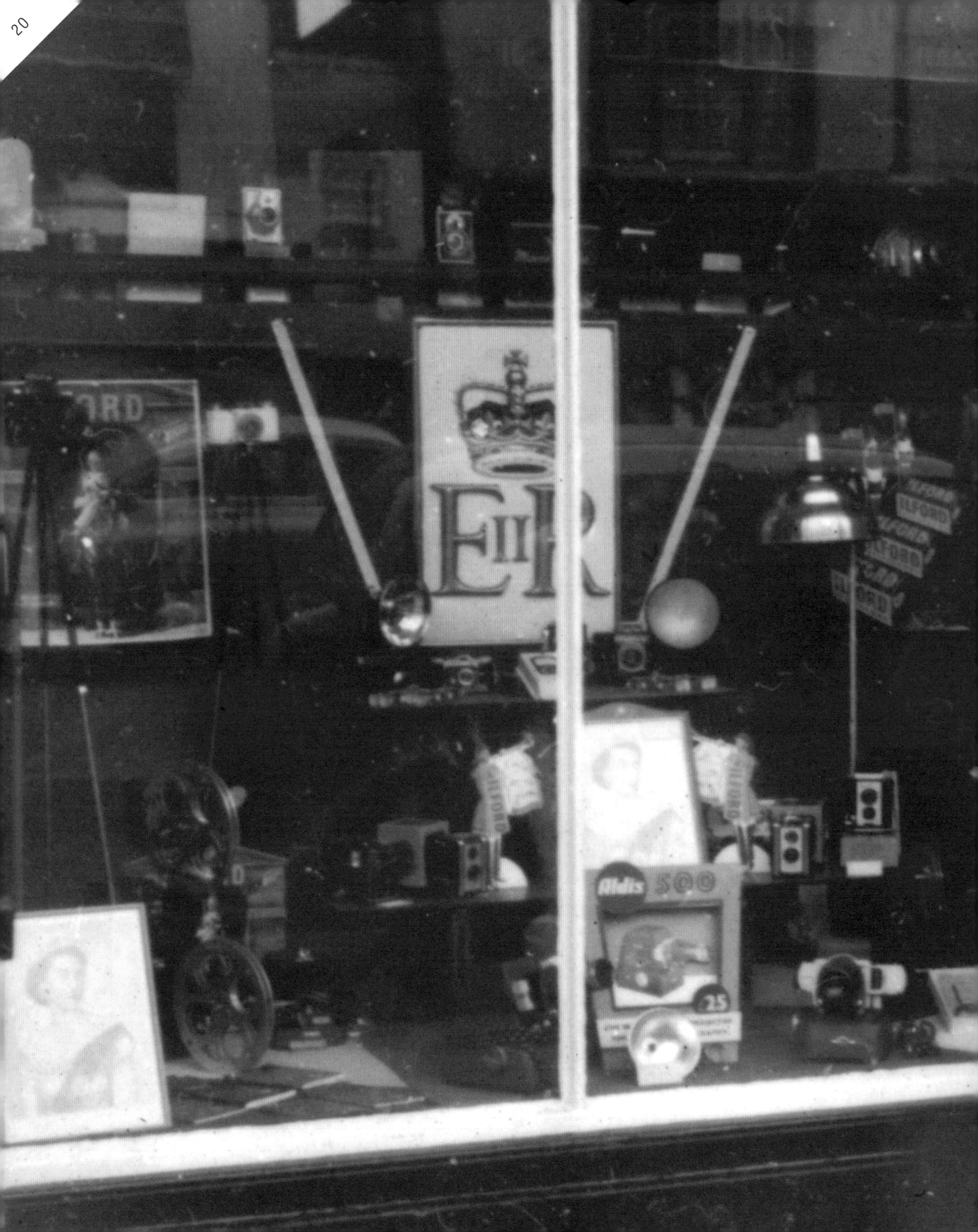
EIIR
Aldis 500
25

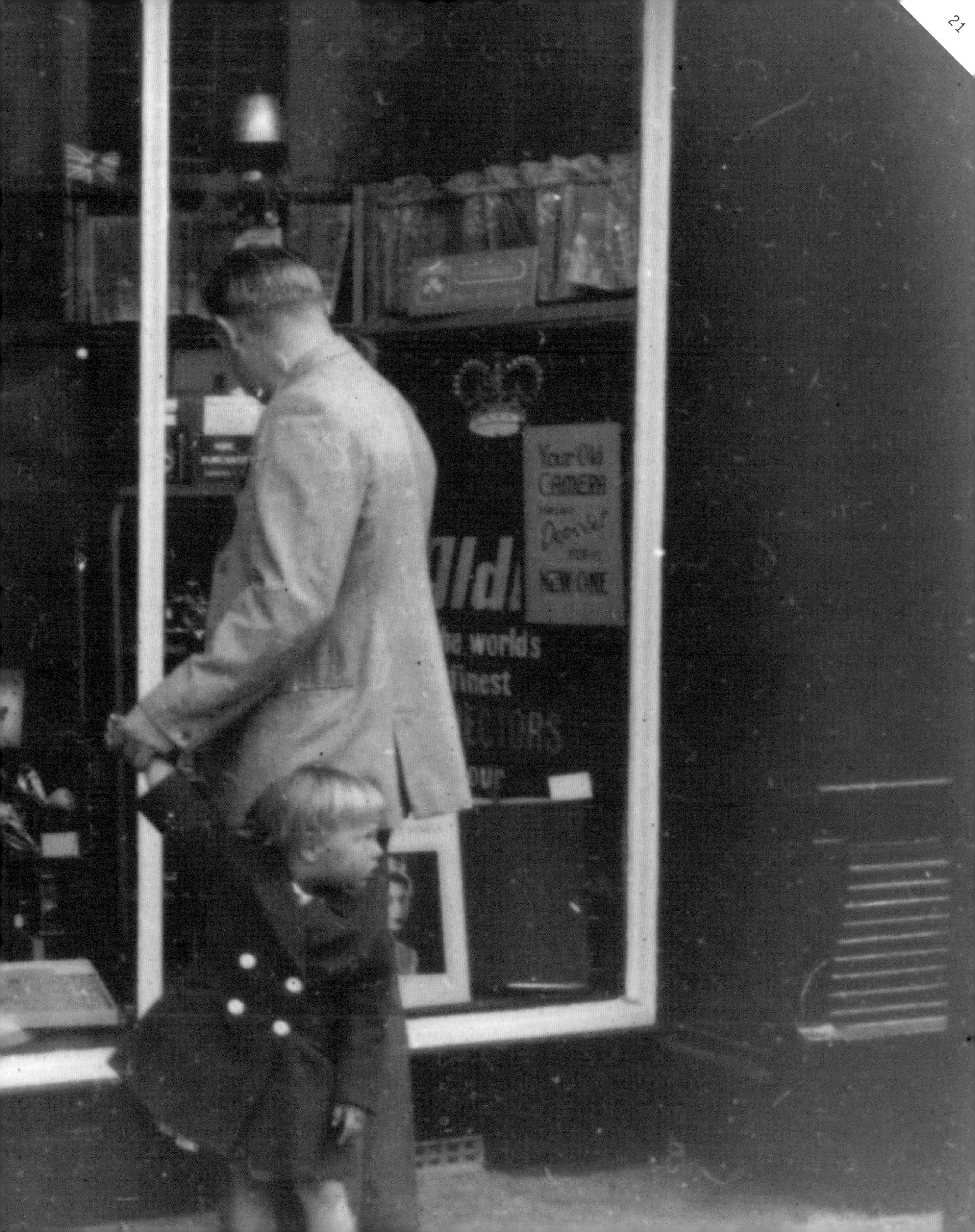
Your Old
CAMERA
Depersited
NEW ONE
9/d
e world's
finest
ECTORS
our

Introduction

In the 1950s Britain was still governed by old-school politeness and the old order in general, most of which was a direct consequence of the discipline instilled by the Second World War and military service. As the decade wore on, however, many people reacted against this old order, culminating in the so-called liberation of the 1960s.

The sixties were a very eventful decade, both internationally and in Britain: it was certainly a decade of change, violence and discontent. On the world-wide stage, many events took place at this time which would influence the present day. The Berlin Wall was built in 1961 and the space race between the United States and the Soviet Union was on in earnest; this culminated in the American Moon landing of 1969. The assassination of President John F. Kennedy in 1963 paved the way for a new kind of vigilance and heralded the modern age, where terror and threat were ever-present, and safety was never to be taken for granted. The civil rights movement was in the vanguard at this time – Dr Martin Luther King, who was shot dead in 1968, made his famous 'I have a dream' speech in 1963, which put the racial debate on the map and had a huge influence on the free society that was to come. In 1969 the murder of actress Sharon Tate, the wife of director Roman Polanski, who directed the iconic film *Rosemary's Baby*, by the hippie Charles Manson and his 'Family', caused widespread outrage. In Greece the monarchy was overthrown in 1967, leading to the King's exile and the establishment of the colonels' junta.

Britain in the 1960s was very different to what it is now. Following on from the 1950s, when rationing was still in place and the country sought to move forward after the war years, the 1960s was a pleasure-seeking decade in which many of the values upheld until then were questioned and ultimately rejected. Up until then, for example, the traditional way of speaking English had been R. P. (Received Pronunciation), based on south-eastern English pronunciation and widely heard in public schools, at Oxford and Cambridge Universities and, of course, in BBC programmes. In the 60s all that changed, however: to be working-class was all right, indeed desirable, and you had to have an accent to match. Regional accents became acceptable and R. P. fell out of favour; people aspired to a classless society – by which they meant that the upper classes were an unwanted anachronism. Labour Prime Minister Harold Wilson, who came to power in 1964, was typical of the decade: although Oxford-educated, he was a working-class boy made good, embodied the populism of the time and spoke shamelessly with a Yorkshire accent.

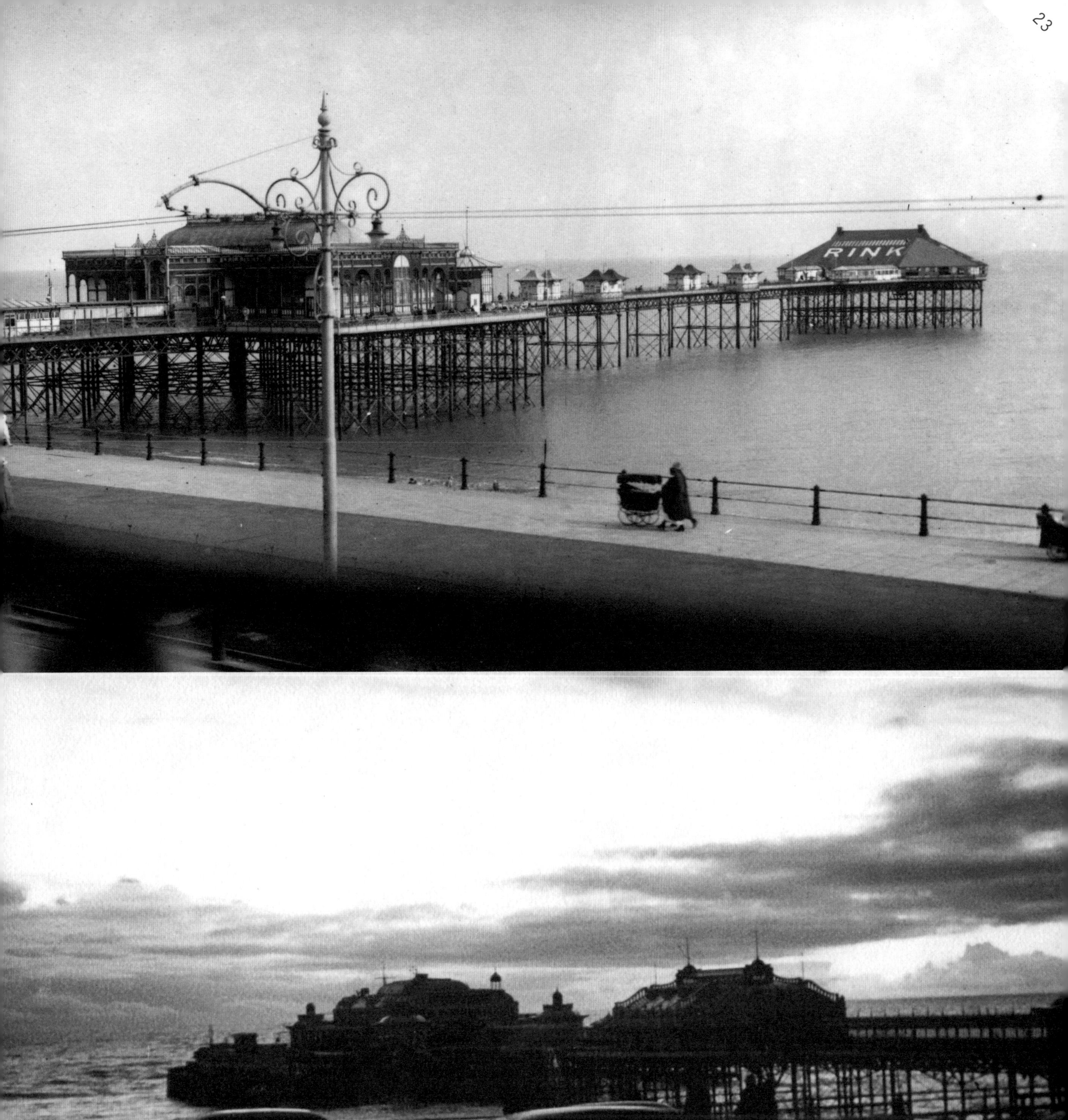
RINK

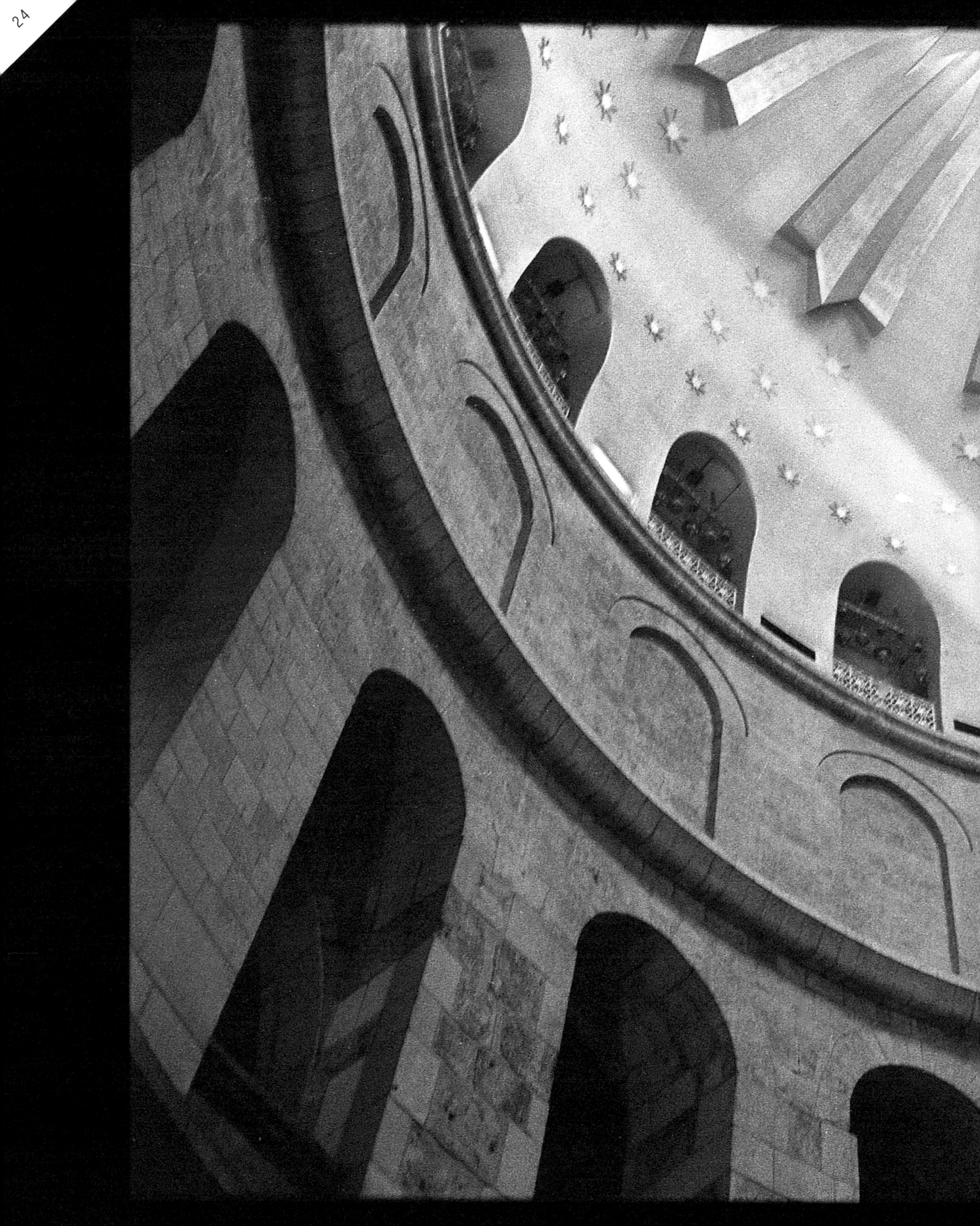

Photography Year Book

1957

Photography

has become an important part of our lives. Its increasing importance has made ever greater demands for quality and reliability in photographic equipment. It is for this reason that every year for more than three decades has brought increased demand for the LEICA.

Since the days when it pioneered miniature photography, LEICA has been regarded by experienced photographers as the ultimate goal — the key to better pictures.
This is not only because the LEICA is a masterpiece of precision but because it has exclusive features which have been designed and built for fast, accurate, and versatile work. And so, LEICA cameras have been carried by experienced men to the farthest corners of the earth in order to bring us photographs which serve to give a better concept of the world we live in.

Wherever your own travels may take you — whether it is to the next city, a neighboring country or the farthest continent — LEICA is the camera you can rely upon to produce the finest possible results under all conditions.

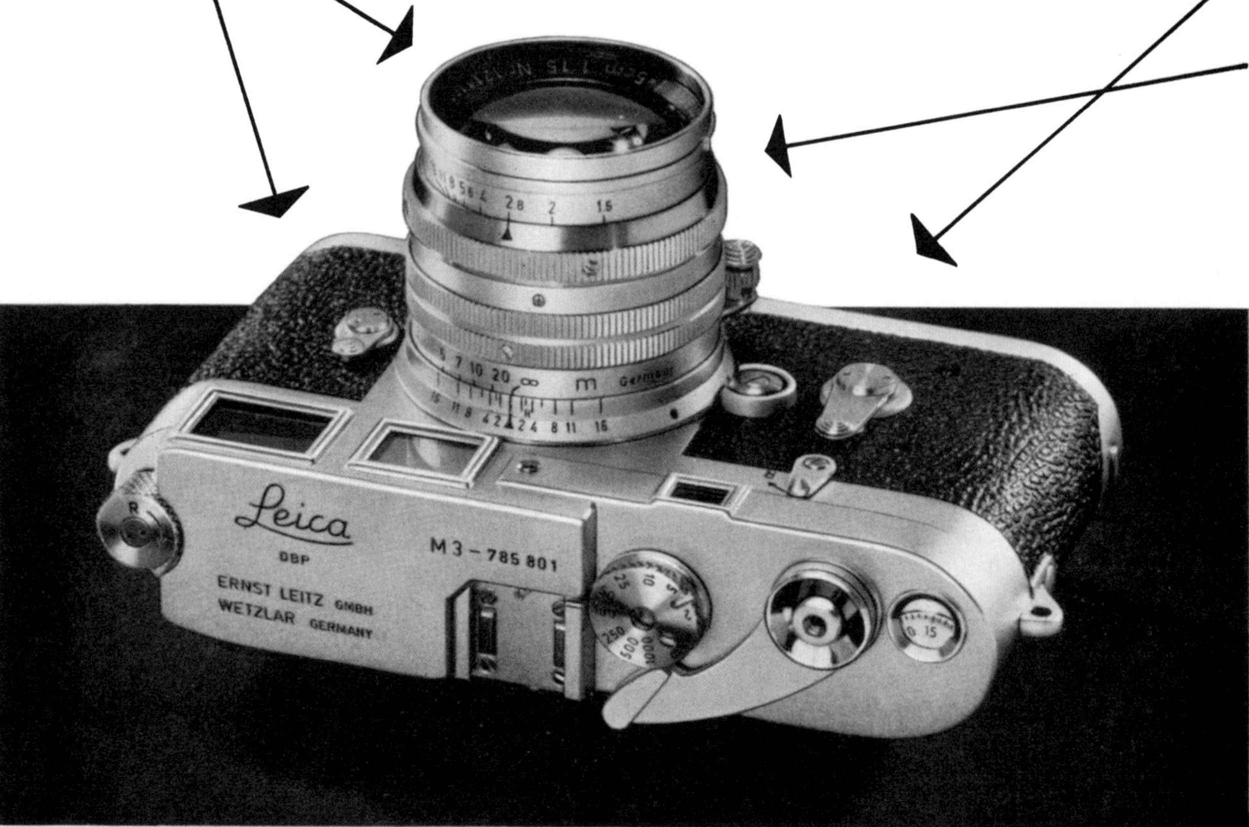

Delivery and service all over the world. Ask your dealer or write to: **ERNST LEITZ** GMBH **WETZLAR** (W.-Germany)

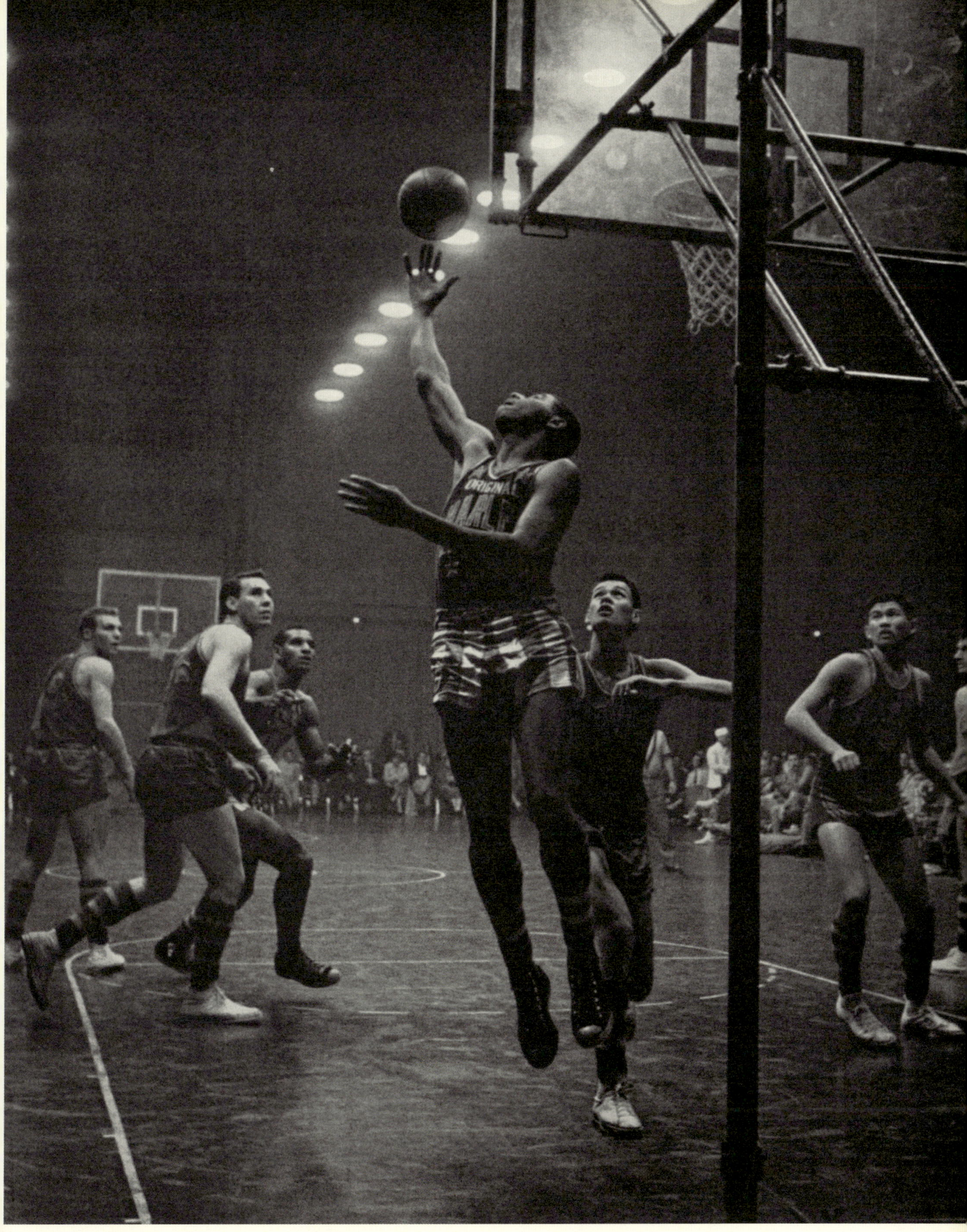

WALTER SCHNEBELE

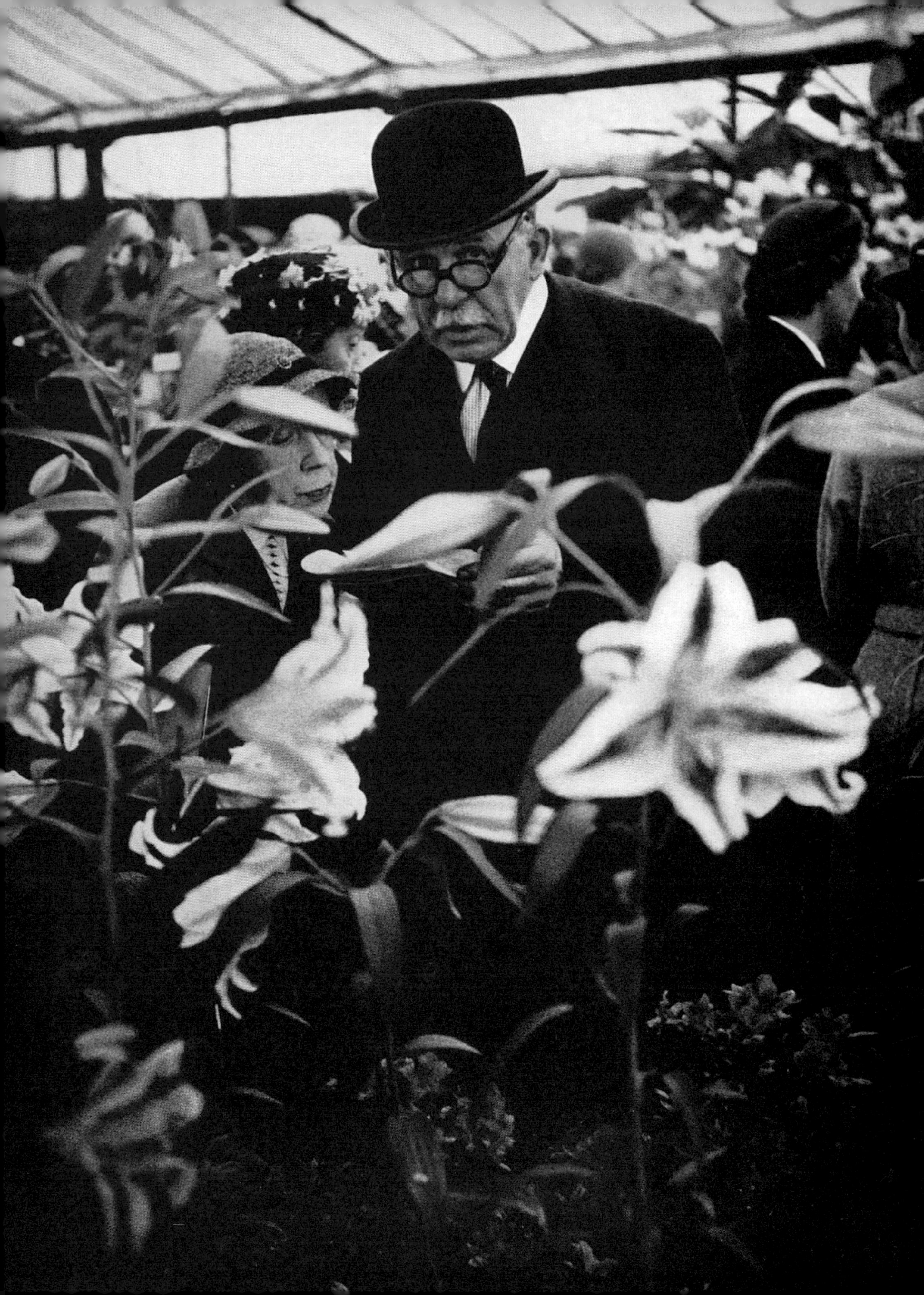

ROBERT FRANK

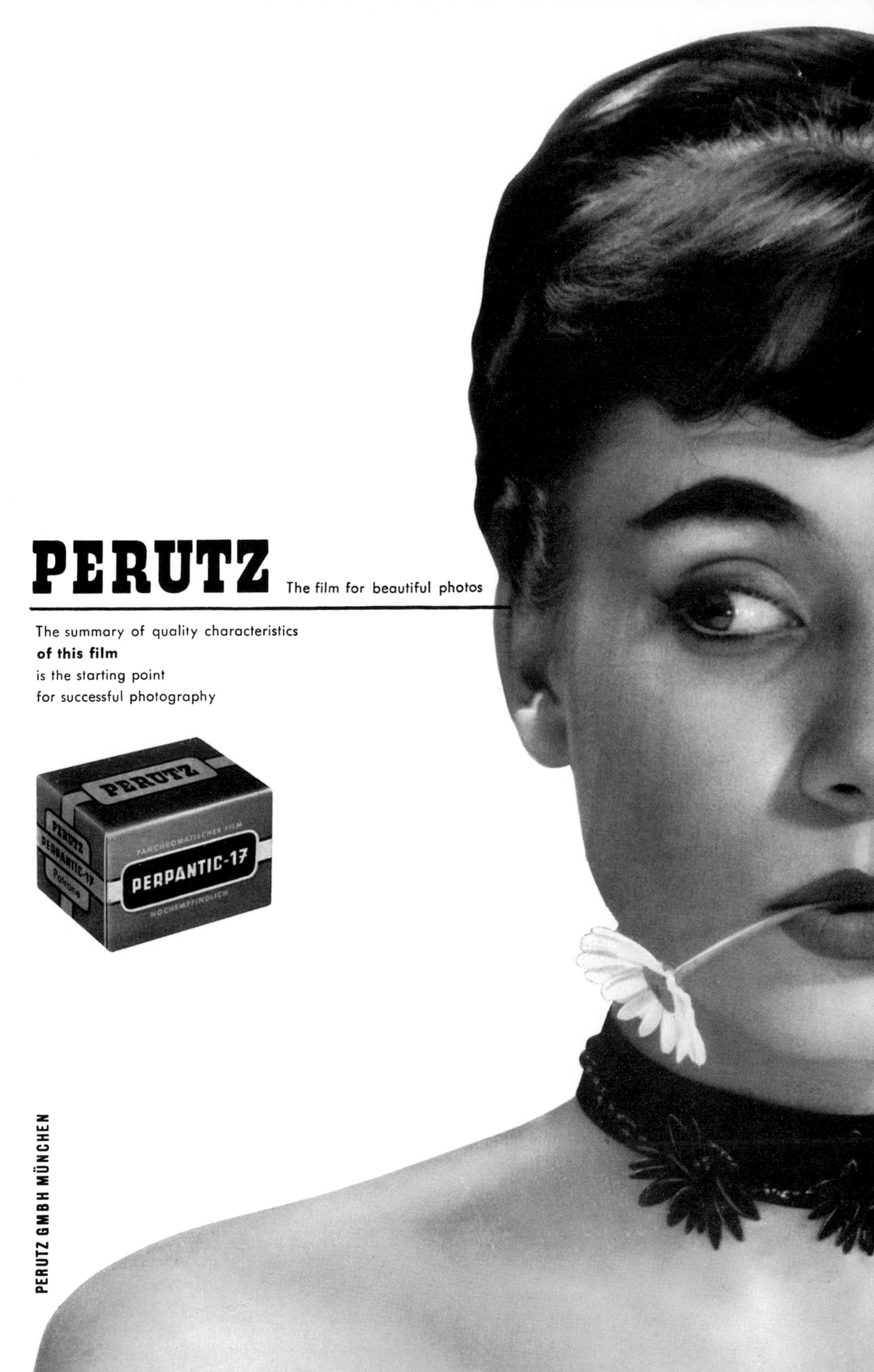

PERUTZ
The film for beautiful photos
The summary of quality characteristics
of this film
is the starting point
for successful photography
PERUTZ
PERUTZ
PERPANTIC-17
Patrone
PANCHROMATISCHER FILM
PERPANTIC-17
HOCHEMPFINDLICH
PERUTZ GMBH MÜNCHEN

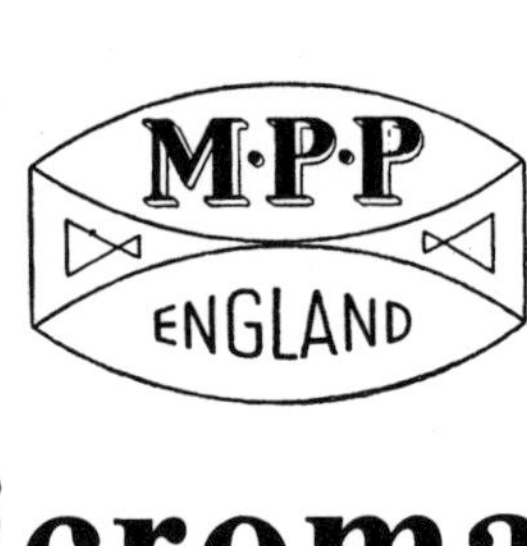

Micromatic

Professional

5×7 ENLARGER

As supplied to
Messrs. ROLLS ROYCE Ltd.

- **AUTOMATIC FOCUSSING**
  - COLD CATHODE LIGHTING
    - GIRDER CONSTRUCTION
      - COUNTER BALANCED HEAD
        - TILTING NEGATIVE STAGE

Rugged Precision-built Enlarger designed
for continuous professional use. Accessories
accept negatives down to $2\frac{1}{4}'' \times 2\frac{1}{4}''$

£125

No Purchase Tax
EX LENS

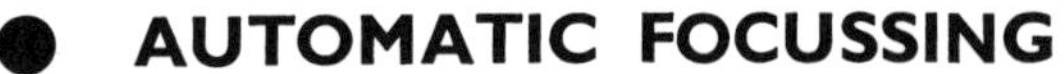

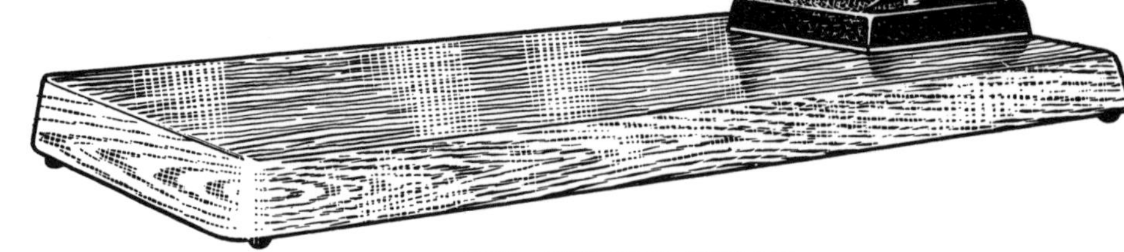

**MPP GIVE YOU PROMPT
AFTER-SALE SERVICE**

Full descriptive literature on request from

MICRO PRECISION PRODUCTS LTD

145 LONDON ROAD, KINGSTON-ON-THAMES   **Tel: KINgston 0153**

JSP. ME2

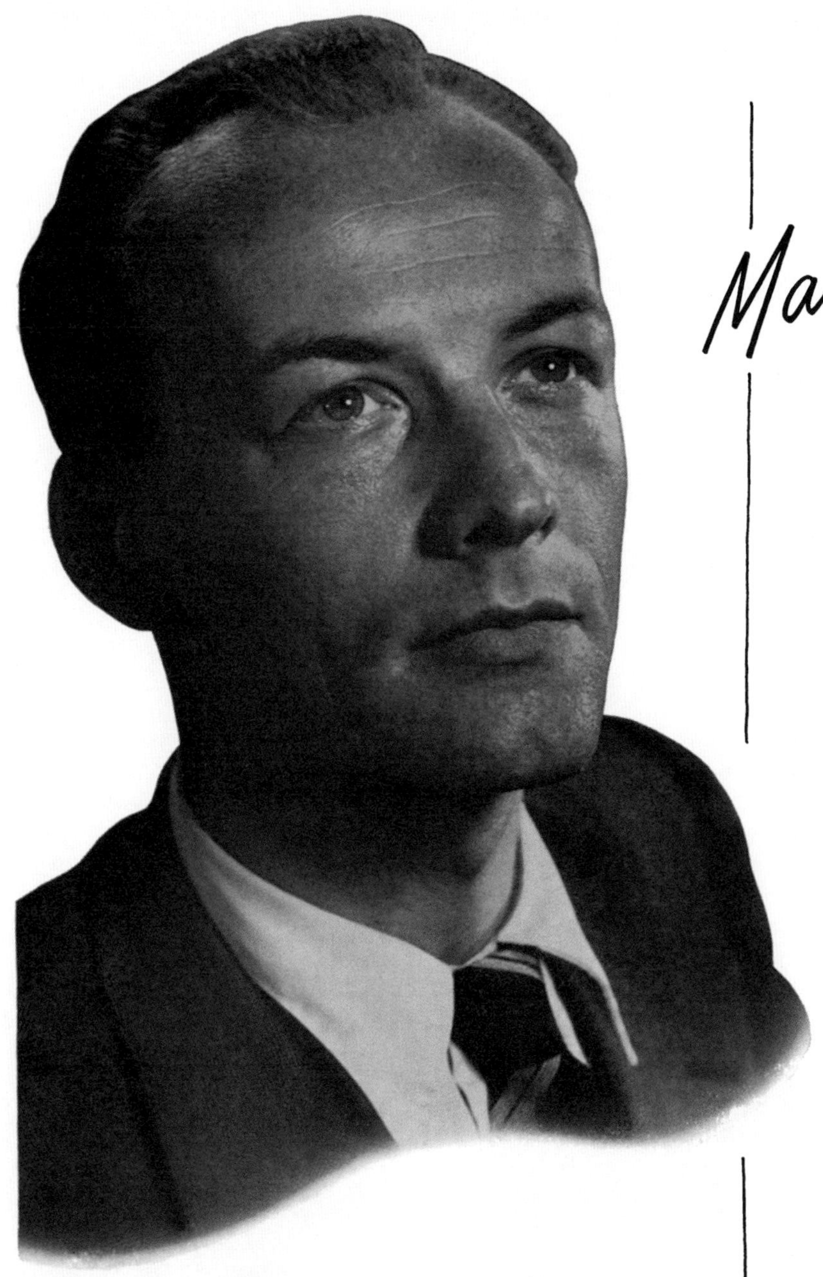

His camera is almost part of him. His the ability to perceive and capture for all time the mood of a fleeting moment. Subordinated to his creative genius, his technique has become second nature. He takes it for granted.

He sets an exacting standard for himself — and for the film he uses. It must be of supreme quality, with the absolute reliability which, like his technique, he can take for granted. That's why he chooses 'Kodak' film.

they come out best on

Kodak FILM

Kodak Limited, Kodak House, Kingsway, London, W.C.2

'Kodak' is a registered trade-mark.

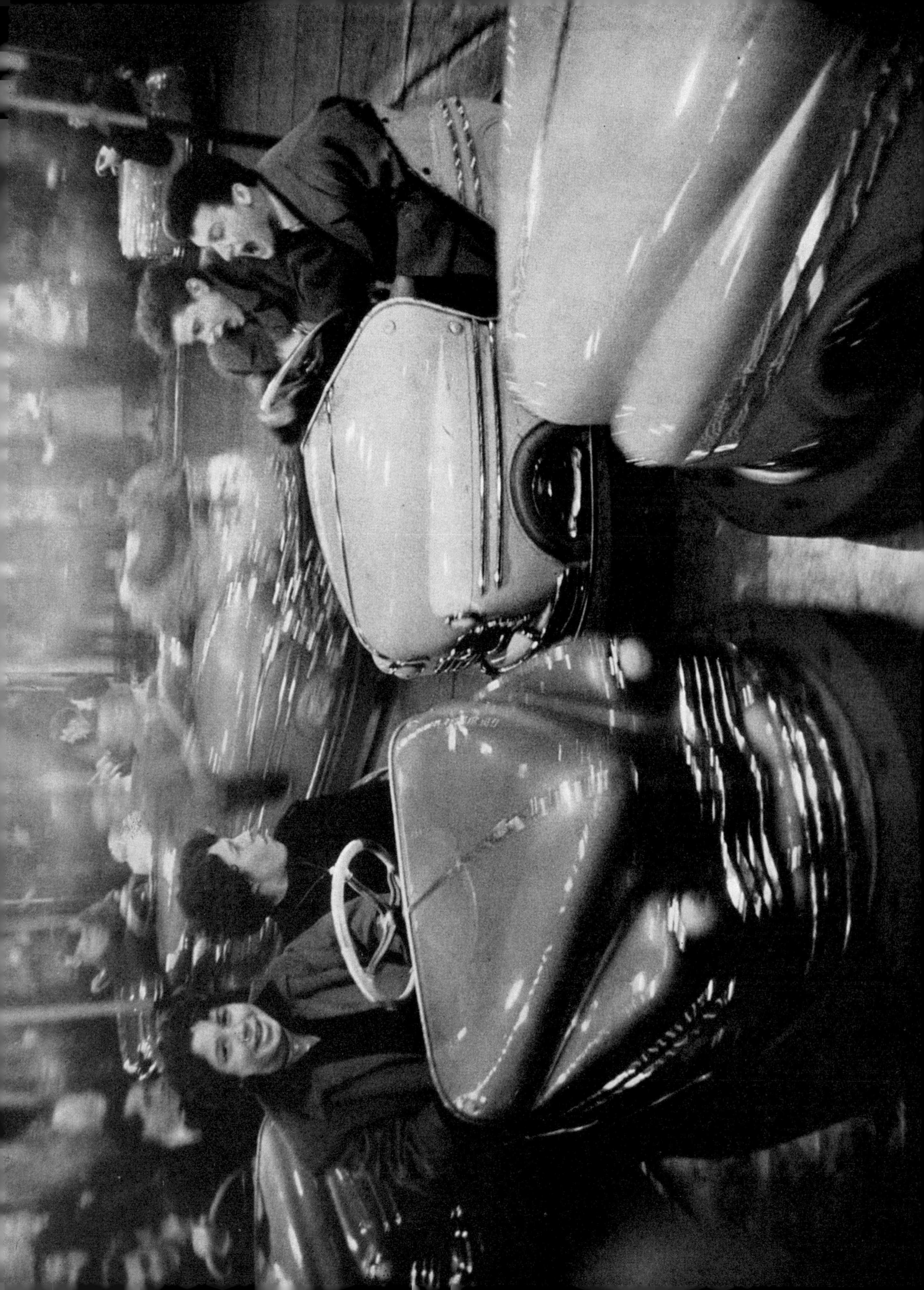

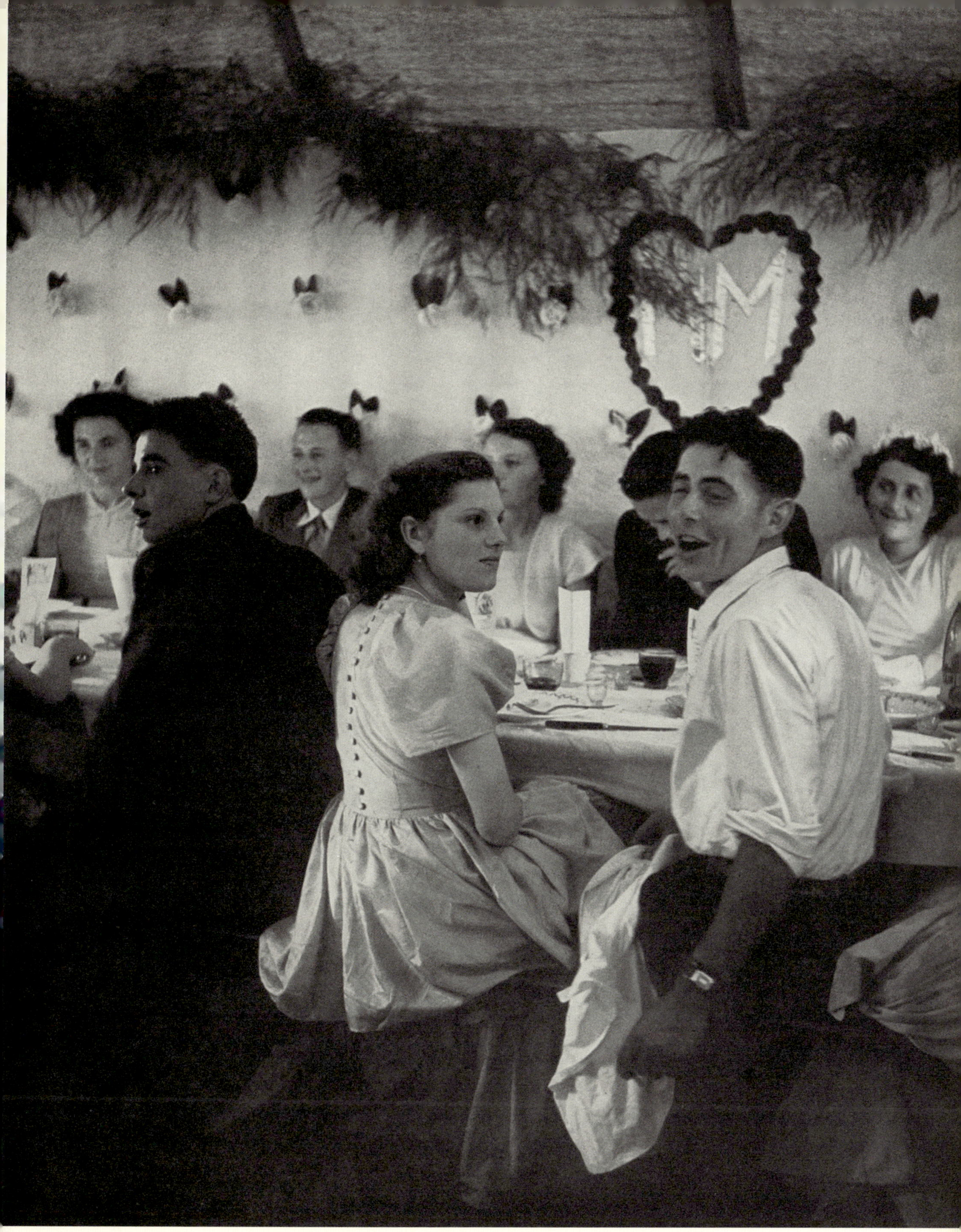

ROBERT DOISNEAU ★

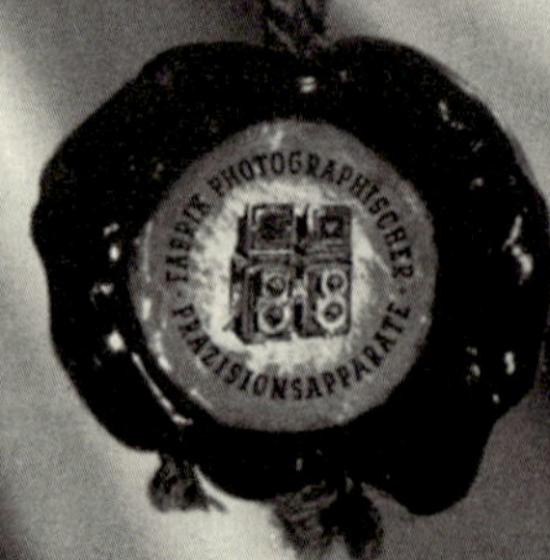
Rolleiflex

THE FAST OPERATING ROLLEI,
WITH SUPERIOR AUTOMATIC
FEATURES, FOR THE MOST
EXACTING WORK
This masterpiece, whose fam...
synonymous with "the be...
leader of the twin-lens ca...
Its natural readiness f...
tion has caused it...
providing f...
speed...
ca...

ROLLEIFLEX

...ra
...thus
...res in
...picture
...e not only
...der stress,
...ve a sur-
...he Rolleiflex
...loading the
...automatically
...ght instant. The
...simultaneously cocked

FRANKE & HEIDECKE
BRAUNSCHWEIG GERMANY

SVEN-GÖSTA JOHANSSON

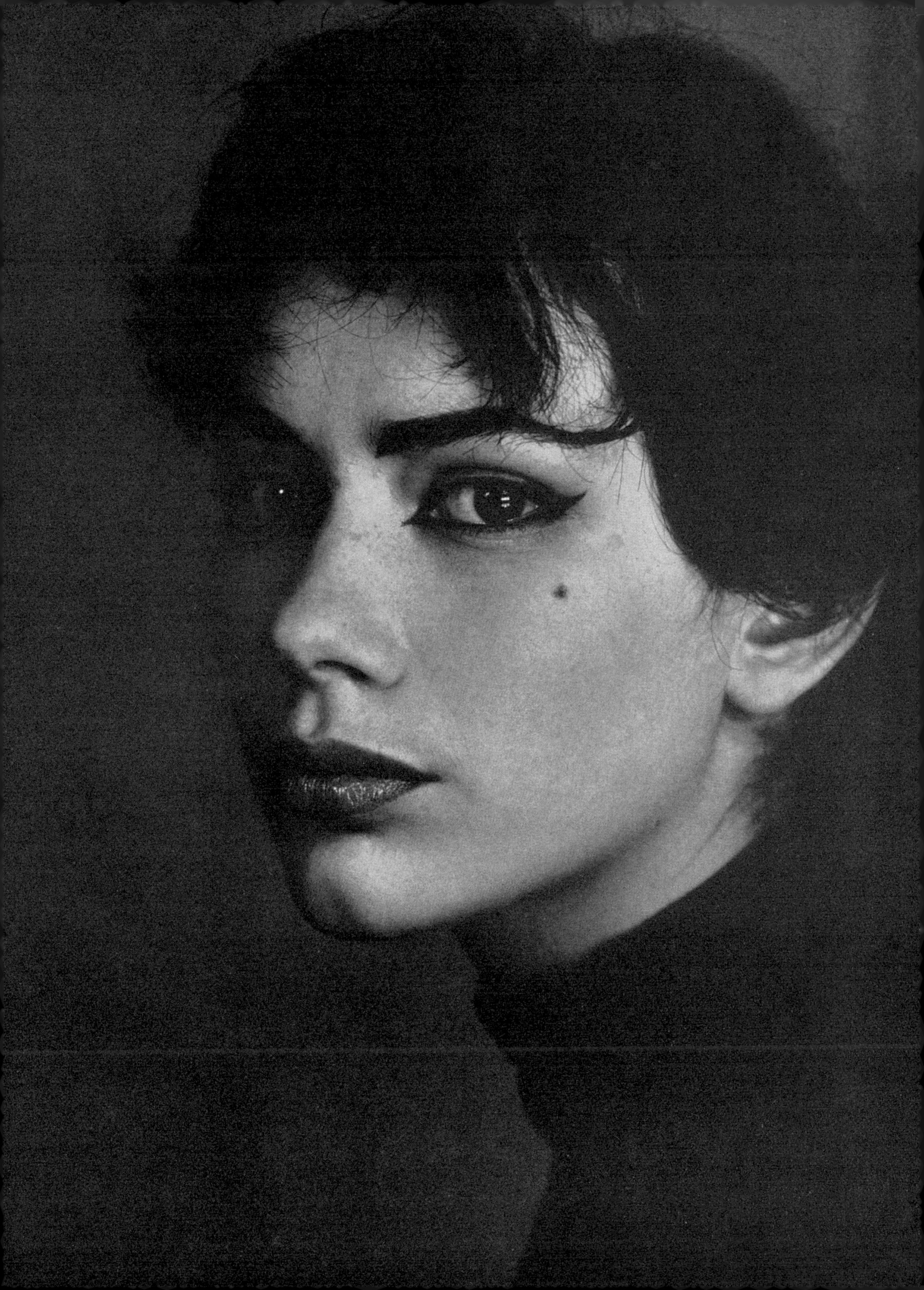

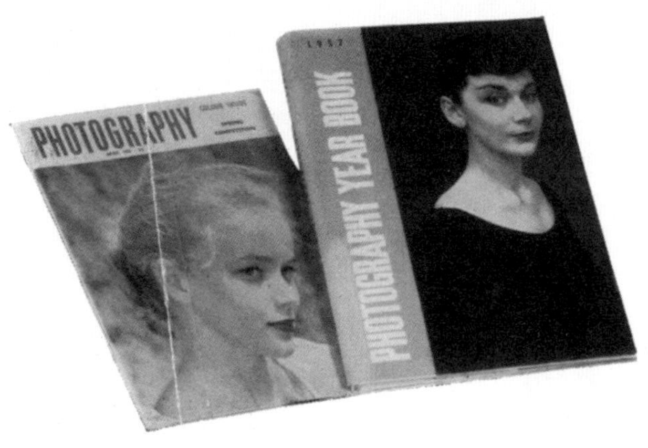

PHOTOGRAPHY MAGAZINE

is obtainable in Great Britain from all newsagents and photographic dealers every month price 2/6. Annual Subscription 31/6d. Postage Free.

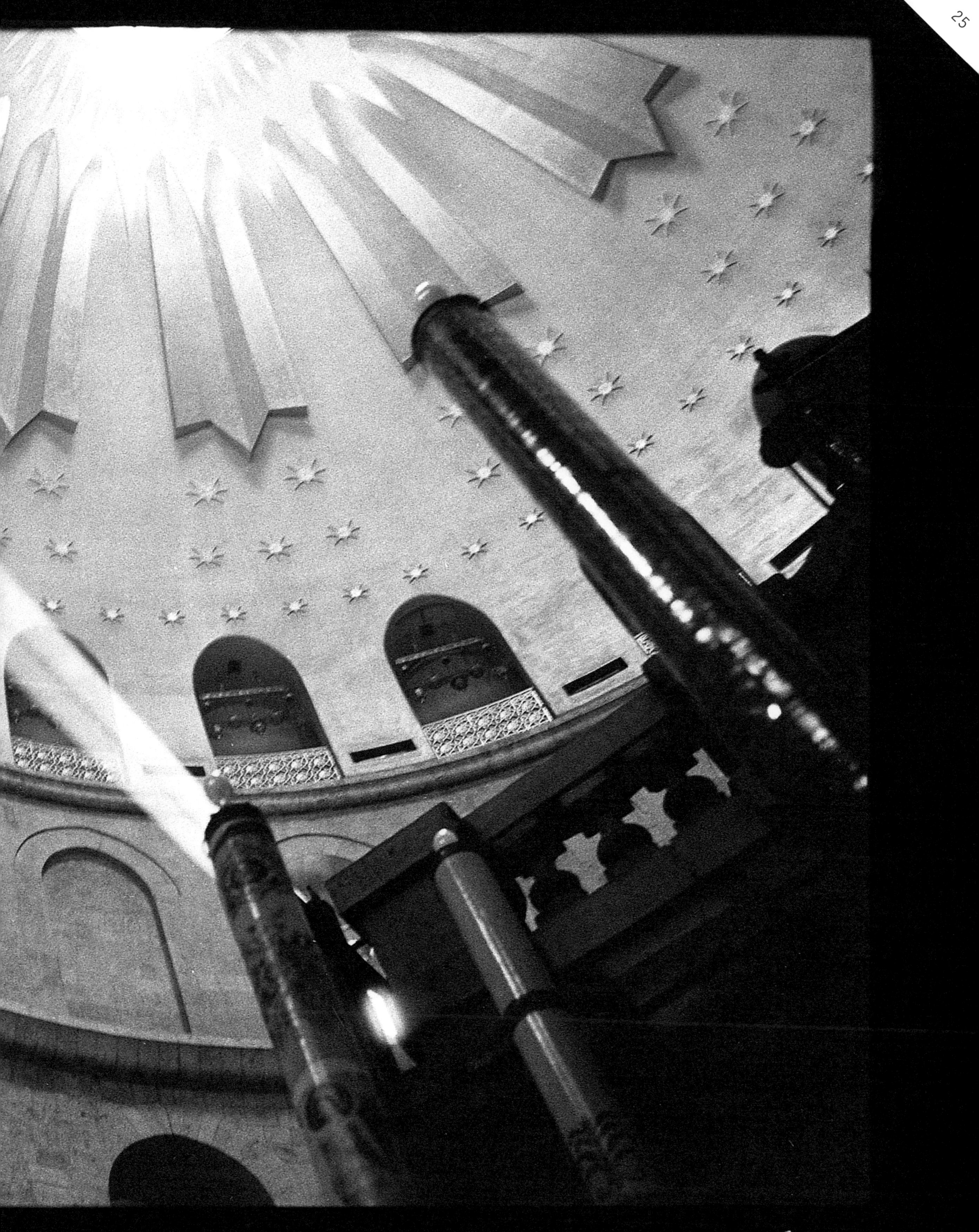

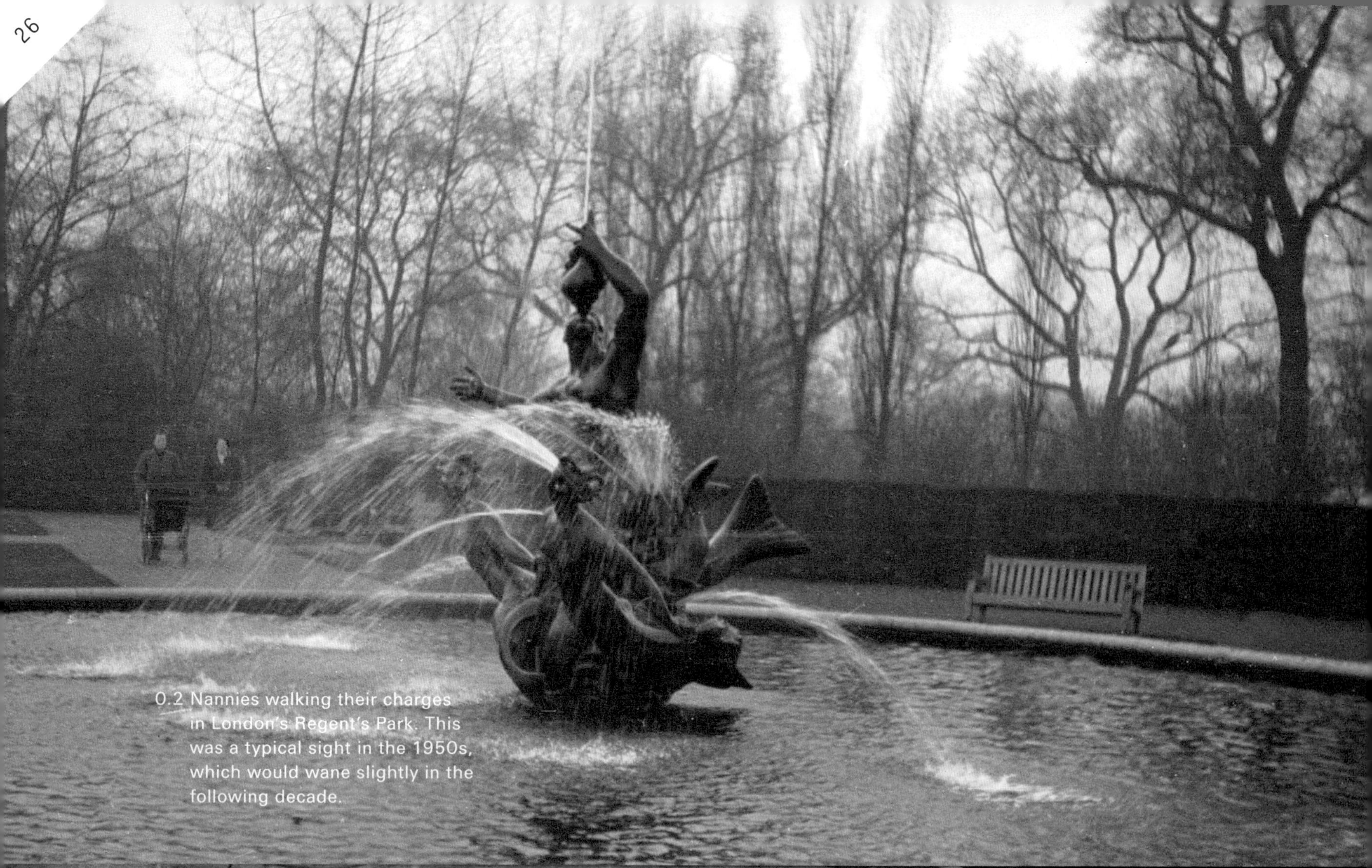

0.2 Nannies walking their charges in London's Regent's Park. This was a typical sight in the 1950s, which would wane slightly in the following decade.

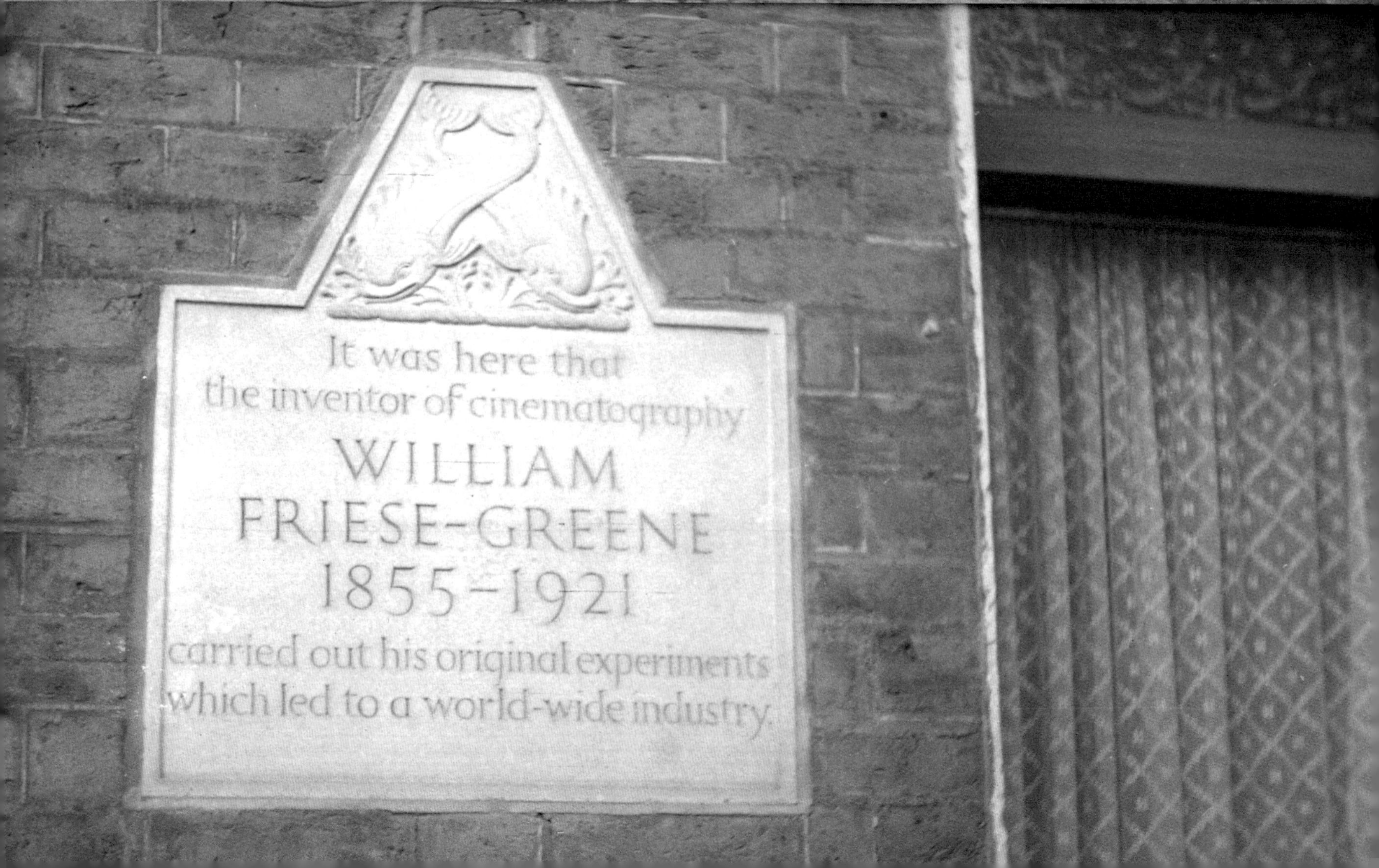

It was here that
the inventor of cinematography
WILLIAM
FRIESE-GREENE
1855 – 1921
carried out his original experiments
which led to a world-wide industry.

The sixties saw the publication of the first colour supplement in
a newspaper (*The Sunday Times Magazine*, in 1962) and the launch
of *The Sun* and *Private Eye*. These were the years of feminism, hippies,
Flower Power, free love, Happenings, Love-Ins, drugs and rebellion.
The establishment was questioned and generally found to be wanting:
in 1968 a protest march in London's Grosvenor Square, against the
Vietnam War, echoed the international mood of disquiet.

They were also very dramatic years in Britain. In 1963 the country
was rocked by the Profumo scandal, in which MP John Profumo lied
to the House of Commons about his involvement with Christine Keeler,
leading to his subsequent resignation and spectacular fall from grace.
Also in 1963 was the Great Train Robbery, in which several men (viewed
by the public as Robin Hood-like heroes) – including Ronald Biggs –
held up a Royal Mail train in Buckinghamshire and stole about £2.6
million, a fortune at the time. In 1966 Ian Brady and Myra Hindley
were convicted at Chester Assizes of the infamous Moors Murders
and were sent down for life. That same year saw the Aberfan Disaster,
in which a waste tip slid down a mountainside, burying a school and
killing 116 children. Britain's winning of the World Cup in 1966 produced
a feeling of euphoria which was utterly in keeping with the times.
The East End of London was ruled by fear in those days: the Kray twins,
well-known gangsters and organised crime figures, were very big at this
time and were sentenced to life imprisonment in 1969. The investiture
of the Prince of Wales took place at Caernarfon Castle in the summer
of 1969, in a mood of sombre nervousness following terrorist threats.

Britain in the 1960s was a different place to the Britain of the 1950s:
many cinemas closed down, to be re-invented as bingo halls, and tower
blocks replaced slum dwellings that were viewed as insanitary, or were
the victims of wartime bombing. Viewed at the time as the cure for
many social evils, these apartments, built in concrete and in the Brutalist
style, nevertheless isolated people who had until then known a spirit
of camaraderie and friendship. One of the most famous tower blocks
of all, Ronan Point in East London, collapsed in 1968 as the result of a
gas explosion, leading to a universal reappraisal of this type of housing.

Popular music underwent a powerful change in 1960s Britain, with
trends which go back to the 1950s when Alma Cogan, Cliff Richard
and Tommy Steele changed our perception of singing. Certainly, in the
1950s much of the hit parade was still dominated by American artists
and it was not until the 1960s that British singers and groups came

into their own. The Beatles burst on to the music scene in 1962, having played in the famous Cavern Club in Liverpool, scoring a modest hit with *Love Me Do* which they followed in 1963 with *Please Please Me*. The Rolling Stones were also very popular at this time – *Satisfaction* was released in 1965 – as was the Merseybeat, a genre of music originating in The Beatles' native Liverpool. These were the years of hits by Cilla Black, Dusty Springfield and The Kinks. The 1960s ended with the BBC banning the broadcast of the song *Je t'aime… moi non plus* by Serge Gainsbourg and Jane Birkin, a record which promptly shot to the number one slot in the charts.

Pirate radio stations, notably Radio Caroline, were very famous during the sixties, years which also saw the advent of the disc jockey – the late Simon Dee was one of the earliest. In 1967 BBC Radio 1 was first broadcast, the first radio station to focus exclusively on popular music. Television, which became widespread in Britain in 1953 with the Coronation of the young Queen Elizabeth, grew in importance in the 1960s, with families gathering together to watch it. The soap opera *Coronation Street* was first broadcast in 1960, *Dr Who* in 1963 and *That Was The Week That Was* was a very popular satirical programme during these years. BBC2 started in the 60s, with *Late Night Line-Up* being broadcast each night, sometimes with the mini-skirted Joan Bakewell (whom Frank Muir famously dubbed the thinking man's crumpet) chairing the studio discussion. *Monty Python's Flying Circus* was first broadcast in 1969. Colour television also began in the sixties. Reality TV and panel shows, so prevalent nowadays, started in the 50s, with *What's My Line?* featuring Barbara Kelly; she was married to Bernard Braden, whose consumer-affairs programme, *On The Braden Beat* (later to become *Braden's Week*) was very popular in the sixties. *Opportunity Knocks*, the famous talent show starring Hughie Green, was also an unmissable programme at the time. And of course the popularity of television sounded the death knell for variety music hall shows.

Films of the 1950s and 1960s have now become classics: from the science fiction *The Day the Earth Stood Still* in 1951, *The War of the Worlds* in 1953 and *Creature from the Black Lagoon* in 1954 to the famous Alfred Hitchcock thrillers, *Strangers on a Train* (1951), *Dial M for Murder* and *Rear Window* (1954), *To Catch a Thief* (1955), *Vertigo* (1958) and the celebrated *North by Northwest* (1959). Hitchcock's *Psycho* came out in 1960 and *The Birds* in 1963, *Mary Poppins* and *Dr Strangelove* in 1964, *The Sound of Music* and *Dr Zhivago* in 1965, *The Graduate* in

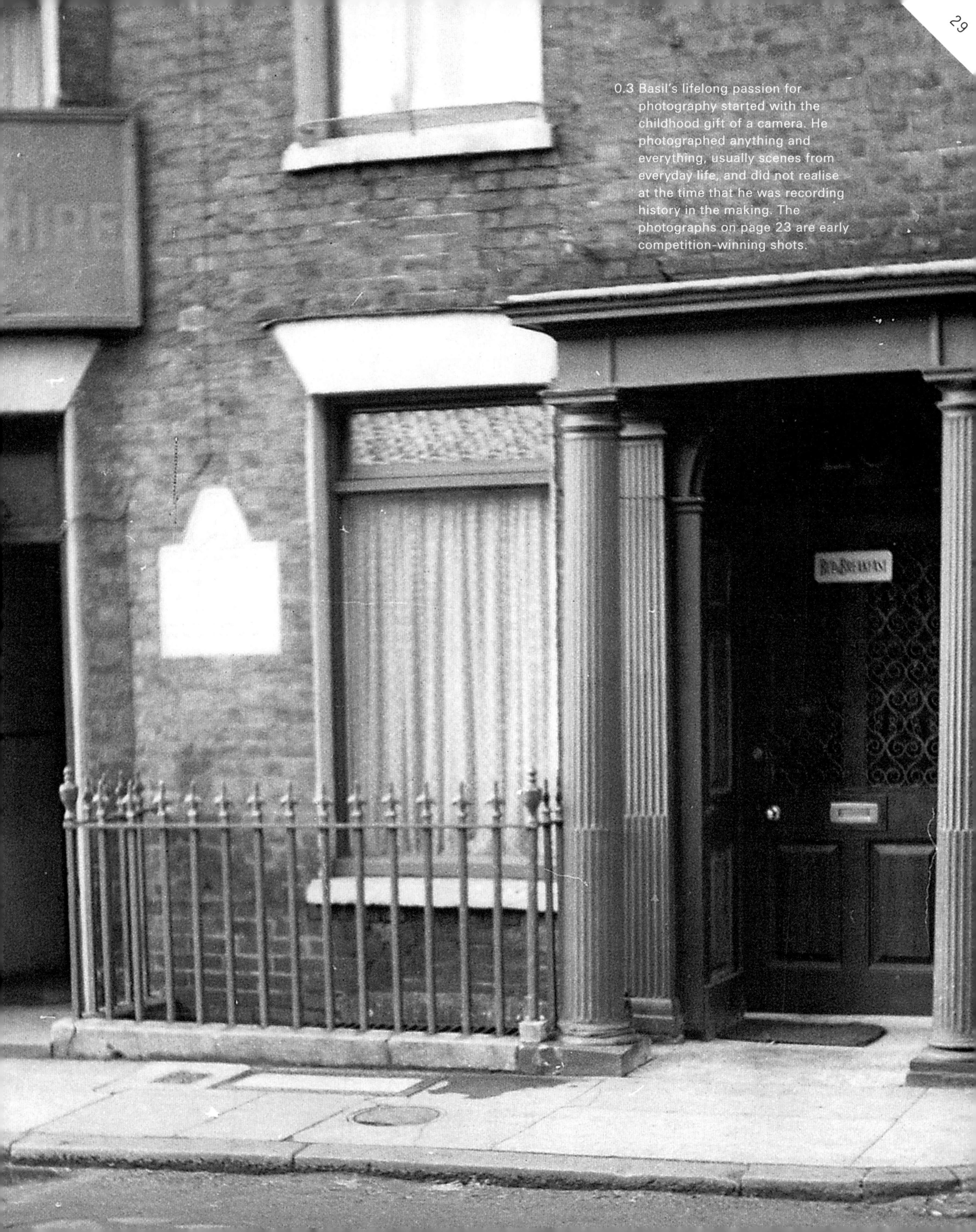

0.3 Basil's lifelong passion for photography started with the childhood gift of a camera. He photographed anything and everything, usually scenes from everyday life, and did not realise at the time that he was recording history in the making. The photographs on page 23 are early competition-winning shots.

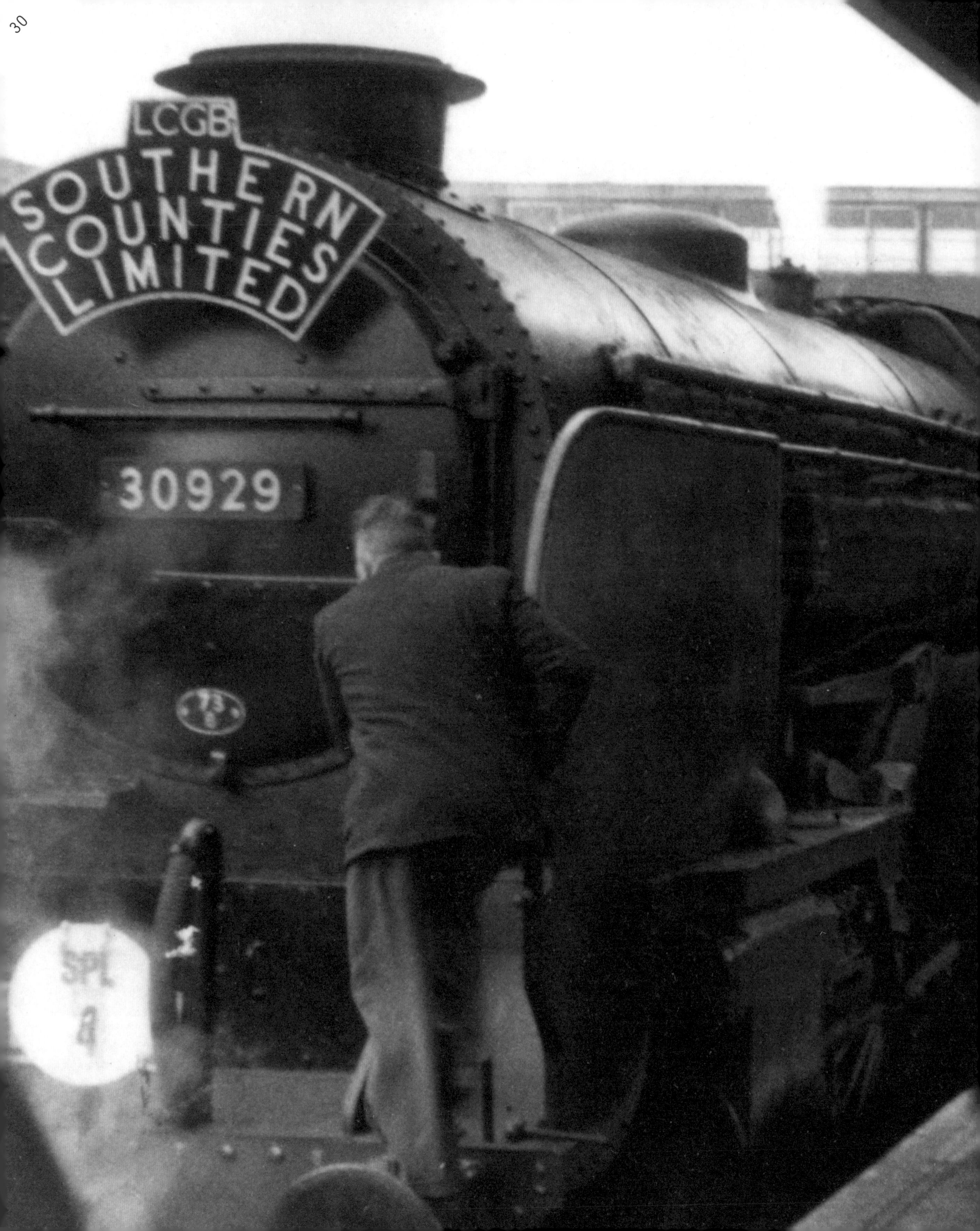
LCGB
SOUTHERN
COUNTIES
LIMITED
30929
SPL
8

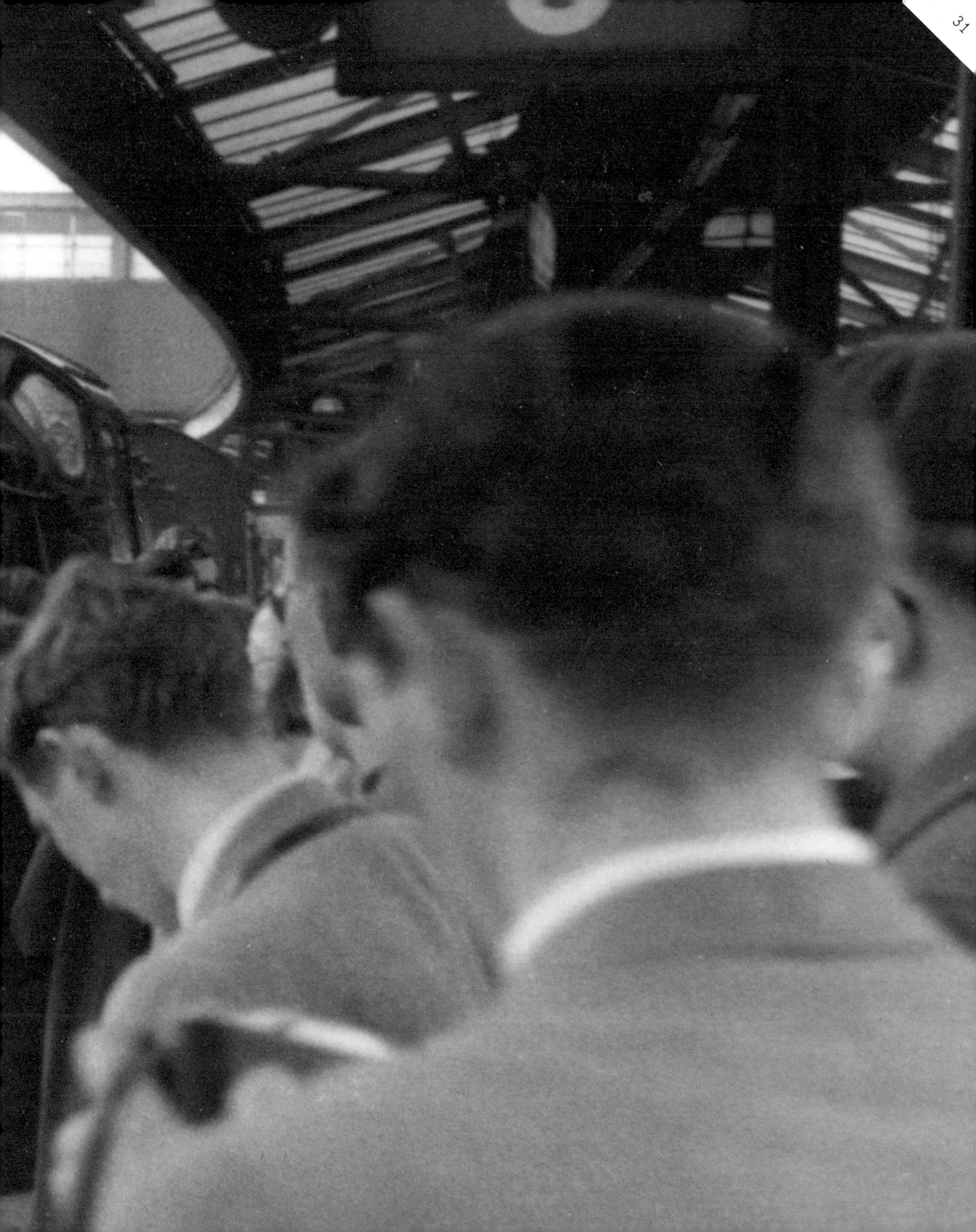

1967 and the now iconic *2001: A Space Odyssey* in 1968. The *Carry On* films began in 1958 and were at the height of their popularity during the 1960s. Books, too, that were very popular in the 1950s and 1960s, have since become classics, from *My Cousin Rachel* (1951) and *The Go-Between* (1953) to *Lord of the Flies* and *Lucky Jim* (1954), *The Talented Mr Ripley* (1955) and *Saturday Night and Sunday Morning* (1958), from *The L-Shaped Room*, *A Burnt-Out Case* and *A Kind of Loving* (1960) to *The Prime of Miss Jean Brodie* (1961) and *The Spy Who Came In From the Cold* (1963). The novelist Len Deighton (who had also been *The Observer*'s cookery editor) created the anti-hero Harry Palmer, who was the antithesis of James Bond. *The Ipcress File*, published in 1962, went on to be filmed in 1965, with Michael Caine in the starring role. *Oh! What A Lovely War*, directed by Richard Attenborough in 1969, was a famous film of the decade.

Transport, which during the fifties was still dogged by petrol rationing, underwent a major revolution in the sixties. Car-ownership soared, motorways became more widespread, the MOT was introduced, as was the breathalyser, and the first traffic wardens started work. Cars had until the sixties been a rare sight on the roads. The QE2 was launched in 1967 and this was the decade of the hovercraft, an easy and quick way to cross the Channel. The way forward for aviation was thought during the sixties to be supersonic travel, with Concorde's maiden flight taking place in 1969. The mini is the car most associated with the sixties, immortalised in the 1969 film *The Italian Job*.

Fashion, which had taken a few tentative steps during the 1950s, came to the fore and some would say rebelled against all that had gone before in the 1960s, from the kipper ties and frilly floral shirts worn by the men to the mini-skirts worn by the women. Tights for women came into vogue during the sixties, putting an end to the tyranny of stockings and suspender belts. London became the fashion capital of the world at this time, with the boutiques of Carnaby Street and the King's Road gaining worldwide attention. Biba, a boutique which began in London's Kensington Church Street, set the tone for an entire generation of women.

The sexual revolution that had begun in the 1950s continued into the 1960s and, with the advent of the contraceptive Pill, liberated women from the fear of pregnancy. The permissive society came of age in the 1960s, when anything went and when radical politics were very 'in' – the new 'redbrick' universities were hotbeds for this sort of attitude to flourish, according to the older generation. In 1960 Penguin Books

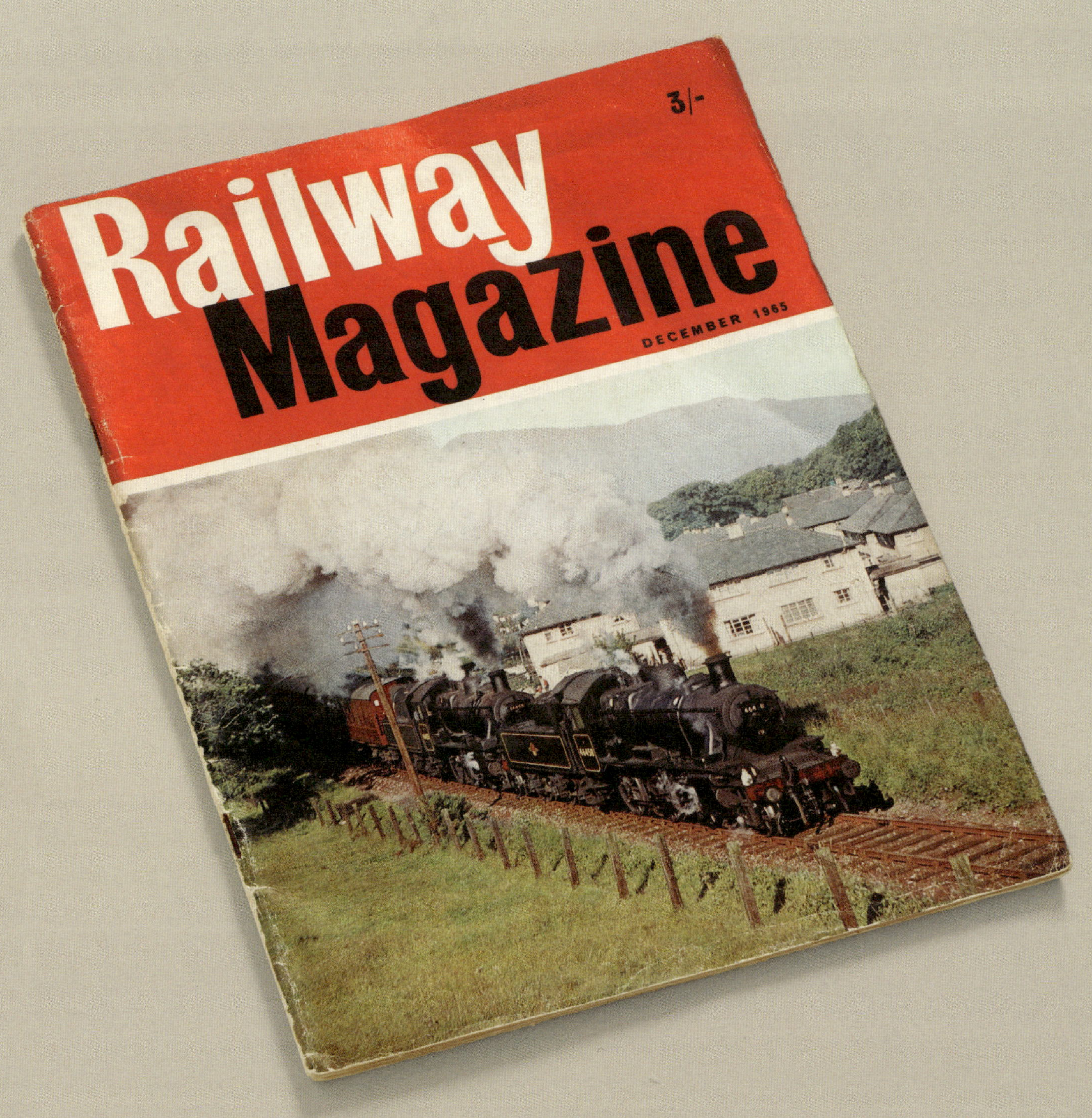
3/-
Railway
Magazine
DECEMBER 1965

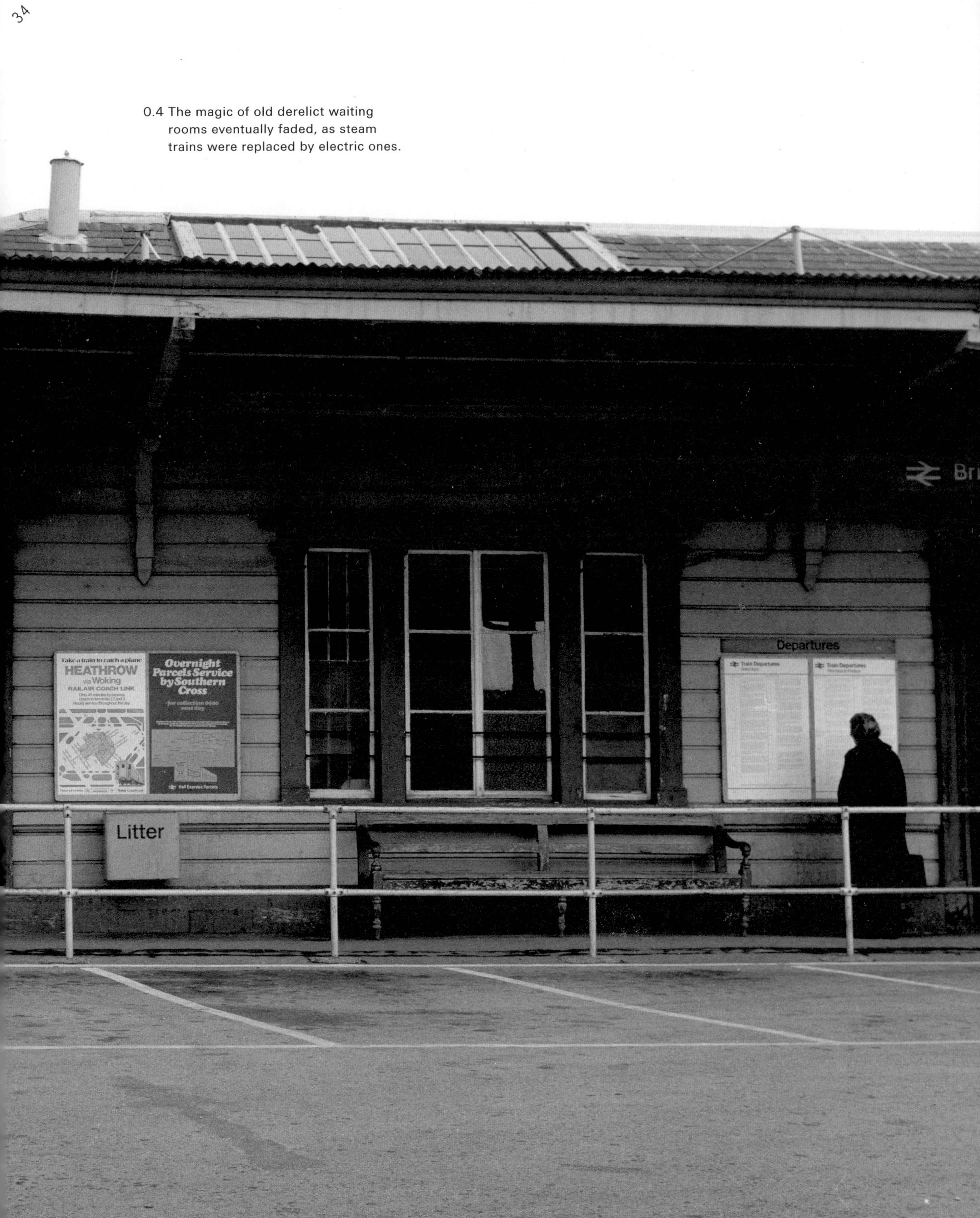

0.4 The magic of old derelict waiting
rooms eventually faded, as steam
trains were replaced by electric ones.

were unsuccessfully prosecuted under the obscenity laws for publishing *Lady Chatterley's Lover* by D. H. Lawrence (as later, in 1964, the American courts ruled *Tropic of Cancer* by Henry Miller to be not obscene). Mary Whitehouse founded The Viewers and Listeners' Association to combat what she saw as overbearing obscenity, and was a self-appointed guardian of the nation's morals. The 1960s sought to shock, to satirise and to overturn the old order, raising two fingers at the establishment, which until then had prevailed, in the old post-war spirit of the 1950s. The musical *Hair*, which opened in the theatres in the 1960s, is a case in point, with scenes of nudity that had never been seen before.

The slogan that most recalls the sixties is 'Make Love Not War', and there was a general feeling that peace was to be sought after at all costs (preferably by the younger generation). The cult of youth, which had begun in the fifties with the predominance of teenagers and nascent rock and roll, continued to prevail in the sixties, and anything that had gone before was to be challenged and rejected. These years were a unique and unforgettable time, one which will never return.

True Romances
FOR THE BEST TRUE-LIFE ROMANTIC READING

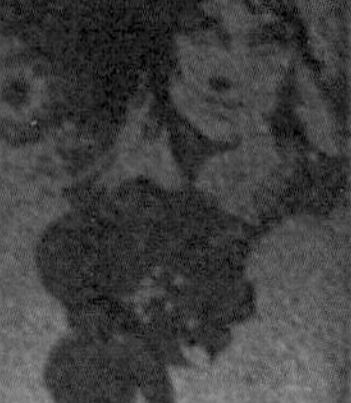

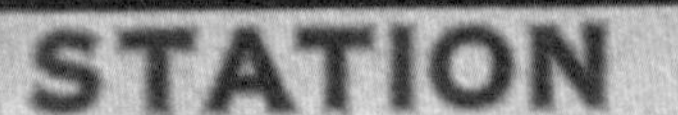
STATION BOOK STALL
73838

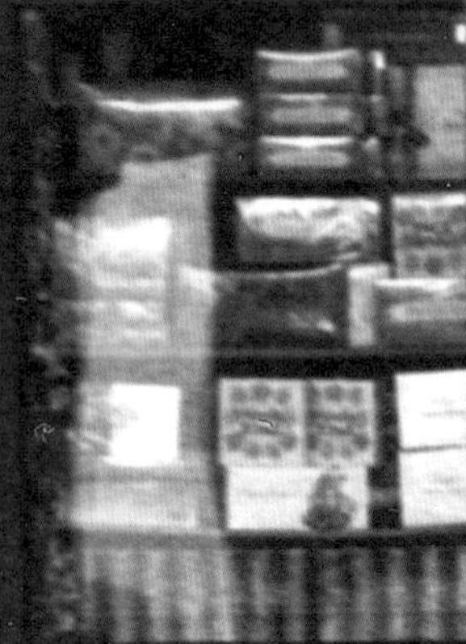

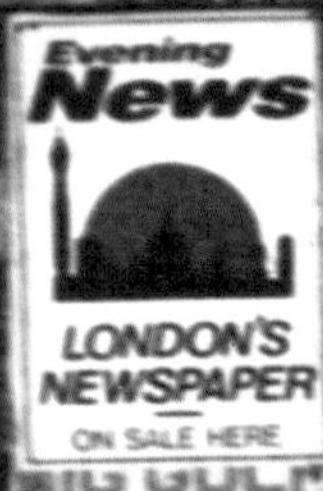
Evening News
LONDON'S NEWSPAPER
ON SALE HERE

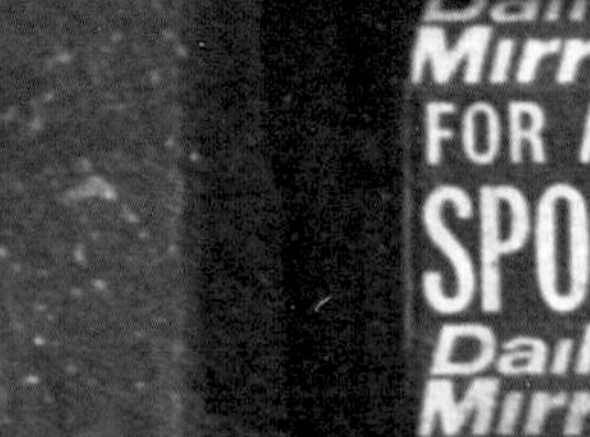
REVEILLE
Dear

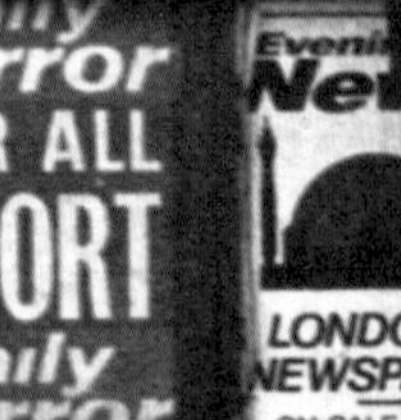
Daily Mirror
FOR ALL SPORT
Daily Mirror

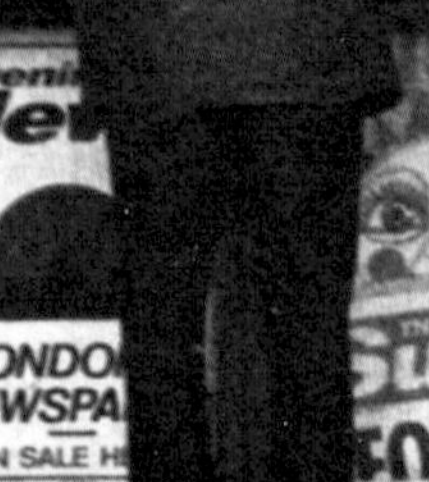
Evening News
LONDON NEWSPAPER
ON SALE HERE

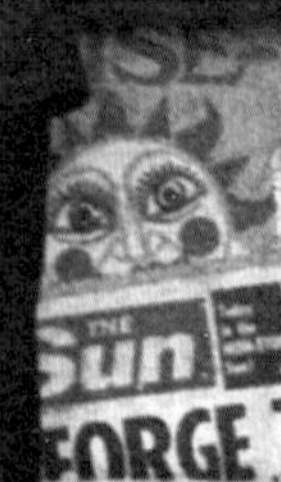
THE Sun
GORGE

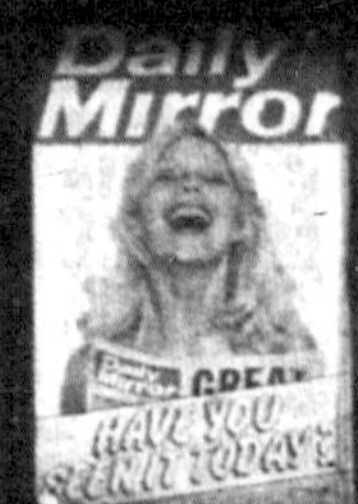
Daily Mirror
GREAT
HAVE YOU
THE Sun

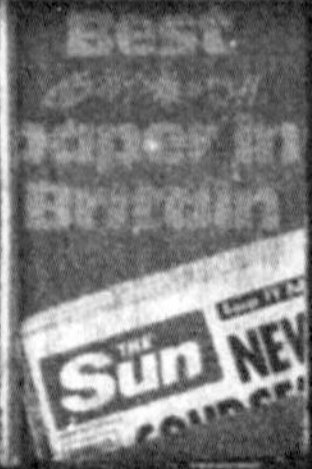
Best
paper in
Britain
THE Sun
NEWS

3
WEYMOUTH
WARNING
Litter

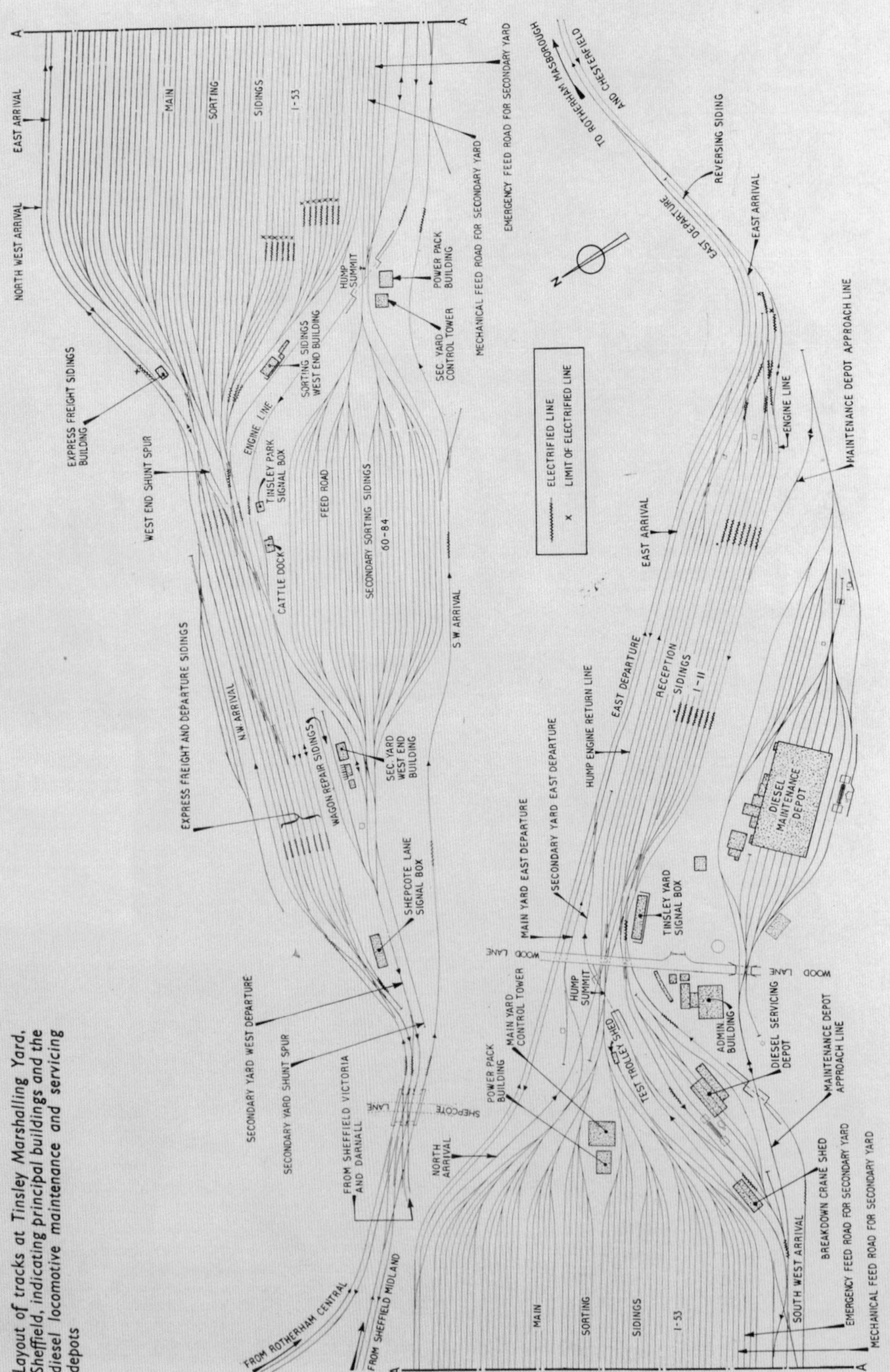

Layout of tracks at Tinsley Marshalling Yard, Sheffield, indicating principal buildings and the diesel locomotive maintenance and servicing depots

in thr
consists
betwee
or traff
trains.
to red
throug
plans i
traffic r

The
occupy
which i
This a
undeve
disturb
residen
to som
provide
who ha
on part
by the f
way wo
powers
acquisi
"comp
British

Whi
access,
conside
be star
had to

The
in all
separat
directi
multipl
of priv
numbe
accom
sidings
second
comm
switchi
in Au

The
betwee
hump
The s
6-11 a
extens
electri
and o
Juncti
locom
area,
faciliti

In t
"ballo
wagor
west
bound
back
siding
a com
in or
possi

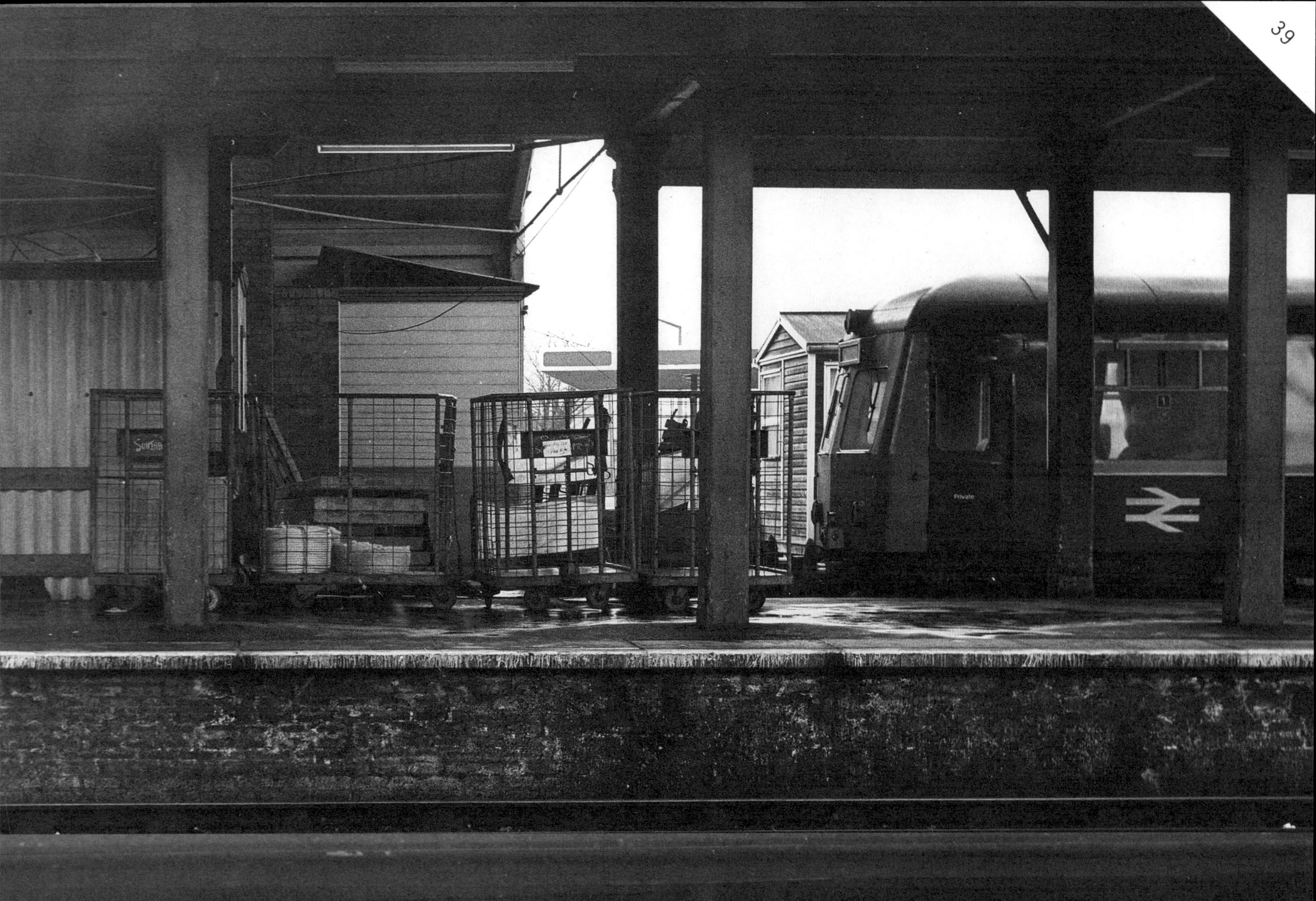

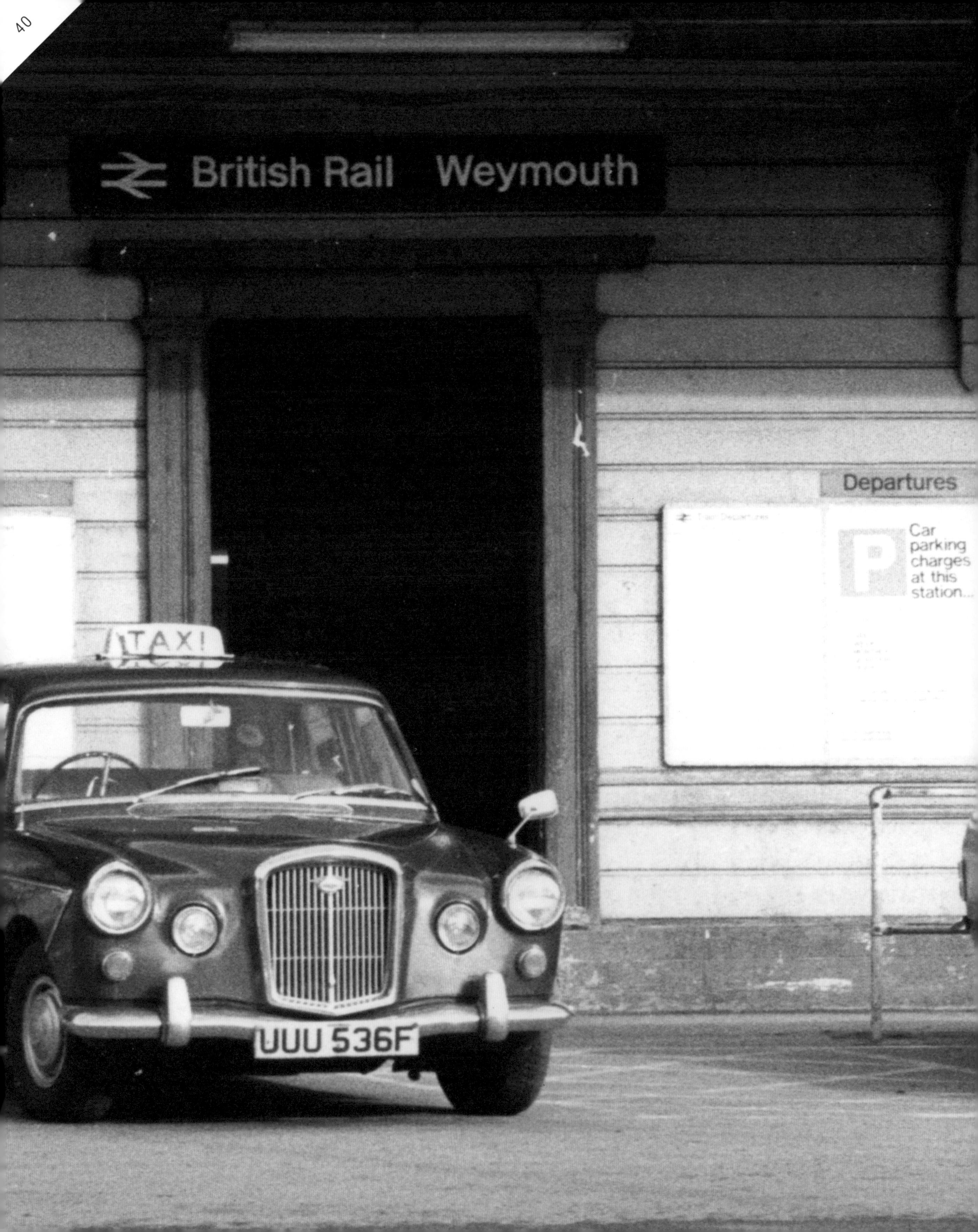

British Rail   Weymouth
Departures
Car
parking
charges
at this
station...
TAXI
UUU 536F

QUIZ
STOP
?
do you
know
the
NEW TRAFFIC SIGNS

7
8
9
10
11
12
7
8
9
10
11
12
GOLDEN
SHRED
page 4

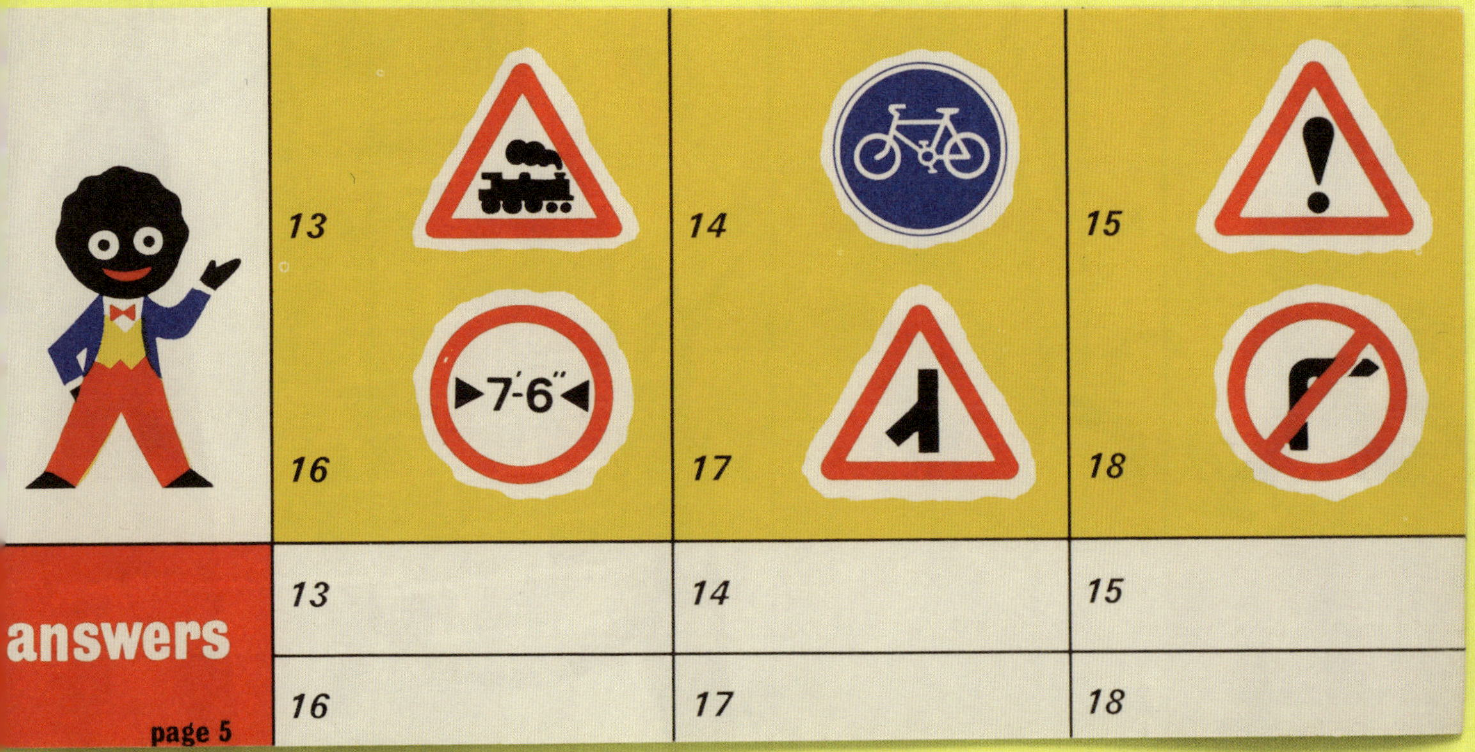

answers

13

14

15

16

17

18

7'-6"

13	14	15
16	17	18

page 5

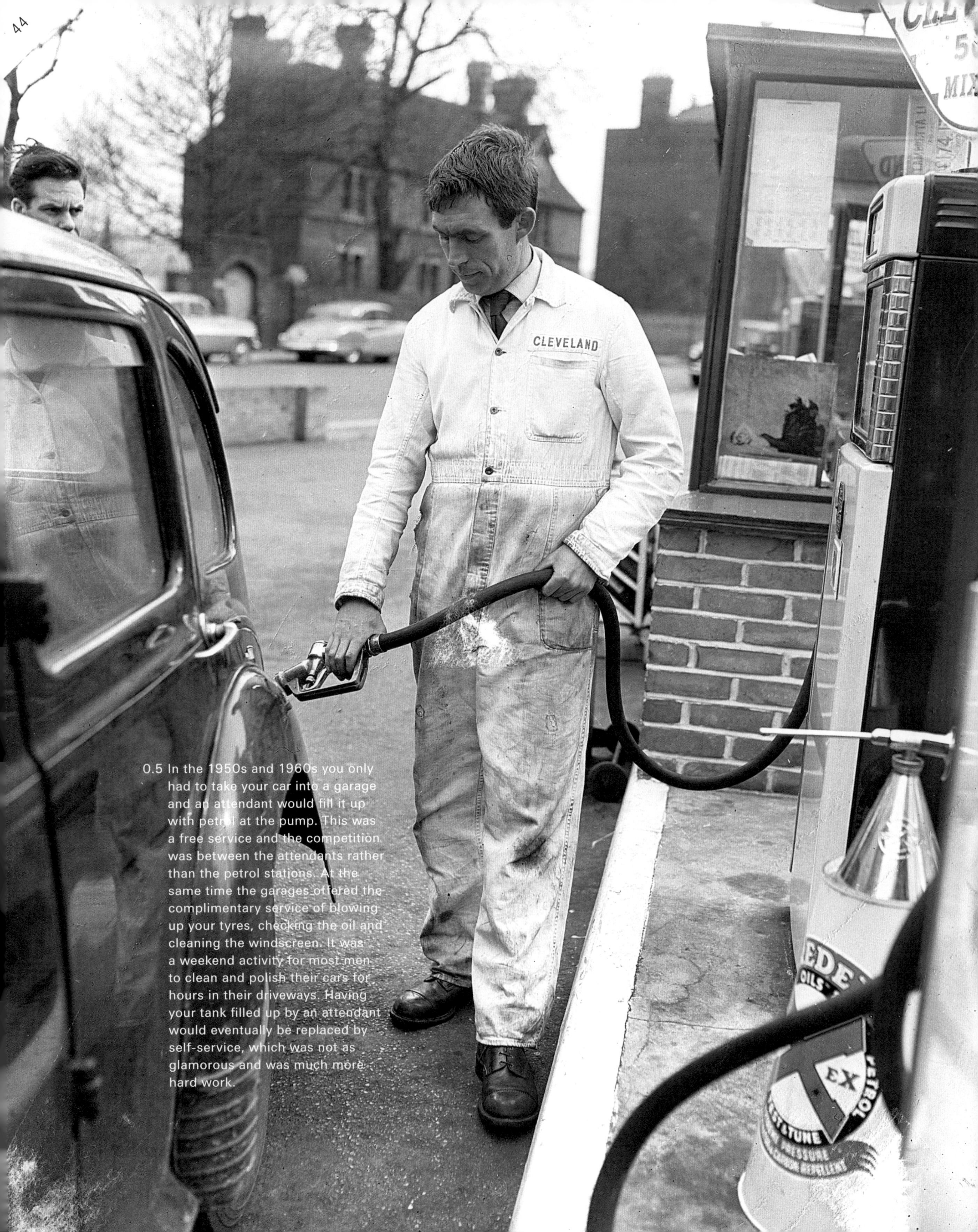

0.5 In the 1950s and 1960s you only had to take your car into a garage and an attendant would fill it up with petrol at the pump. This was a free service and the competition was between the attendants rather than the petrol stations. At the same time the garages offered the complimentary service of blowing up your tyres, checking the oil and cleaning the windscreen. It was a weekend activity for most men to clean and polish their cars for hours in their driveways. Having your tank filled up by an attendant would eventually be replaced by self-service, which was not as glamorous and was much more hard work.

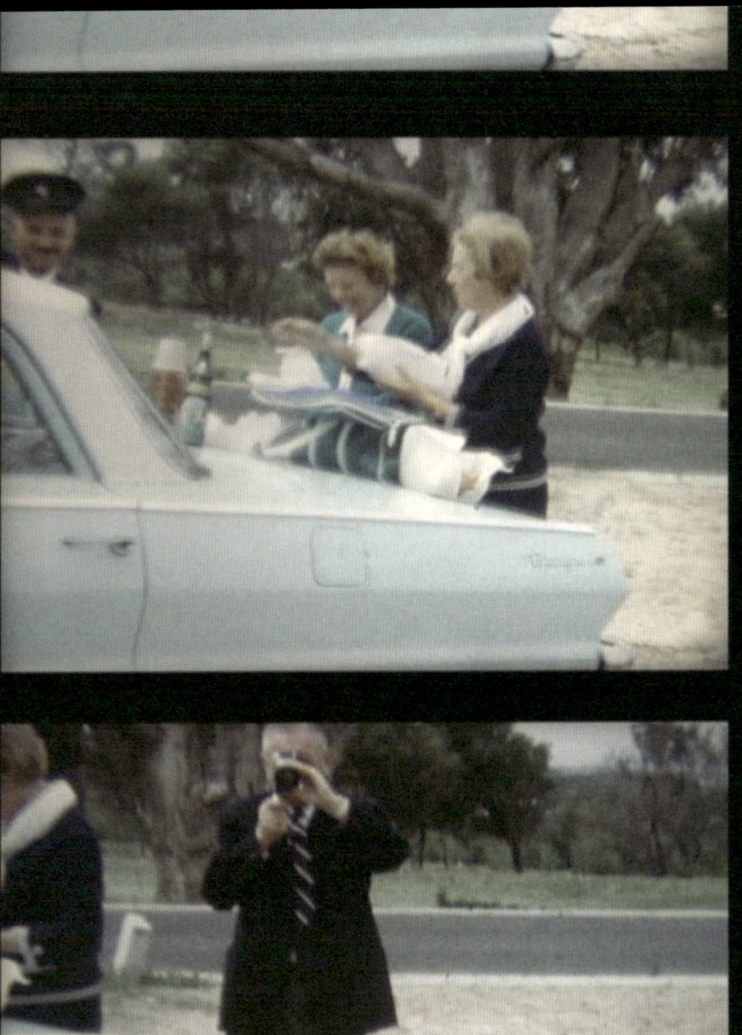

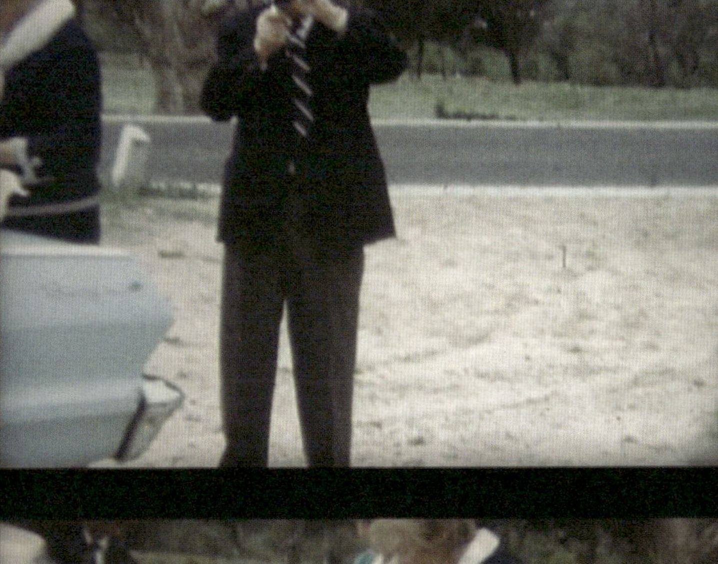

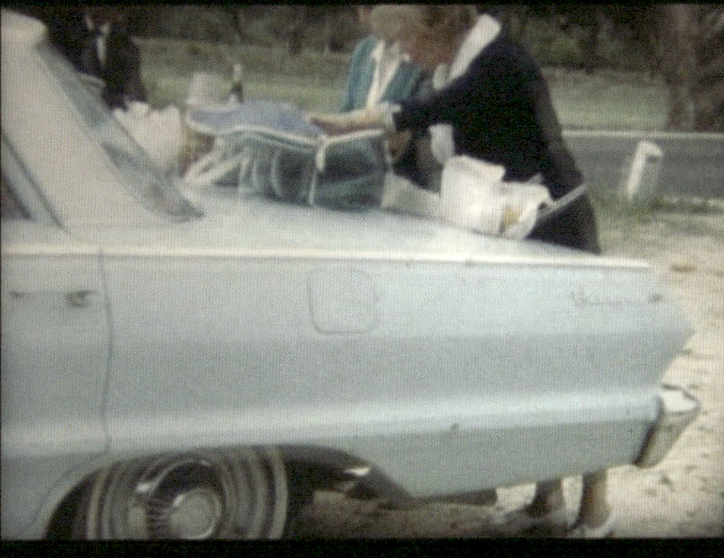

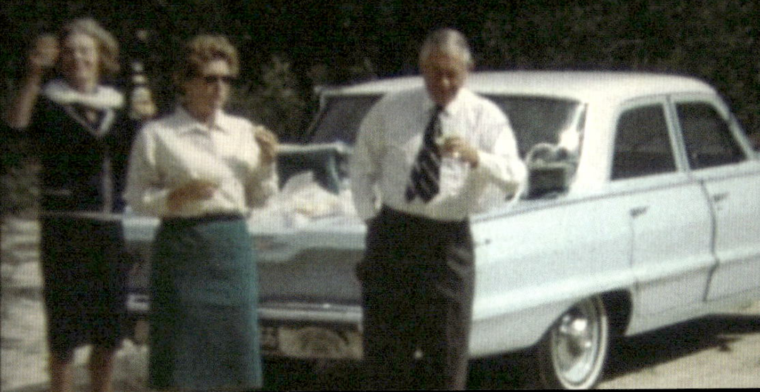

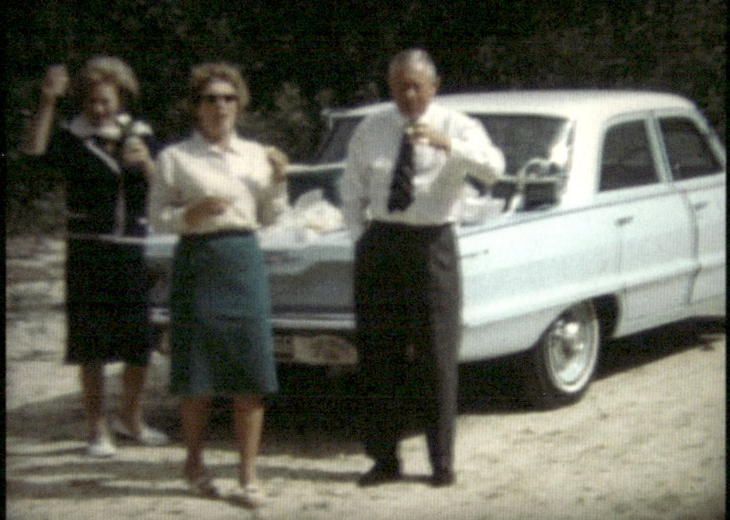

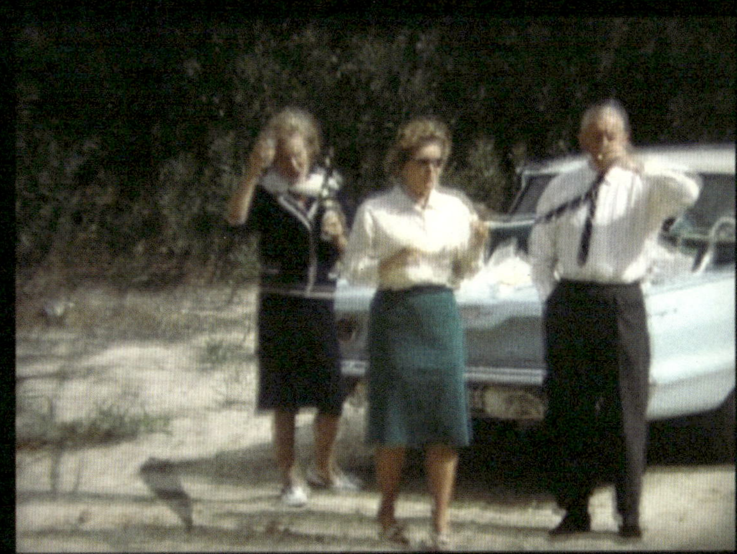

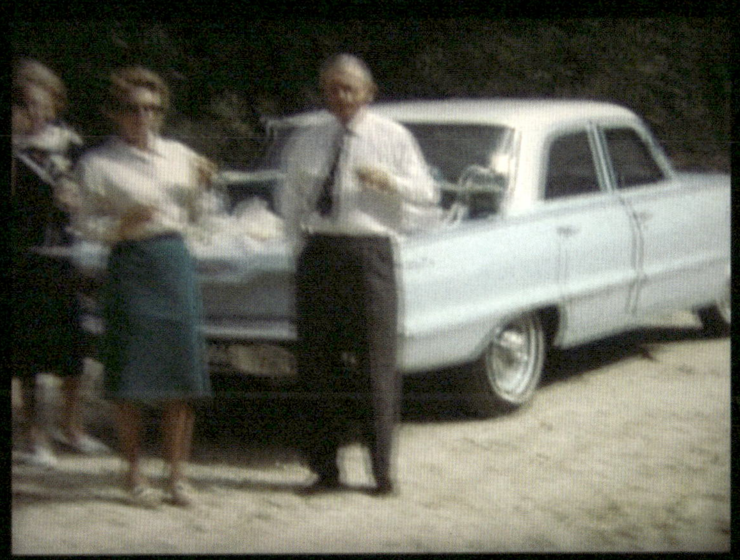

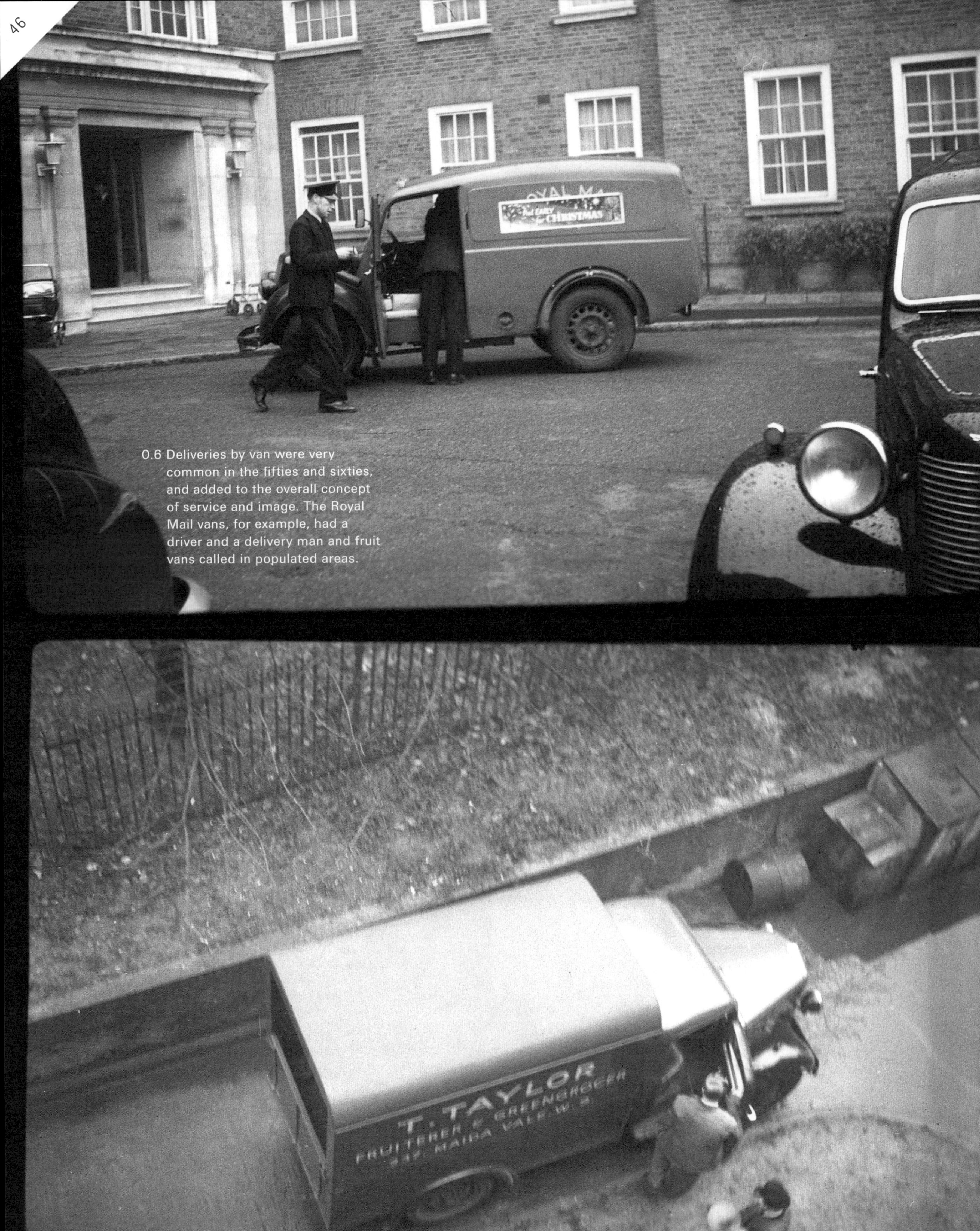

0.6 Deliveries by van were very common in the fifties and sixties, and added to the overall concept of service and image. The Royal Mail vans, for example, had a driver and a delivery man and fruit vans called in populated areas.

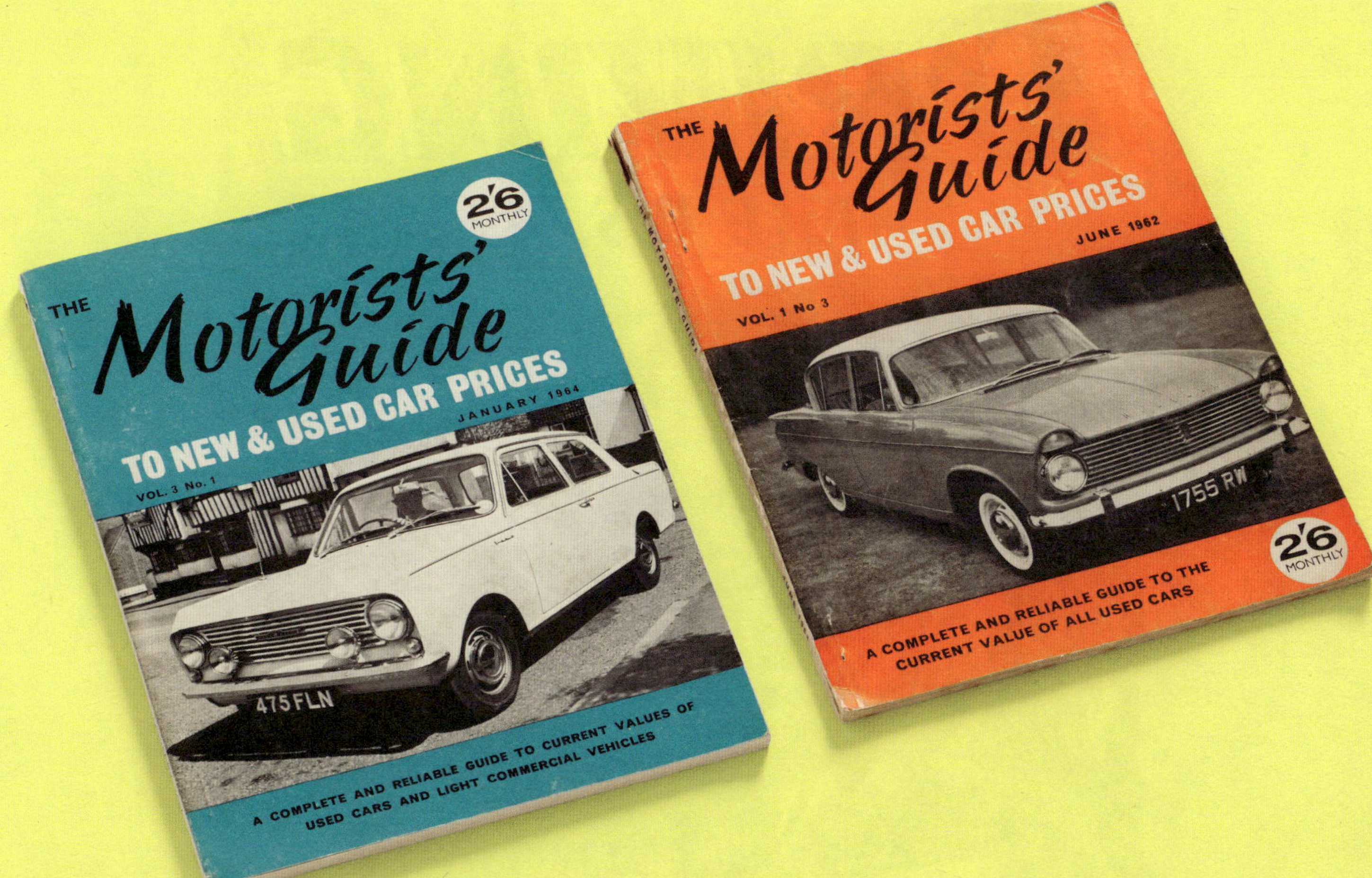
THE
Motorists' Guide
TO NEW & USED CAR PRICES
VOL. 3 No. 1
JANUARY 1964
2'6 MONTHLY
475 FLN
A COMPLETE AND RELIABLE GUIDE TO CURRENT VALUES OF
USED CARS AND LIGHT COMMERCIAL VEHICLES
THE
Motorists' Guide
TO NEW & USED CAR PRICES
VOL. 1 No 3
JUNE 1962
1755 RW
2'6 MONTHLY
A COMPLETE AND RELIABLE GUIDE TO THE
CURRENT VALUE OF ALL USED CARS

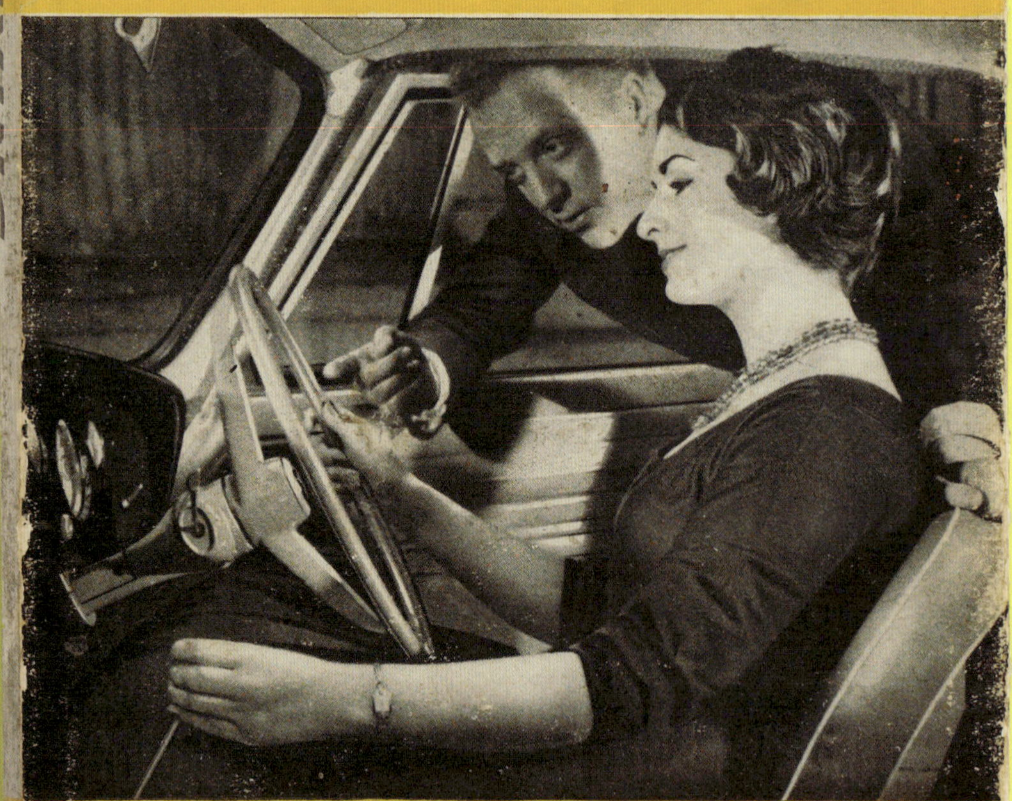

THE BETTER SAFER MOTORING SERIES
GOOD DRIVING
—THE B.S.M. WAY
RONALD PRIESTLEY and TOM WISDOM

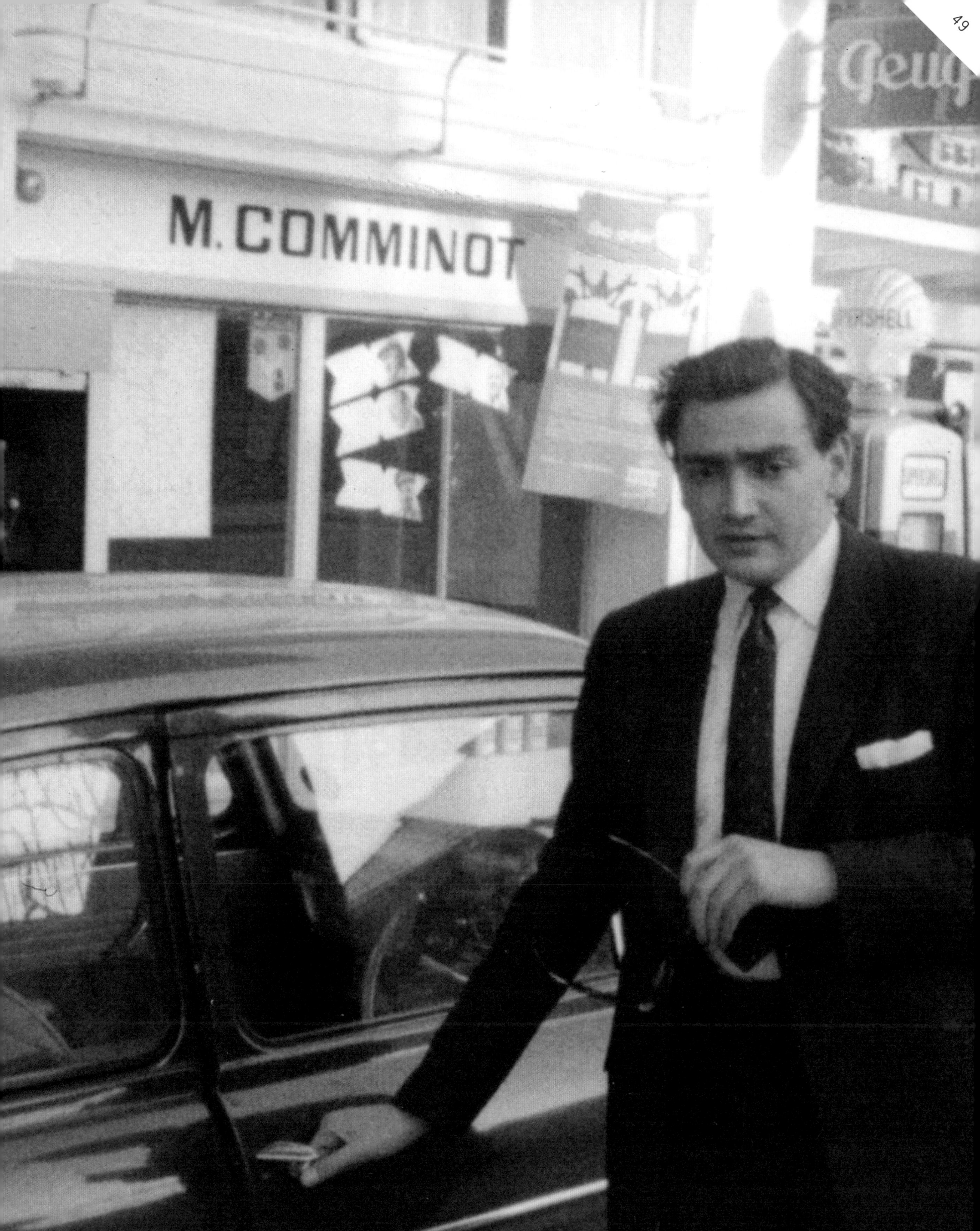
M. COMMINOT
Geu
SHELL

Butlins

For those who chose to holiday in Britain there were always Butlins holiday camps, where many activities were presided over by the Redcoats (staff in red blazers whose duties included stewarding, or being an adult or children's entertainer). These activities, which would be in part geared towards grown-ups and in part towards children, were part of the price of the holiday and formed an essential part of the Butlins experience.

Created by Billy Butlin in the 1930s at Skegness to provide cheap holidays for everyone, regardless of class, Butlins holiday camps were much visited in the fifties and sixties and afforded an organised, action-packed day. Billy Butlin created a major business which gave pleasure to thousands. Slogans included, up to the 1950s, 'Holidays are Jollidays' and, from the 1960s, 'You'll have a really wonderful time at Butlins by the sea'.

Butlins also had a very broad-minded approach to unmarried couples staying in the same room, unlike other hotels where you had to produce your passport to prove you were married.

On arrival campers would be given a badge to ensure re-admission to the camp (this would be worn throughout their stay) and would be shown to their chalet. Adults could go out in the evening and rely on the babysitting service provided for children. Every morning at 8 o'clock campers would be woken up to music over the tannoy in order to get to breakfast without delay. There are many stories people can tell about the fun they had at Butlins. To this day it still has excellent rides, entertainment for the children and many theme bars. The Butlins atmosphere was always one of jollity and enjoyment, undimmed after all these years.

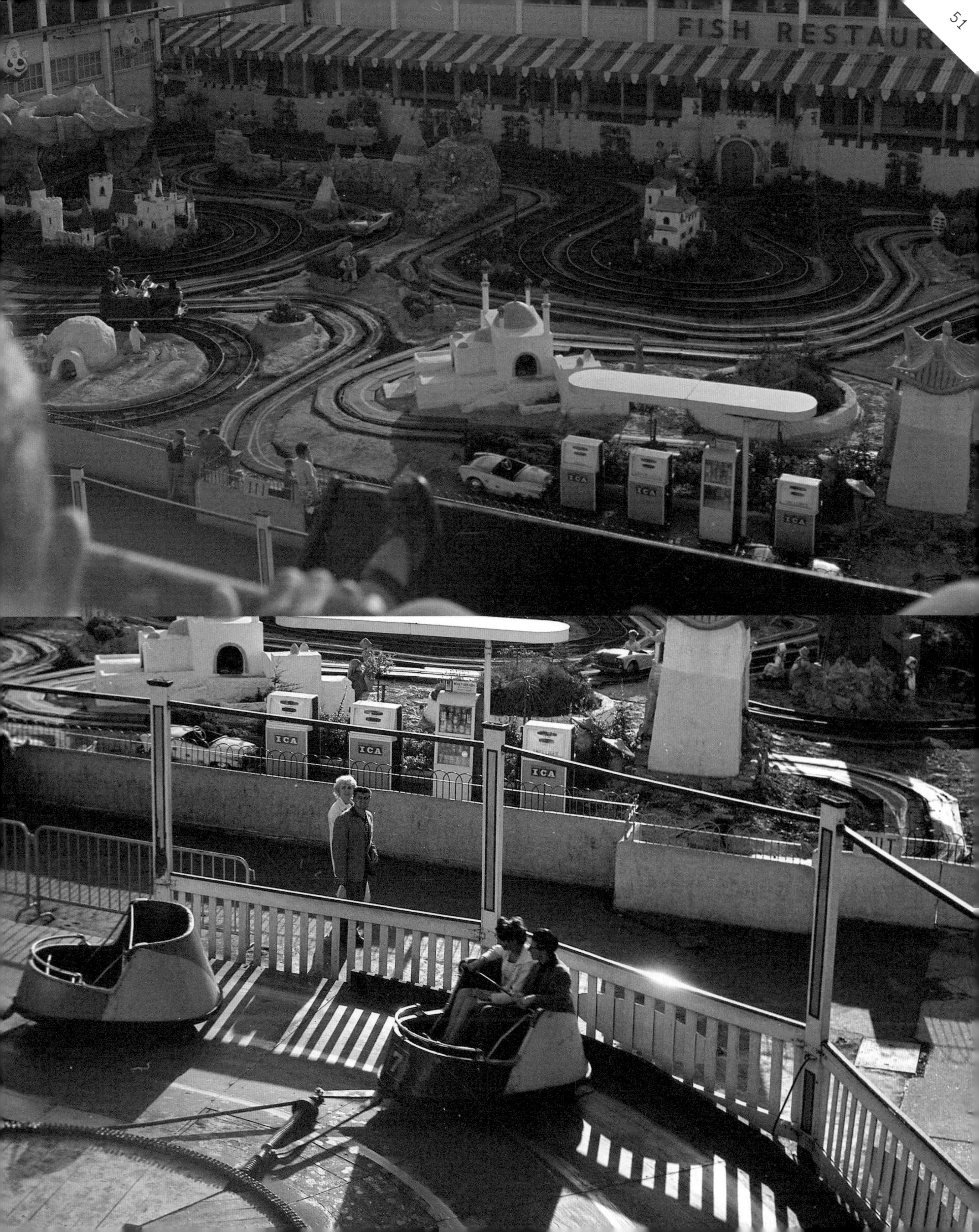
FISH RESTAUR
ICA
ICA
ICA
ICA

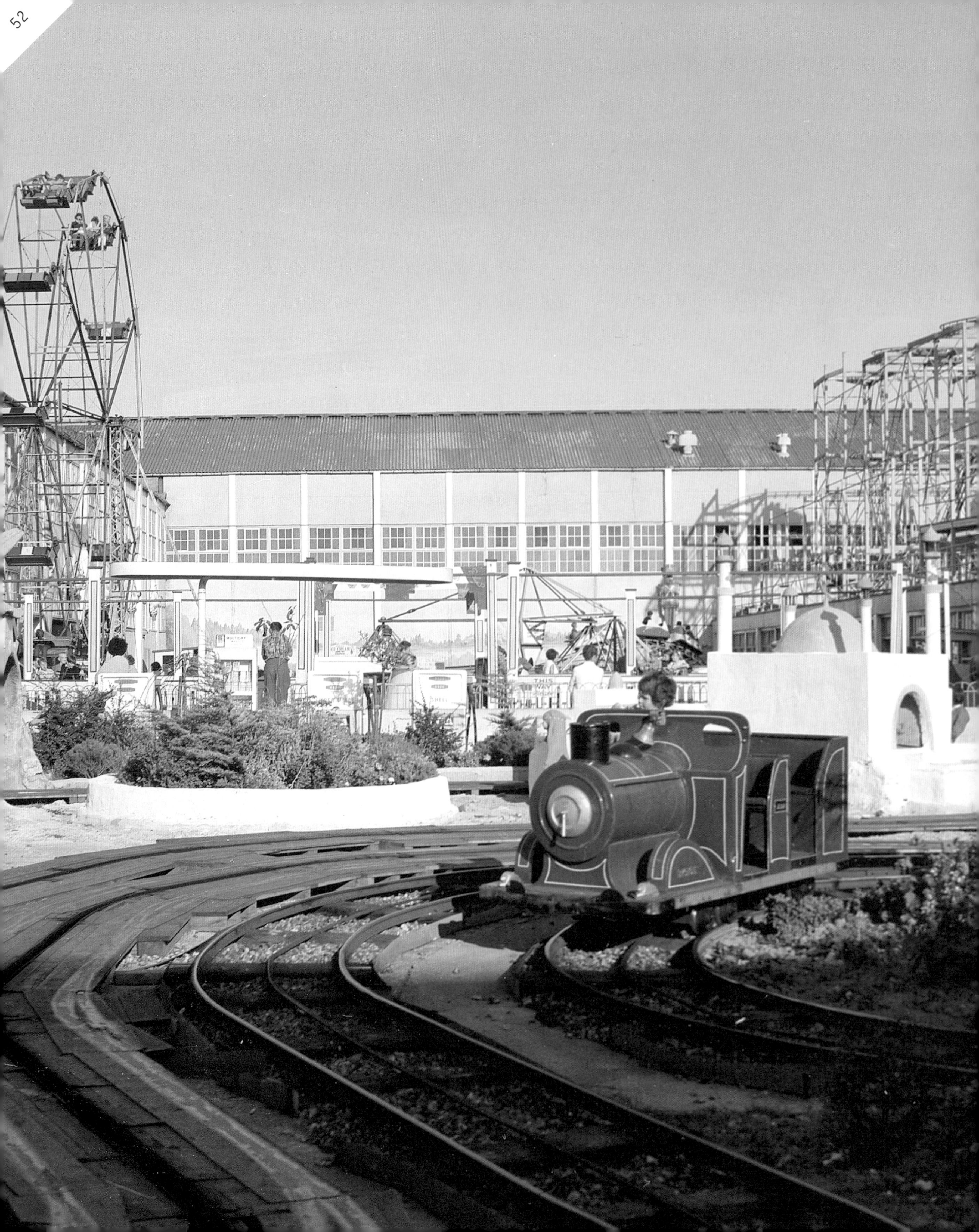

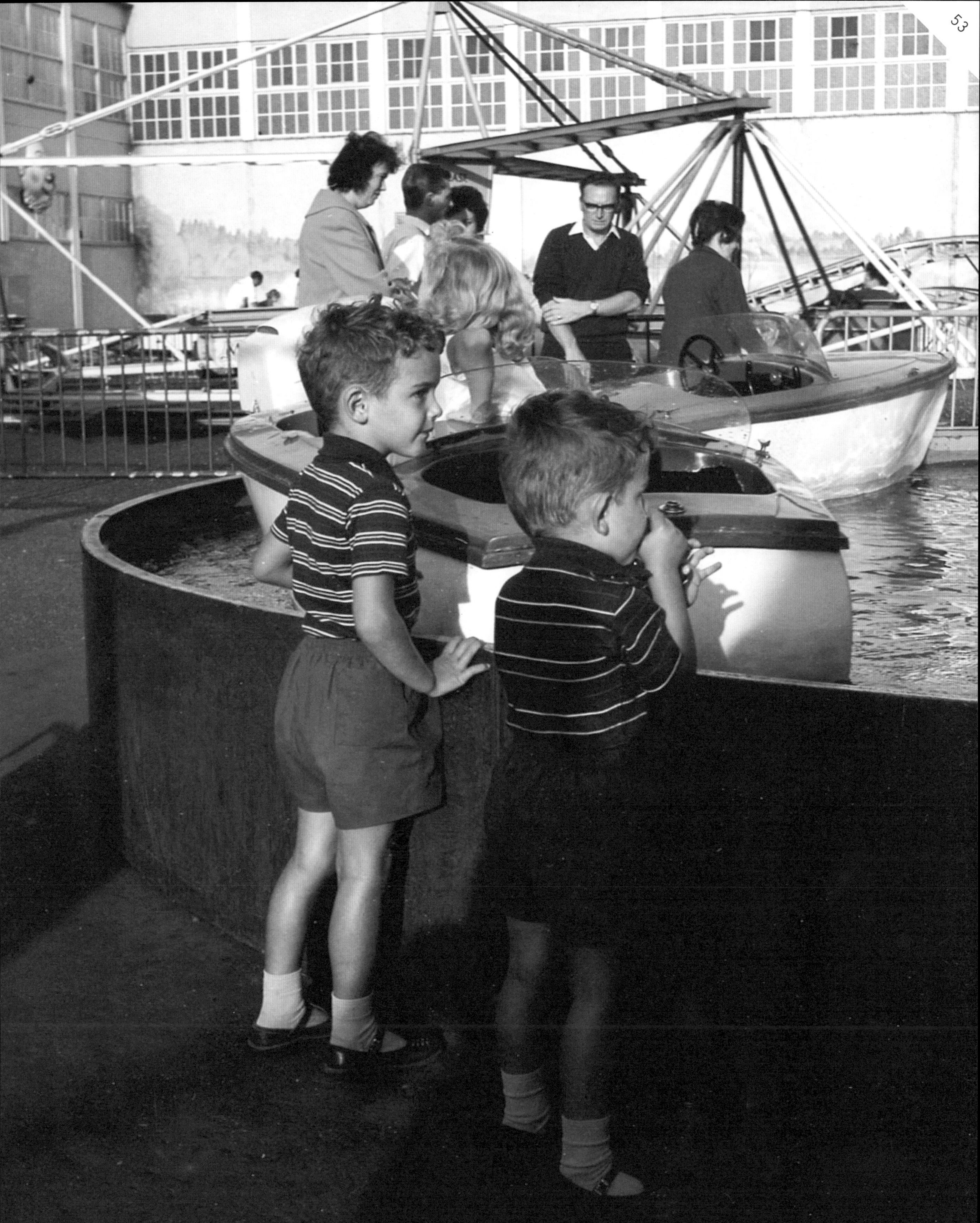

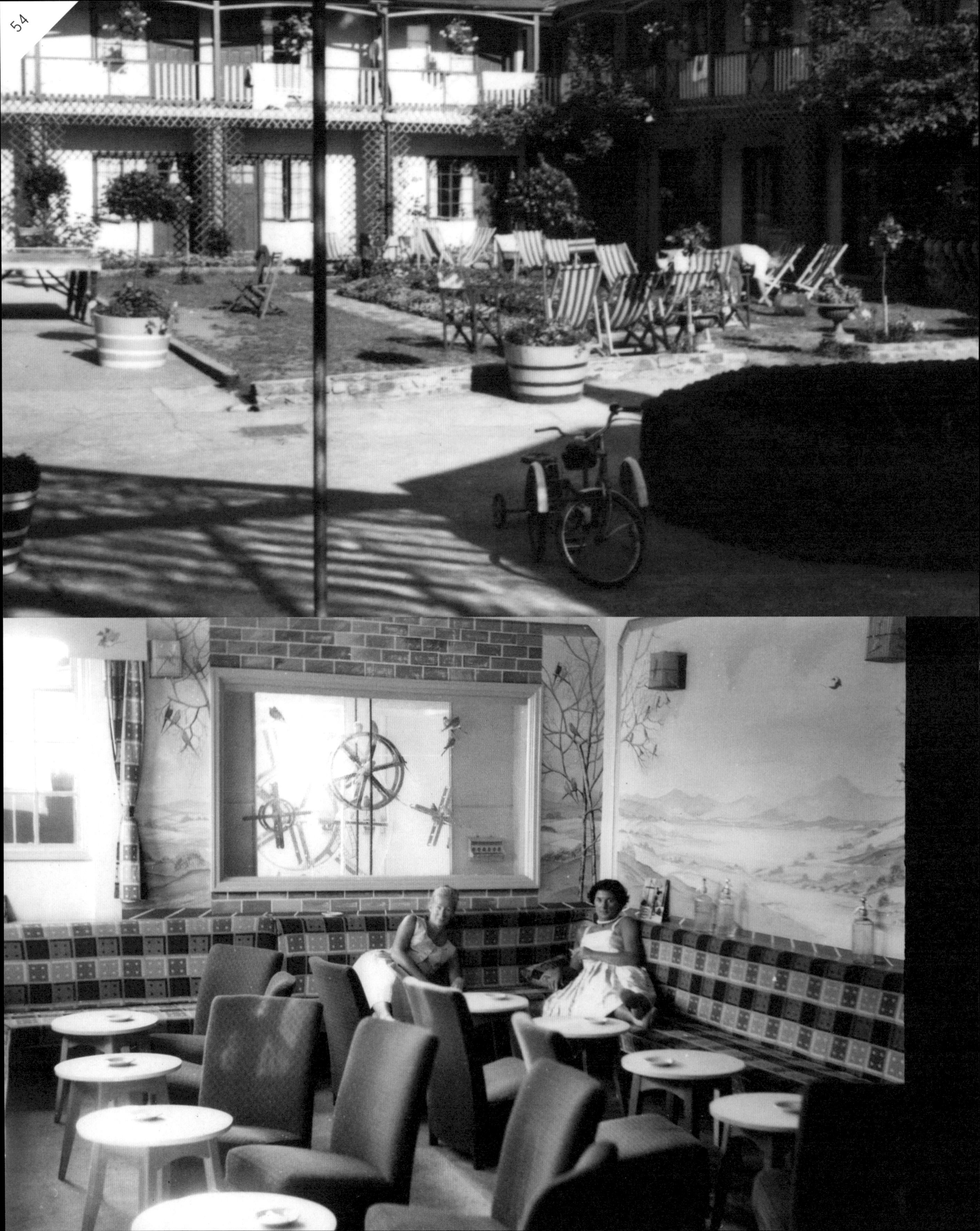

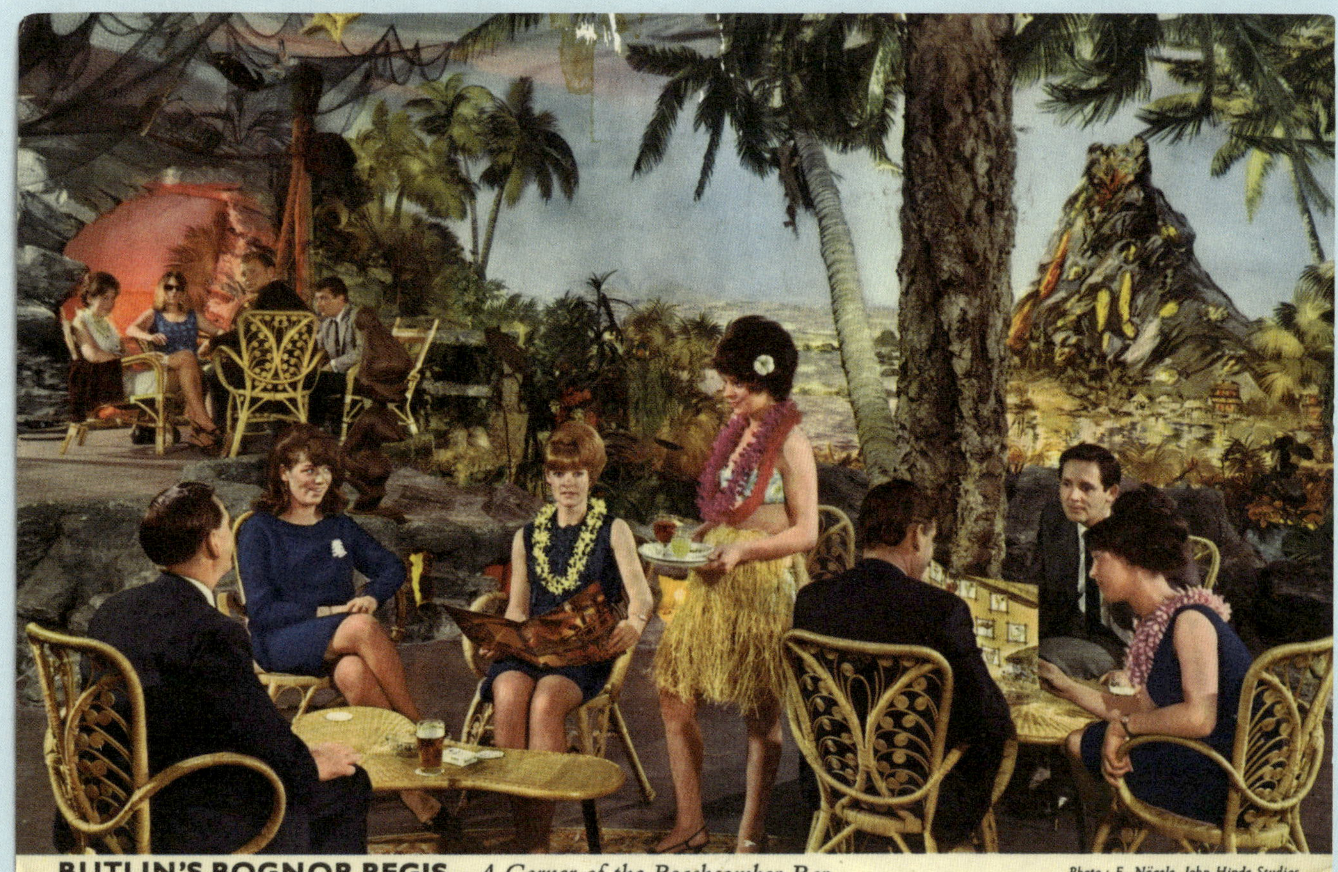

BUTLIN'S BOGNOR REGIS—*A Corner of the Beachcomber Bar*

Photo : E. Nägele, John Hinde Studios.

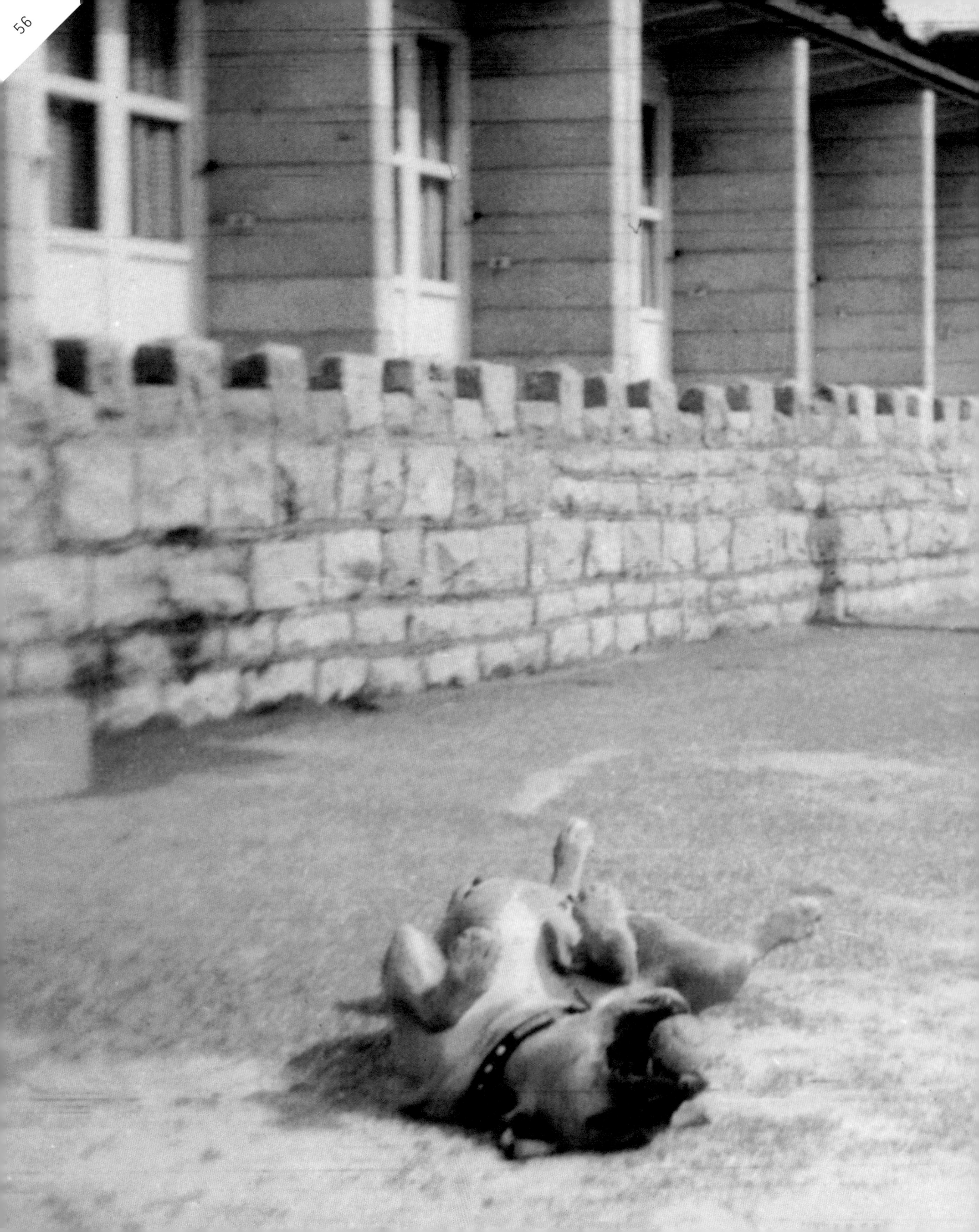

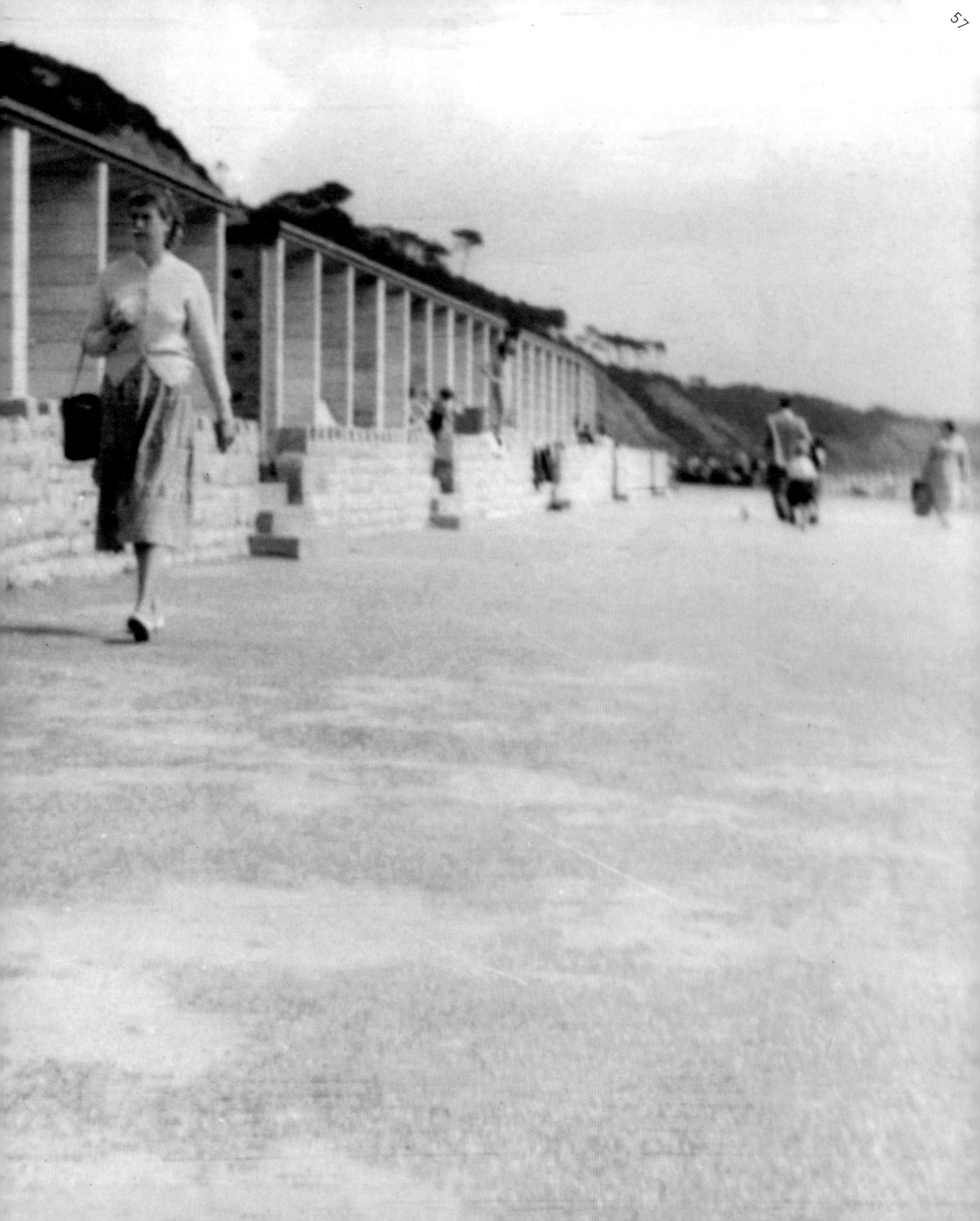

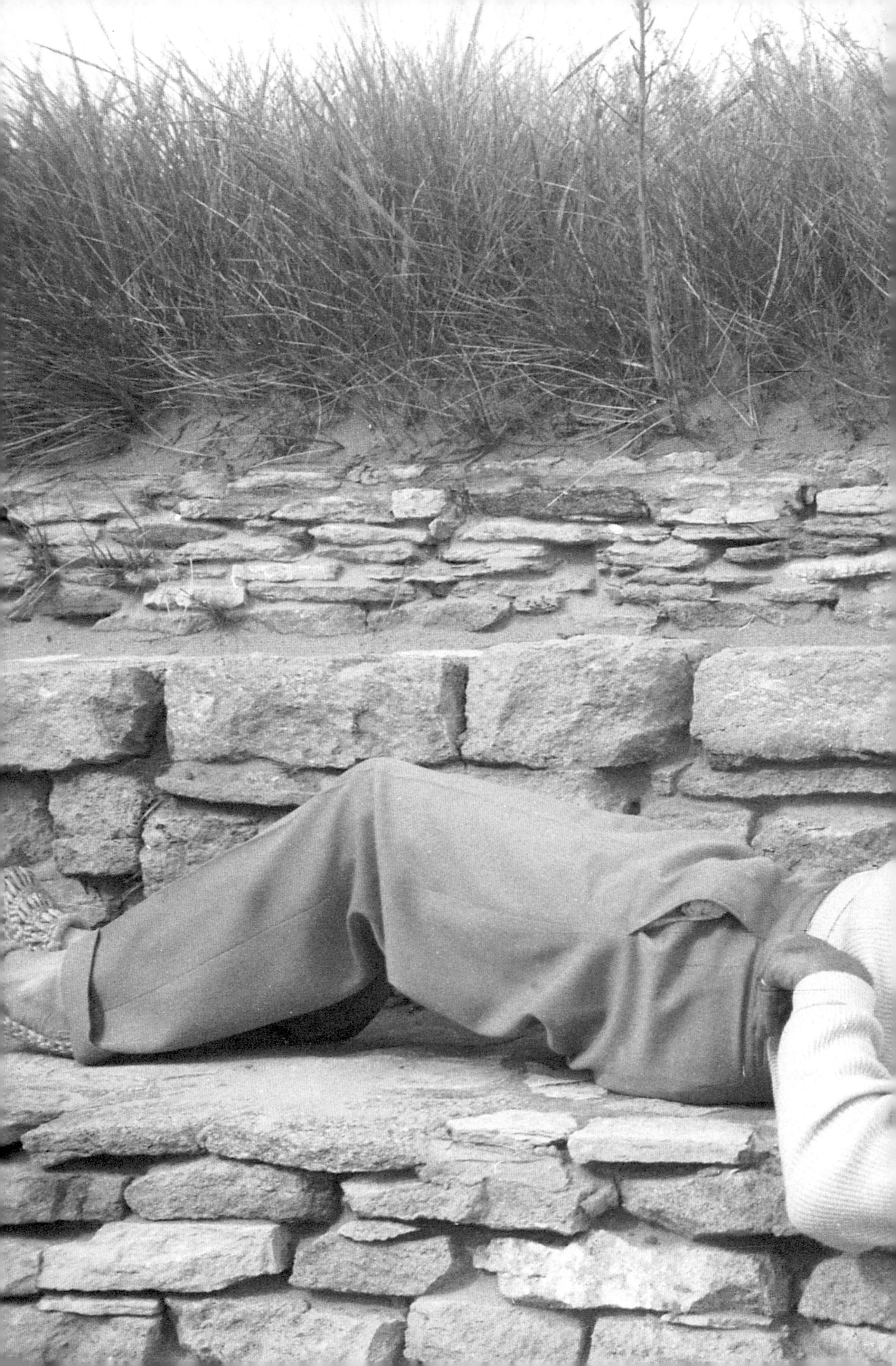

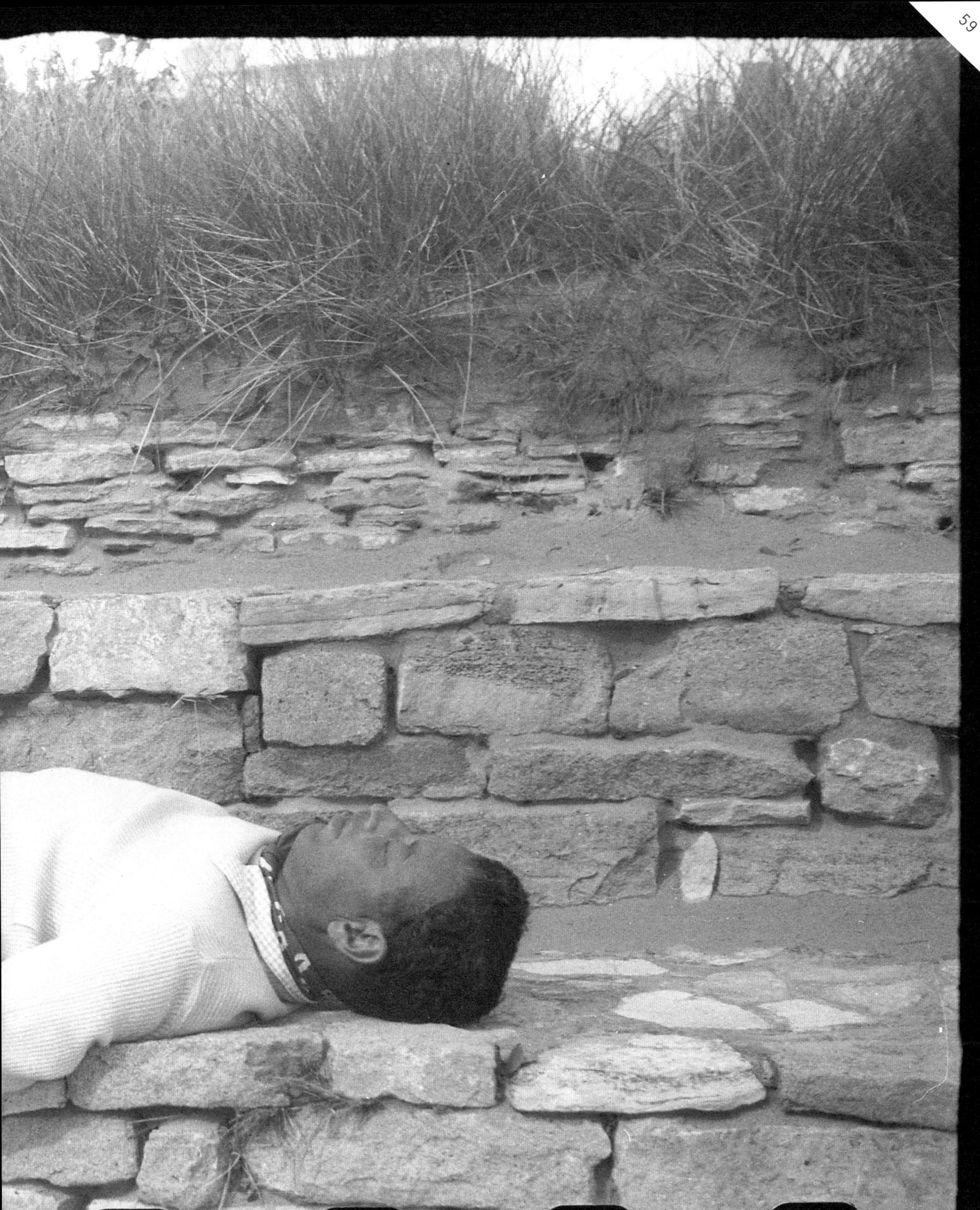

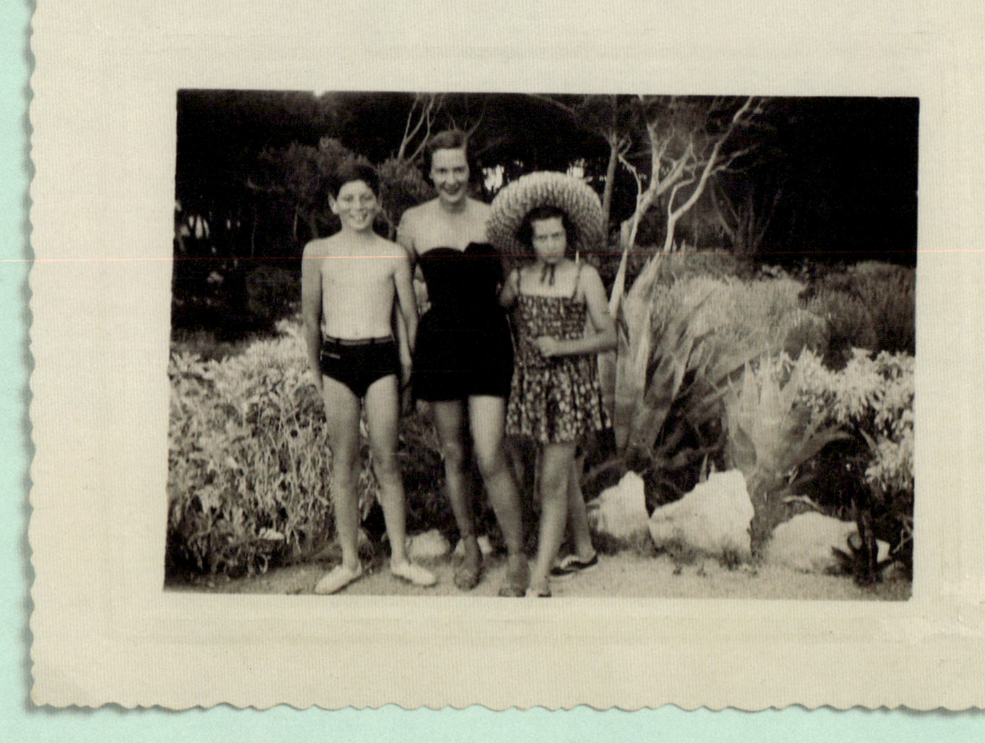

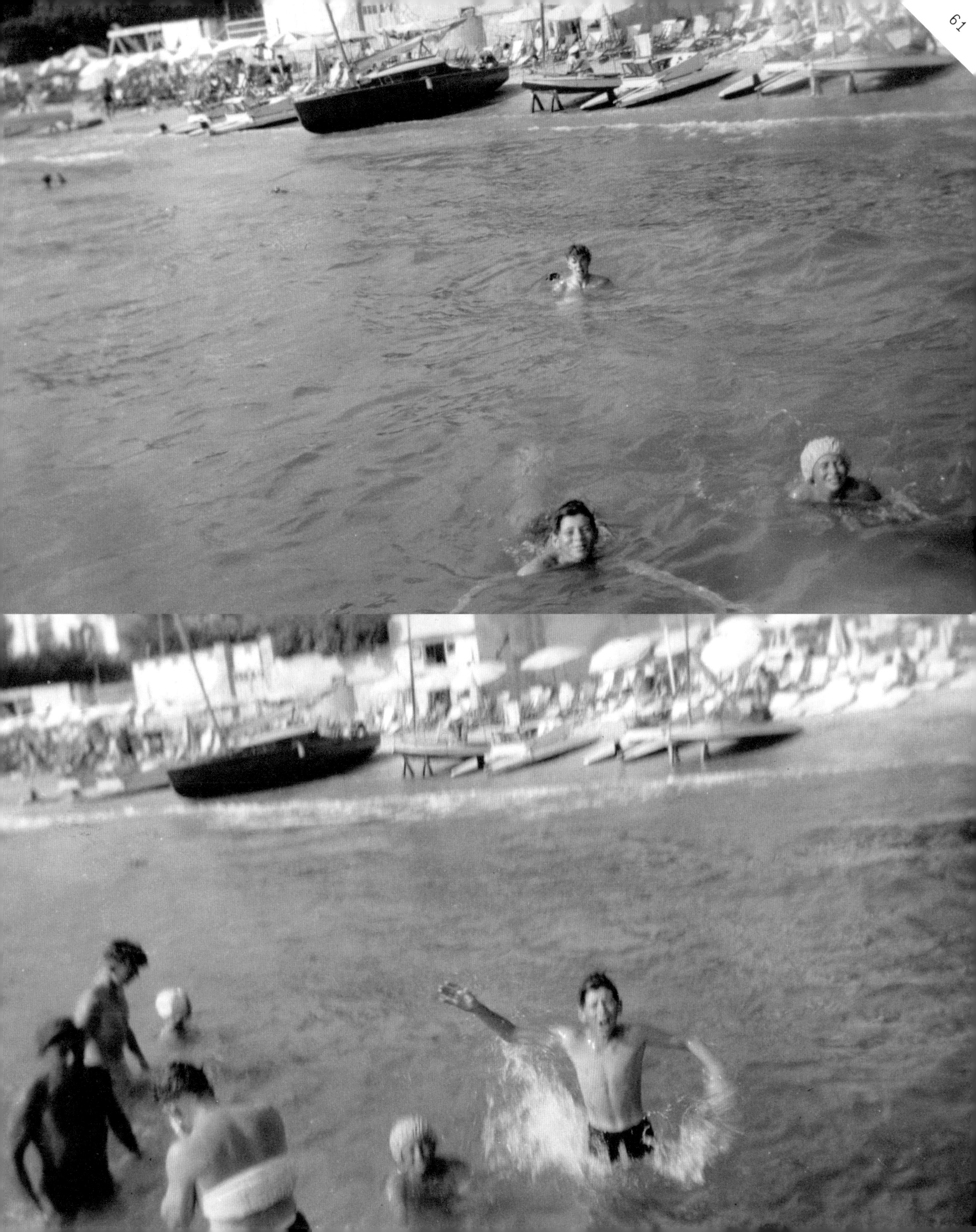

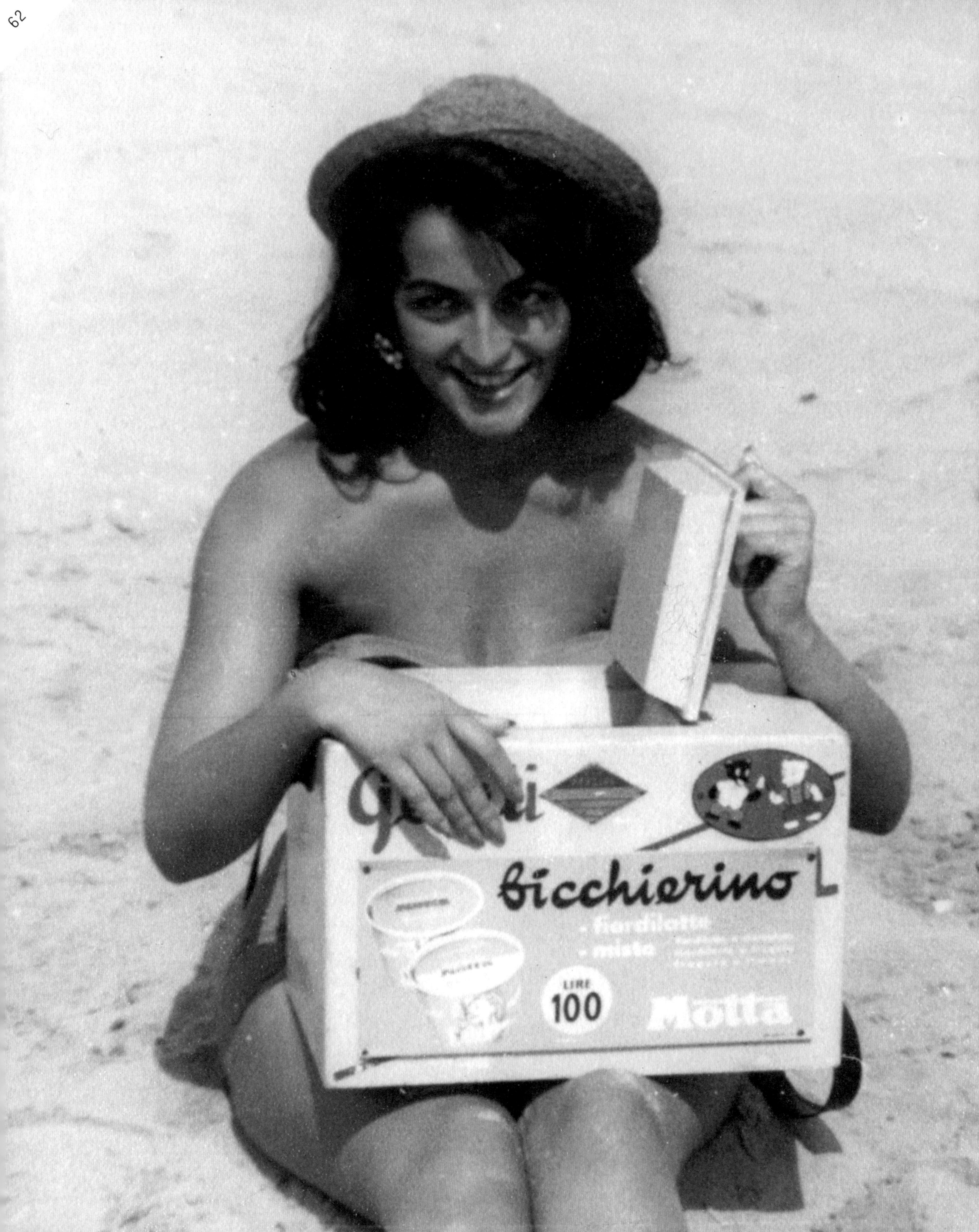
bicchierino
- fiordilatte
- misto
LIRE
100
Motta

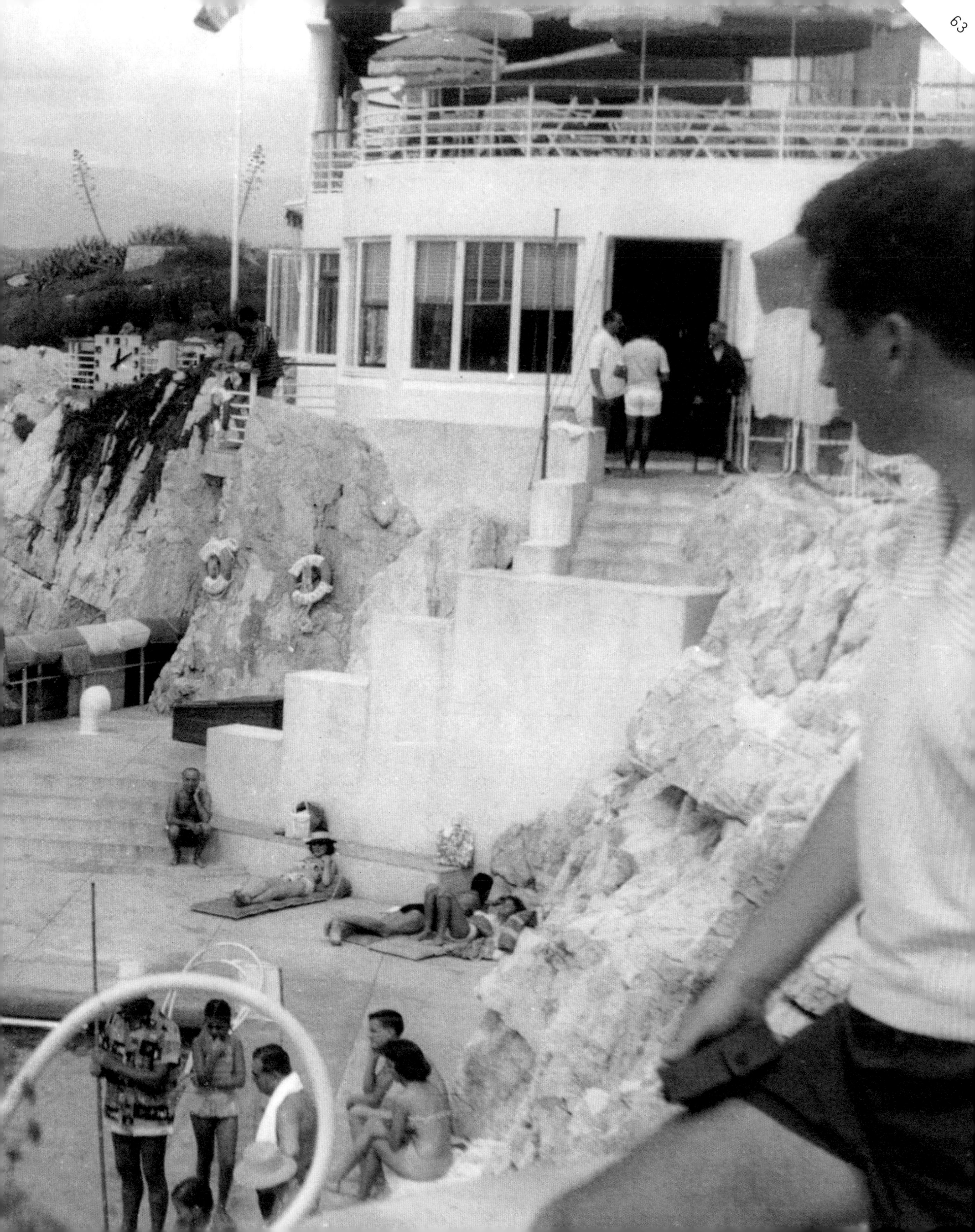

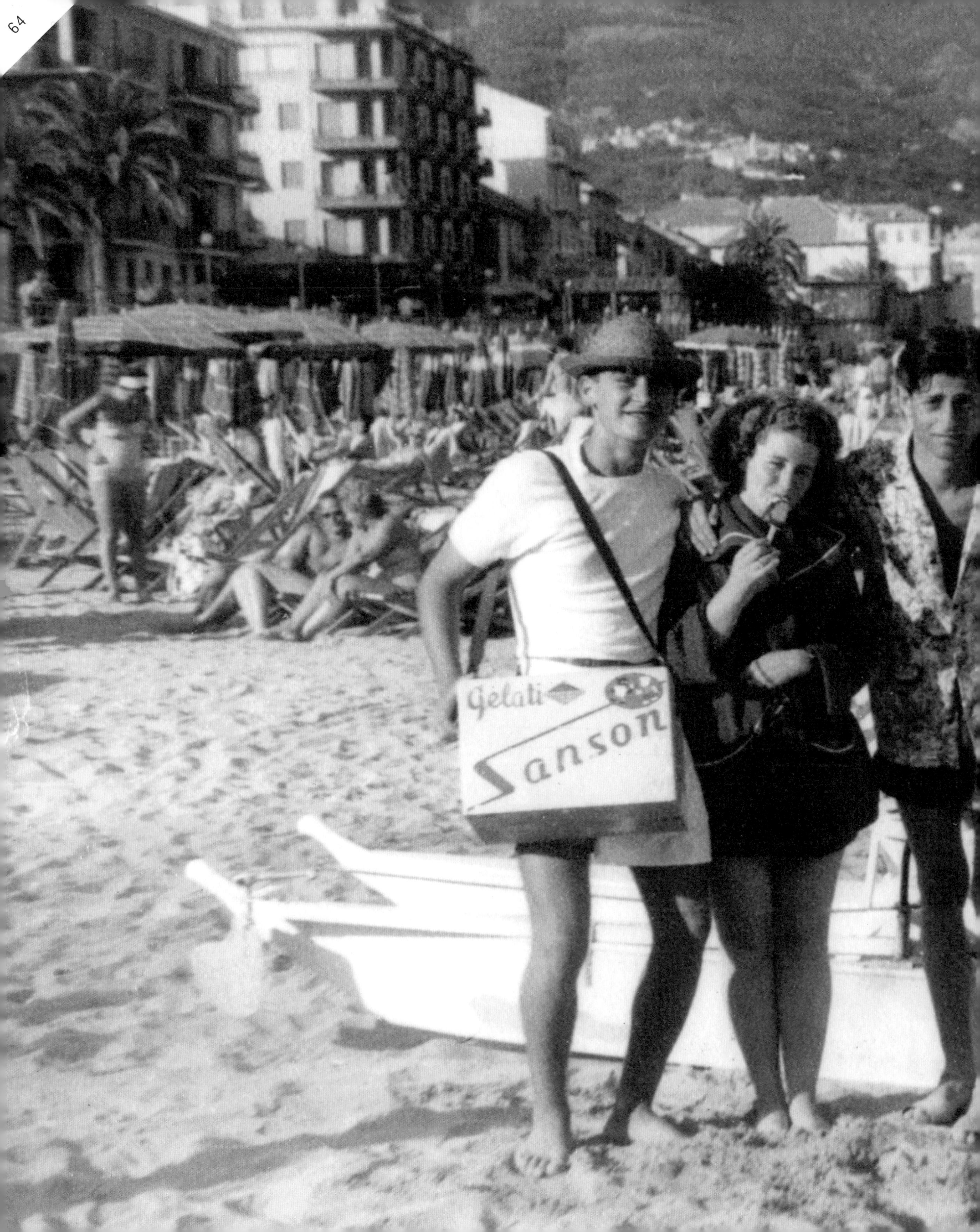
Gelati
Sanson

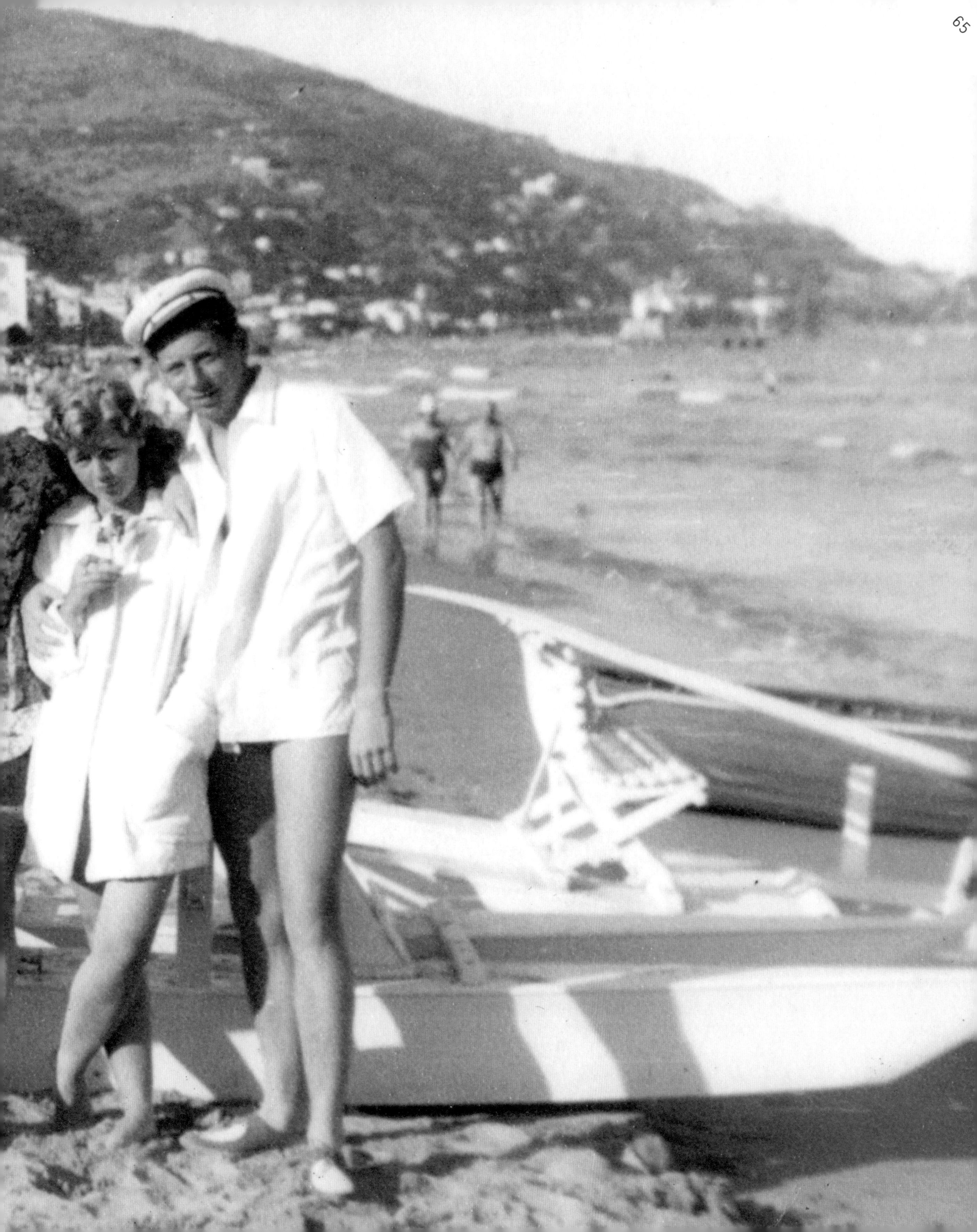

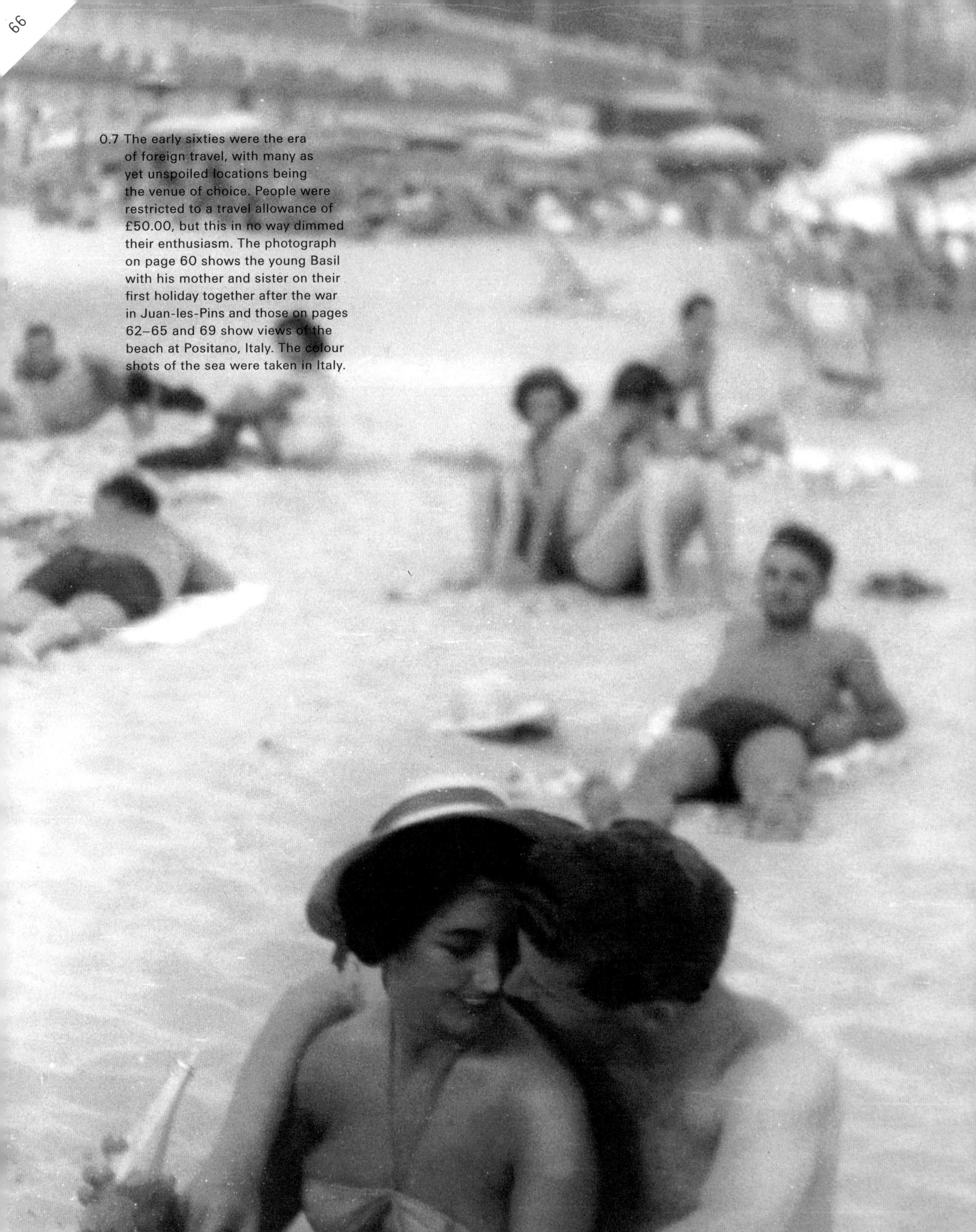

0.7 The early sixties were the era
of foreign travel, with many as
yet unspoiled locations being
the venue of choice. People were
restricted to a travel allowance of
£50.00, but this in no way dimmed
their enthusiasm. The photograph
on page 60 shows the young Basil
with his mother and sister on their
first holiday together after the war
in Juan-les-Pins and those on pages
62–65 and 69 show views of the
beach at Positano, Italy. The colour
shots of the sea were taken in Italy.

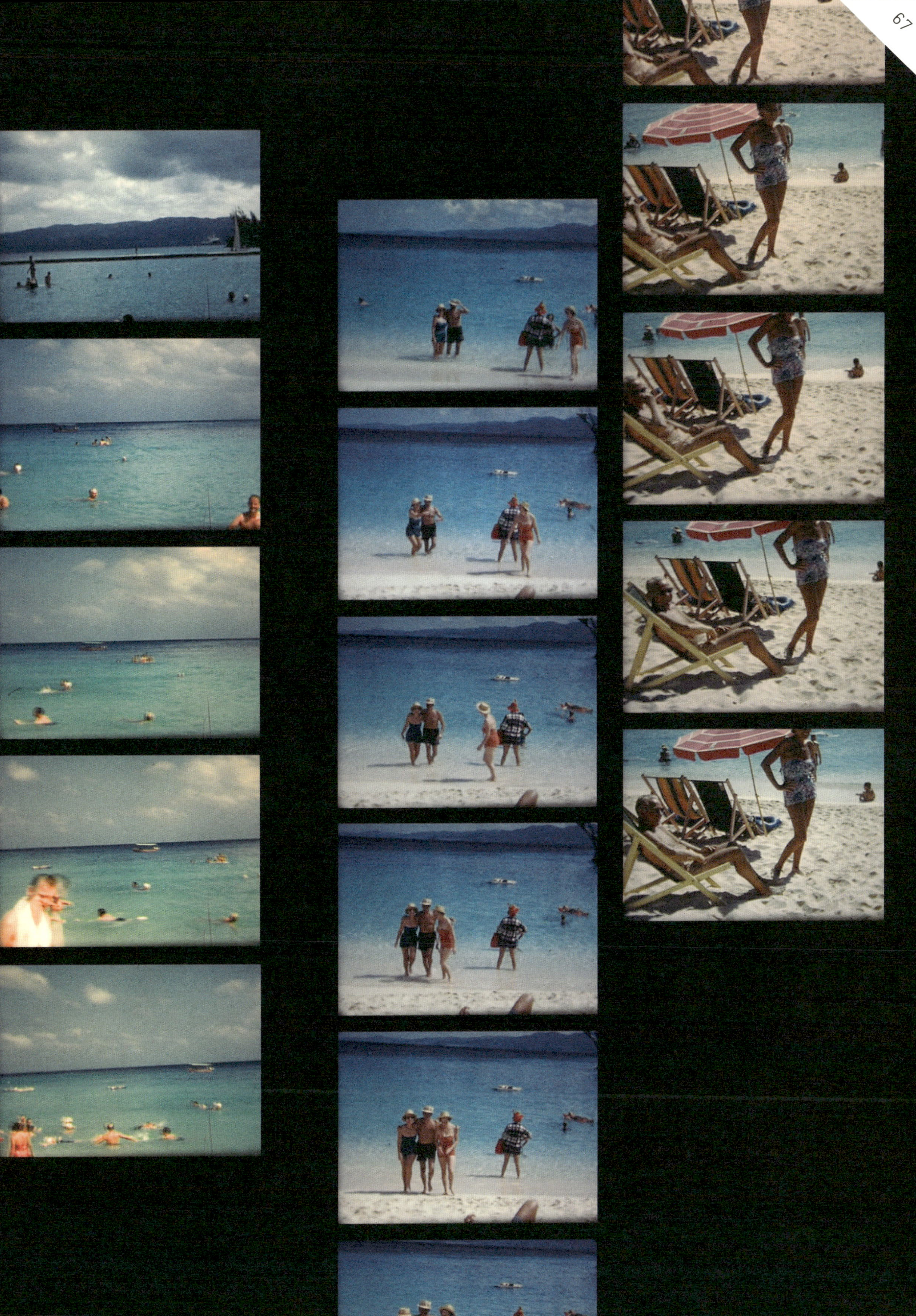

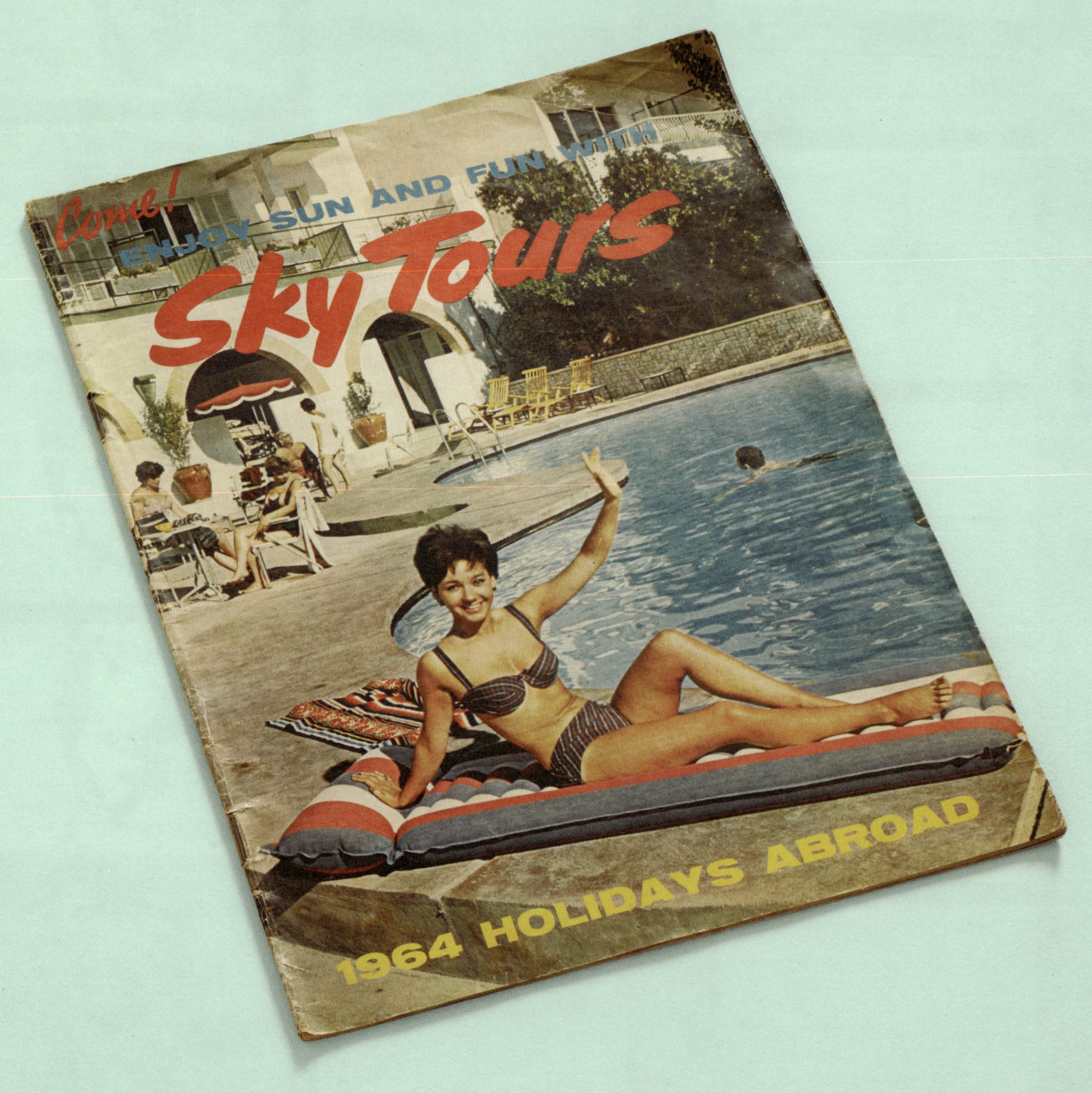
Come!
ENJOY SUN AND FUN WITH
Sky Tours
1964 HOLIDAYS ABROAD

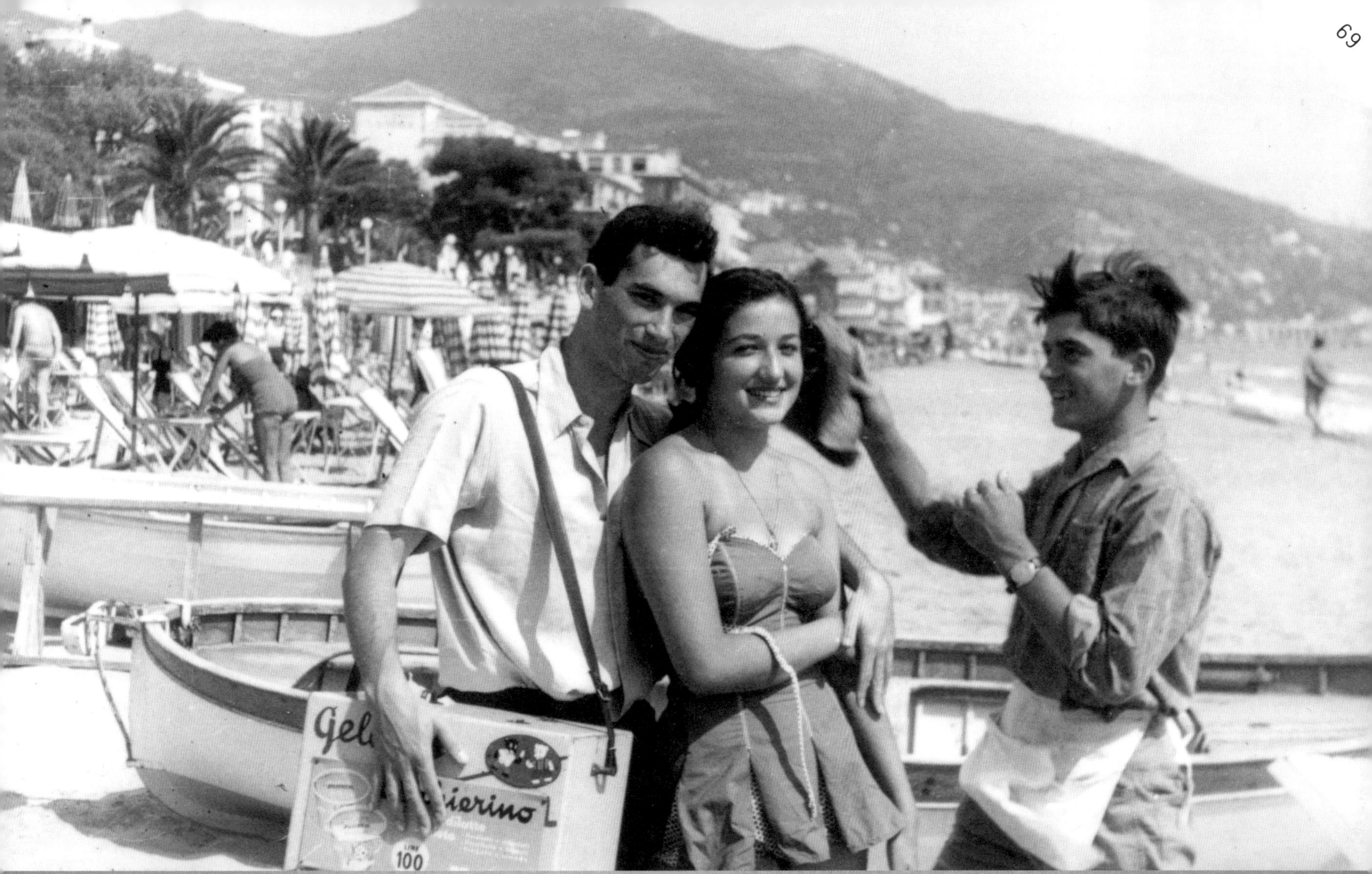

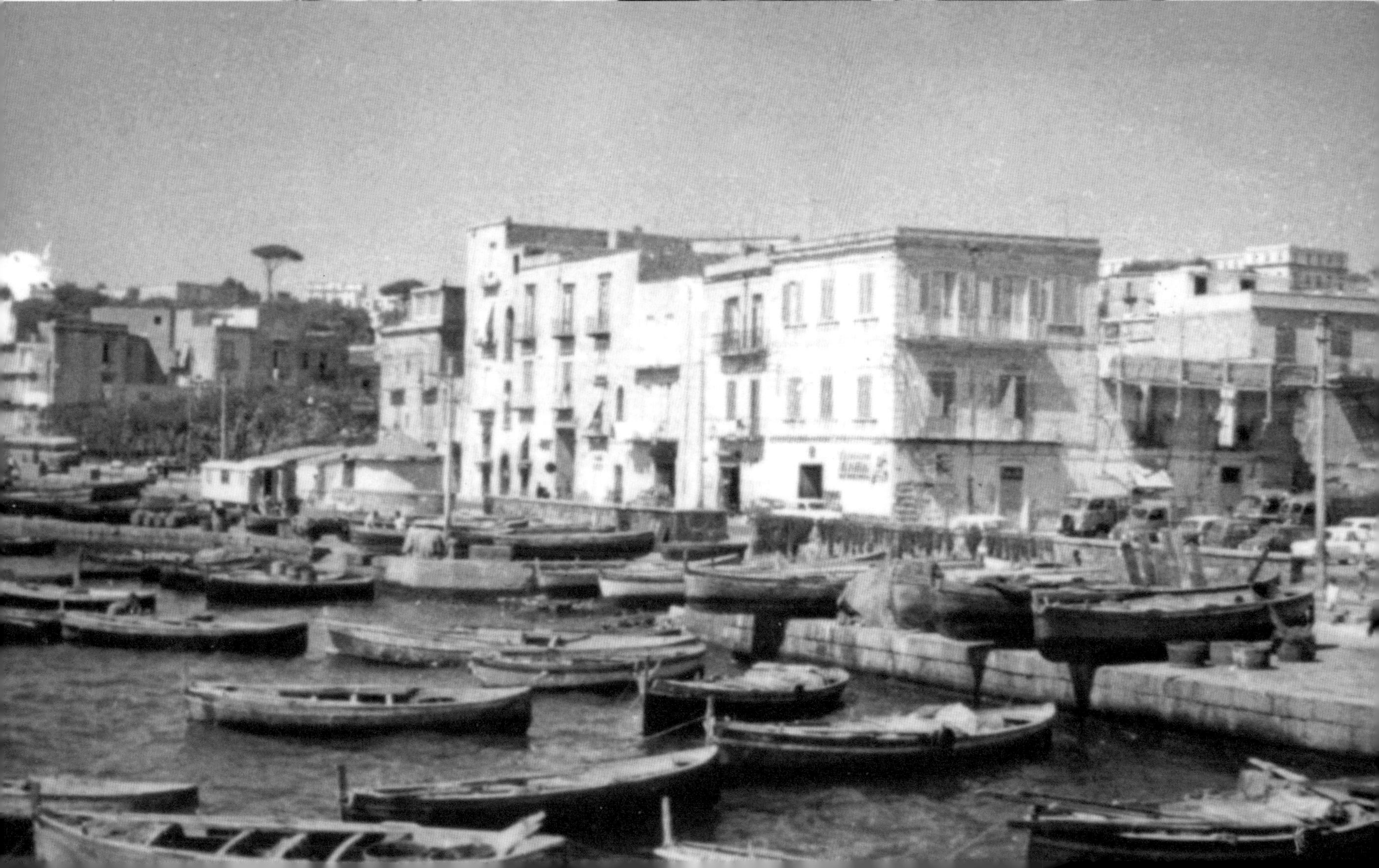

0.8 No holiday in Spain in the 1960s would be complete without a visit to a bullfight, which sounded so exciting after all that had been published on the subject (Hemingway et al). Celebrity-led, the *corrida*, during which the matadors would bait the bull and eventually kill it was startling, but in no way pleasant. Now, not surprisingly, banned in many parts of the world, the bullfight nevertheless remains an undying symbol of Spain. It is now regarded as outdated and unkind to animals but in the sixties this was not considered.

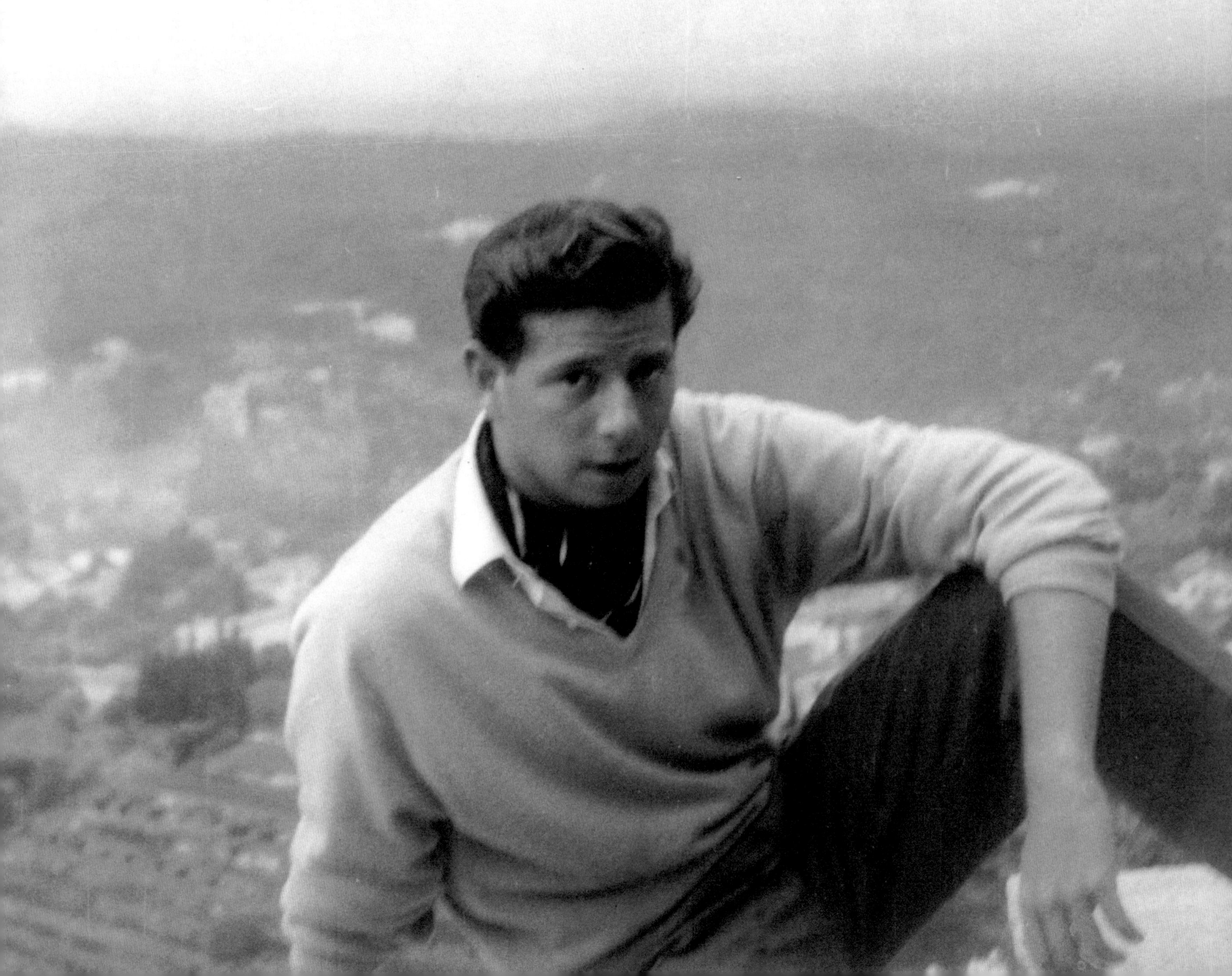

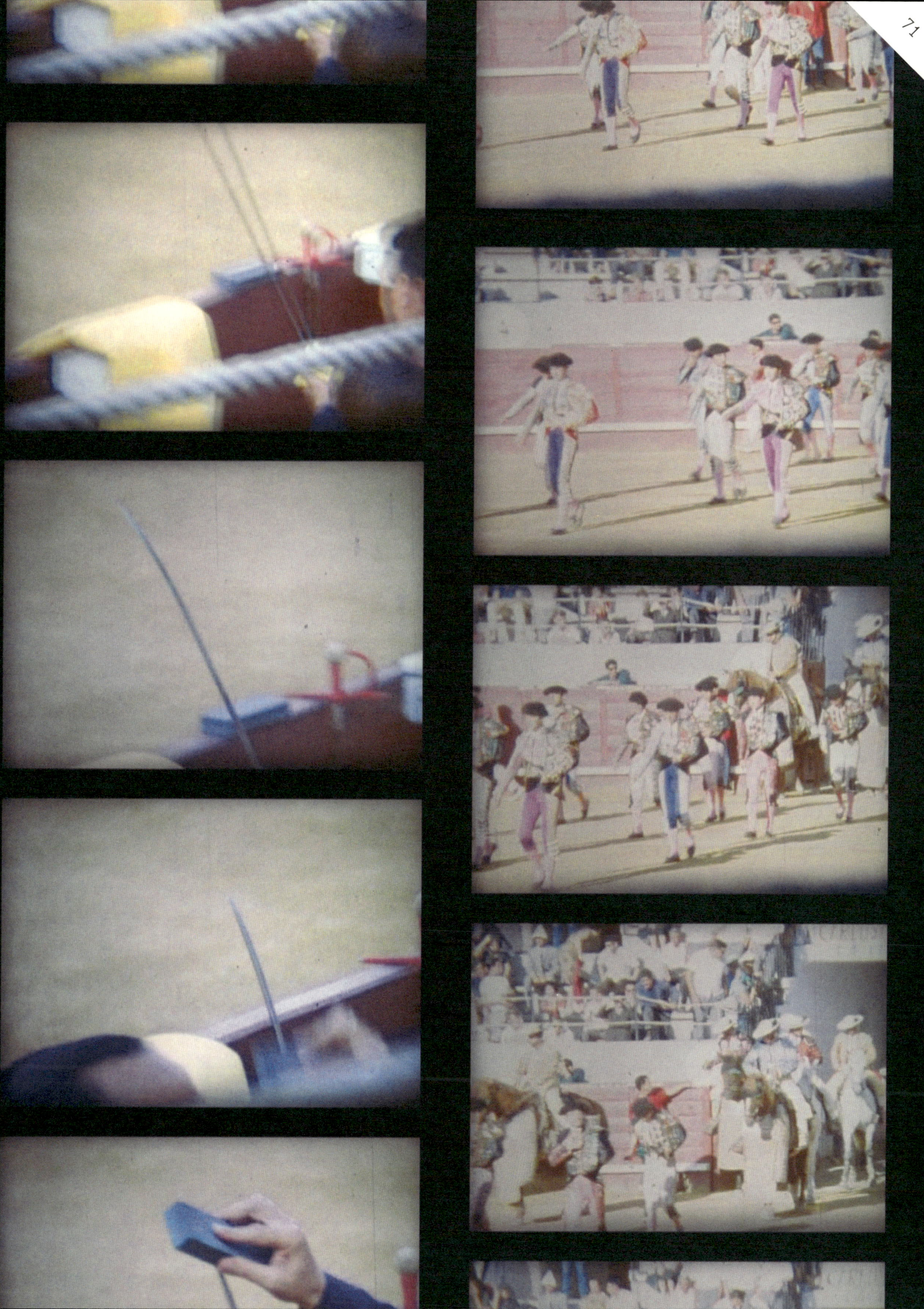

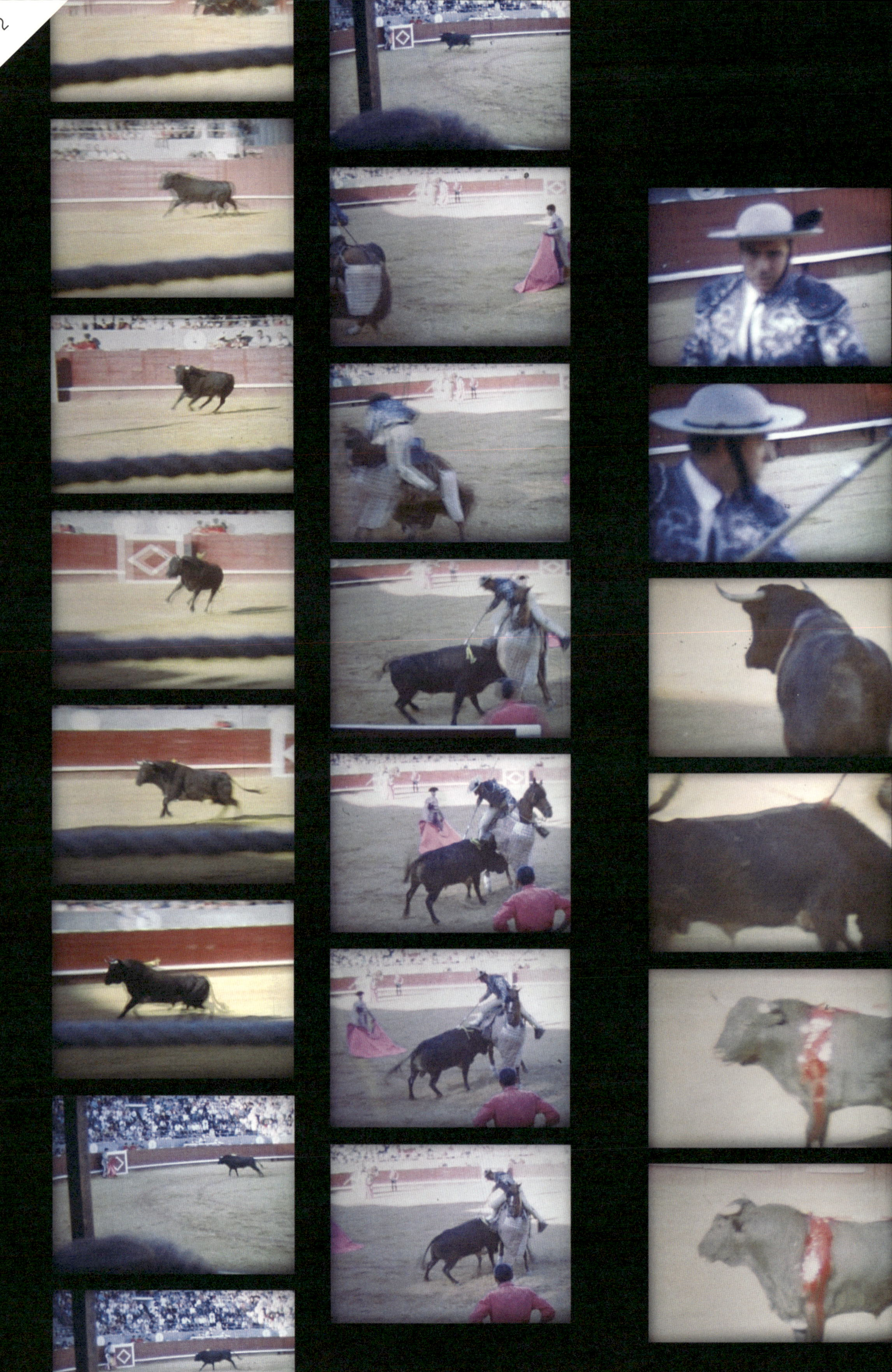

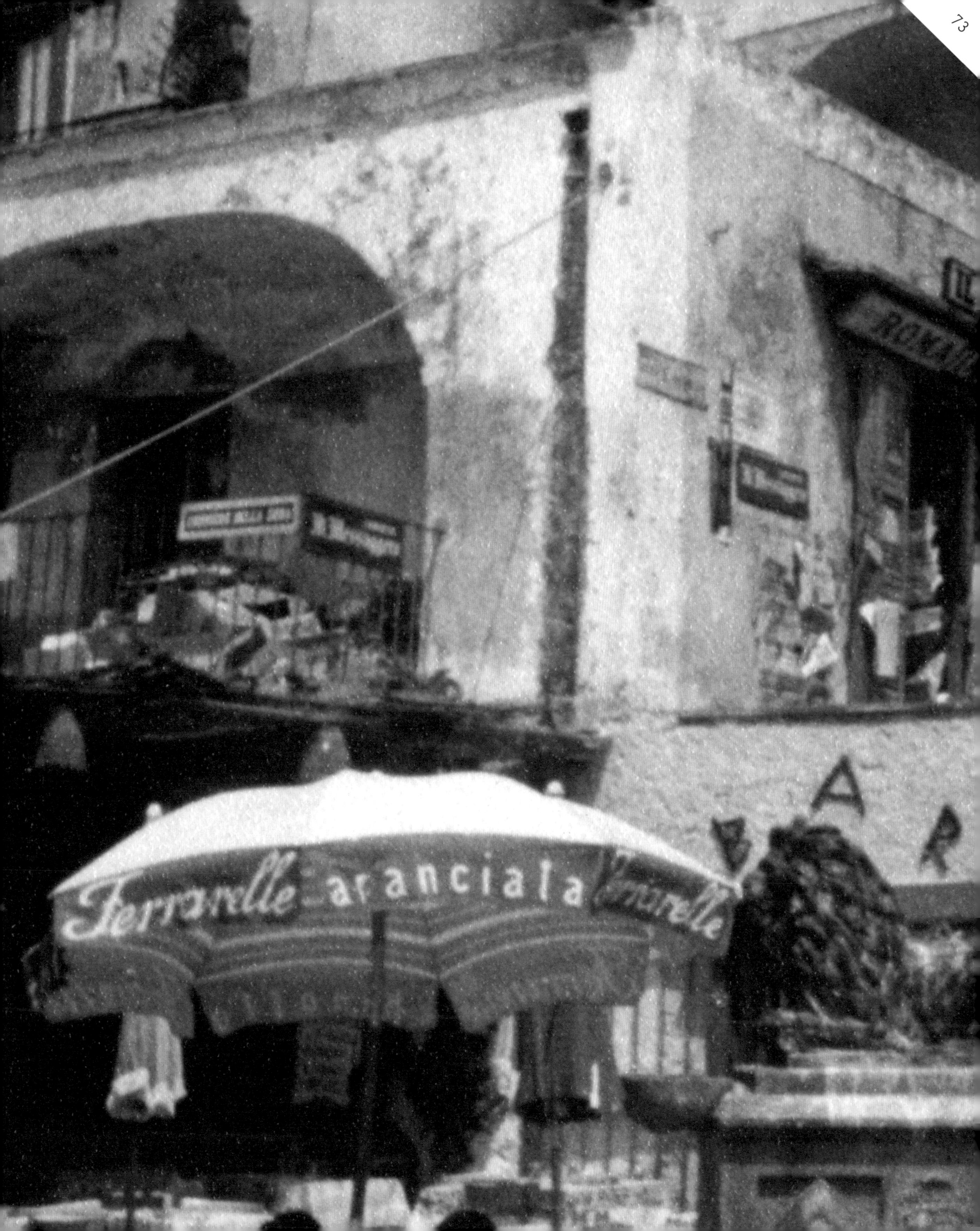
Ferrarelle aranciata Ferrarelle
BAR

TRAVELLING ABROAD

ON A SMALL INCOME
By J. ALLAN CASH

2/6 NET

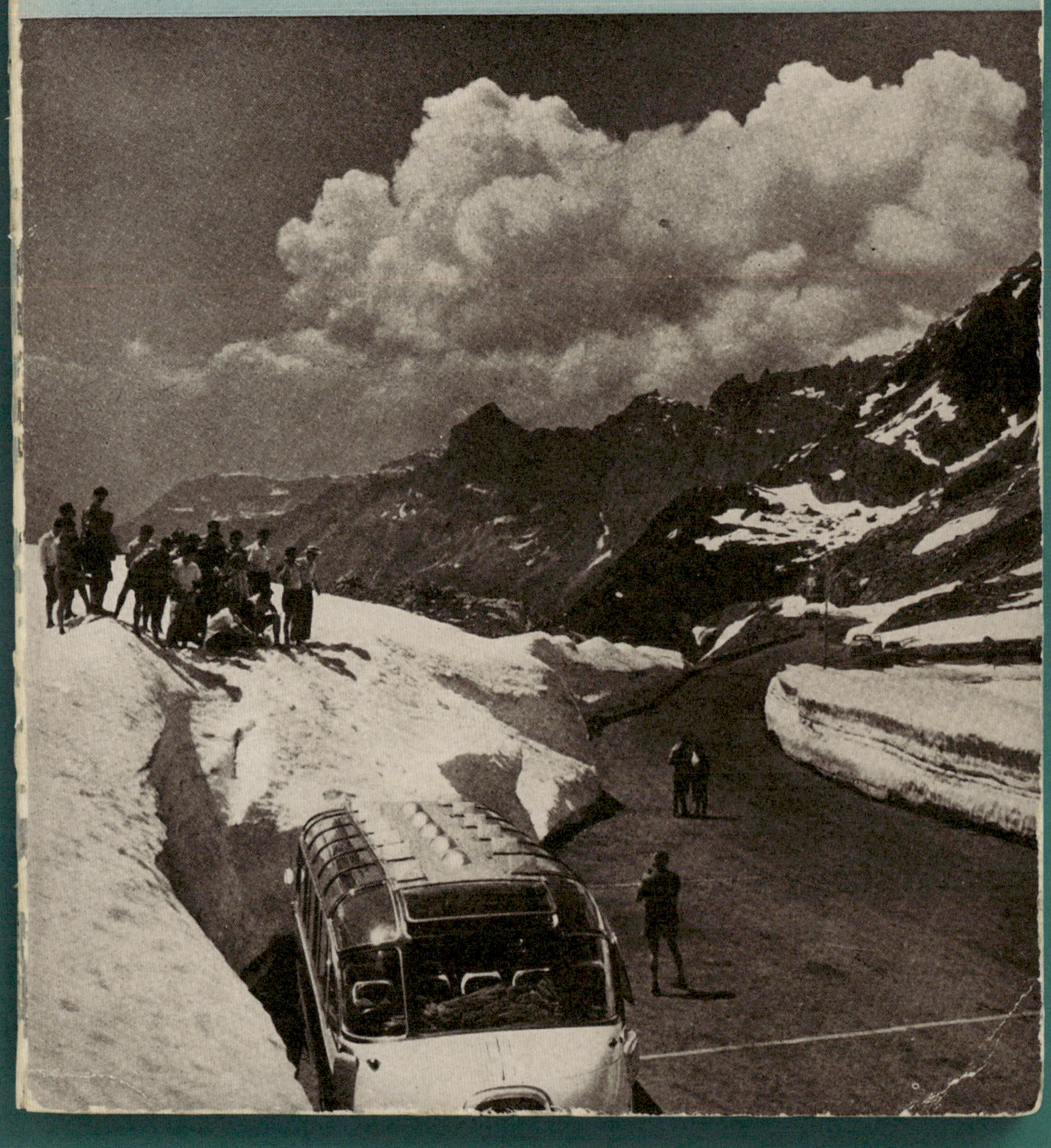

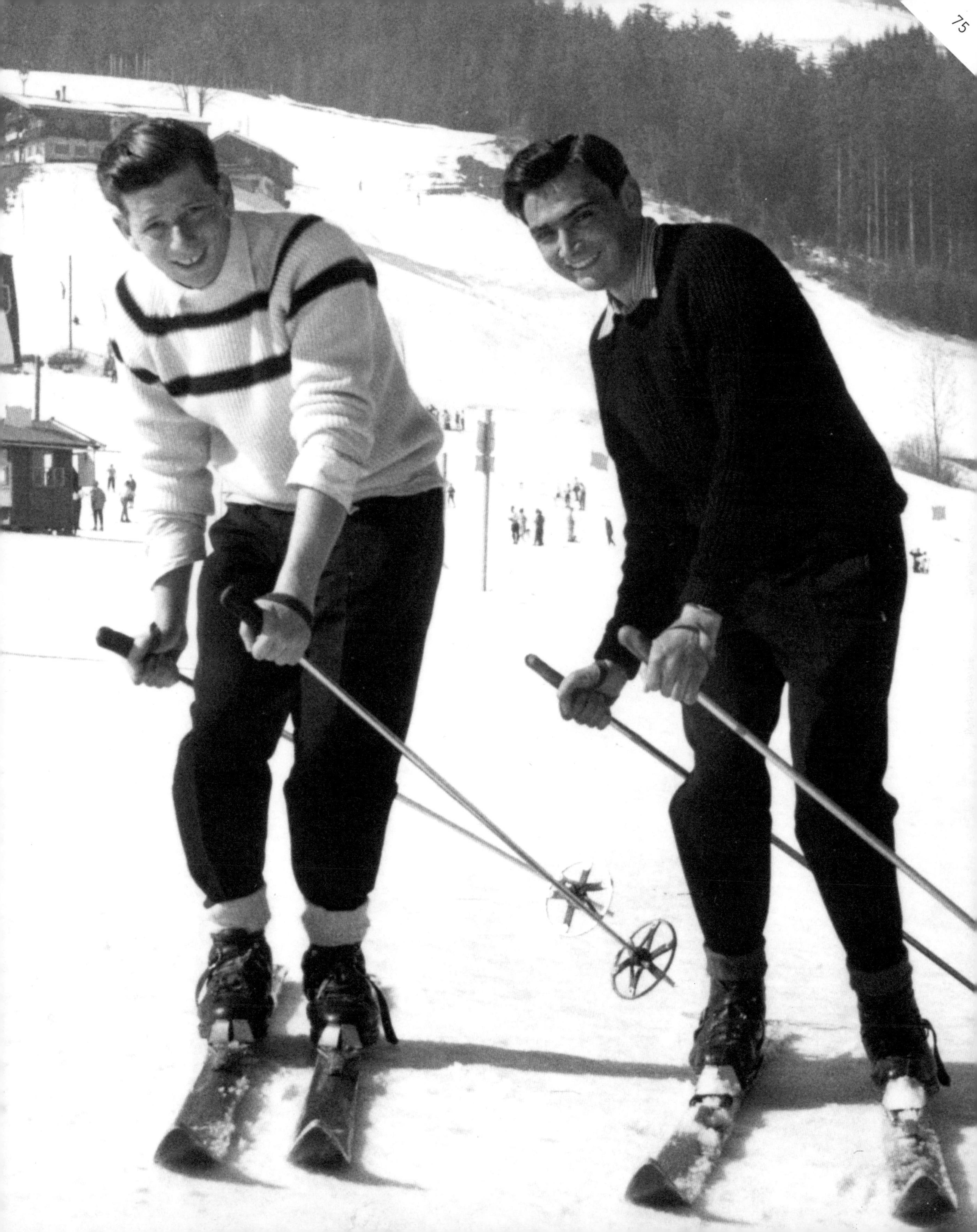

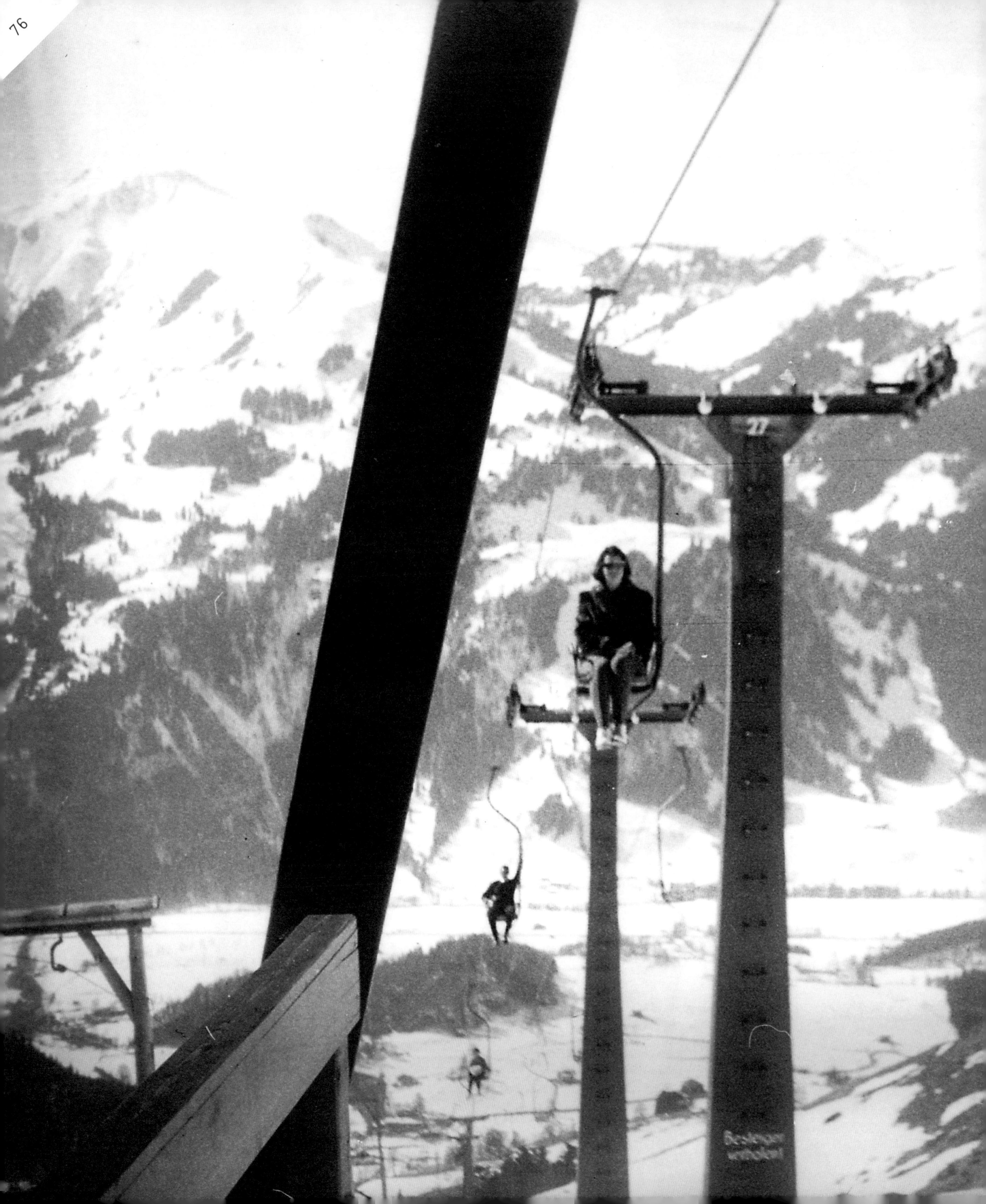

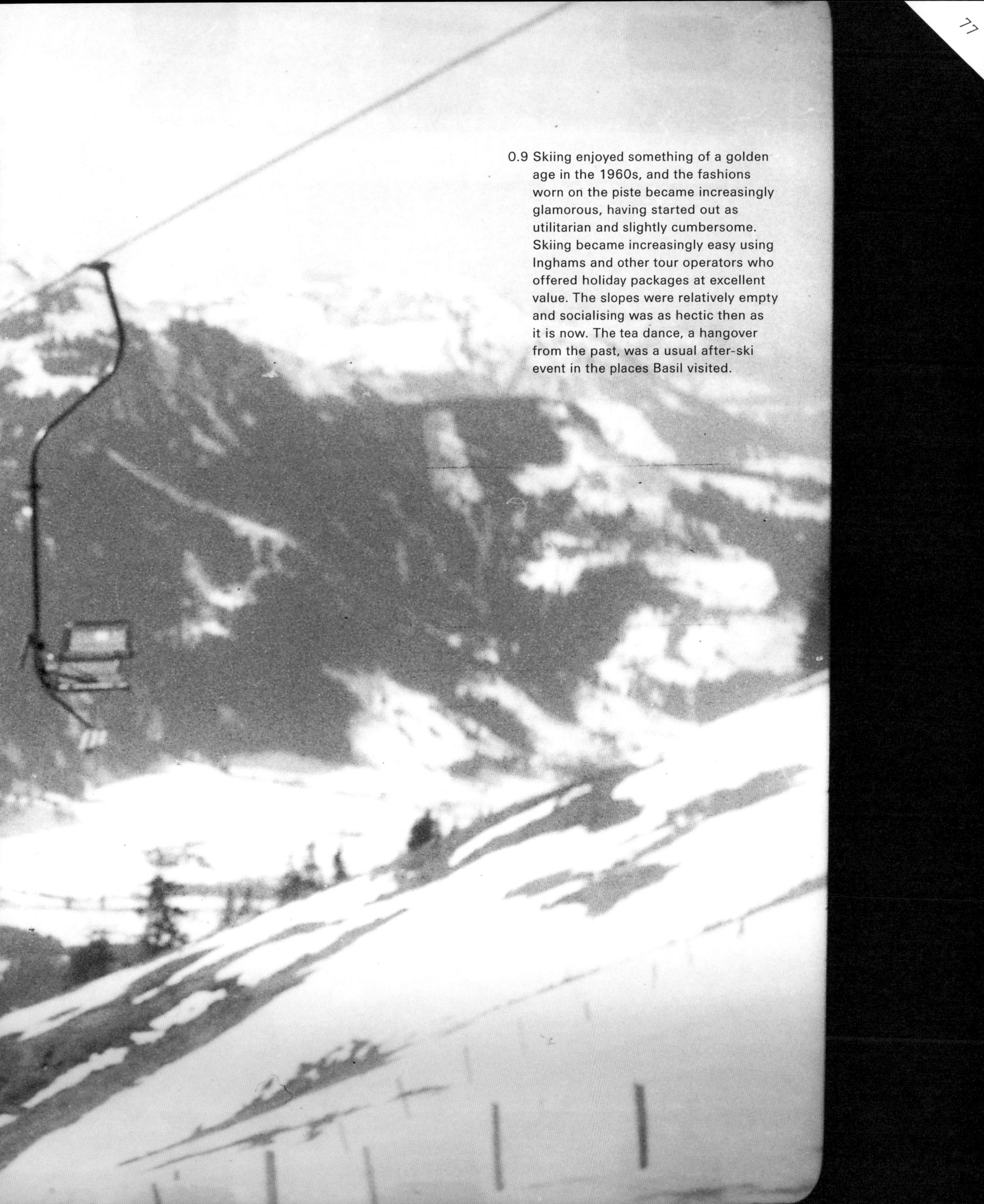

0.9 Skiing enjoyed something of a golden age in the 1960s, and the fashions worn on the piste became increasingly glamorous, having started out as utilitarian and slightly cumbersome. Skiing became increasingly easy using Inghams and other tour operators who offered holiday packages at excellent value. The slopes were relatively empty and socialising was as hectic then as it is now. The tea dance, a hangover from the past, was a usual after-ski event in the places Basil visited.

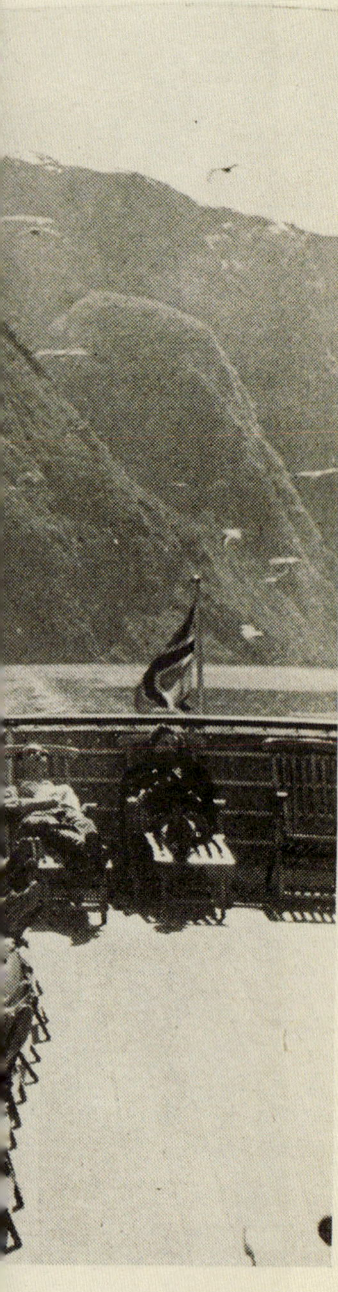

he Sognefjord, a

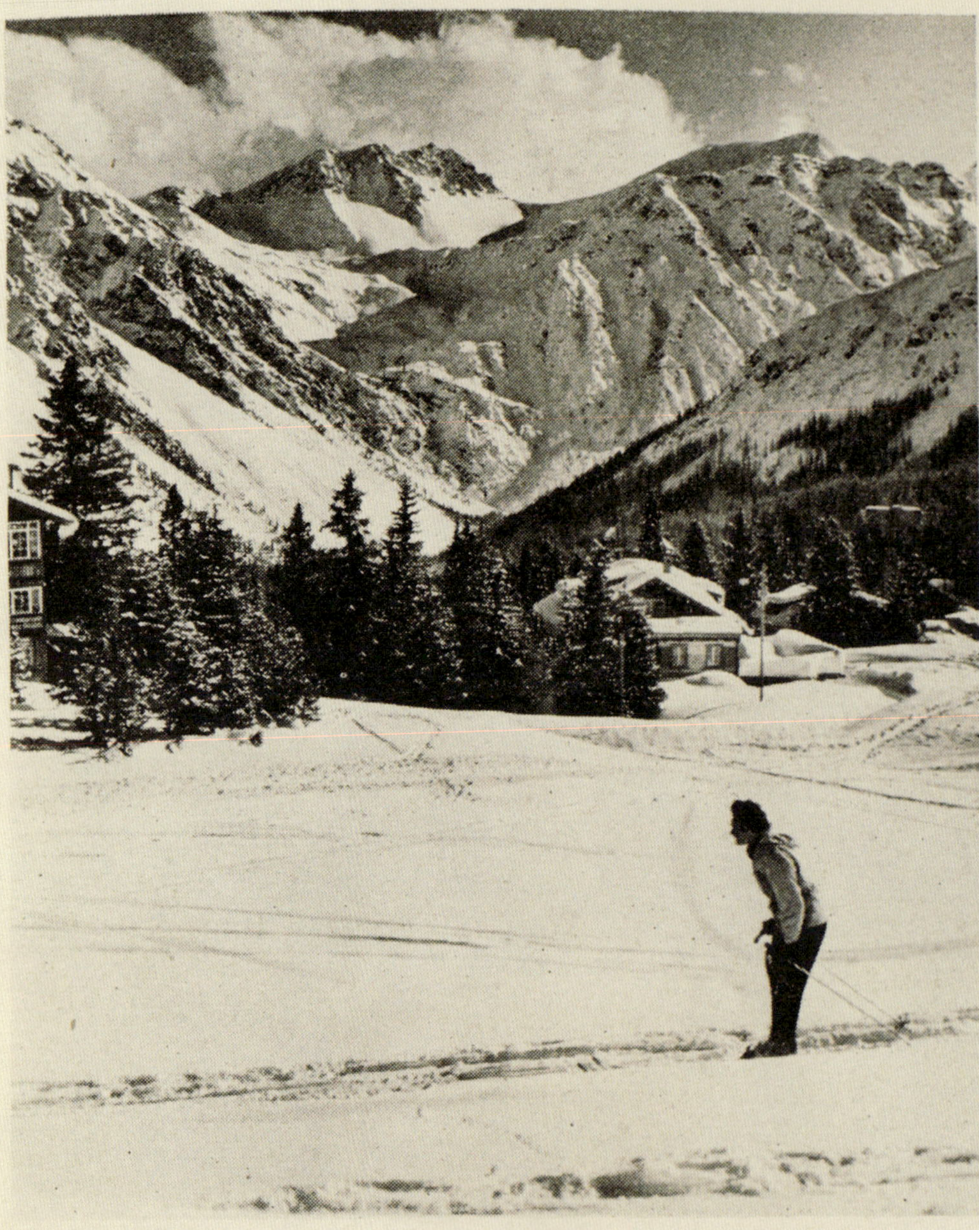

13. Winter Sports at Arosa, in Switzerland. There are hundreds of such places in the whole Alpine area, from France to Austria

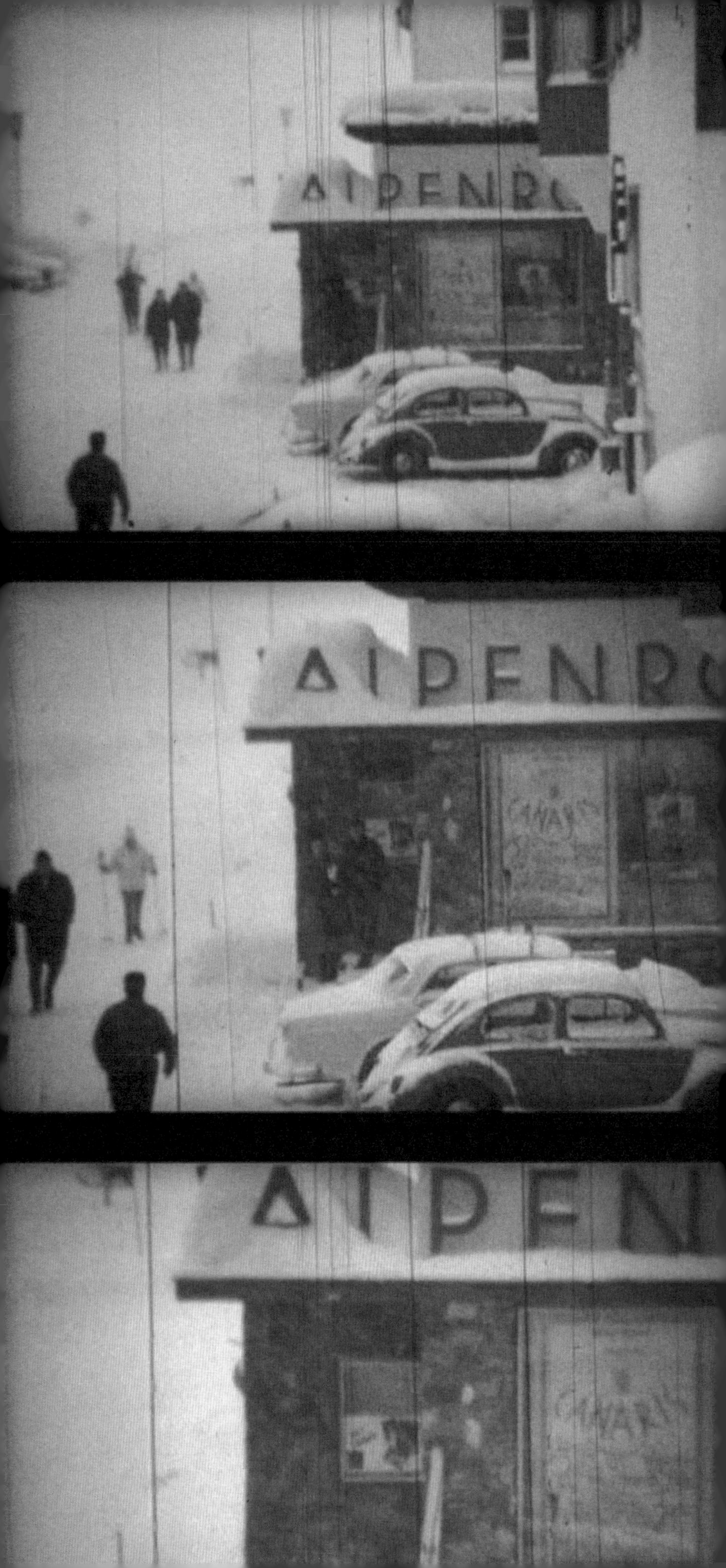

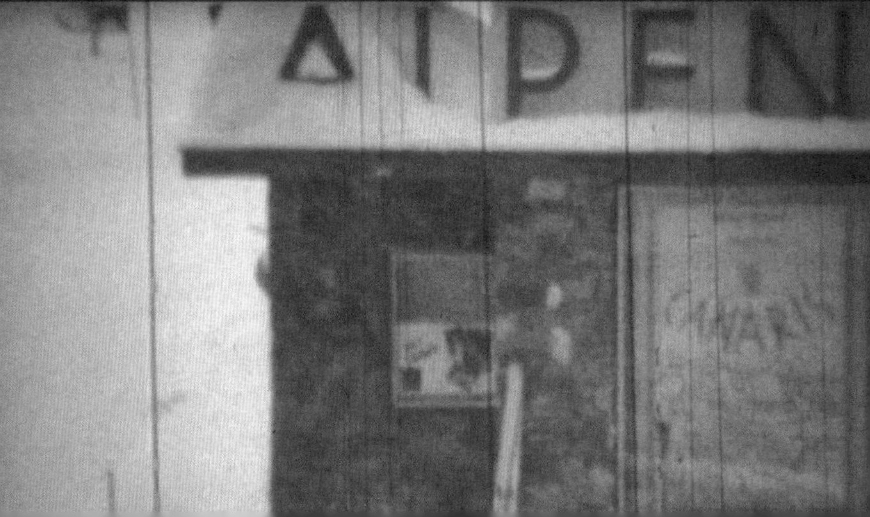
ALPENR

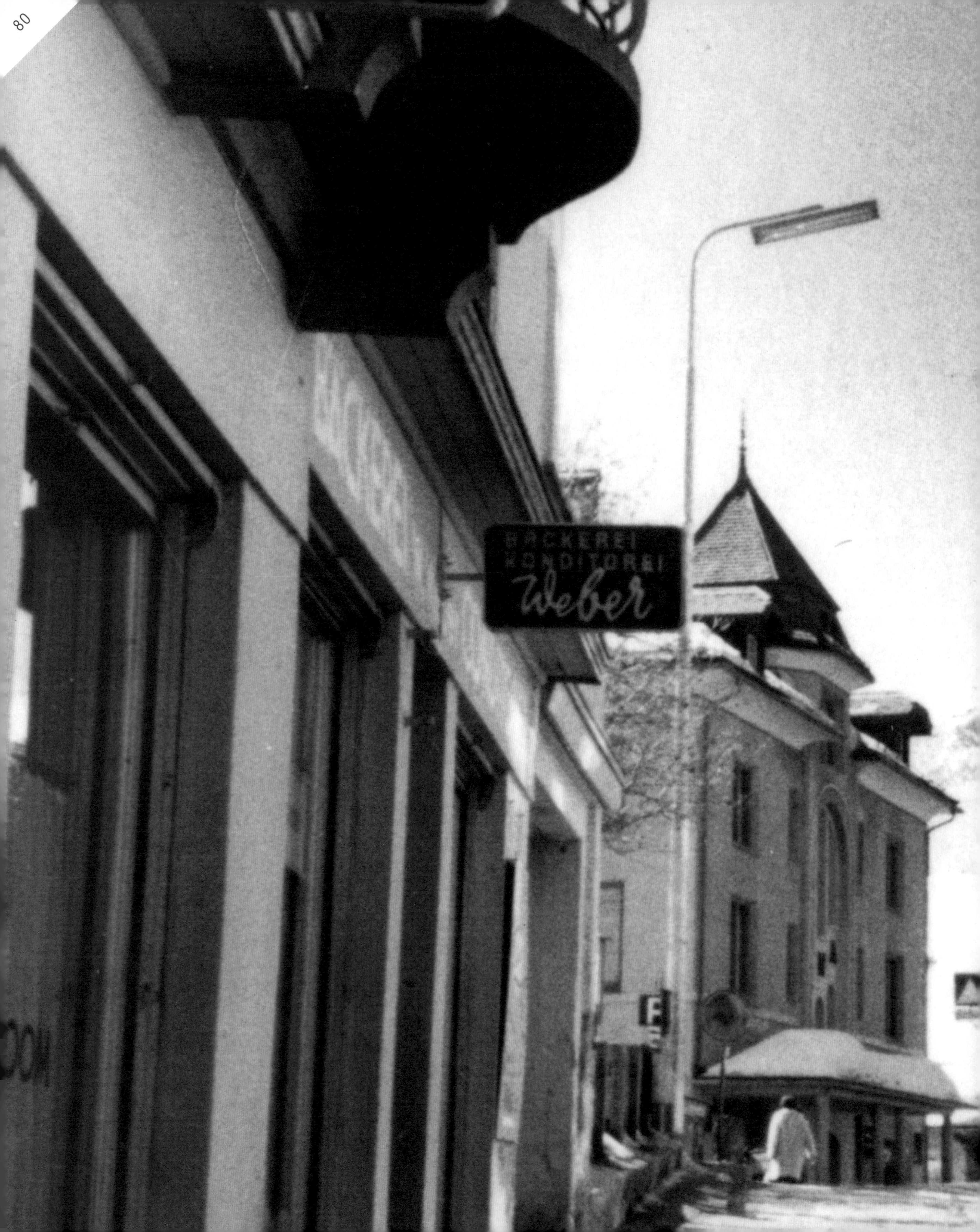
BÄCKEREI
KONDITOREI
Weber

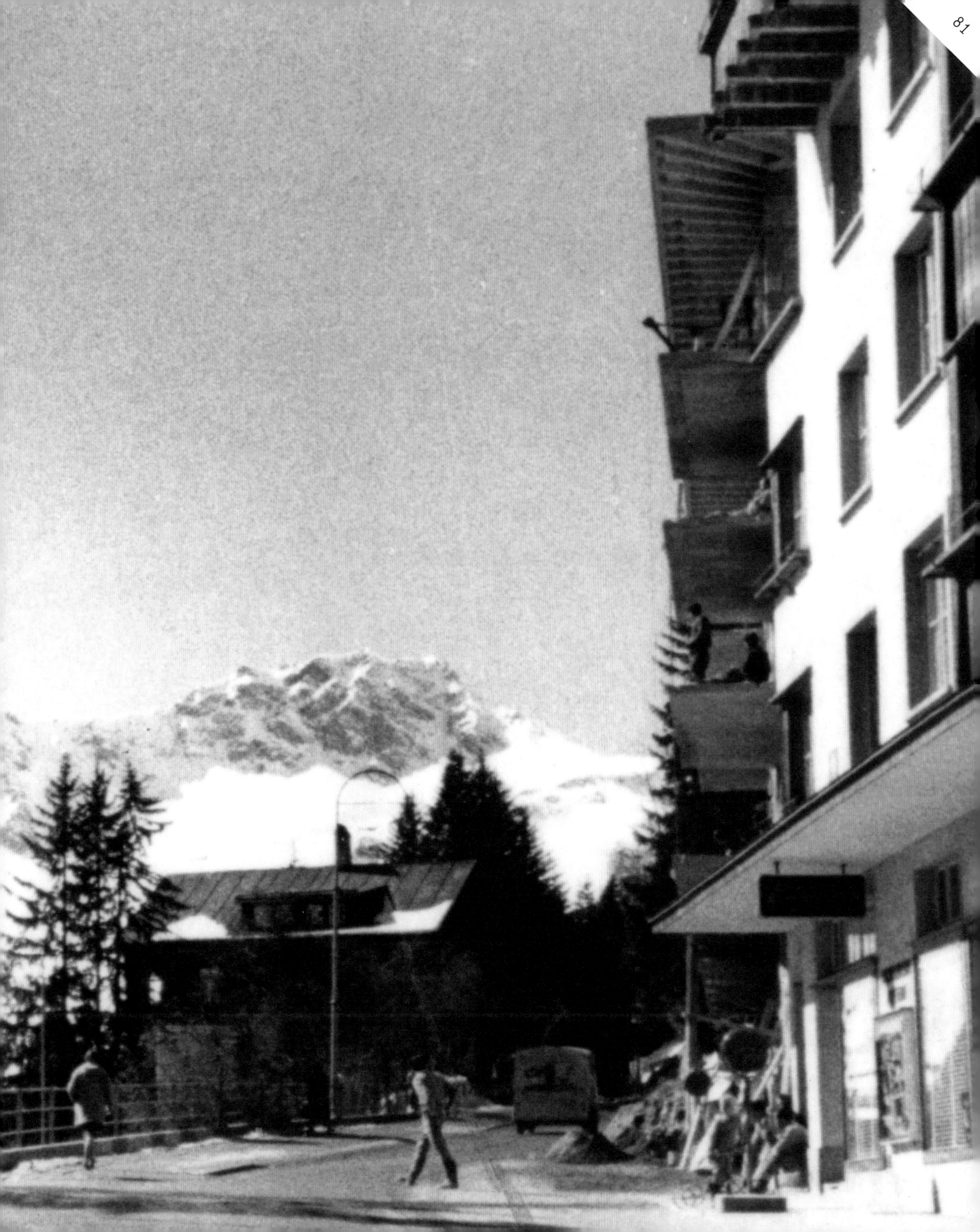

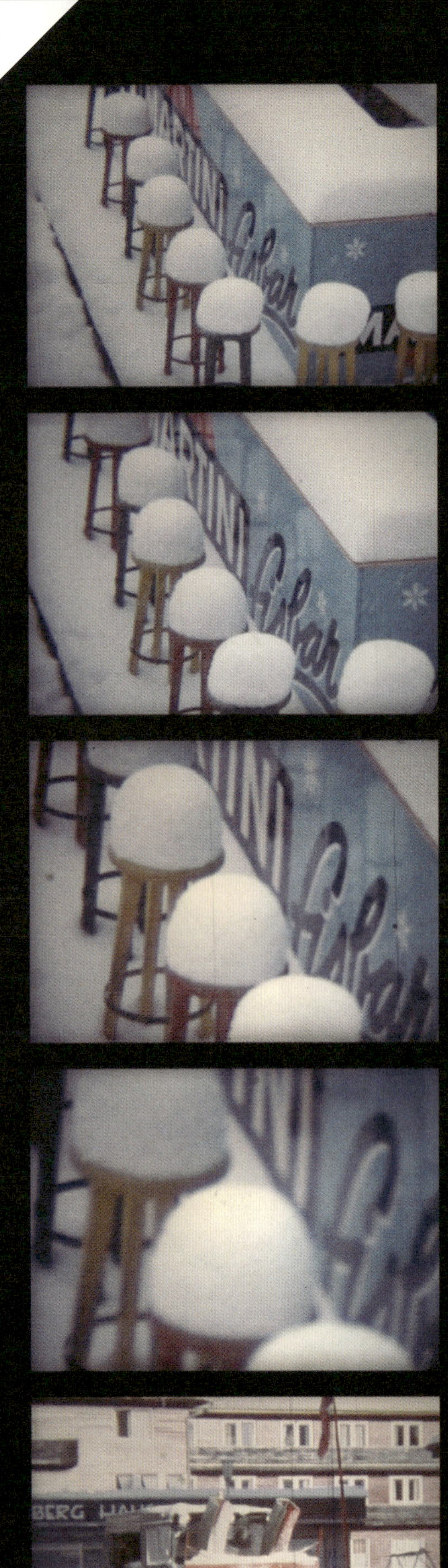
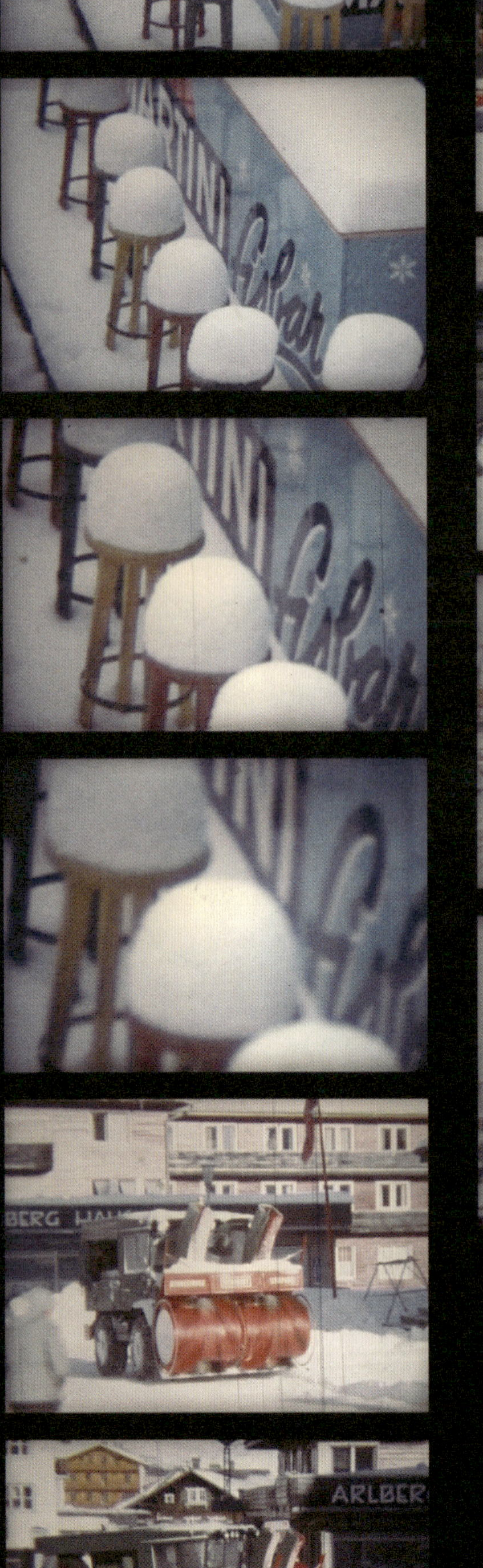
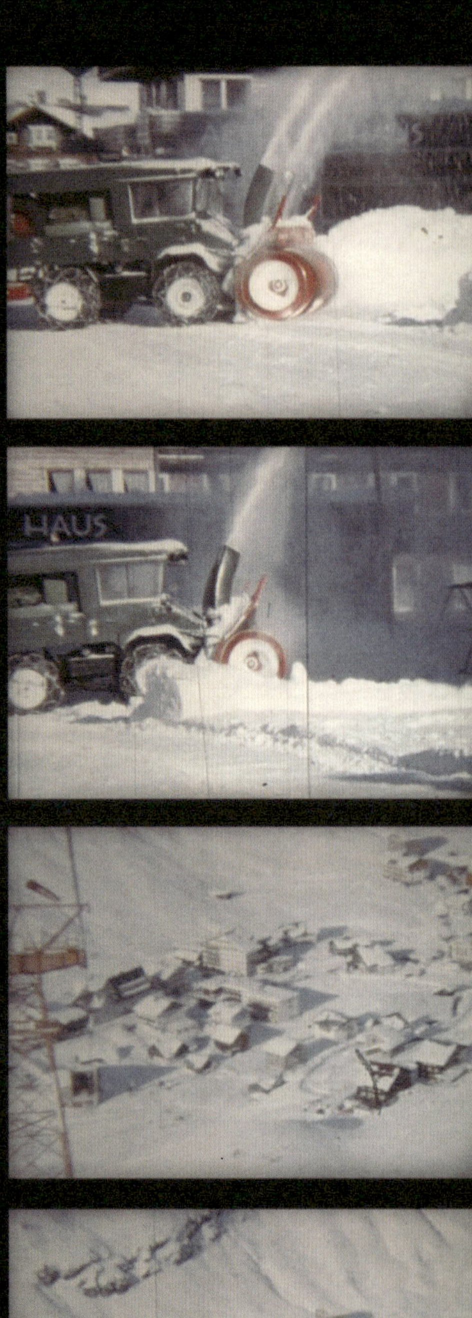
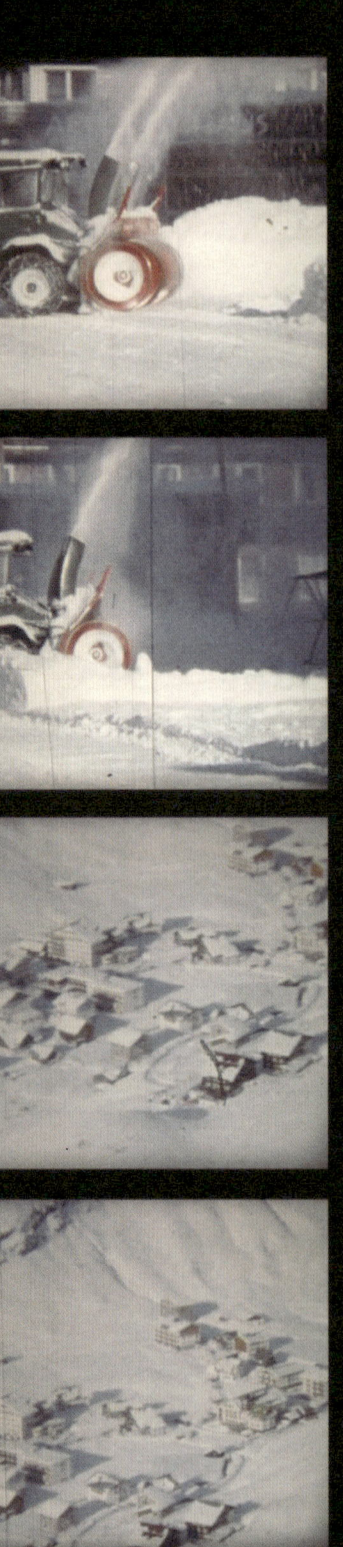
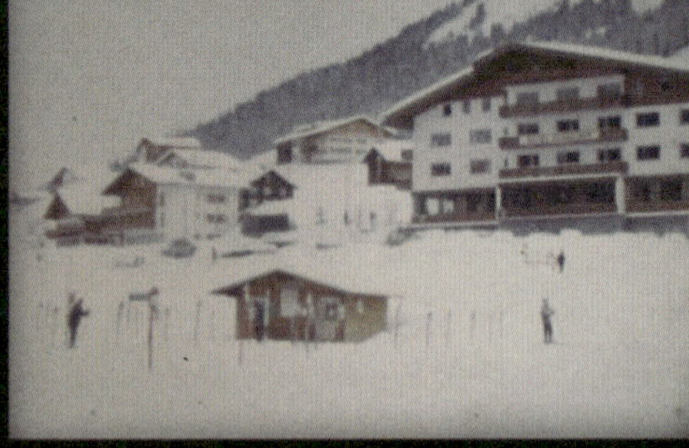
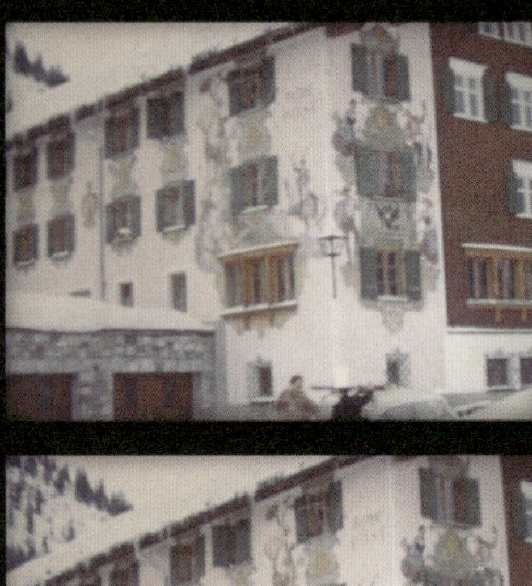
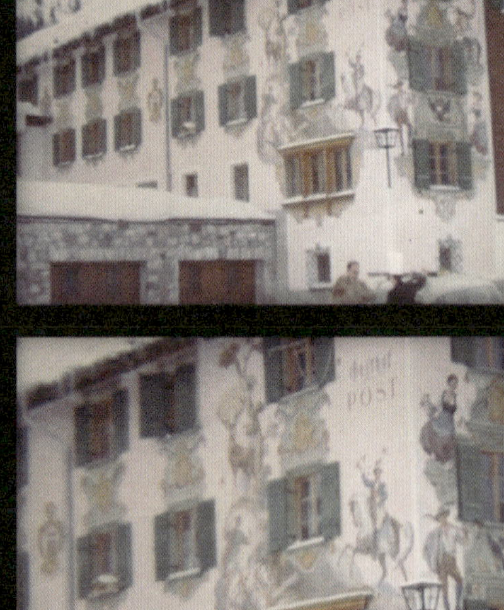

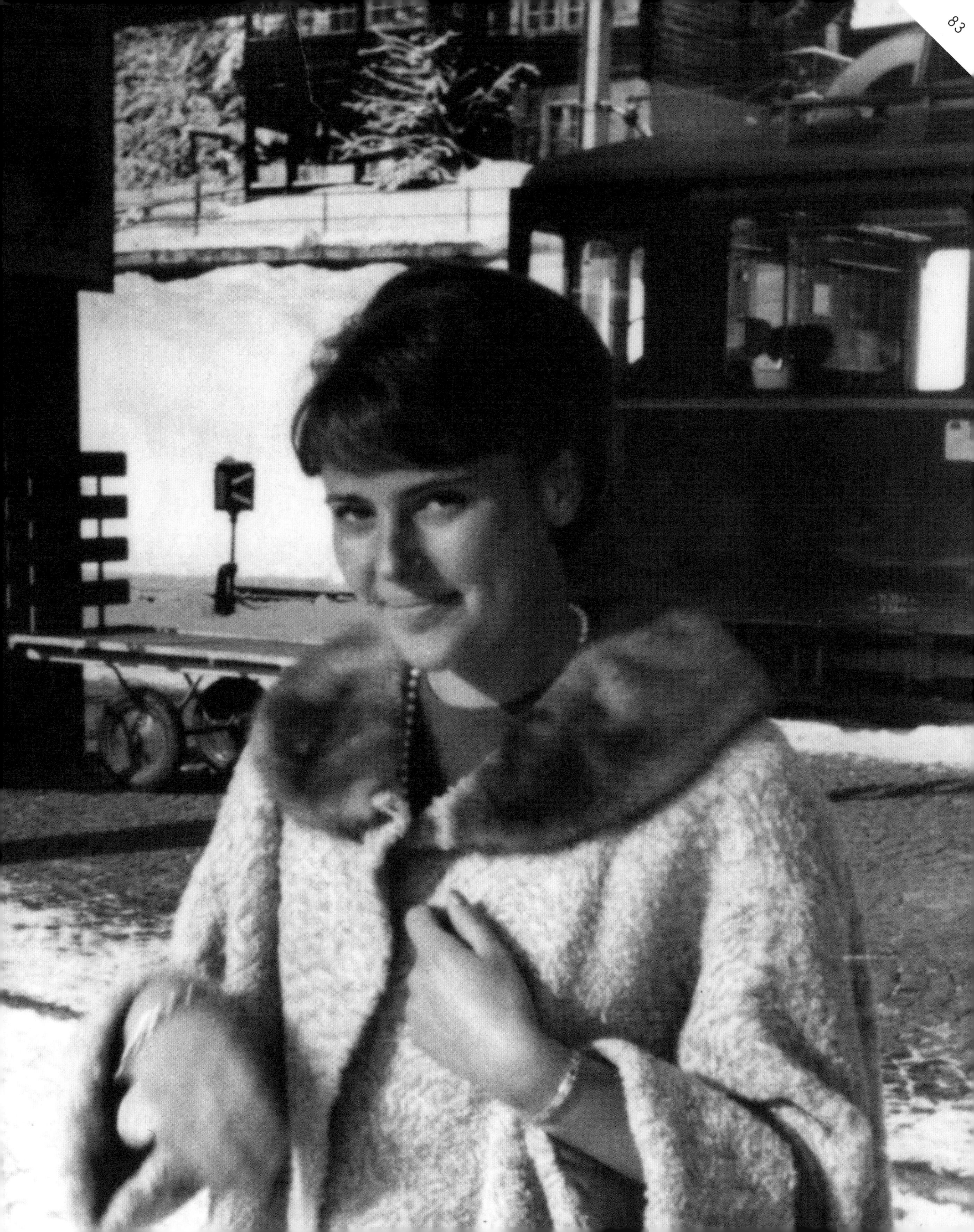

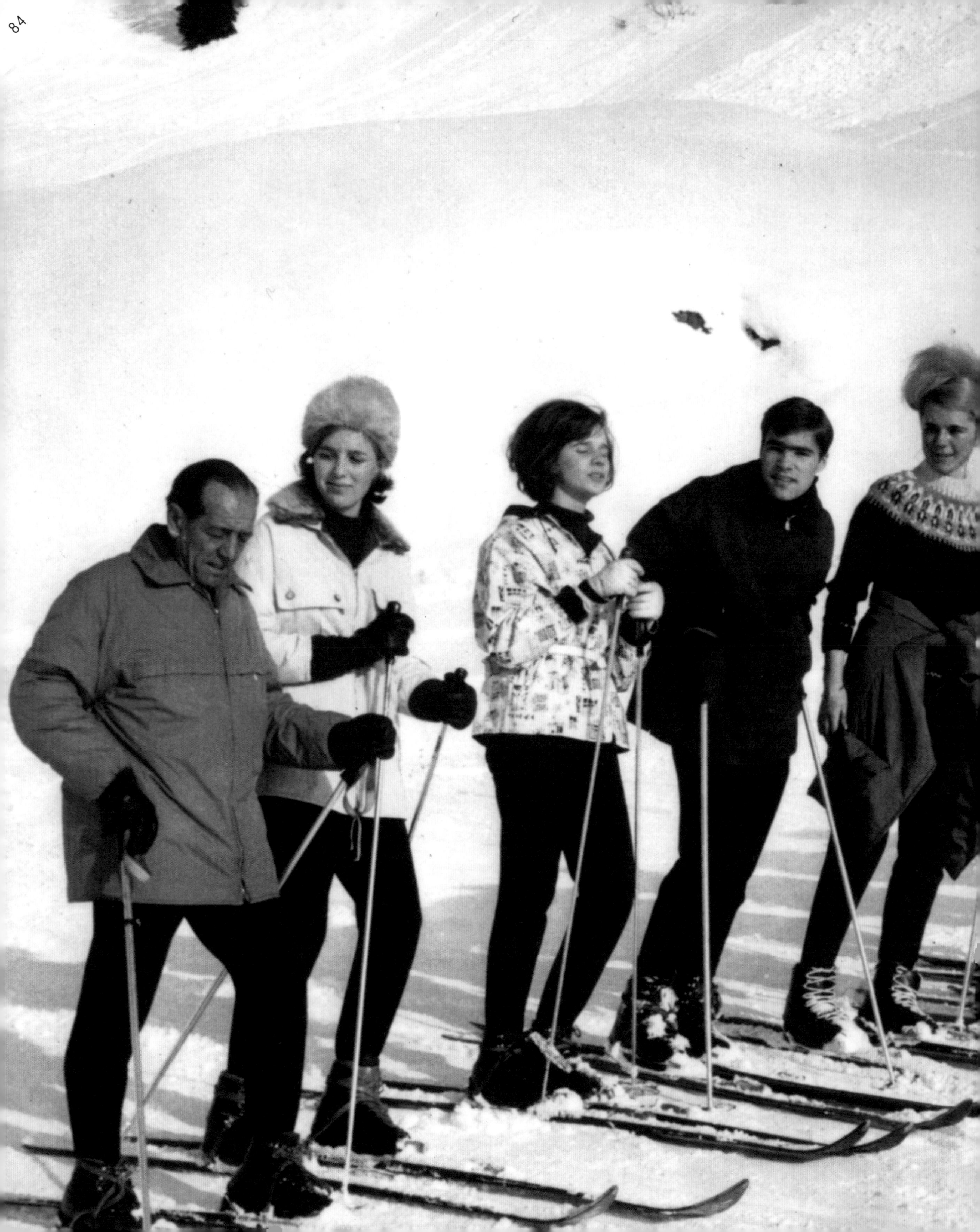

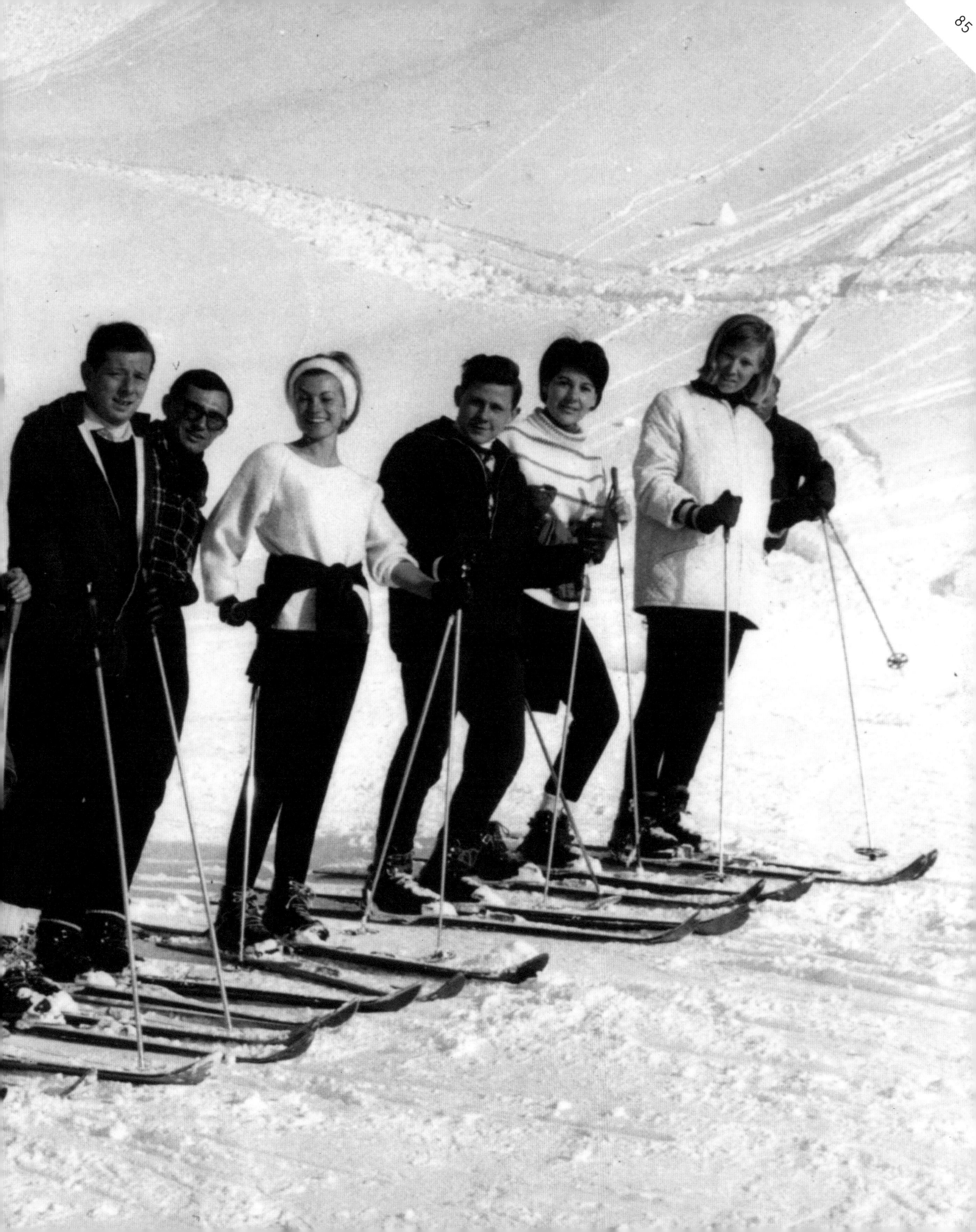

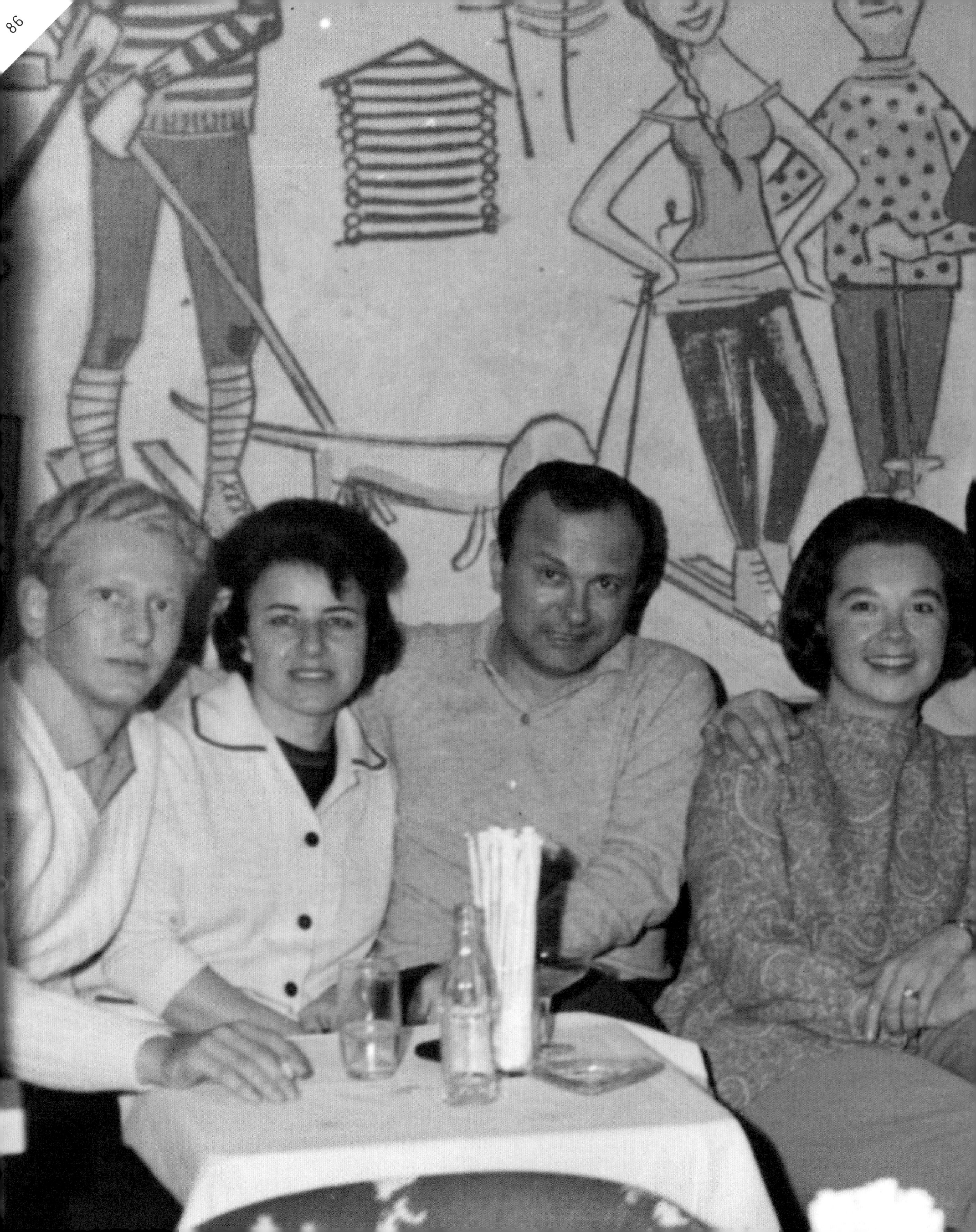

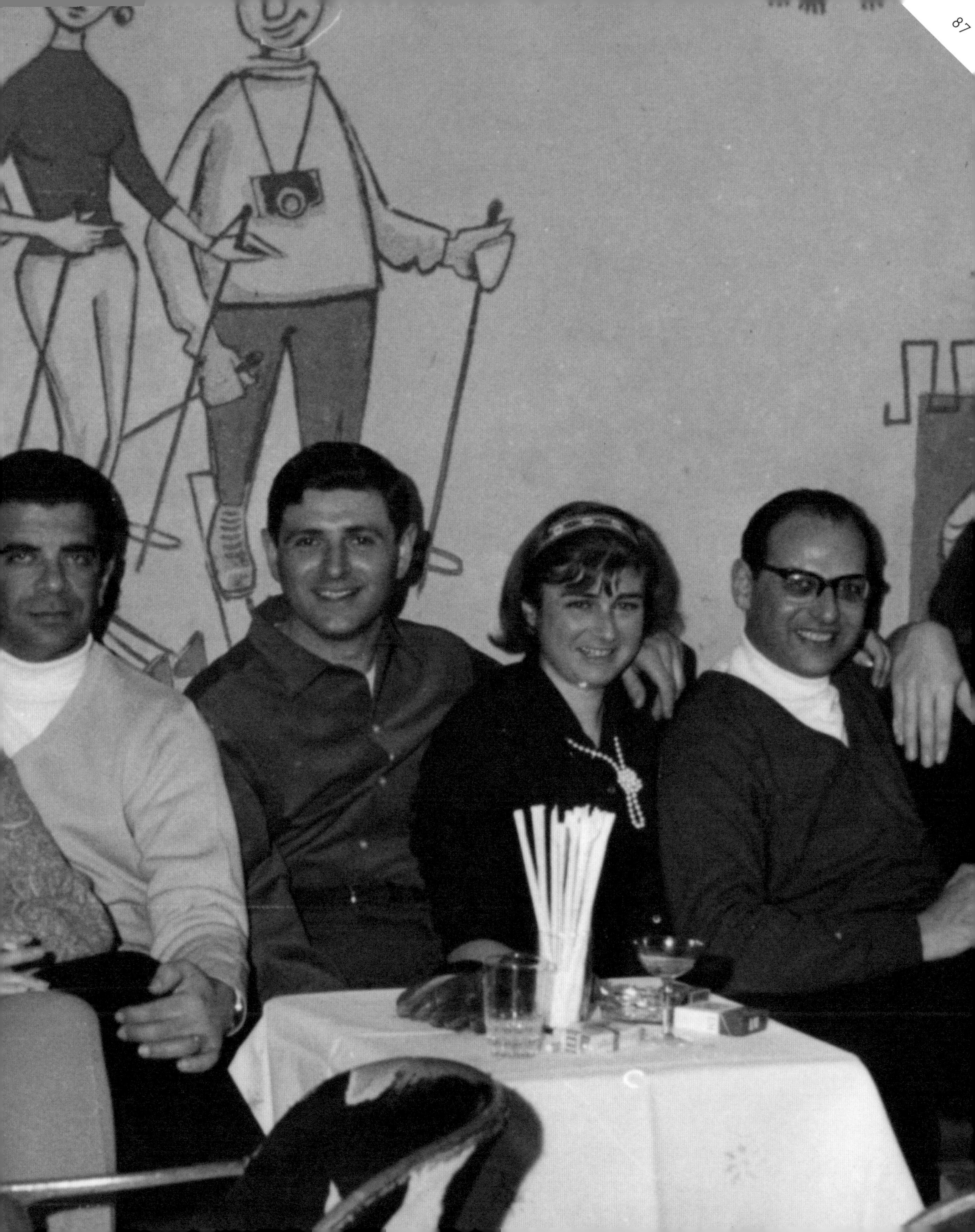

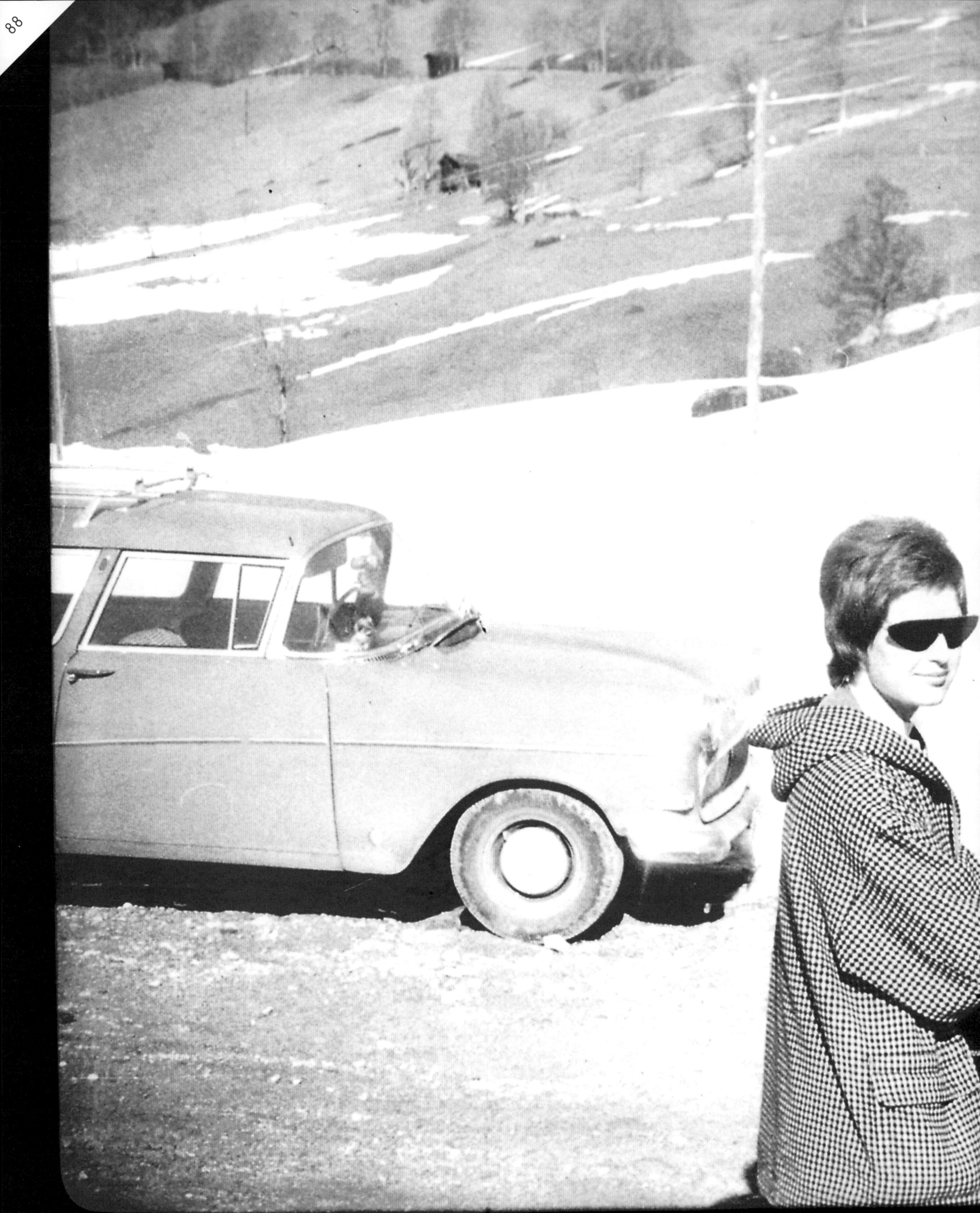

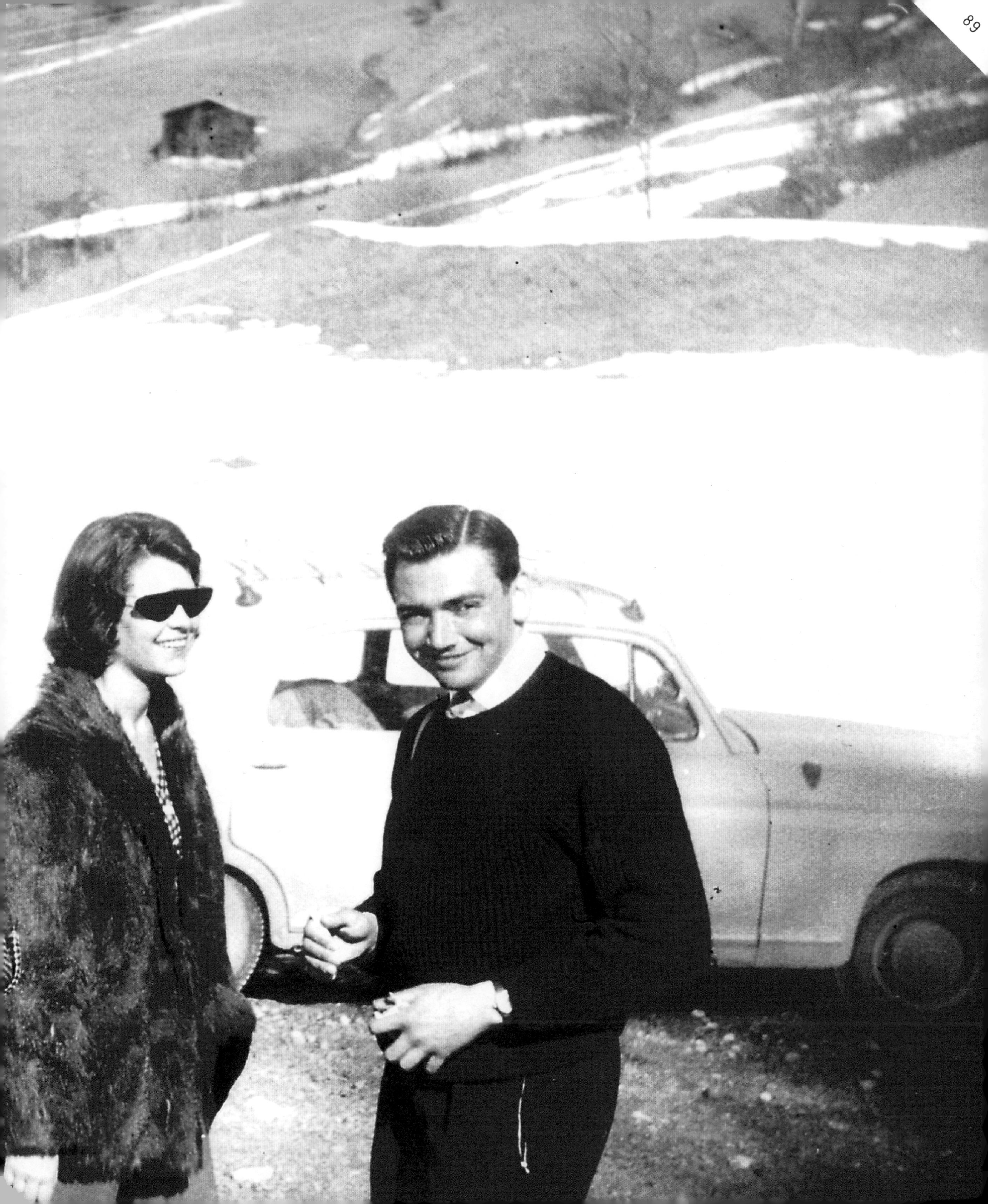

1.0 In the 1960s passengers walked on
to aircraft by means of staircases on
wheels. This was a very glamorous
age for air travel, quite unlike now in
that it was like travelling on a private
jet, and you dressed up in order to go
to the airport. A typical evening out
was to look at the planes from the
viewing terrace on the roof of the now
demolished Queen's Building
at London's Heathrow.

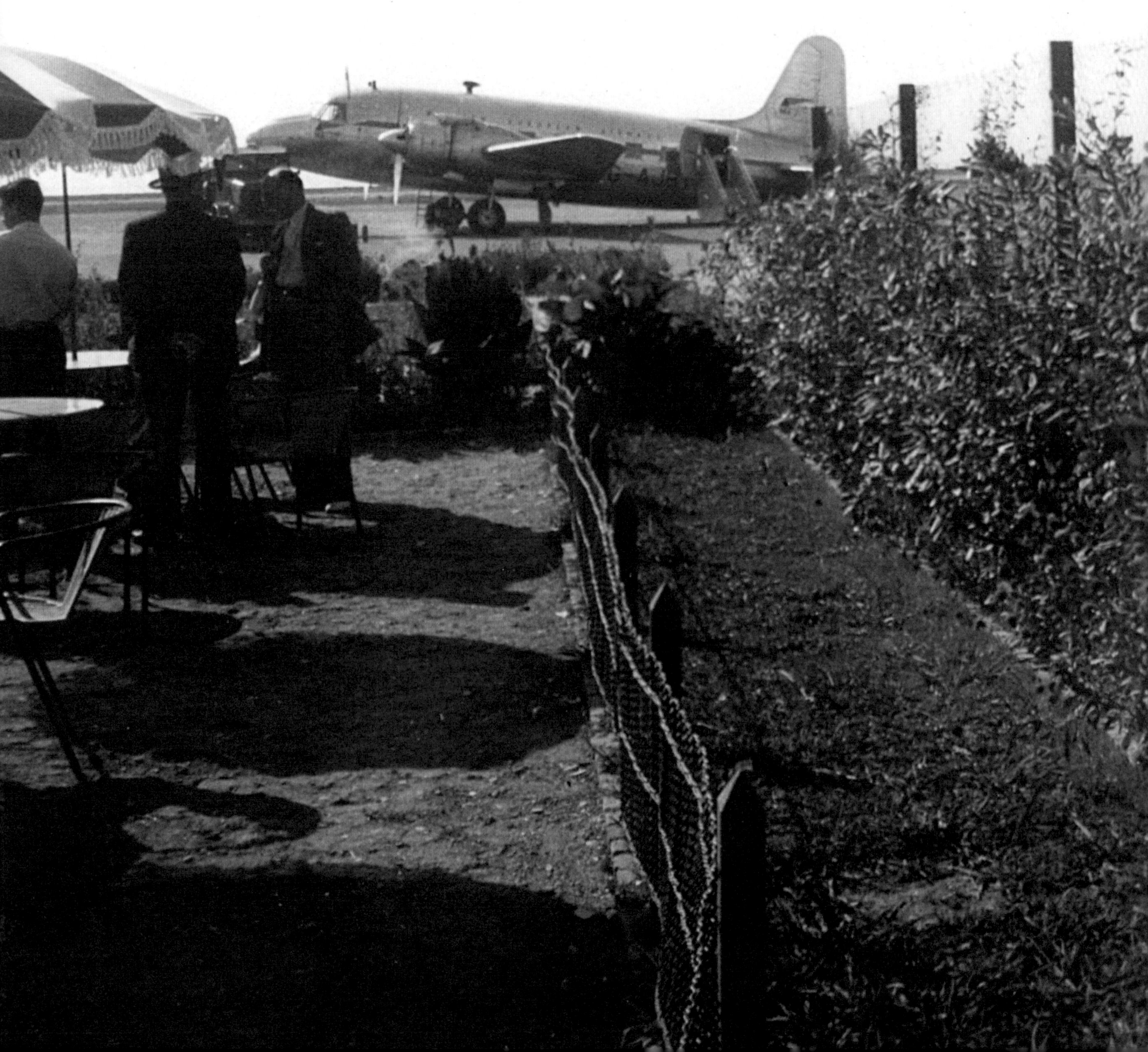

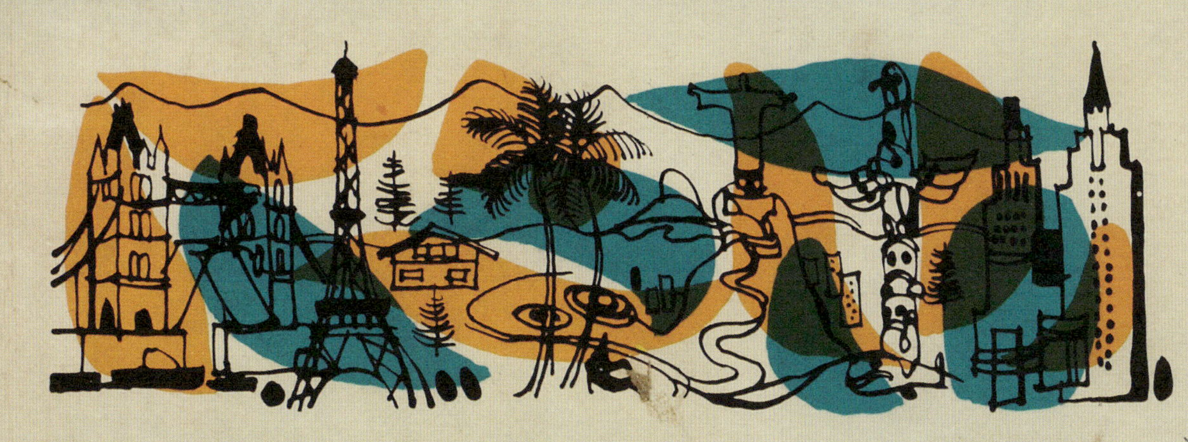

B·O·A·C

travellers digest

NORTH AMERICA · SOUTH AMERICA
PACIFIC · CARIBBEAN
EUROPE · ISRAEL

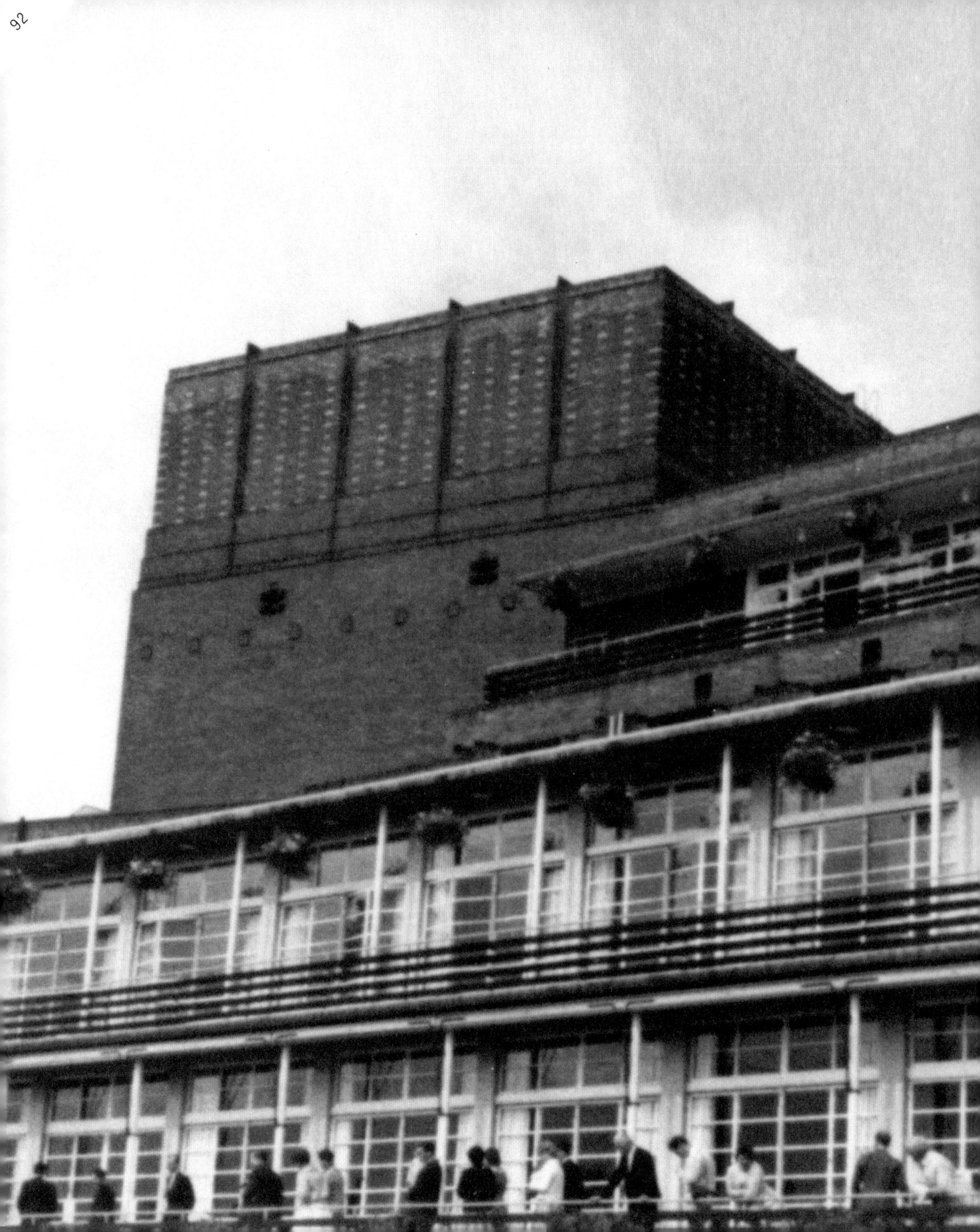

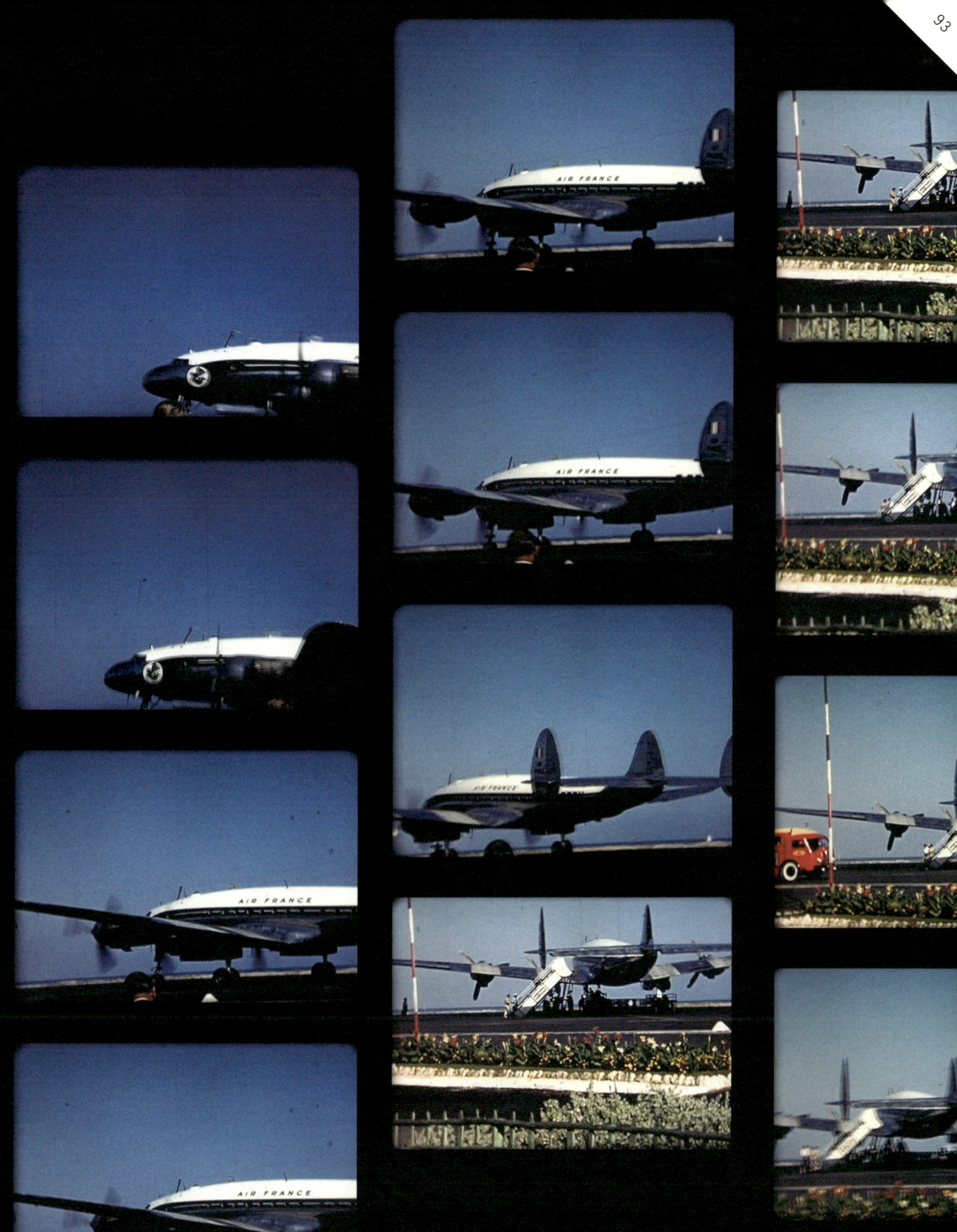

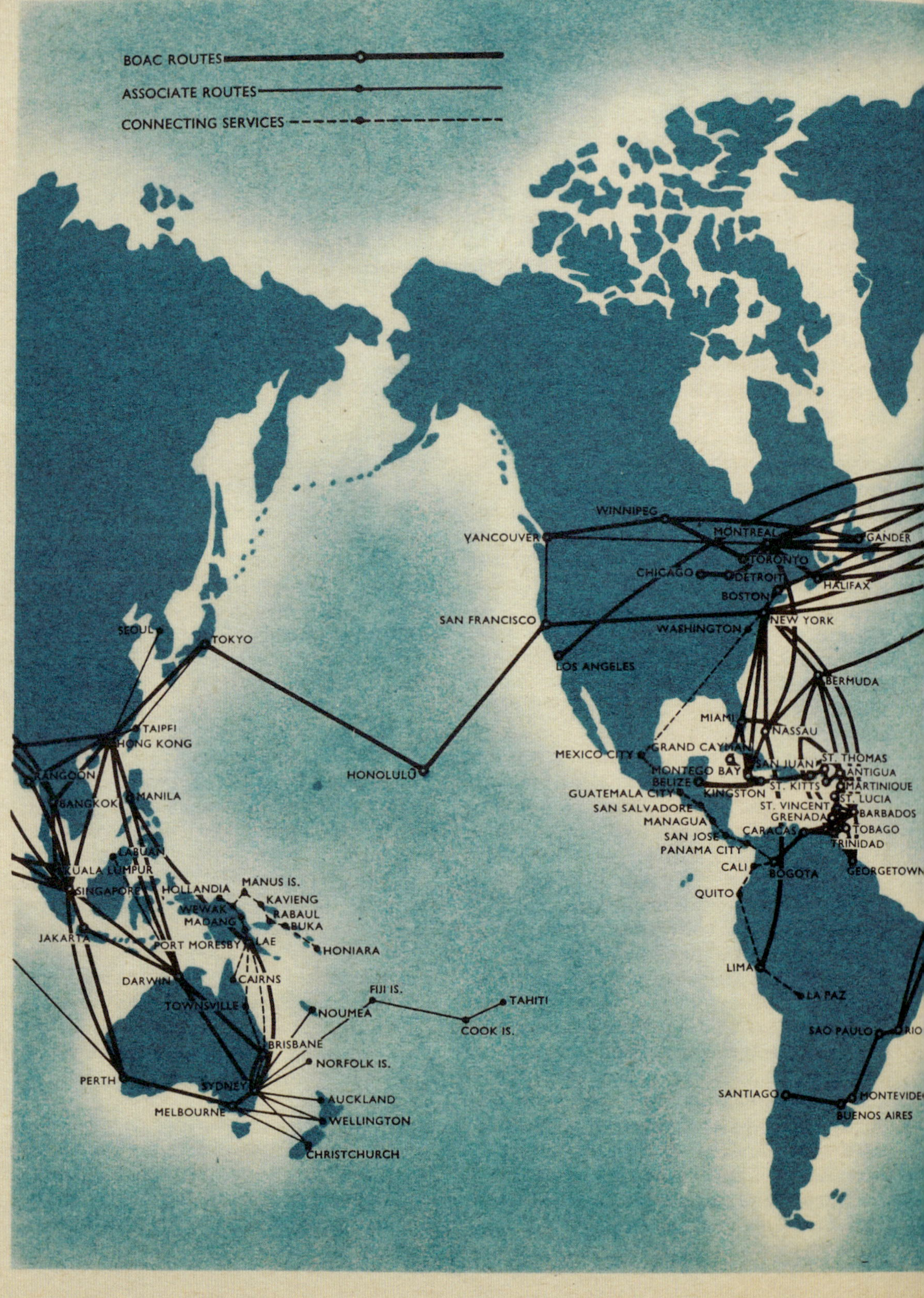

BOAC ROUTES
ASSOCIATE ROUTES
CONNECTING SERVICES
WINNIPEG
MONTREAL
GANDER
VANCOUVER
TORONTO
CHICAGO
DETROIT
HALIFAX
BOSTON
SAN FRANCISCO
NEW YORK
WASHINGTON
SEOUL
TOKYO
LOS ANGELES
BERMUDA
MIAMI
NASSAU
TAIPEI
HONG KONG
MEXICO CITY
GRAND CAYMAN
ST. THOMAS
MONTEGO BAY
SAN JUAN
ANTIGUA
RANGOON
BELIZE
MARTINIQUE
MANILA
GUATEMALA CITY
KINGSTON
ST. KITTS
ST. LUCIA
BANGKOK
SAN SALVADOR
ST. VINCENT
MANAGUA
GRENADA
BARBADOS
HONOLULU
SAN JOSE
CARACAS
TOBAGO
LABUAN
PANAMA CITY
TRINIDAD
KUALA LUMPUR
CALI
SINGAPORE
HOLLANDIA
MANUS IS.
BOGOTA
GEORGETOWN
KAVIENG
QUITO
WEWAK
RABAUL
MADANG
BUKA
JAKARTA
PORT MORESBY
LAE
HONIARA
LIMA
DARWIN
CAIRNS
FIJI IS.
TAHITI
TOWNSVILLE
NOUMEA
LA PAZ
COOK IS.
BRISBANE
SAO PAULO
RIO
PERTH
NORFOLK IS.
SYDNEY
AUCKLAND
MELBOURNE
SANTIAGO
MONTEVIDEO
WELLINGTON
BUENOS AIRES
CHRISTCHURCH

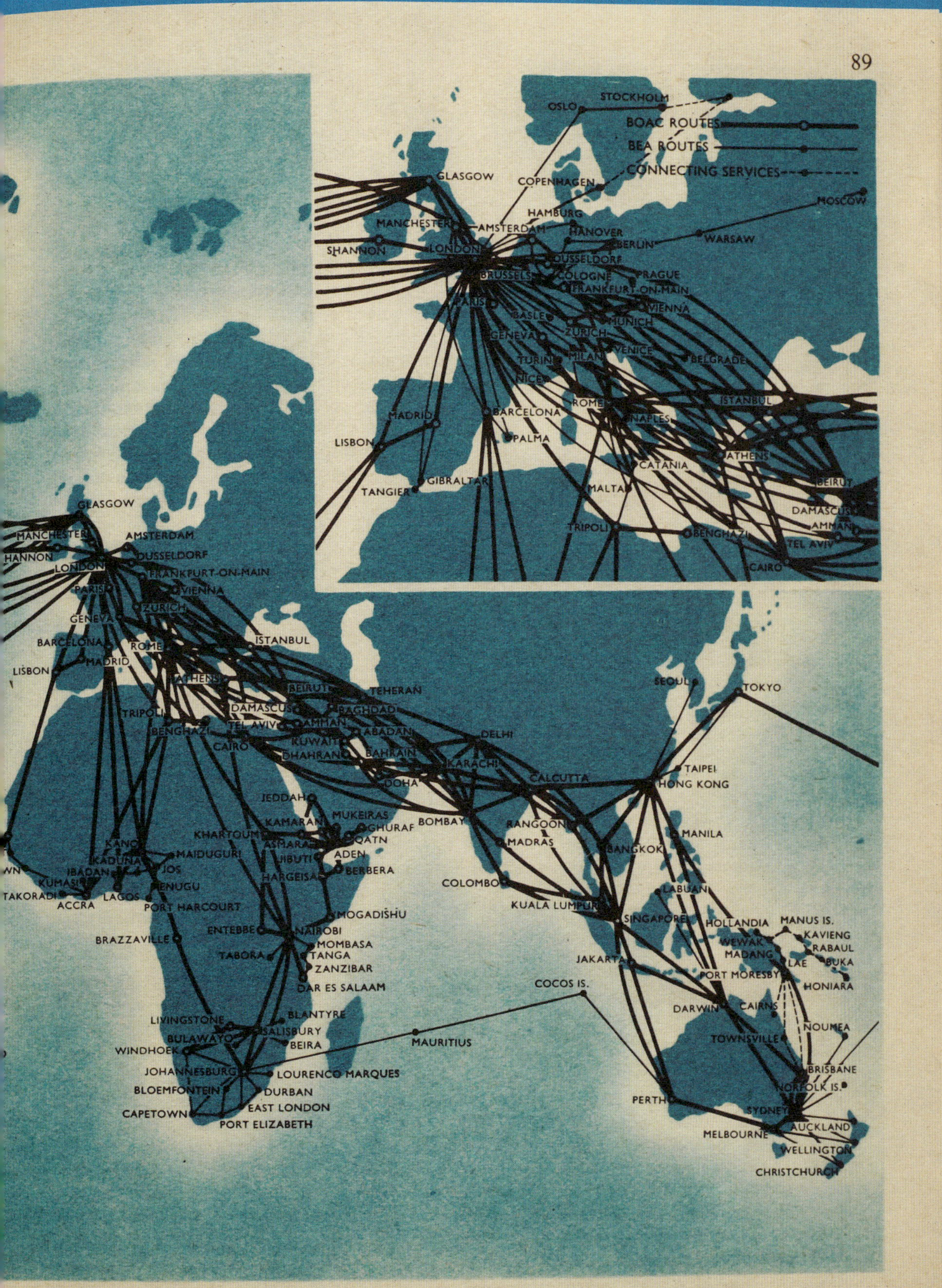
OSLO
STOCKHOLM
BOAC ROUTES
BEA ROUTES
CONNECTING SERVICES
GLASGOW
COPENNAGEN
HAMBURG
MOSCOW
MANCHESTER
AMSTERDAM
HANOVER
BERLIN
WARSAW
SHANNON
LONDON
DUSSELDORF
BRUSSELS
COLOGNE
PRAGUE
PARIS
FRANKFURT-ON-MAIN
BASLE
VIENNA
GENEVA
ZURICH
MUNICH
TURIN
MILAN
VENICE
BELGRADE
NICE
ROME
ISTANBUL
MADRID
BARCELONA
NAPLES
LISBON
PALMA
ATHENS
TANGIER
GIBRALTAR
CATANIA
MALTA
BEIRUT
DAMASCUS
AMMAN
TRIPOLI
BENGHAZI
TEL AVIV
CAIRO
GEASGOW
MANCHESTER
AMSTERDAM
HANNON
LONDON
DUSSELDORF
PARIS
FRANKFURT-ON-MAIN
GENEVA
VIENNA
ZURICH
BARCELONA
ROME
ISTANBUL
LISBON
MADRID
ATHENS
BEIRUT
TEHERAN
TRIPOLI
DAMASCUS
BAGHDAD
BENGHAZI
TEL AVIV
AMMAN
SEOUL
TOKYO
CAIRO
KUWAIT
ABADAN
DHAHRAN
BAHRAIN
DELHI
DOHA
KARACHI
CALCUTTA
TAIPEI
HONG KONG
JEDDAH
MUKEIRAS
KAMARAN
GHURAF
BOMBAY
RANGOON
KHARTOUM
ASHARA
QATN
MADRAS
MANILA
KANO
ASMARA
ADEN
BANGKOK
KADUNA
MAIDUGURI
JIBUTI
BERBERA
IBADAN
JOS
HARGEISA
COLOMBO
LABUAN
KUMASI
ENUGU
KUALA LUMPUR
TAKORADI
LAGOS
SINGAPORE
HOLLANDIA
MANUS IS.
ACCRA
PORT HARCOURT
WEWAK
KAVIENG
MOGADISHU
MADANG
RABAUL
BRAZZAVILLE
ENTEBBE
NAIROBI
LAE
BUKA
TABORA
MOMBASA
PORT MORESBY
HONIARA
TANGA
ZANZIBAR
JAKARTA
DAR ES SALAAM
COCOS IS.
DARWIN
CAIRNS
LIVINGSTONE
BLANTYRE
NOUMEA
BULAWAYO
SALISBURY
MAURITIUS
TOWNSVILLE
WINDHOEK
BEIRA
JOHANNESBURG
LOURENCO MARQUES
BRISBANE
NORFOLK IS.
BLOEMFONTEIN
DURBAN
PERTH
CAPETOWN
EAST LONDON
SYDNEY
AUCKLAND
PORT ELIZABETH
MELBOURNE
WELLINGTON
CHRISTCHURCH

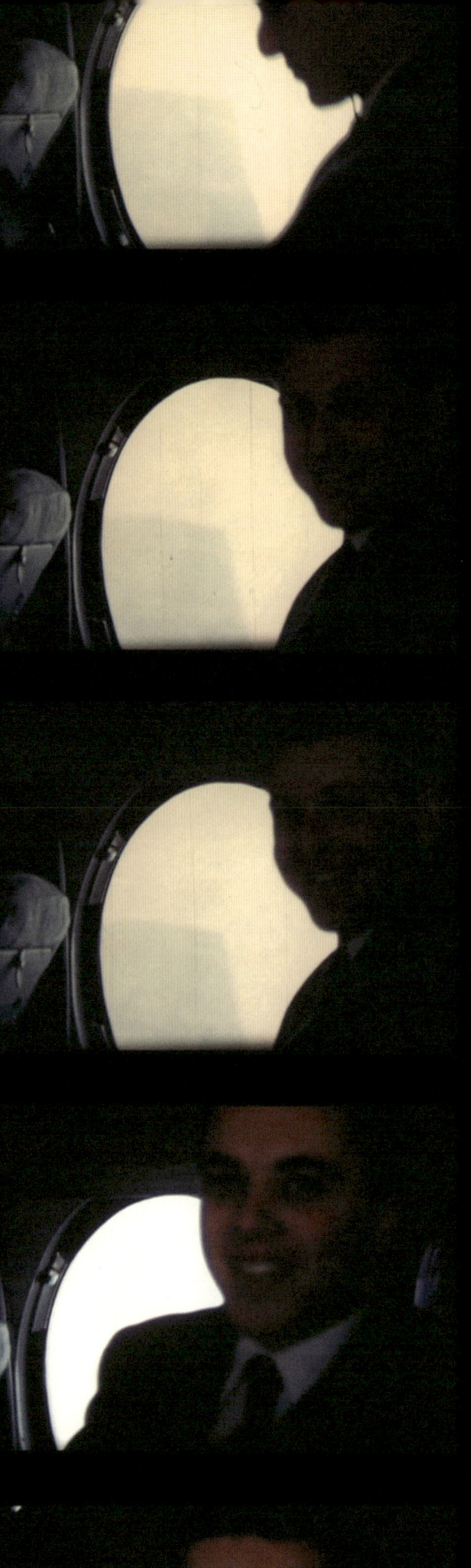
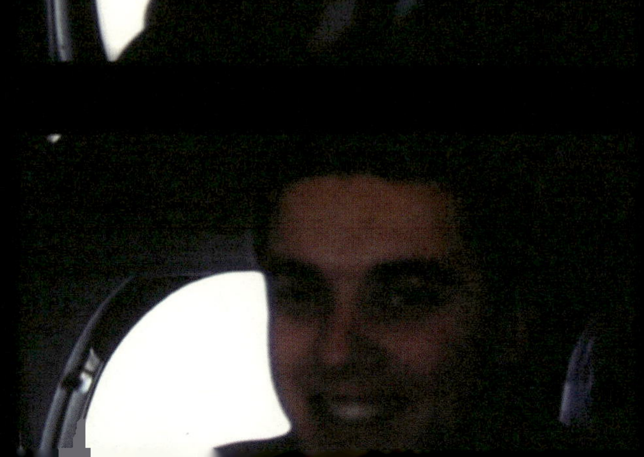

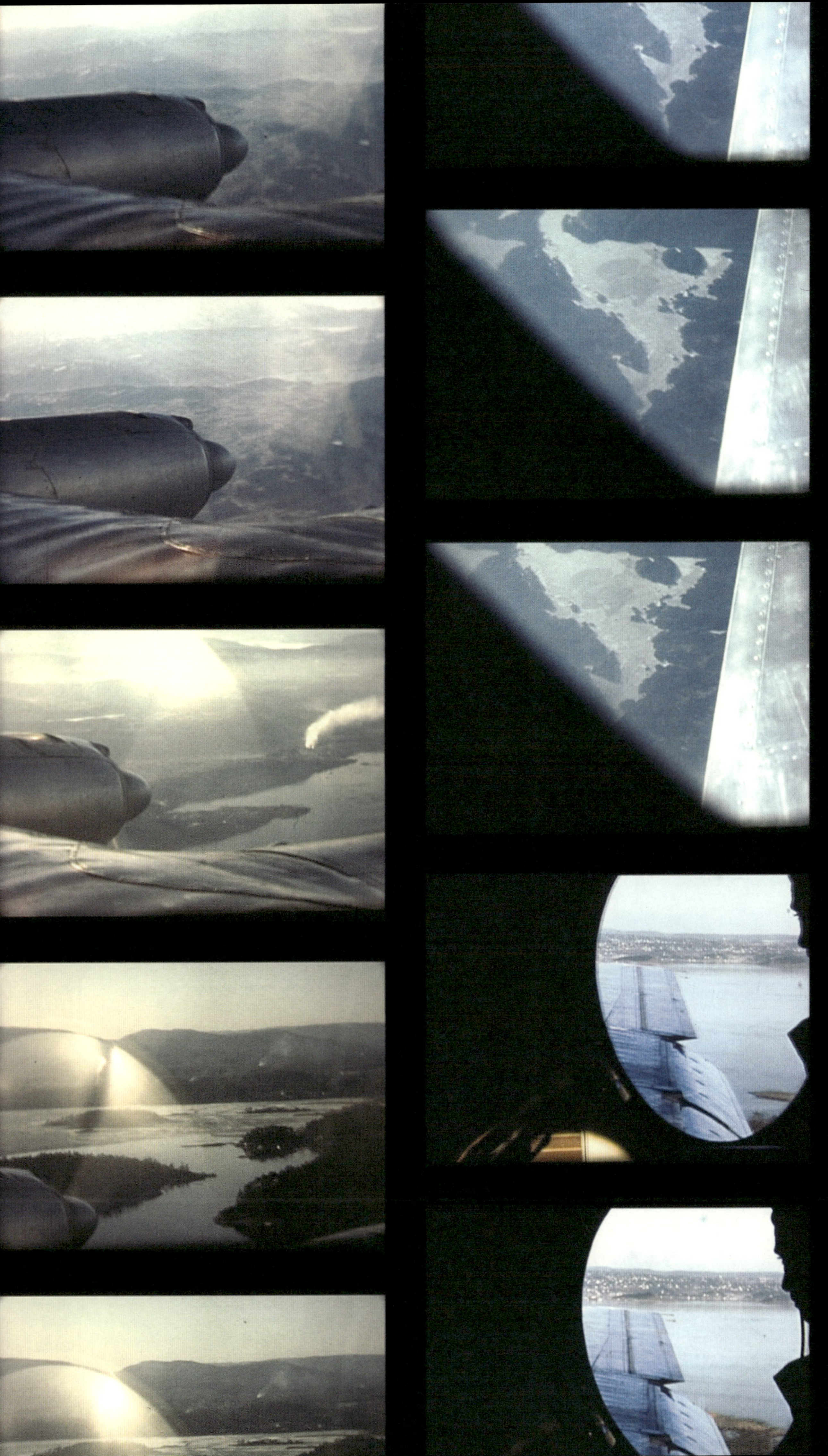

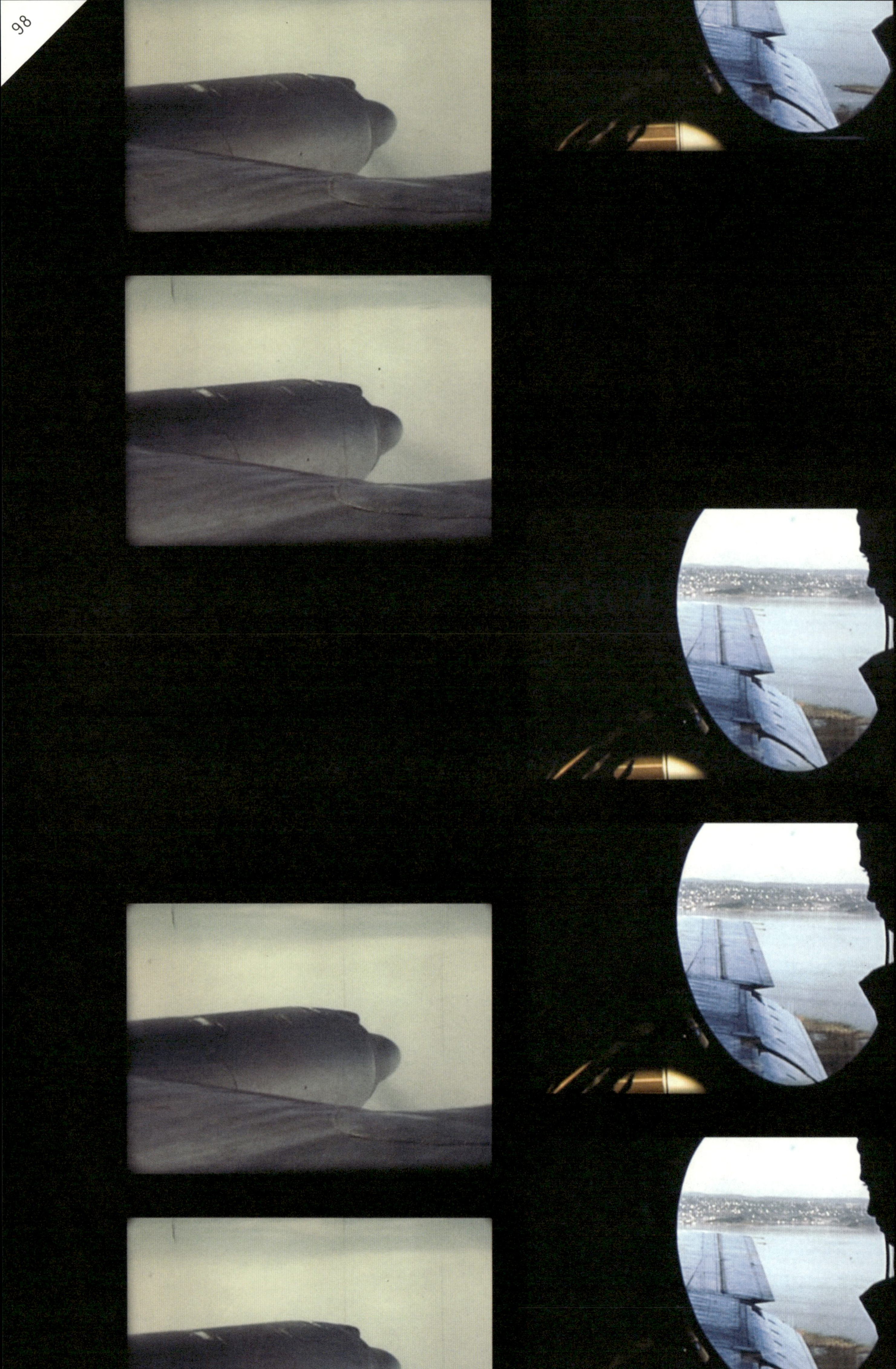

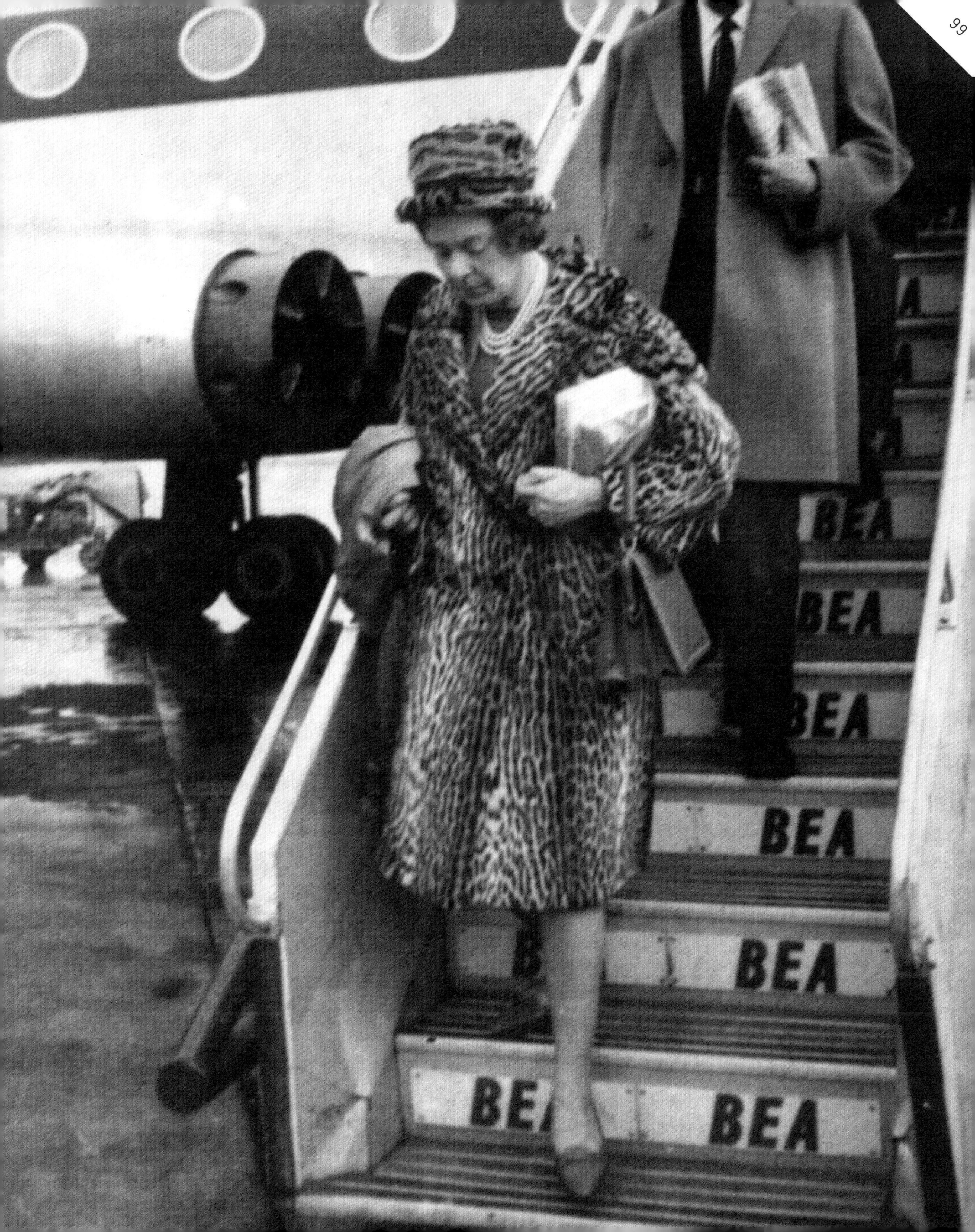
BEA
BEA
BEA
BEA
BEA
BEA
BEA

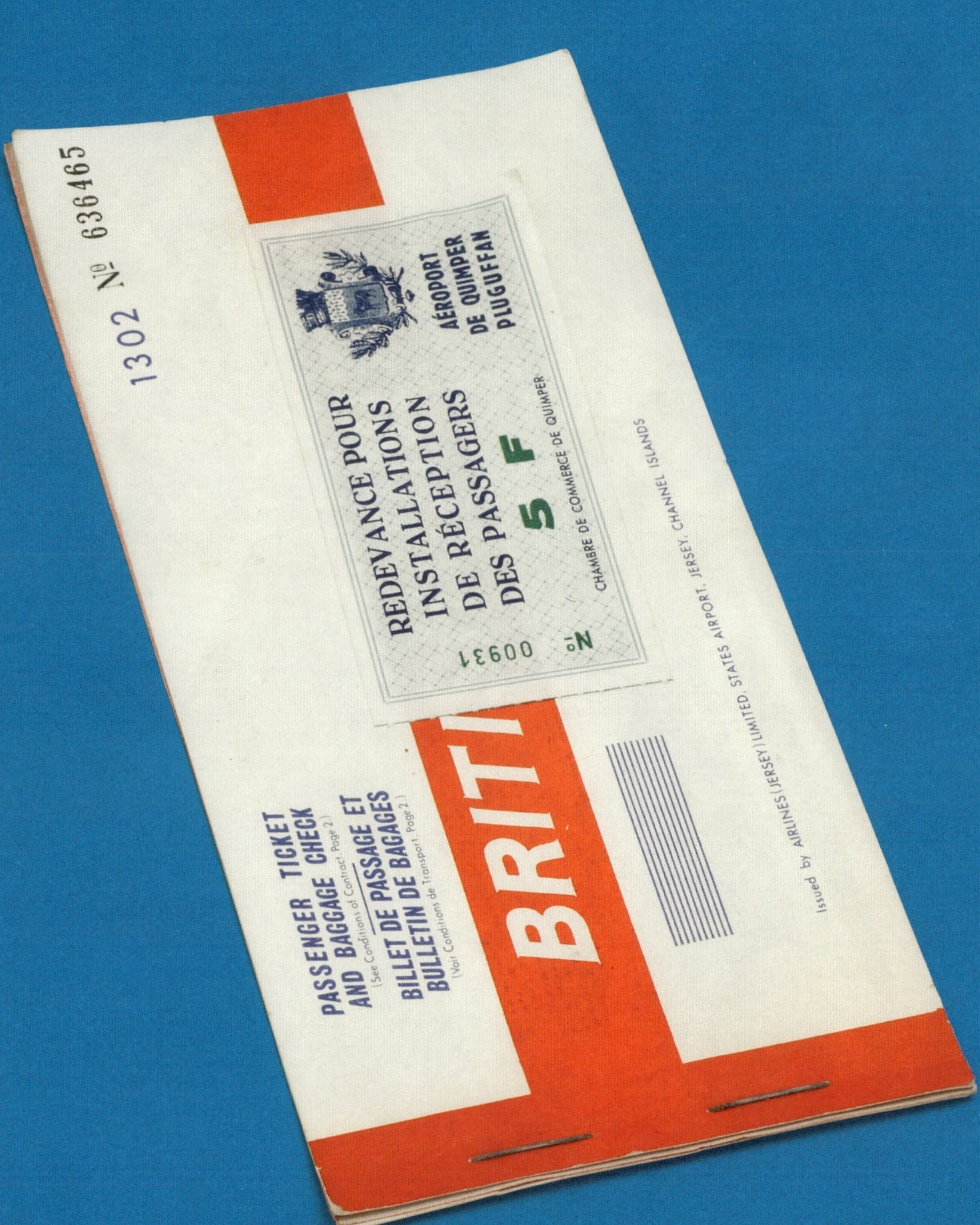
1302 Nº 636465
REDEVANCE POUR
INSTALLATIONS
DE RÉCEPTION
DES PASSAGERS
AÉROPORT
DE QUIMPER
PLUGUFFAN
5 F
CHAMBRE DE COMMERCE DE QUIMPER
Nº 00931
PASSENGER TICKET
AND BAGGAGE CHECK
(See Conditions of Contract-Page 2)
BILLET DE PASSAGE ET
BULLETIN DE BAGAGES
(Voir Conditions de Transport-Page 2)
BRIT
Issued by AIRLINES (JERSEY) LIMITED STATES AIRPORT, JERSEY, CHANNEL ISLANDS

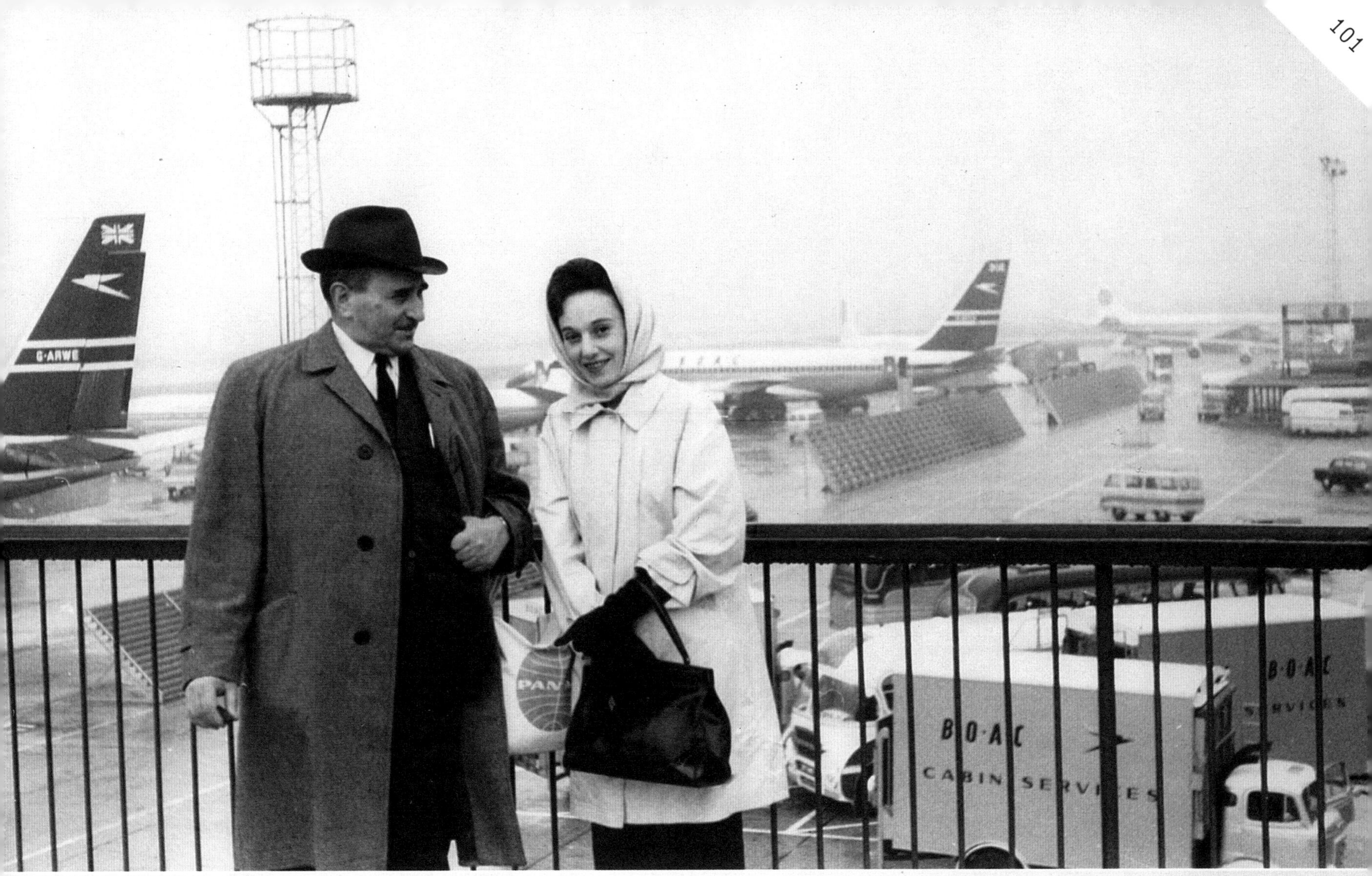

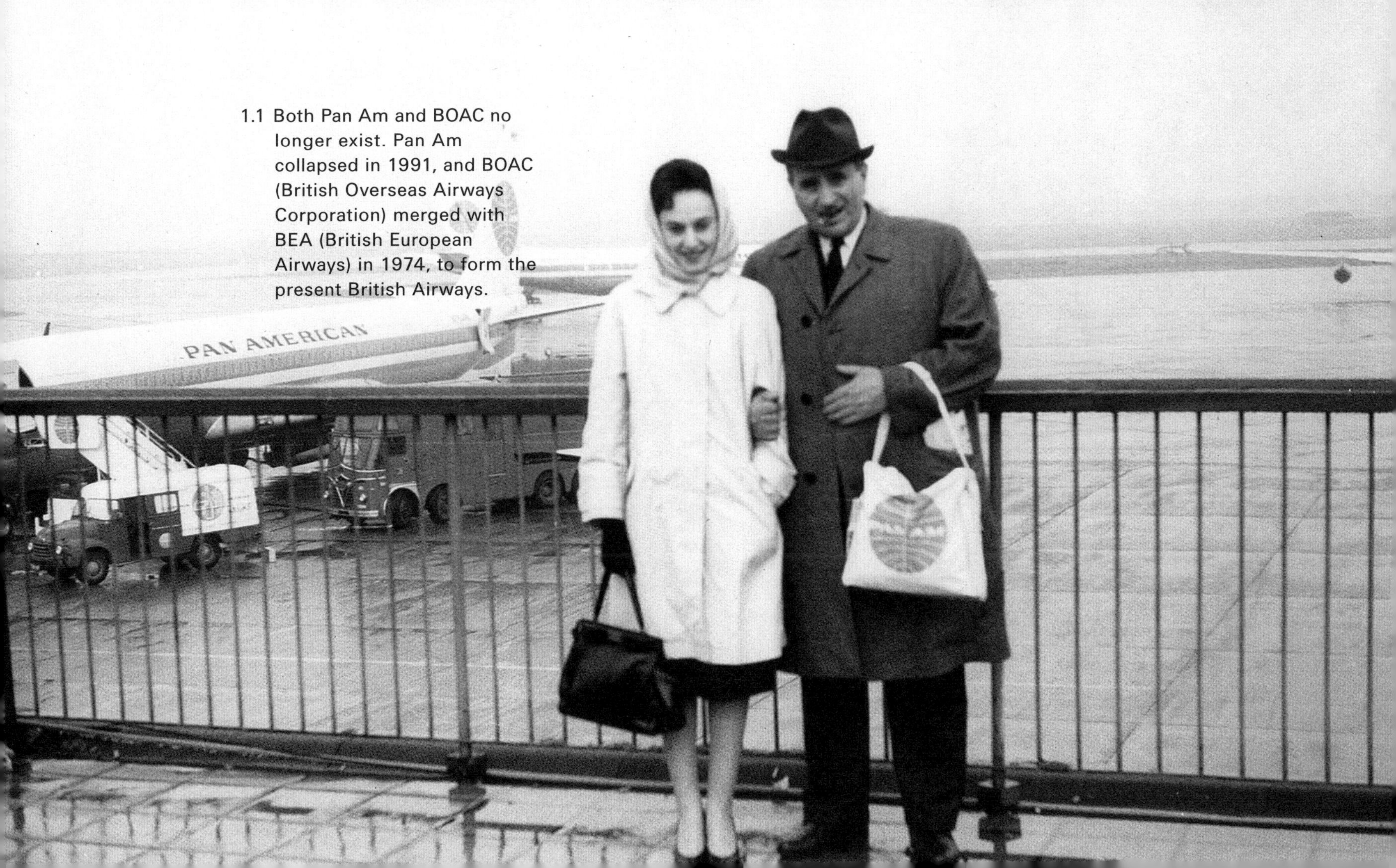

1.1 Both Pan Am and BOAC no longer exist. Pan Am collapsed in 1991, and BOAC (British Overseas Airways Corporation) merged with BEA (British European Airways) in 1974, to form the present British Airways.

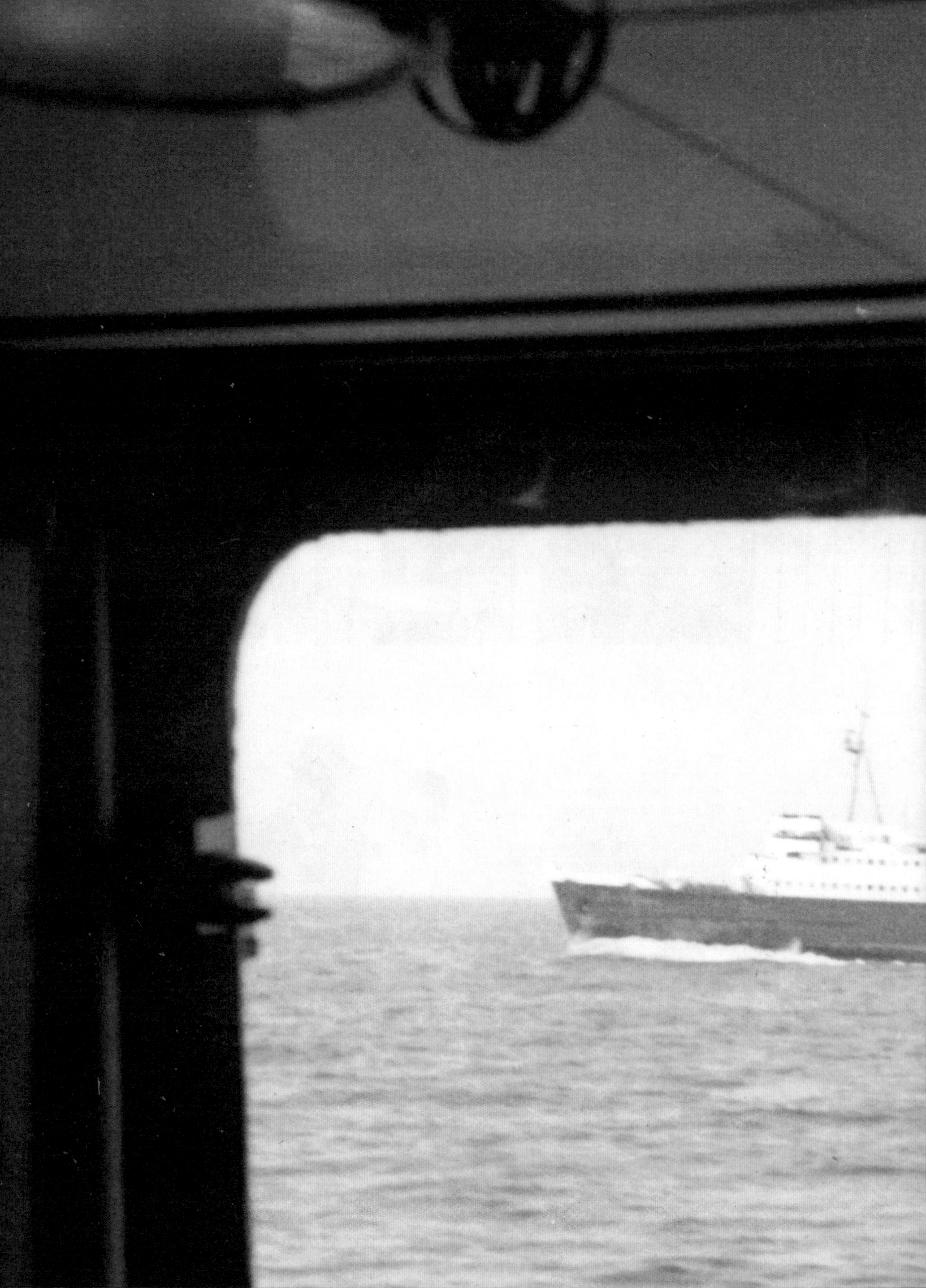

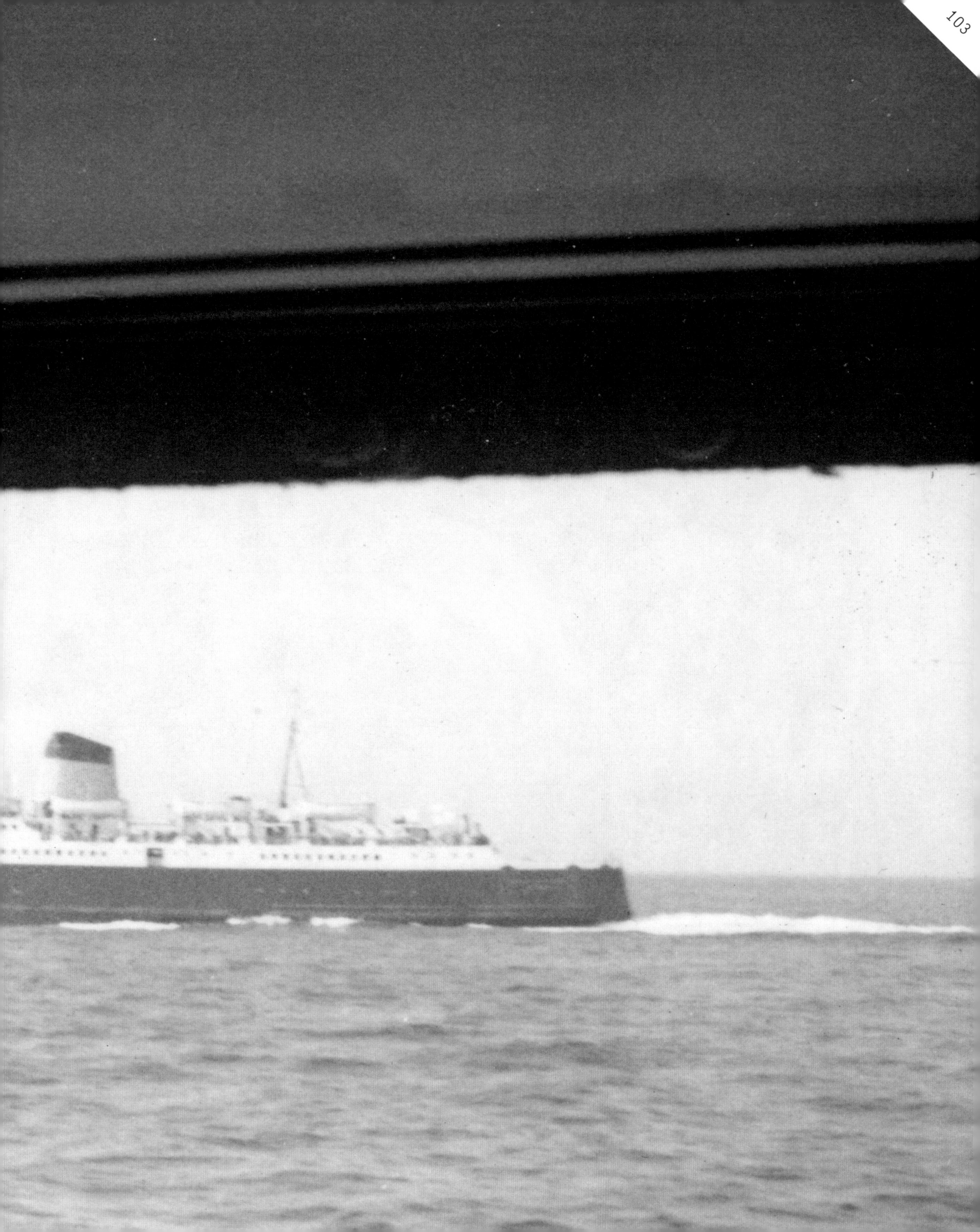

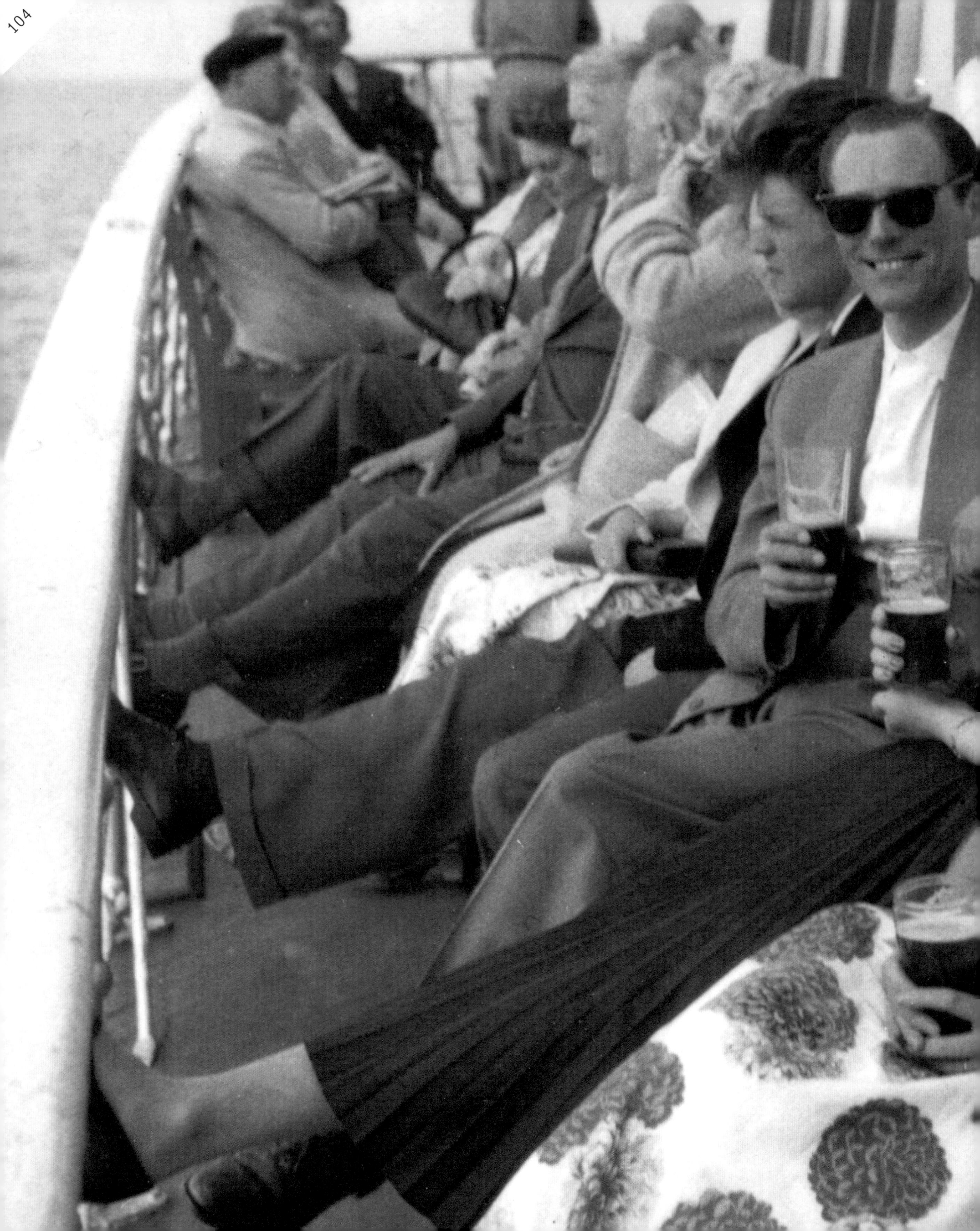

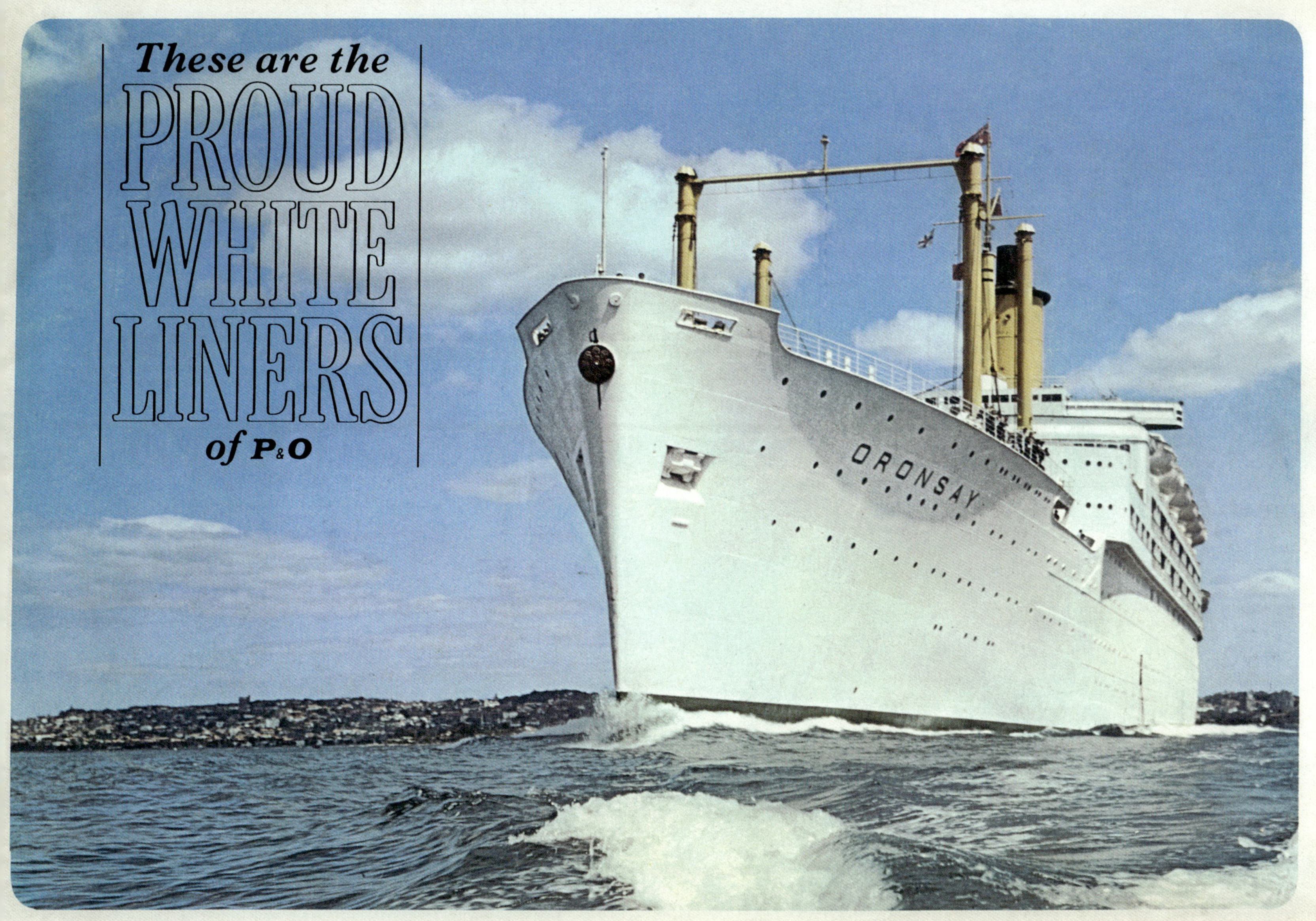
These are the
PROUD
WHITE
LINERS
of P&O
ORONSAY

CANBERRA

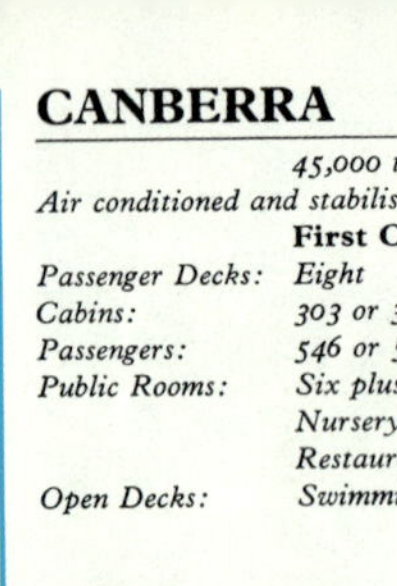

	45,000 tons	Length 818 feet
Air conditioned and stabilised		
	First Class	**Tourist Class**
Passenger Decks:	Eight	Ten
Cabins:	303 or 333	492 or 522
Passengers:	546 or 596	1,616 or 1,716
Public Rooms:	Six plus Cinema, Nursery and Restaurant	Eight plus Cinema, Nursery and Restaurant
Open Decks:	Swimming Pool	Two Swimming Pools and Paddling Pool
Crew:	938	

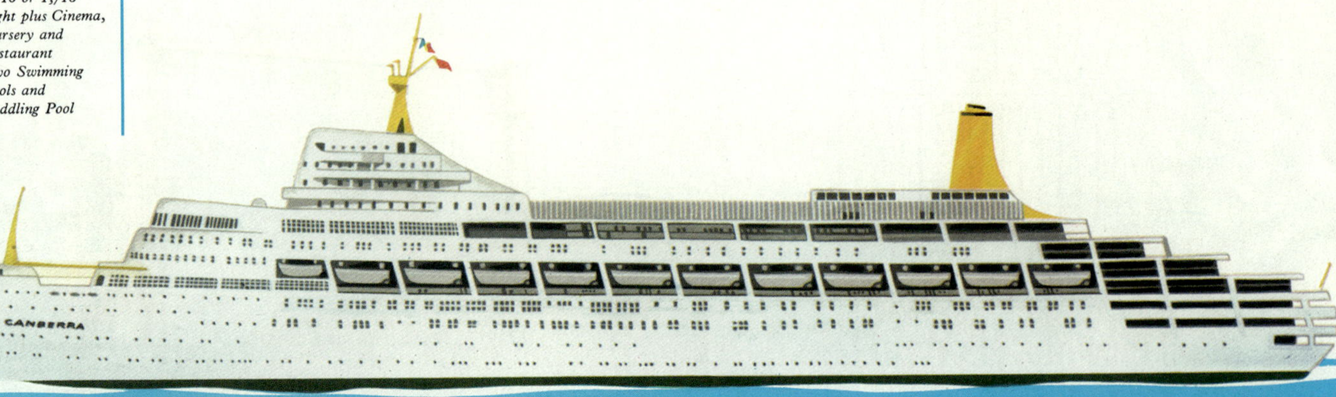

ORIANA

	42,000 tons	Length 804 feet
Air conditioned and stabilised		
	First Class	**Tourist Class**
Passenger Decks:	Eight	Nine
Cabins:	283 or 337	512 or 566
Passengers:	528 or 636	1,492 or 1,650
Public Rooms:	Nine plus Cinema, Nursery, Playroom and Restaurant	Eight plus Cinema, Nursery, Playroom and Restaurant
Open Decks:	Swimming Pool and Two Paddling Pools	Two Swimming Pools and Three Paddling Pools
Crew:	889	

ARCADIA

	30,000 tons	Length 721 feet
Air conditioned and stabilised		
	First Class	**Tourist Class**
Passenger Decks:	Six	Seven
Cabins:	354	208
Passengers:	644	735
Public Rooms:	Eight plus Cinema, Nursery and Restaurant	Five plus Cinema, Nursery and Restaurant
Open Decks:	Swimming Pool	Swimming Pool
Crew:	716	

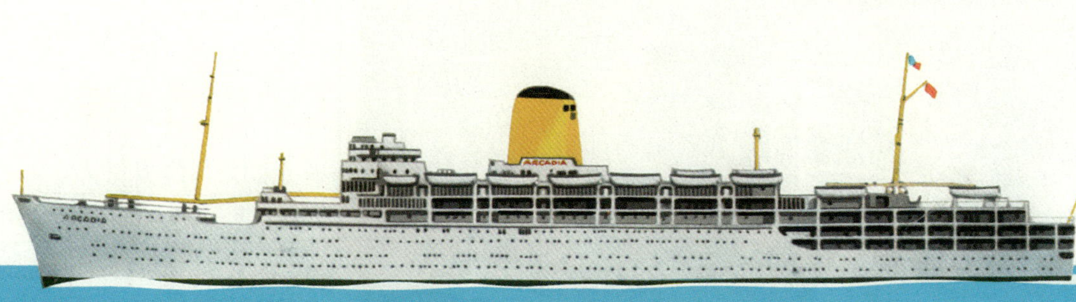

IBERIA

	30,000 tons	Length 719 feet
Air conditioned and stabilised		
	First Class	**Tourist Class**
Passenger Decks:	Six	Seven
Cabins:	351	206
Passengers:	650	733
Public Rooms:	Eight plus Cinema, Nursery and Restaurant	Five plus Cinema, Nursery and Restaurant
Open Decks:	Swimming Pool	Swimming Pool
Crew:	708	

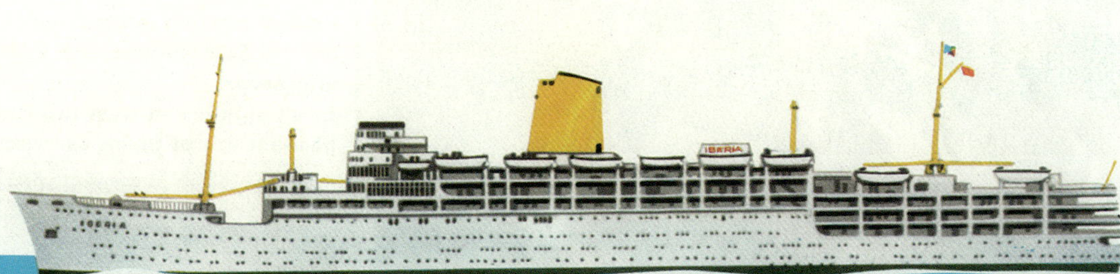

ORSOVA

	29,000 tons	Length 722 feet
Air conditioned and stabilised		
	First Class	**Tourist Class**
Passenger Decks:	Six	Six
Cabins:	370	257
Passengers:	688	809
Public Rooms:	Eight plus Cinema, Nursery and Restaurant	Four plus Cinema, Nursery and Restaurant
Open Decks:	Swimming Pool and Paddling Pool	Swimming Pool and Paddling Pool
Crew:	639	

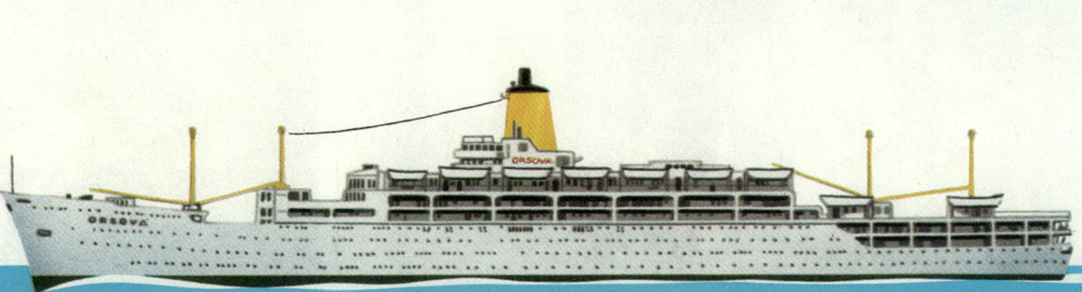

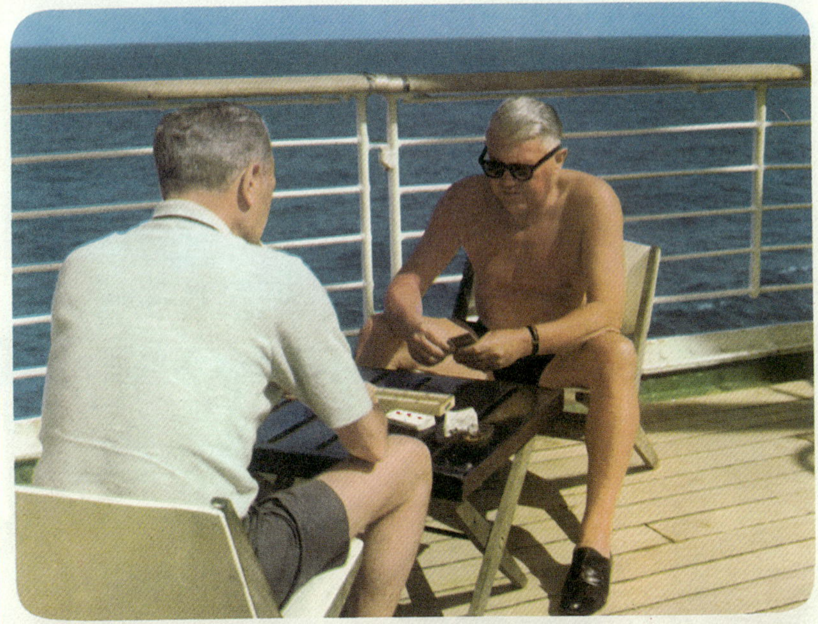

EVERYTHING YOU NEED

P & O have thought of everything (so they should; they've been in the business over a century). You left your toothbrush behind? The shop has a selection. It even has woollies for cold climes and swimming costumes for warm ones. And cameras and film and souvenirs. All duty-free.

Good, imaginative and experienced hairdressers run a fully-equipped salon on board every ship. And men can have their modest locks shorn in the mornings.

The latest films on release are hired for showing on board ship. Some have permanent cinemas, others convert the ballroom temporarily. And normally there are two first features each week — apart from documentaries etc. shown in the afternoons.

Every ship has at least two good table tennis tables in each class. A mild and pleasant way of taking exercise.

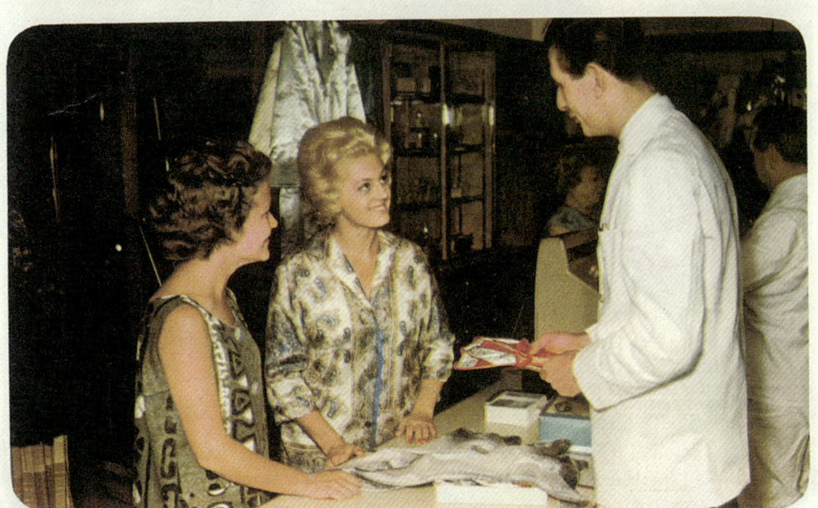

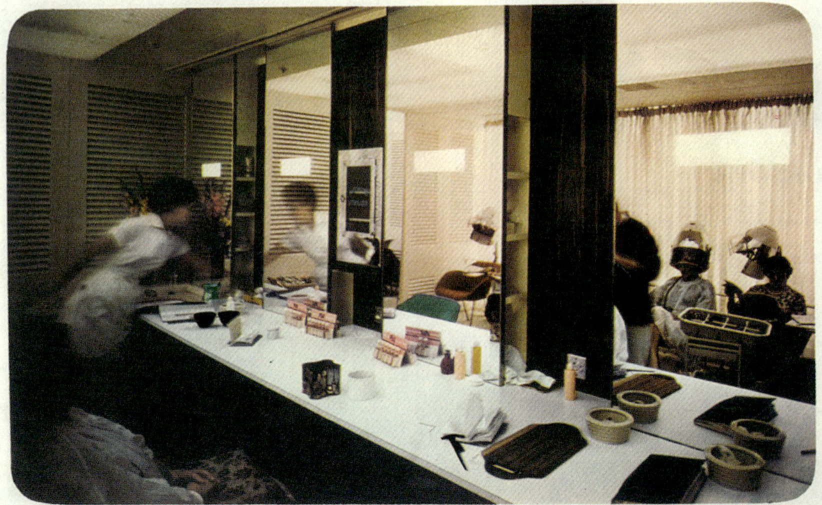

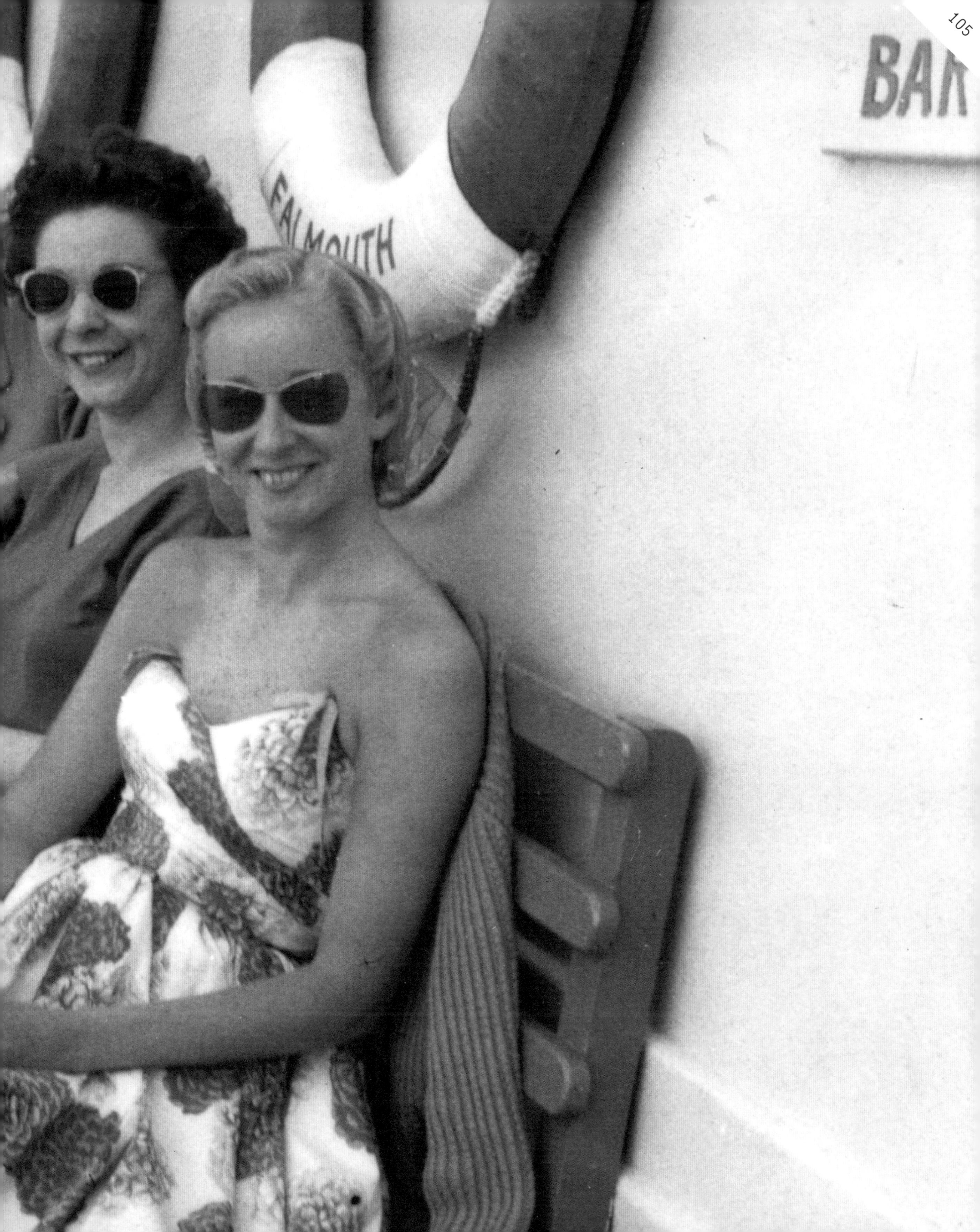
FALMOUTH
BAR

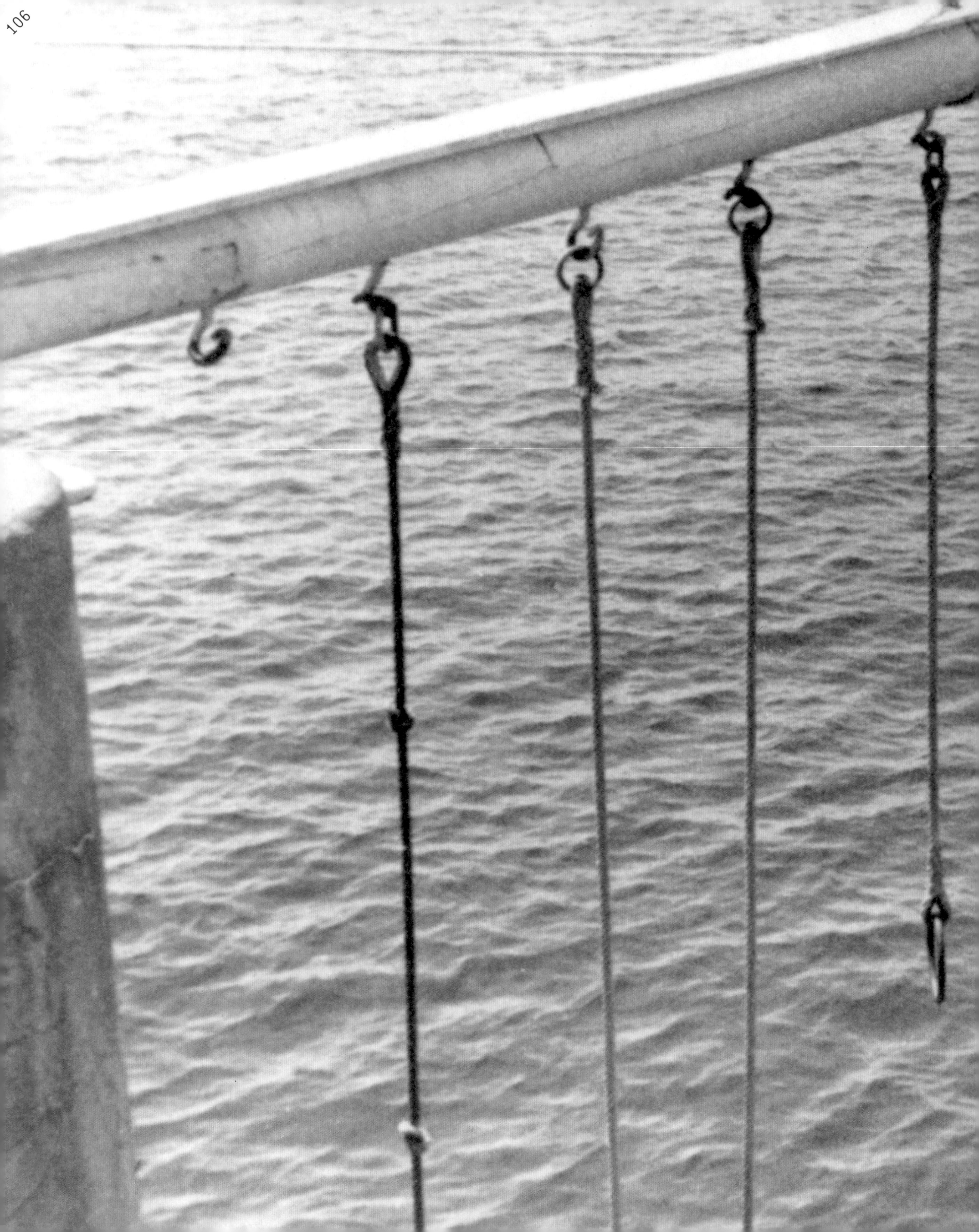

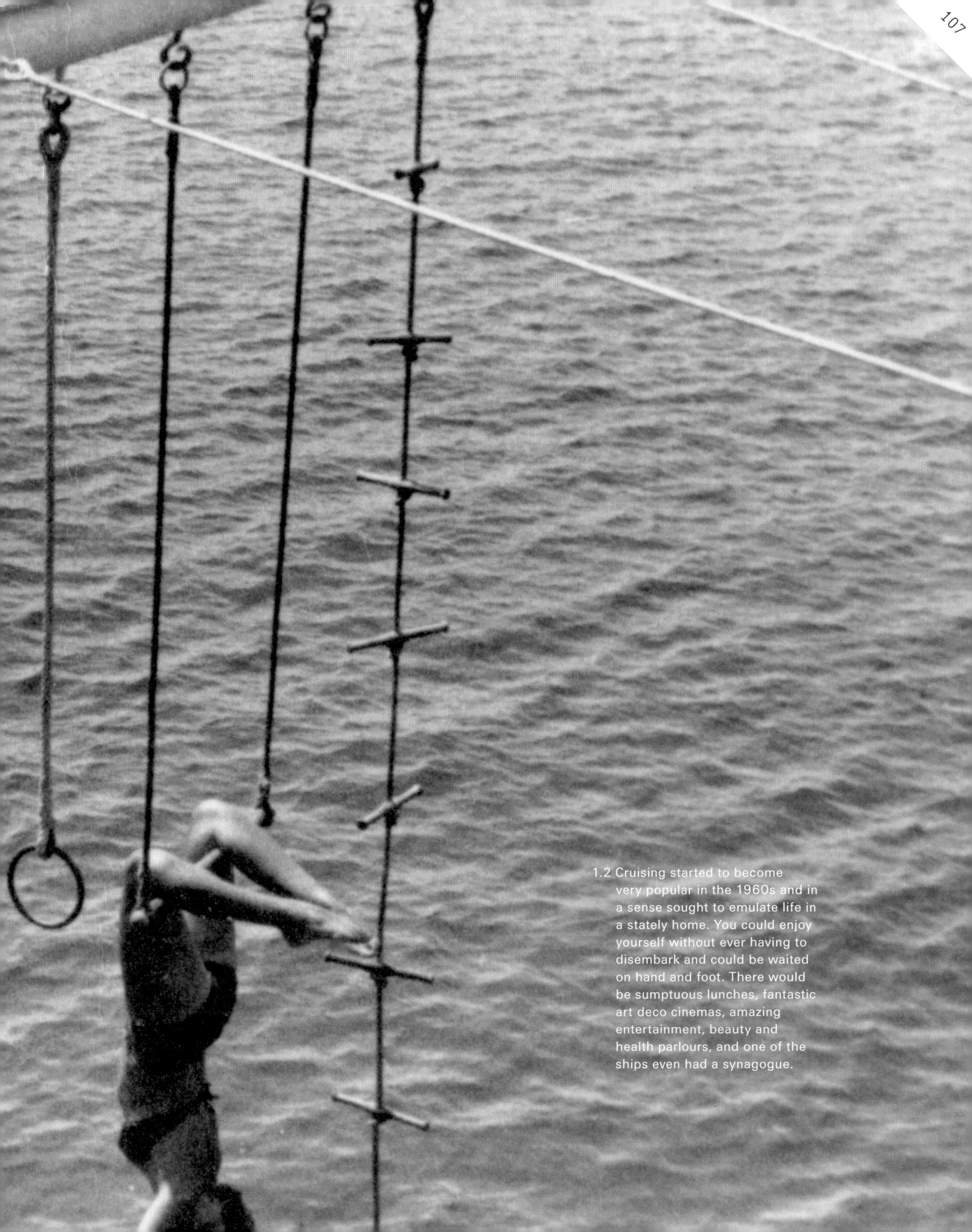

1.2 Cruising started to become very popular in the 1960s and in a sense sought to emulate life in a stately home. You could enjoy yourself without ever having to disembark and could be waited on hand and foot. There would be sumptuous lunches, fantastic art deco cinemas, amazing entertainment, beauty and health parlours, and one of the ships even had a synagogue.

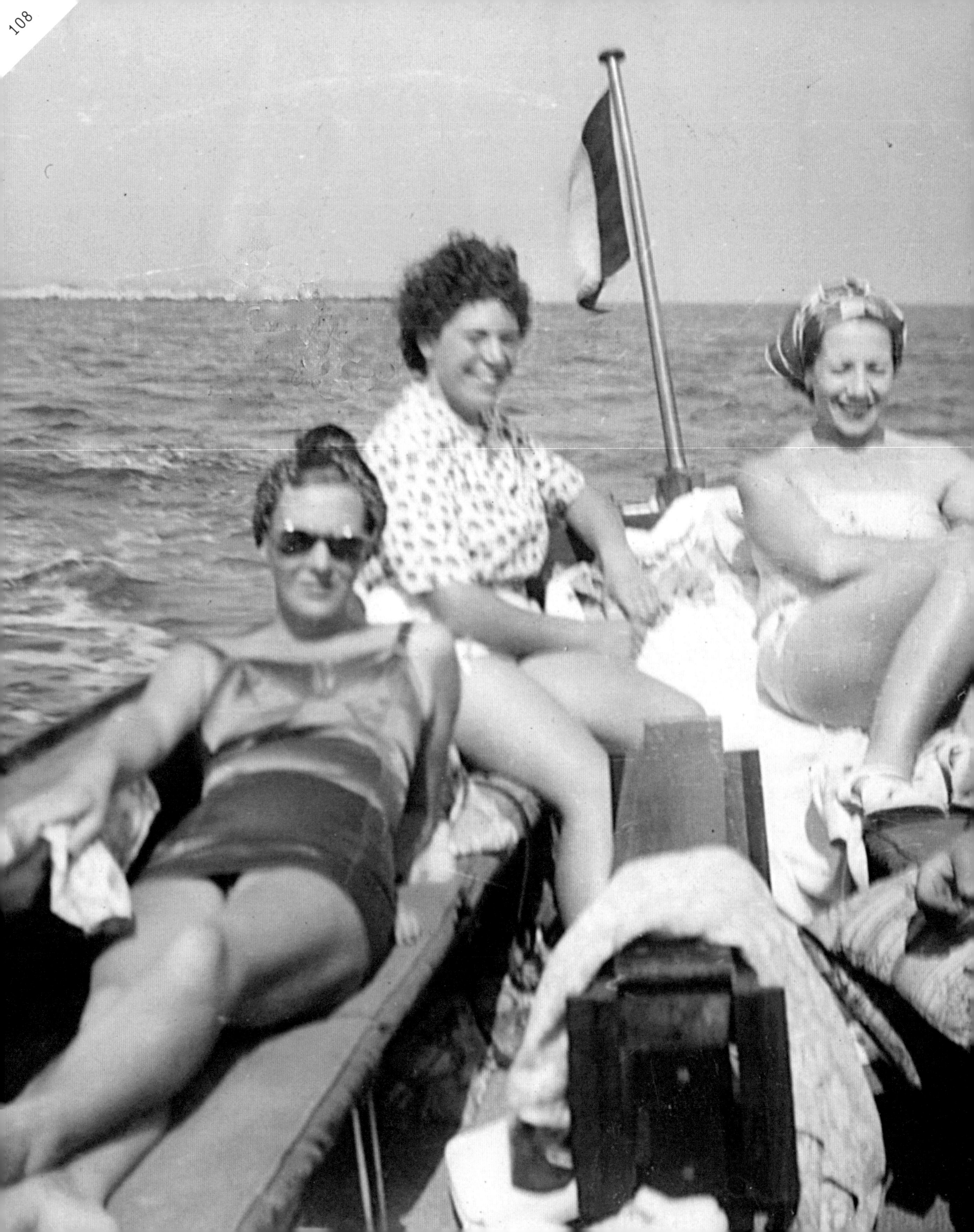

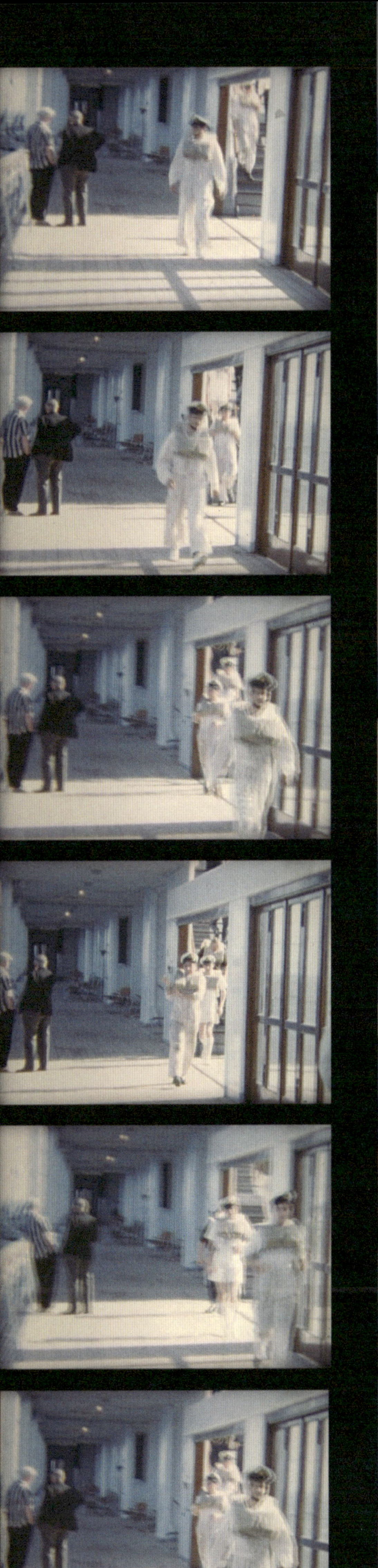
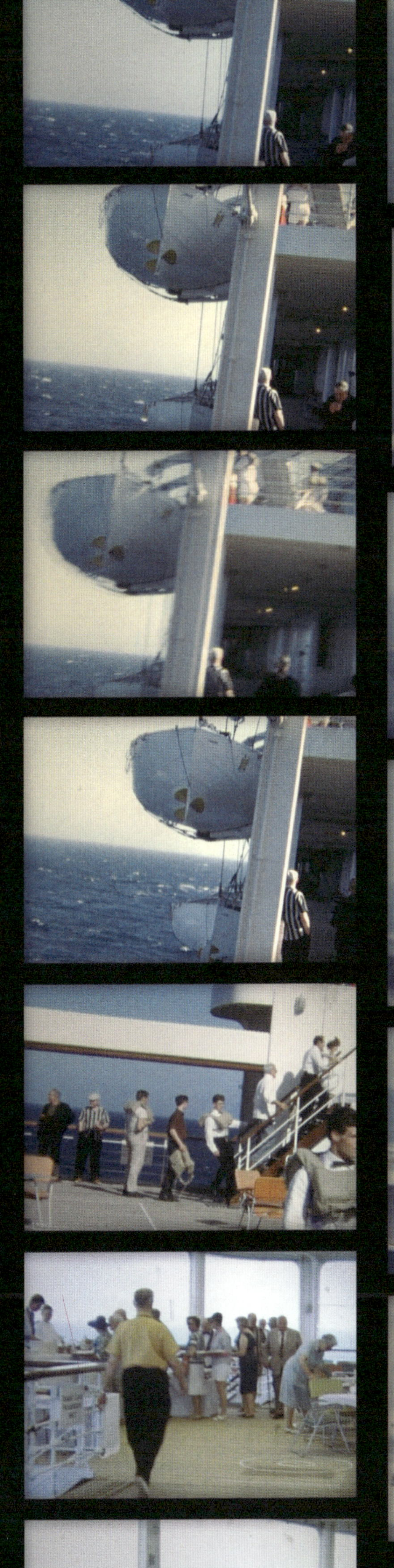
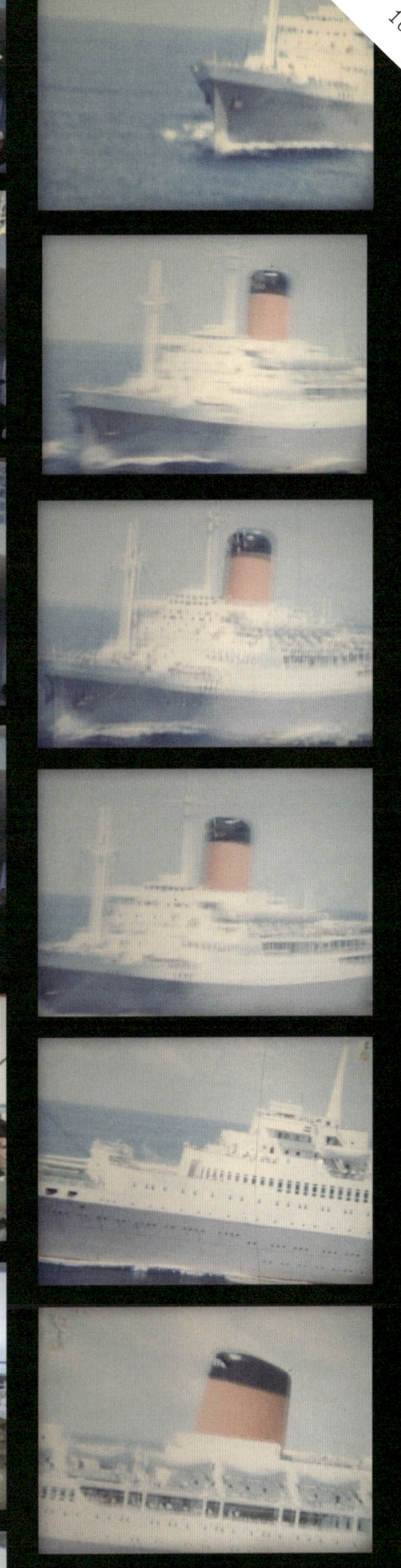

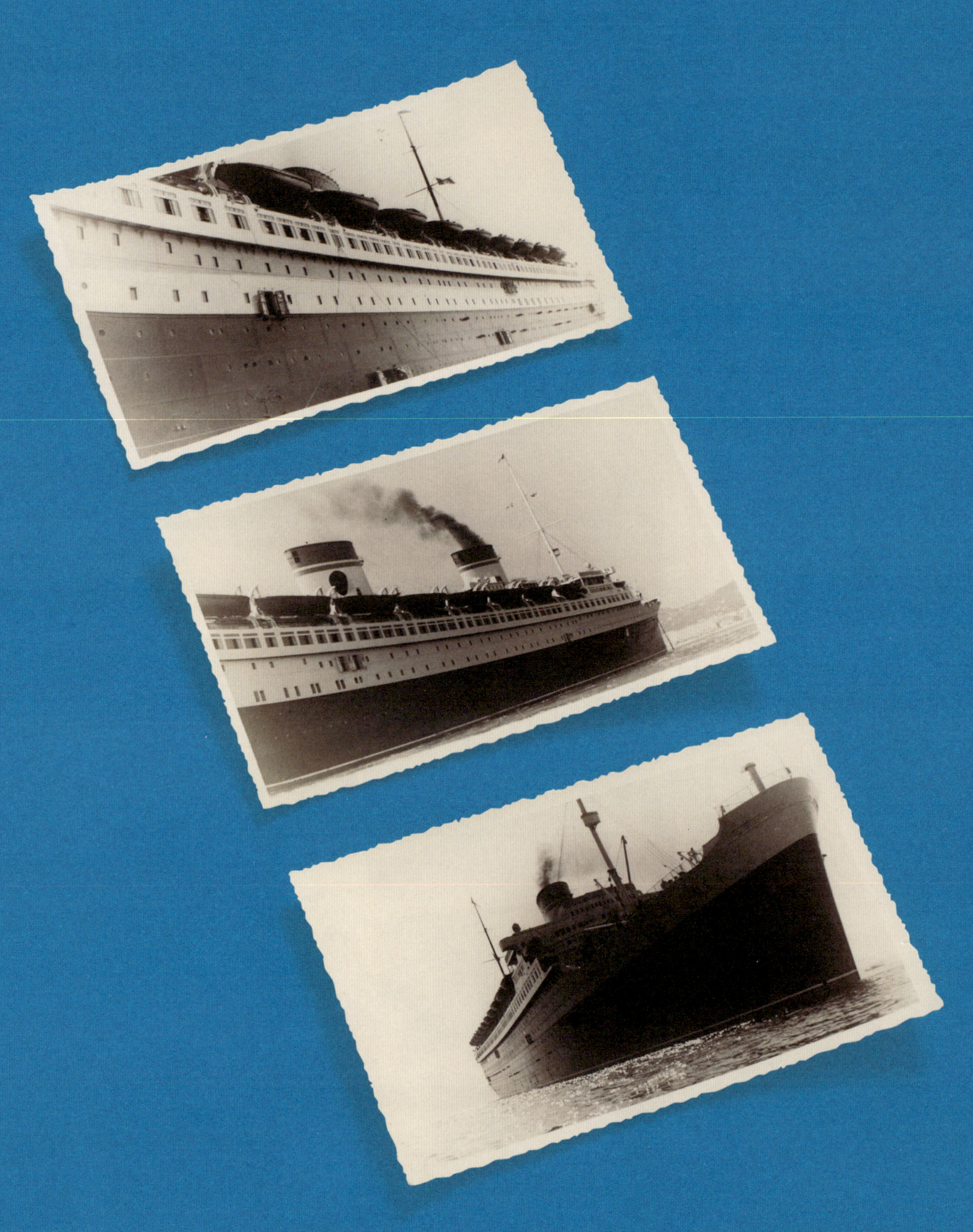

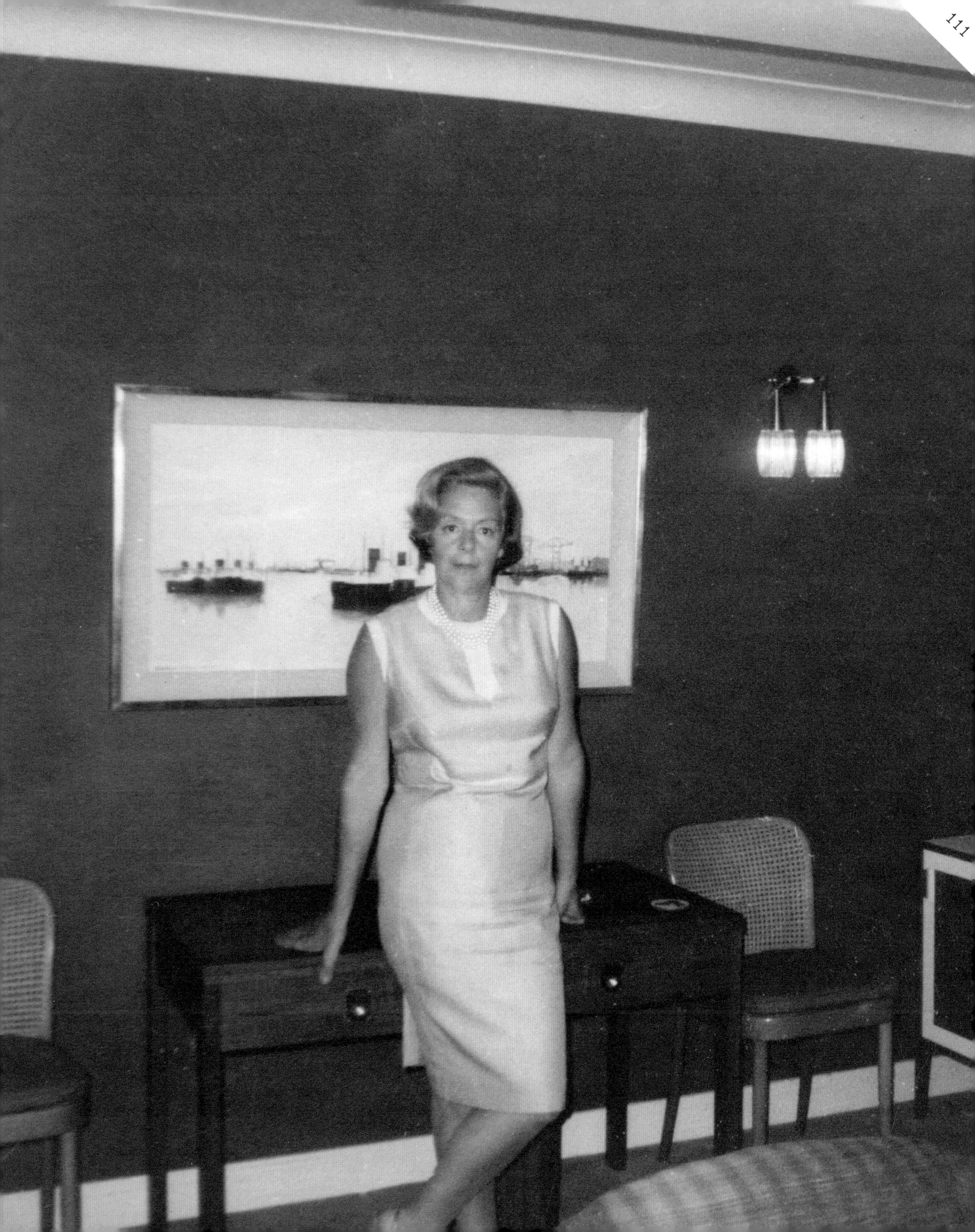

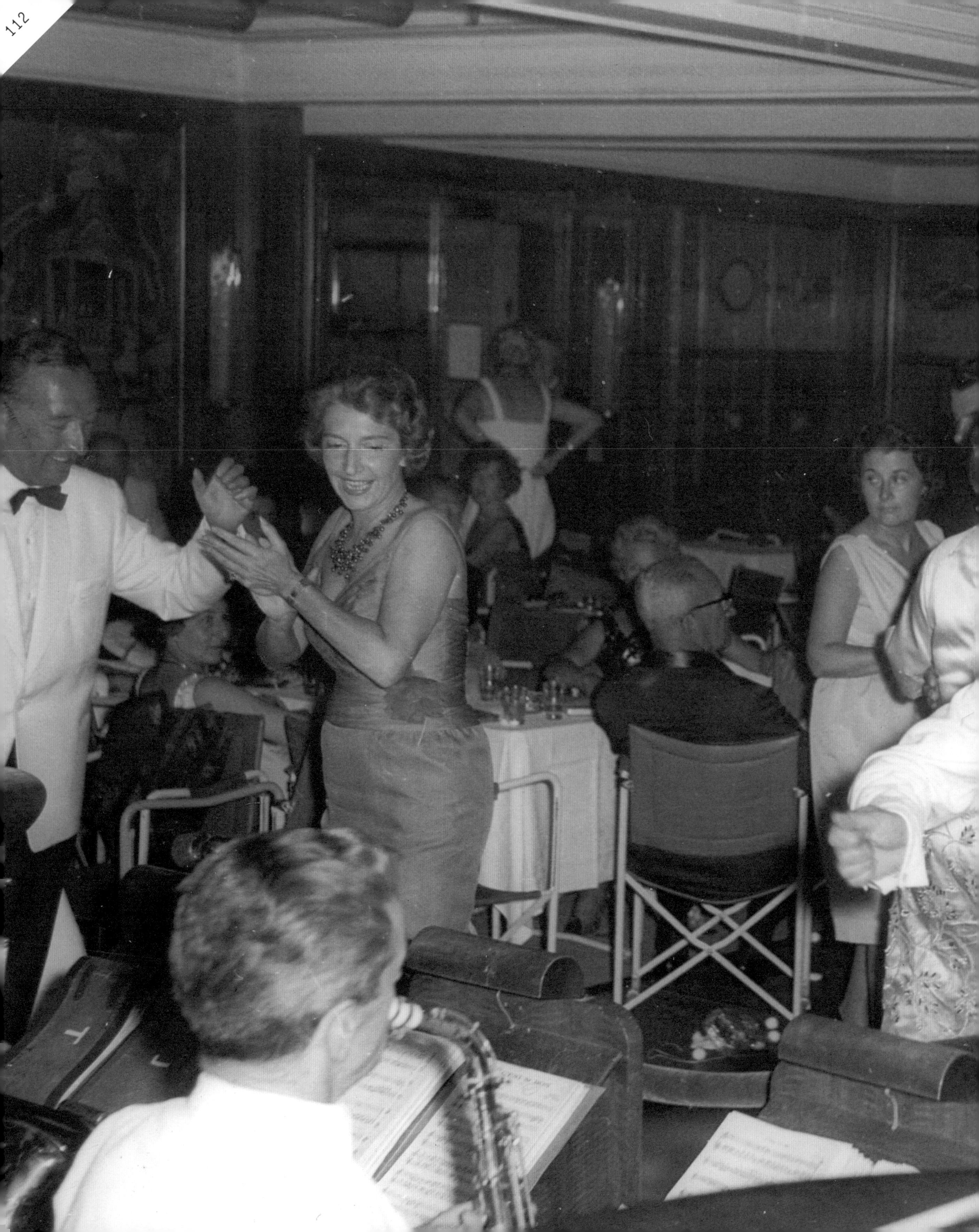

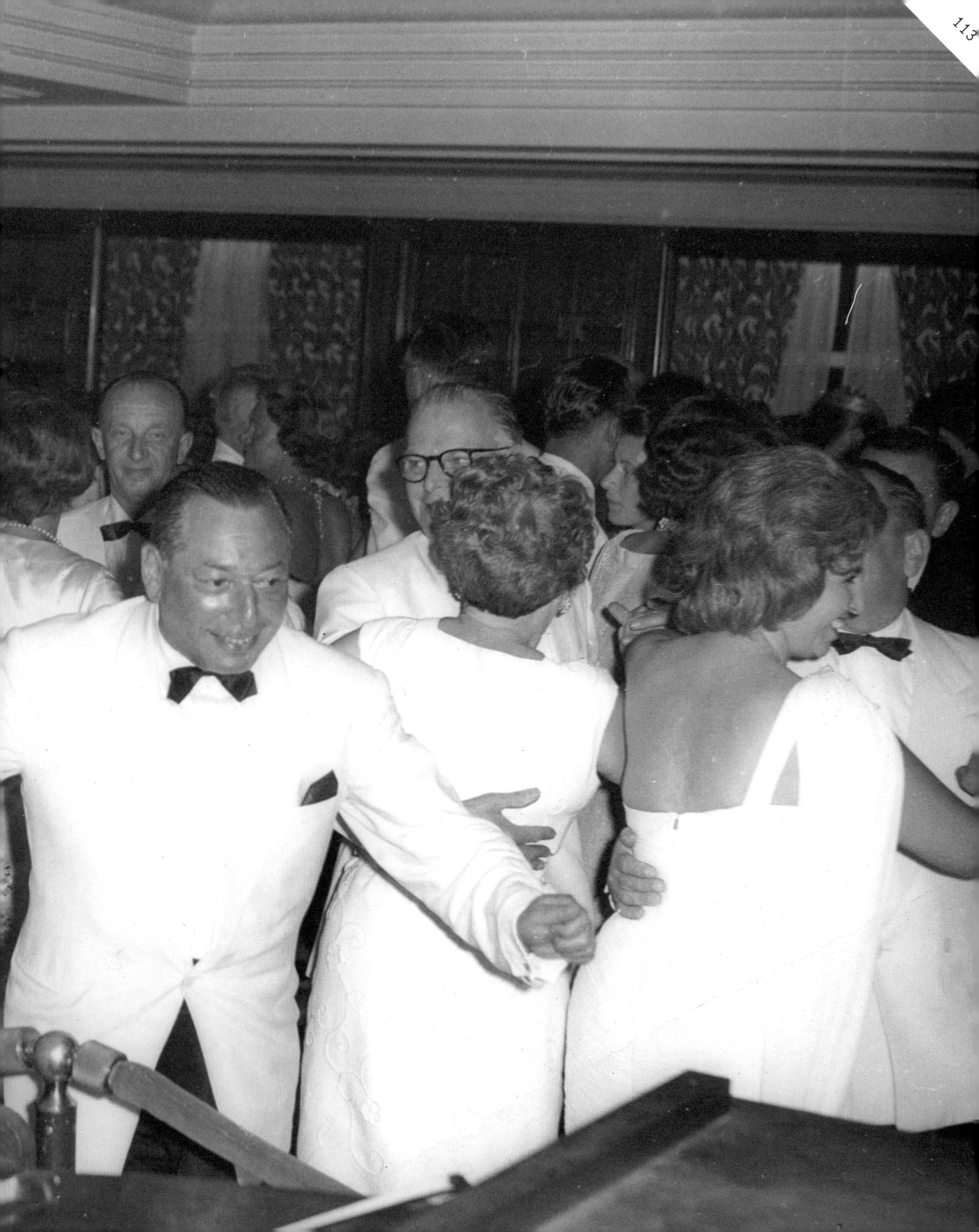

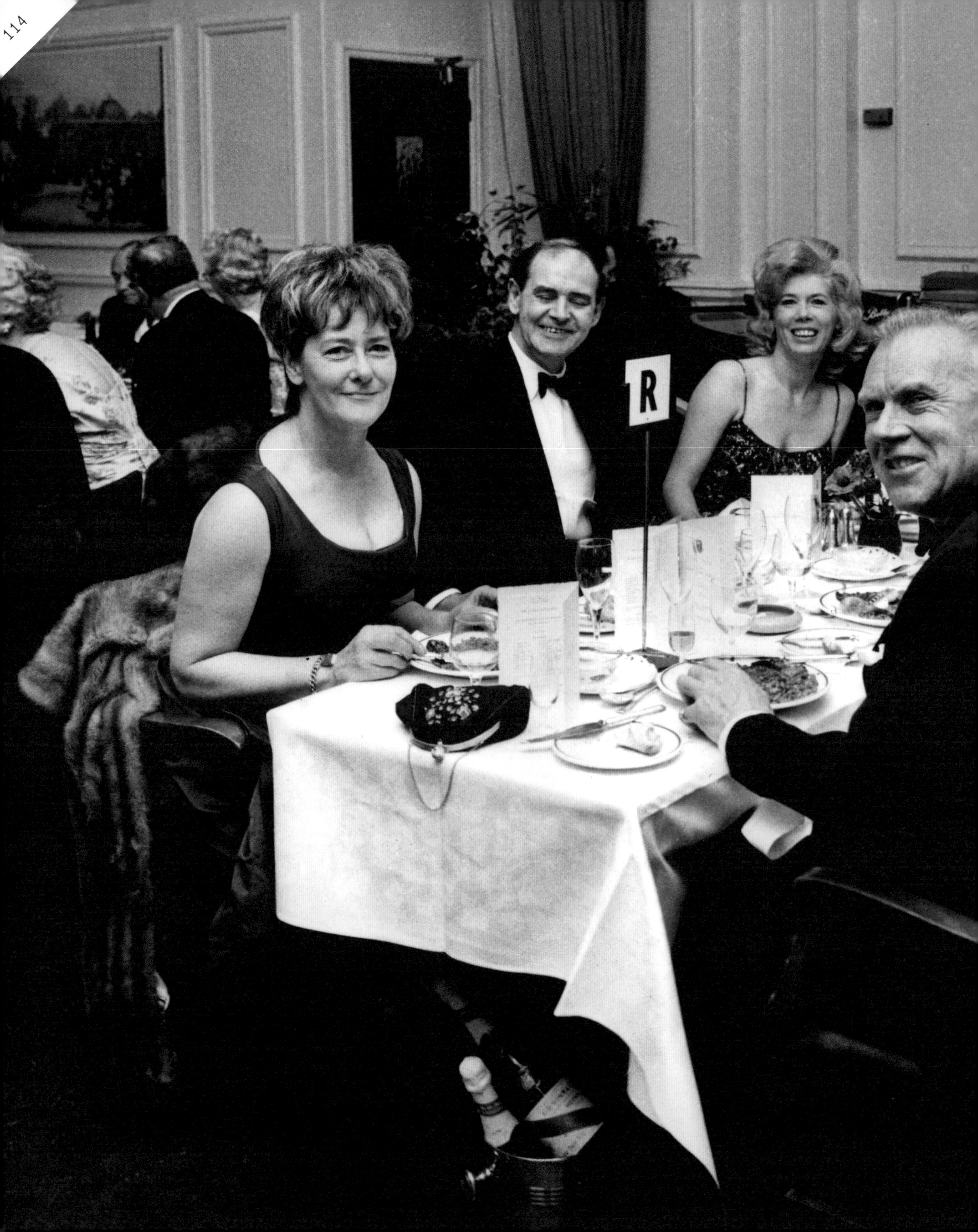

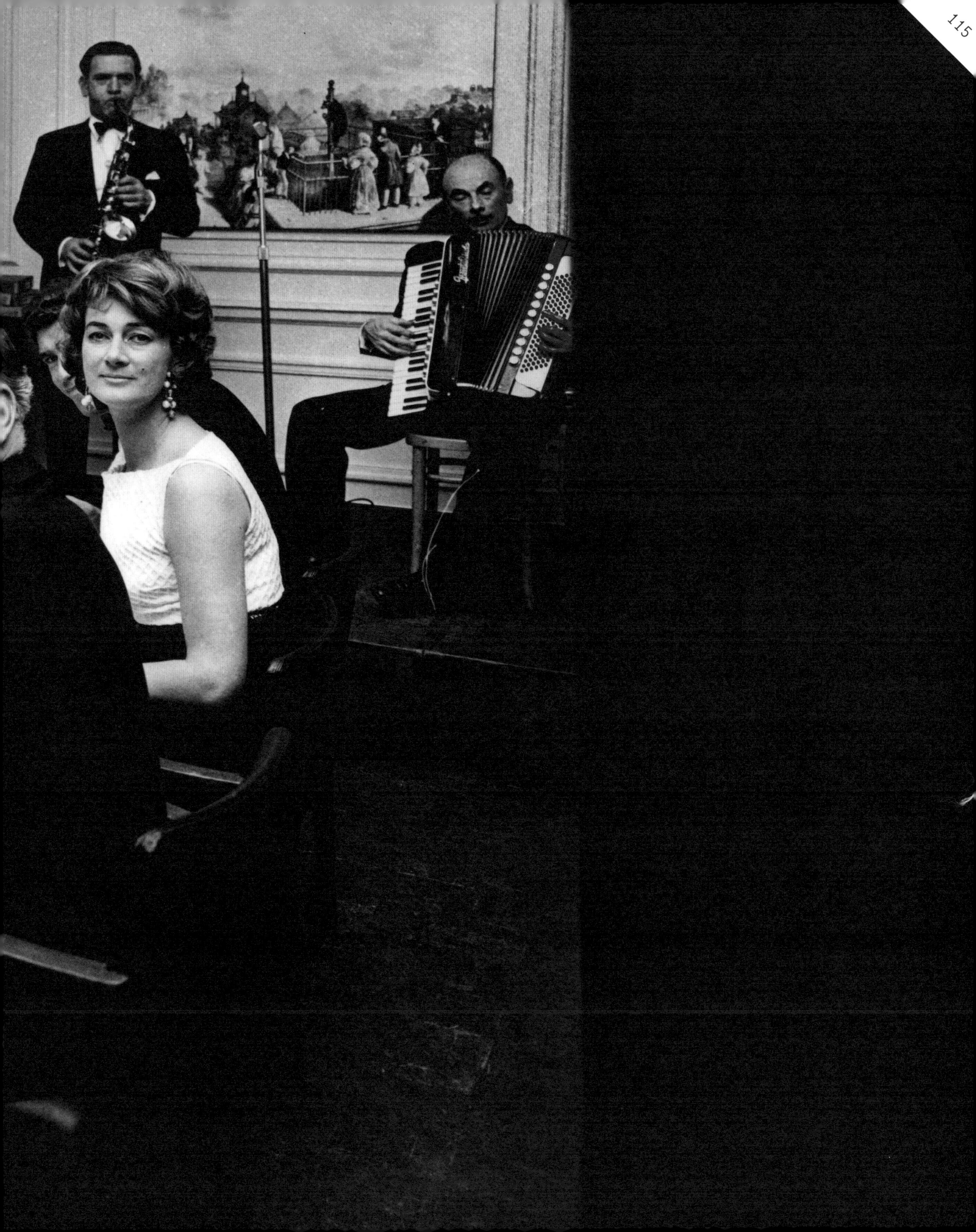

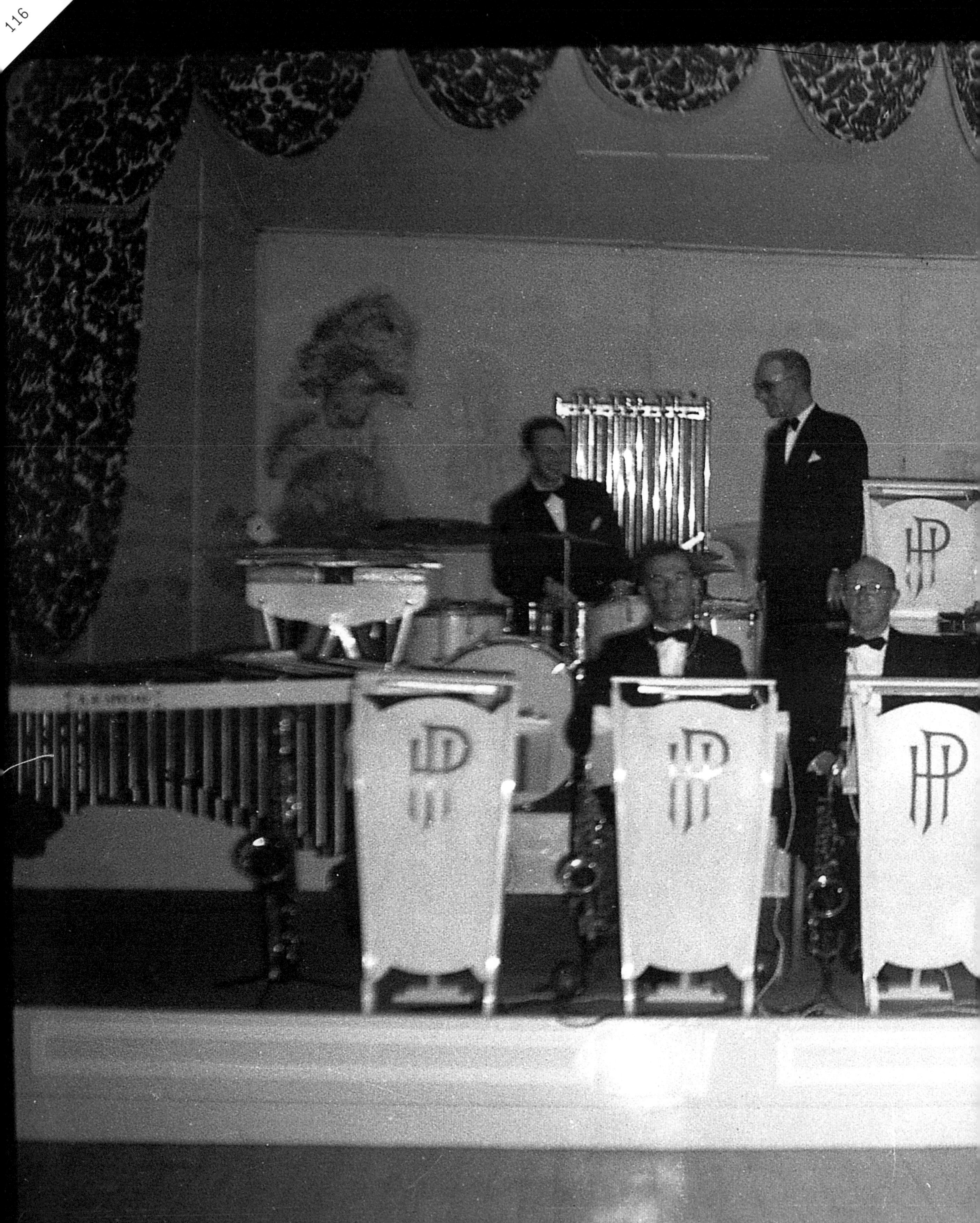

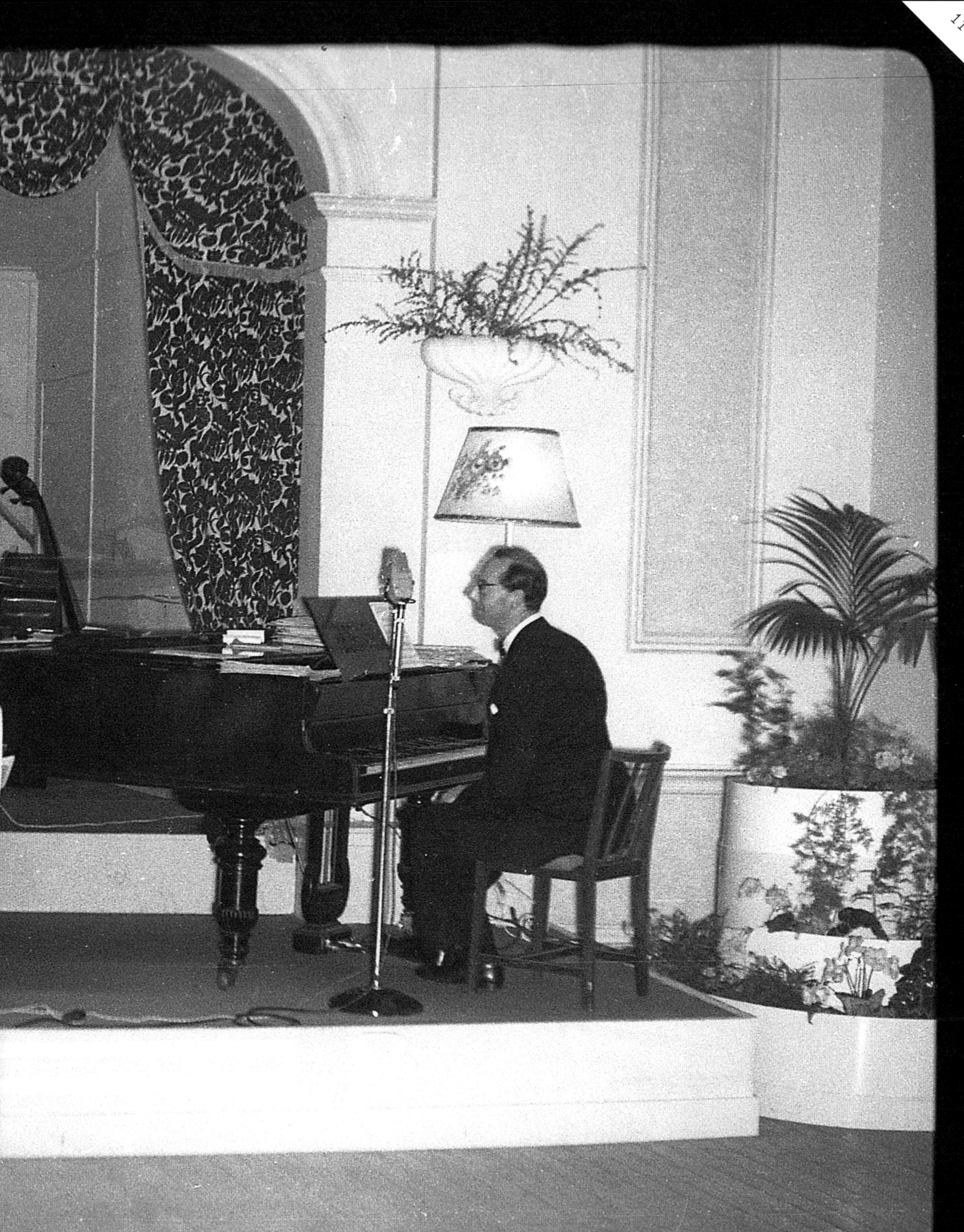

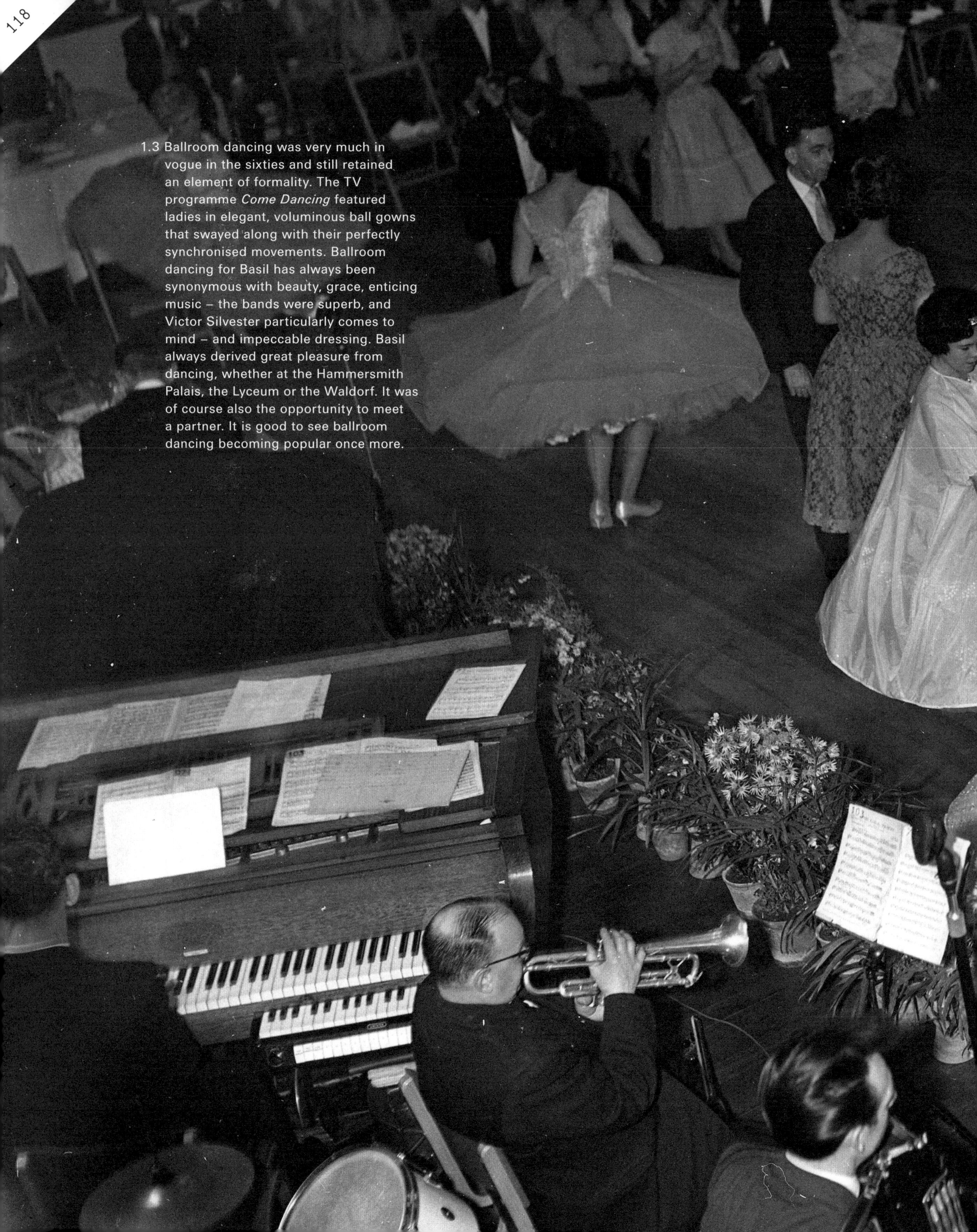

1.3 Ballroom dancing was very much in vogue in the sixties and still retained an element of formality. The TV programme *Come Dancing* featured ladies in elegant, voluminous ball gowns that swayed along with their perfectly synchronised movements. Ballroom dancing for Basil has always been synonymous with beauty, grace, enticing music – the bands were superb, and Victor Silvester particularly comes to mind – and impeccable dressing. Basil always derived great pleasure from dancing, whether at the Hammersmith Palais, the Lyceum or the Waldorf. It was of course also the opportunity to meet a partner. It is good to see ballroom dancing becoming popular once more.

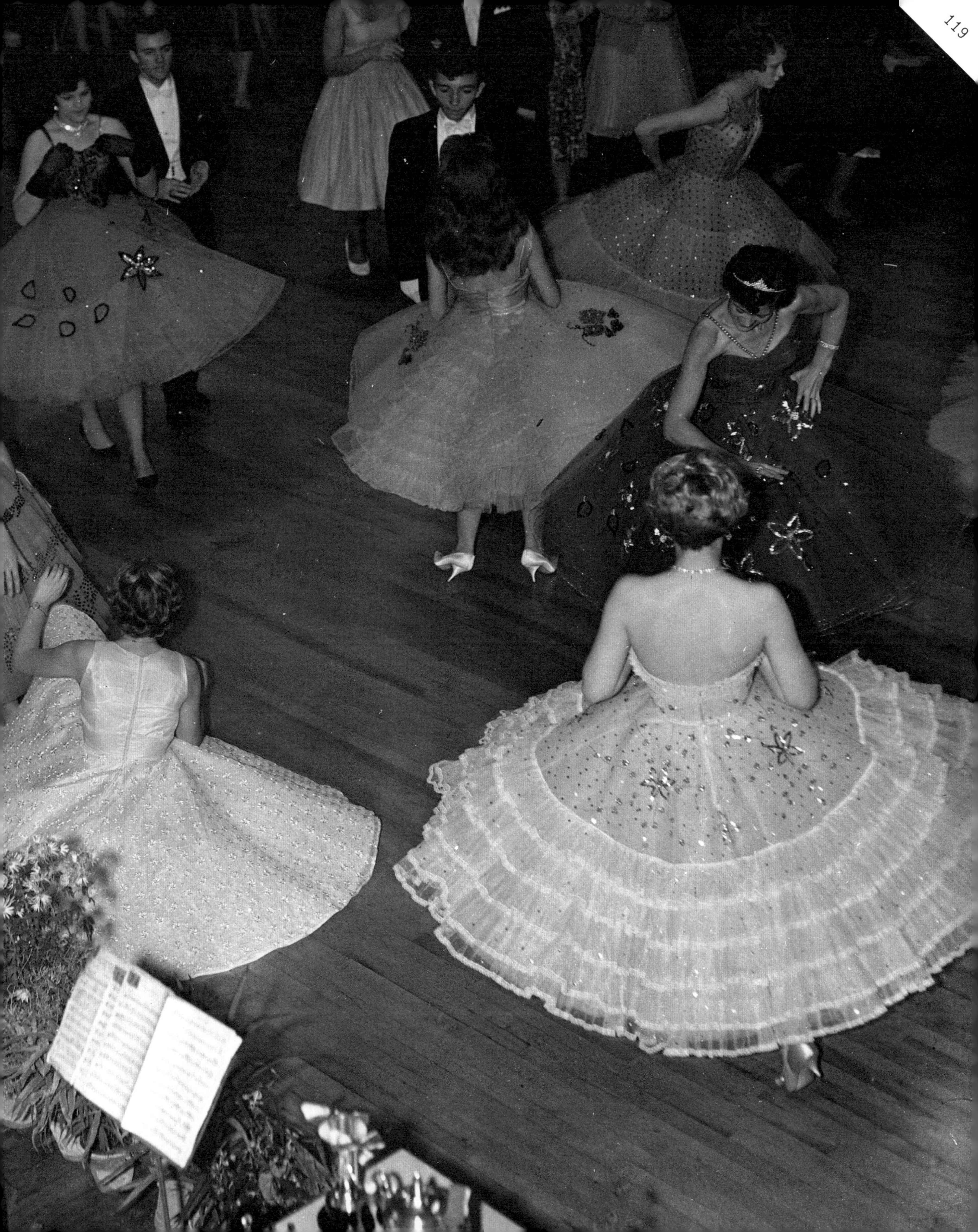

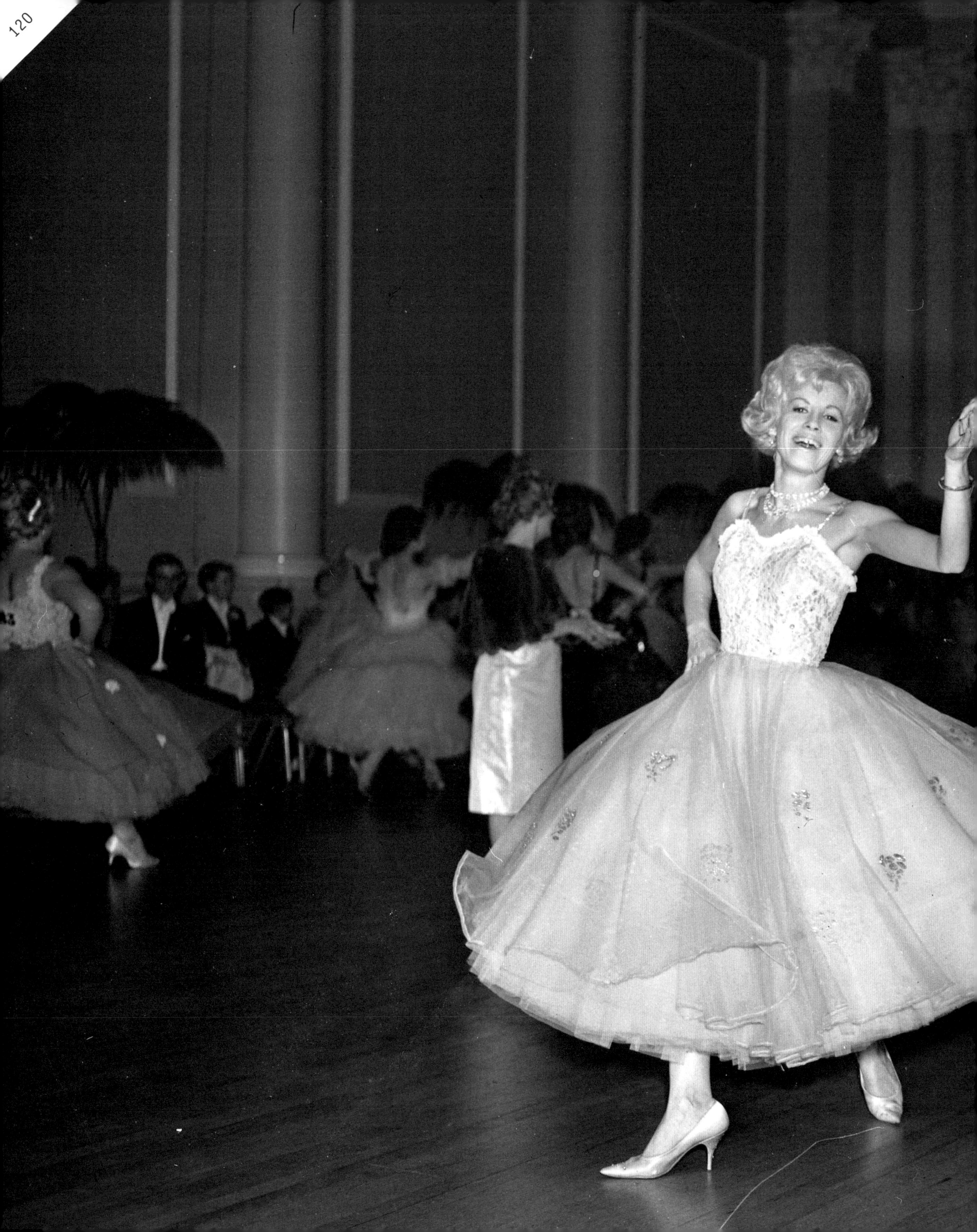

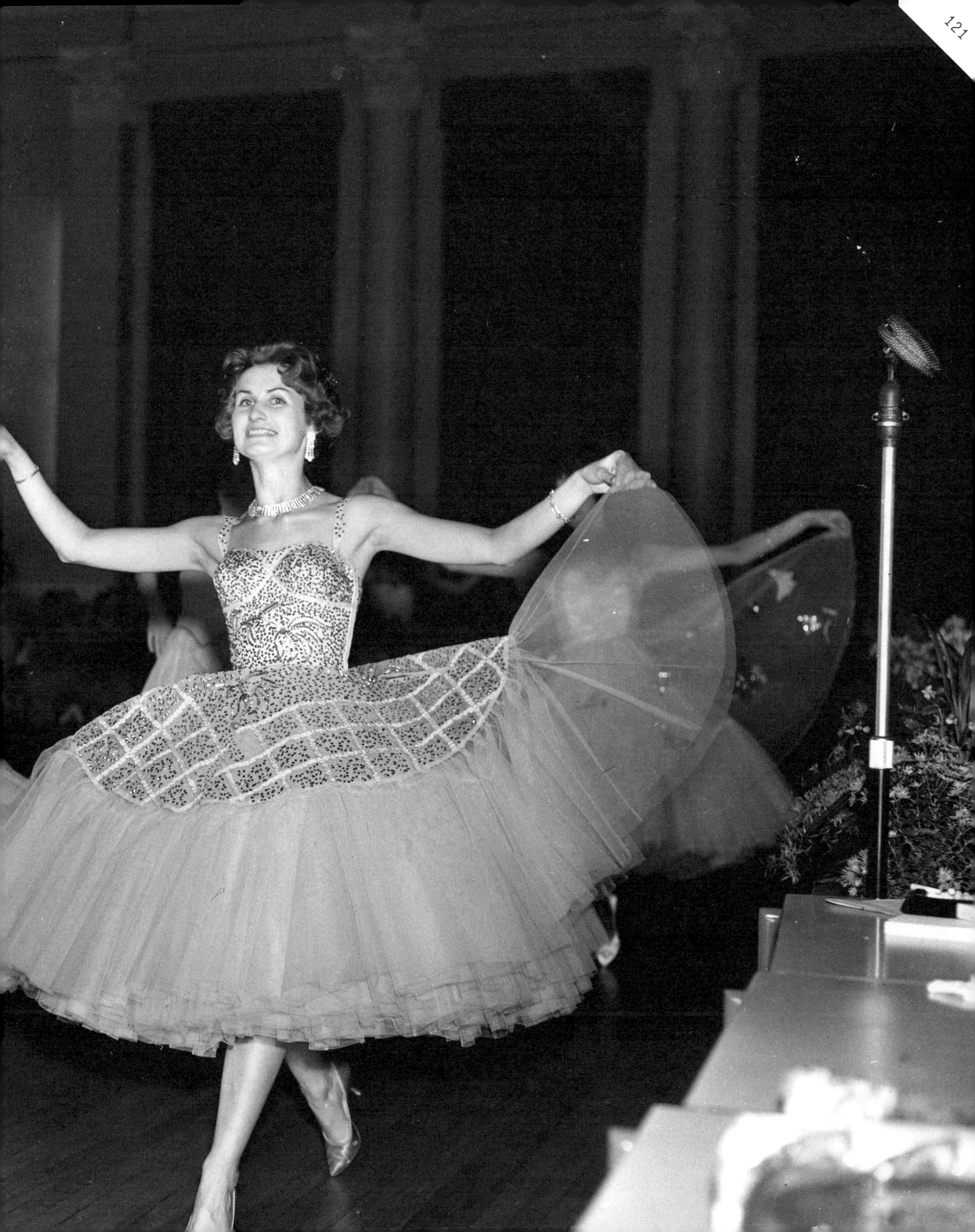

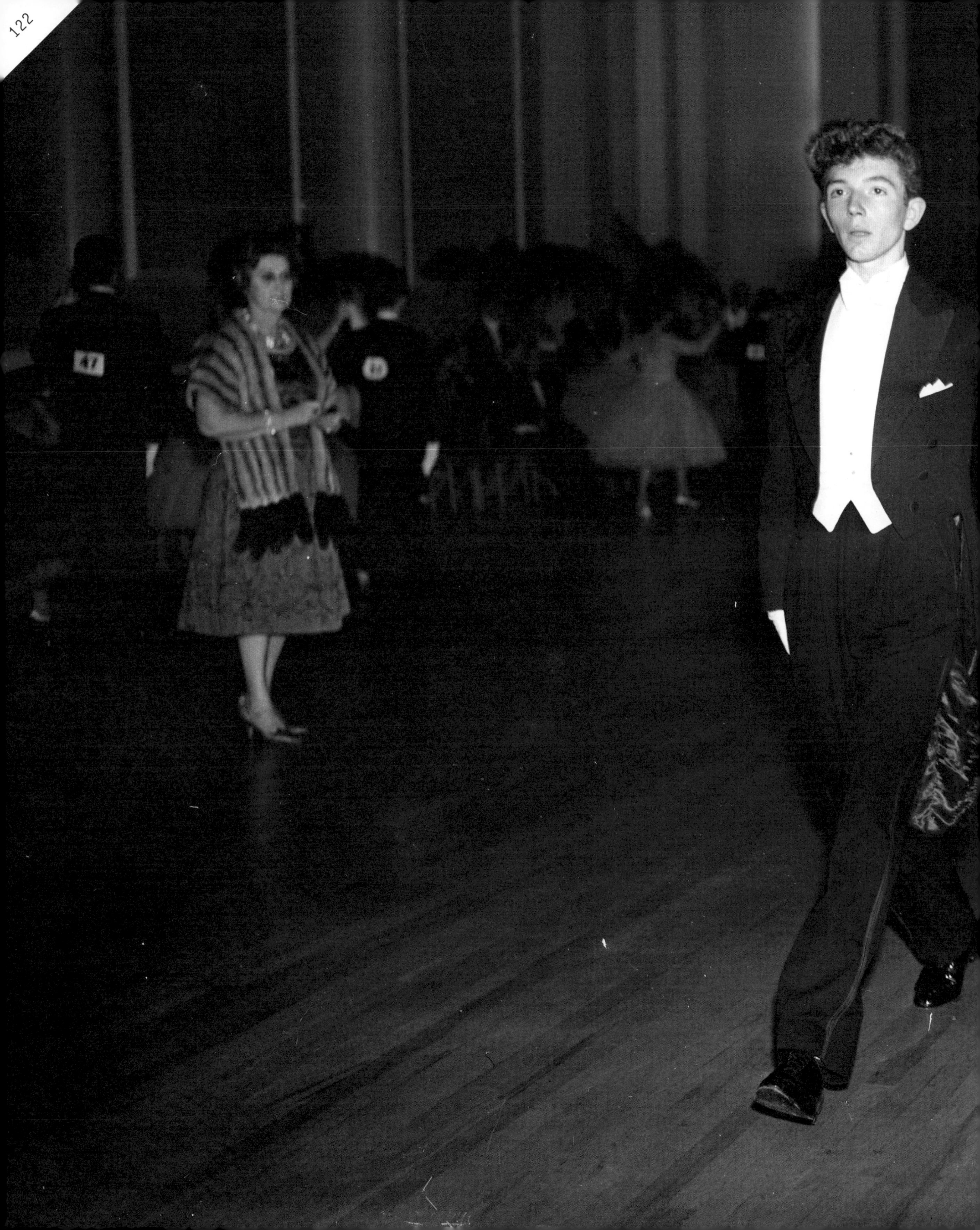

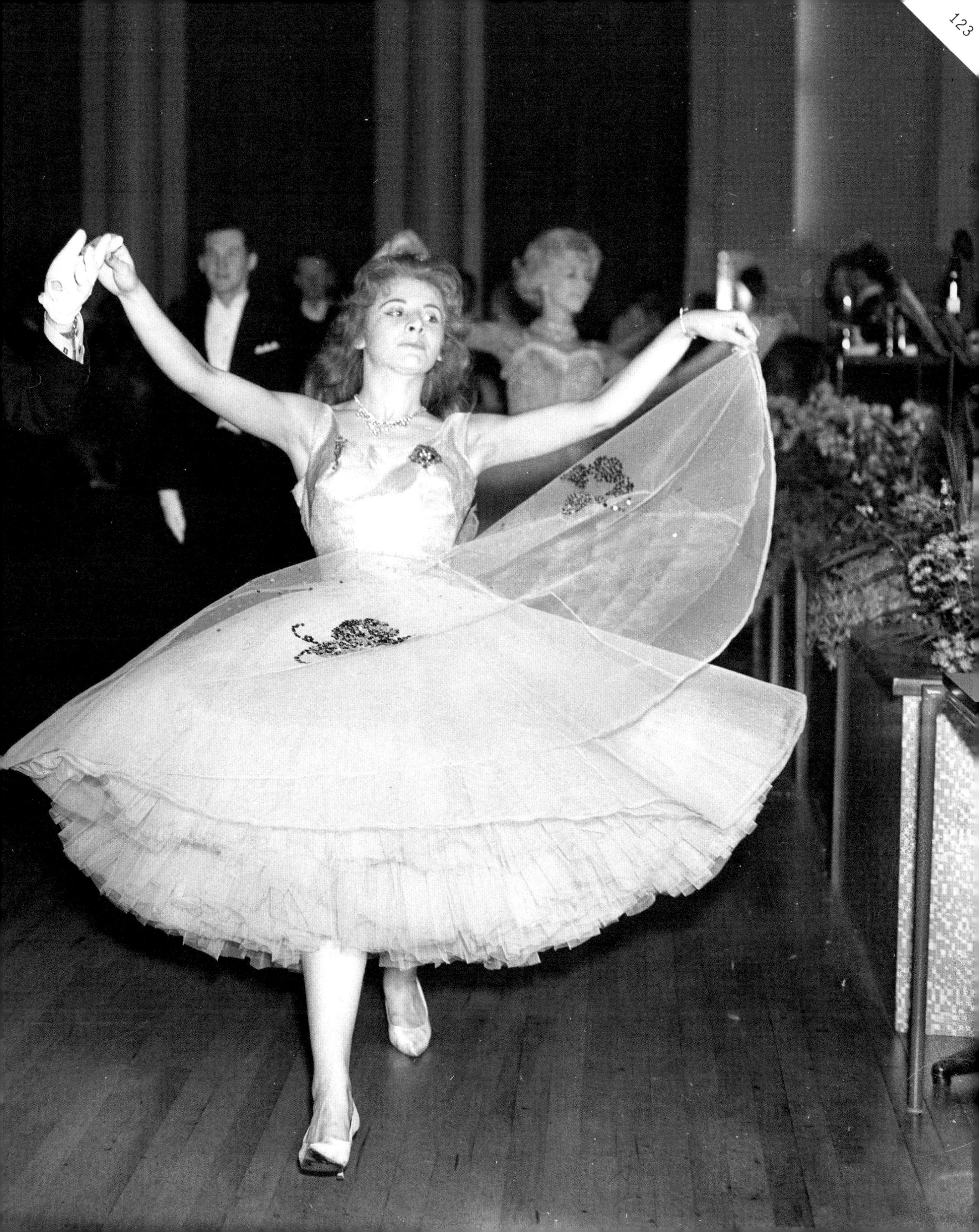

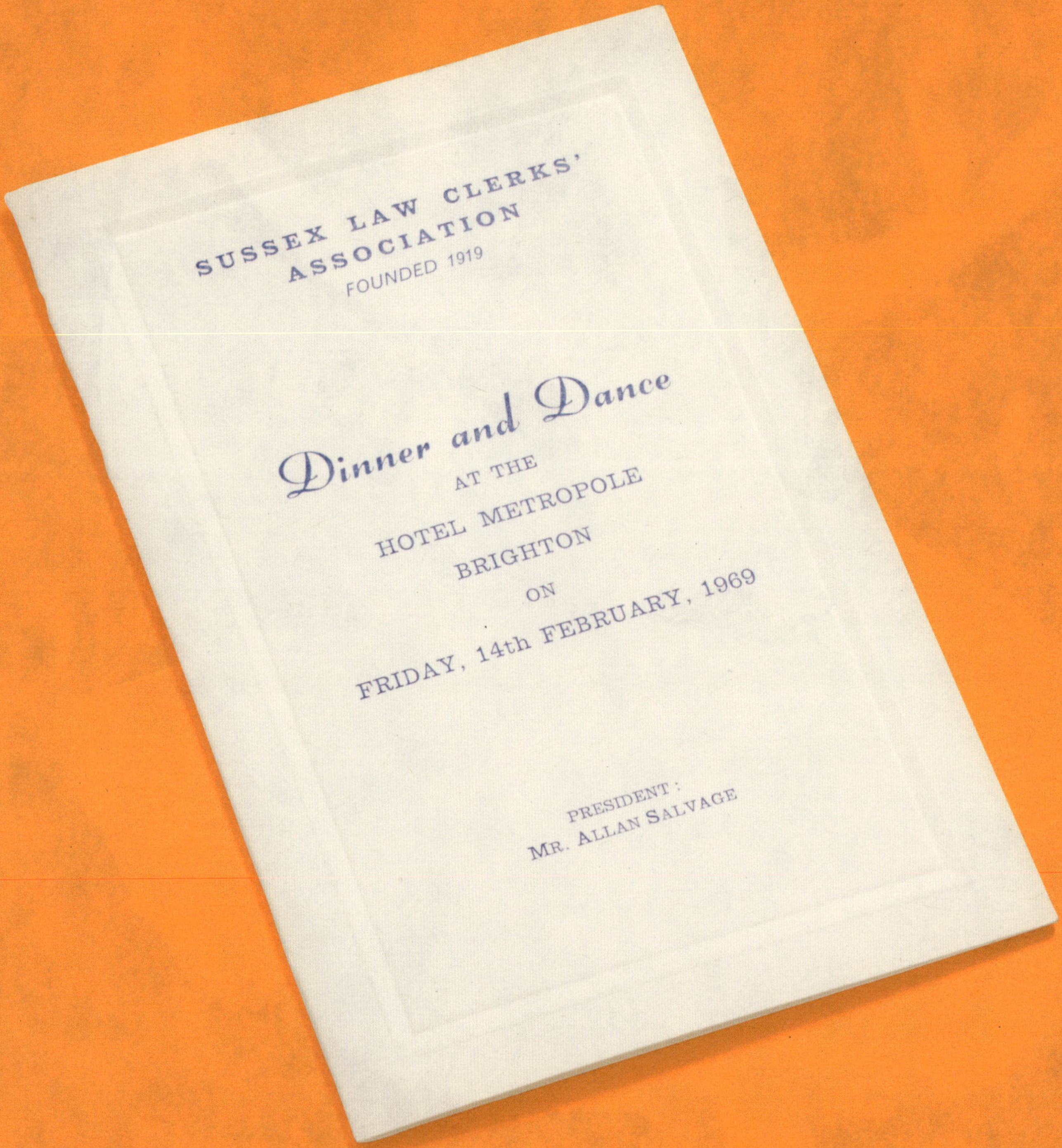

SUSSEX LAW CLERKS'
ASSOCIATION
FOUNDED 1919

Dinner and Dance

AT THE

HOTEL METROPOLE

BRIGHTON

ON

FRIDAY, 14th FEBRUARY, 1969

PRESIDENT :
MR. ALLAN SALVAGE

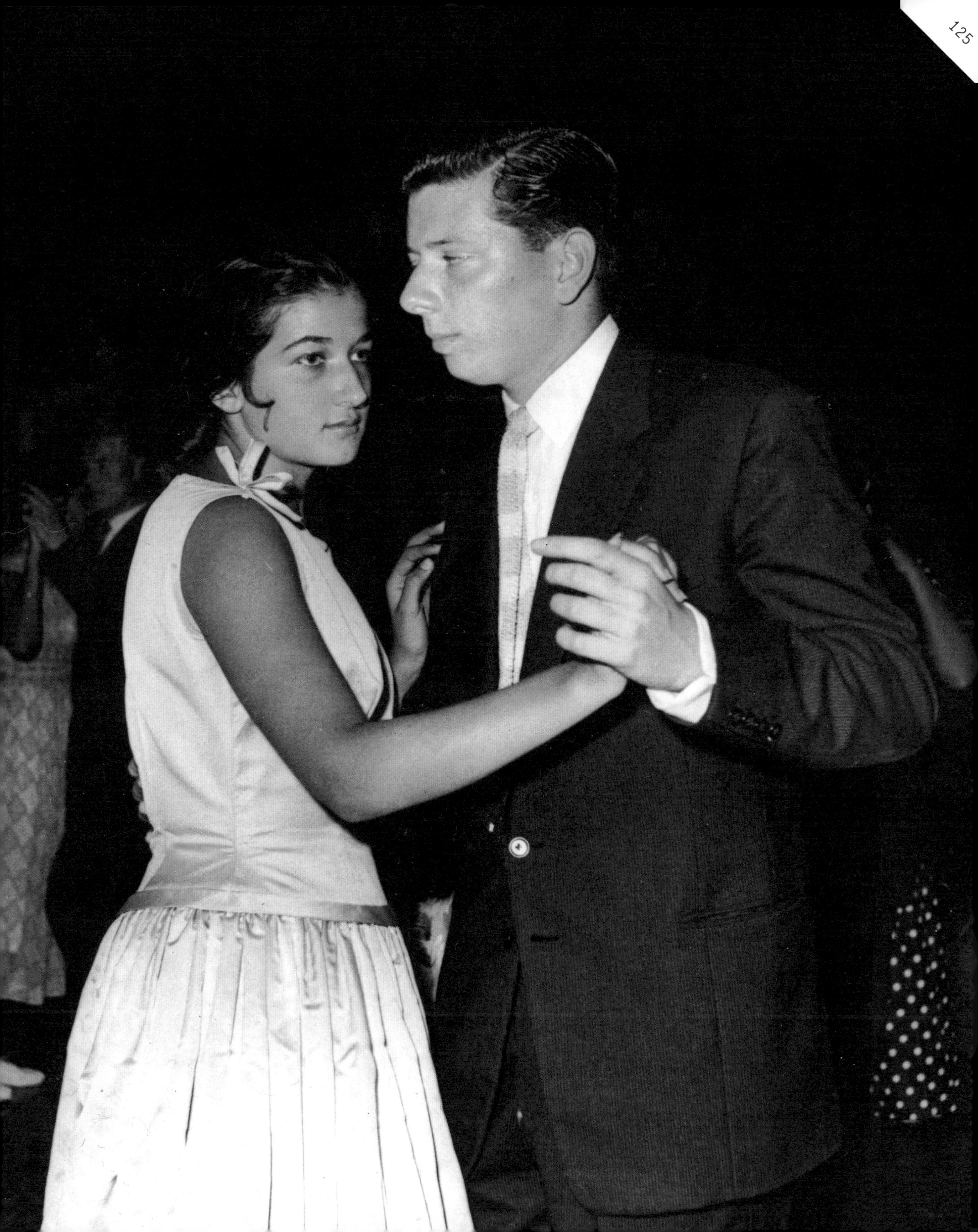

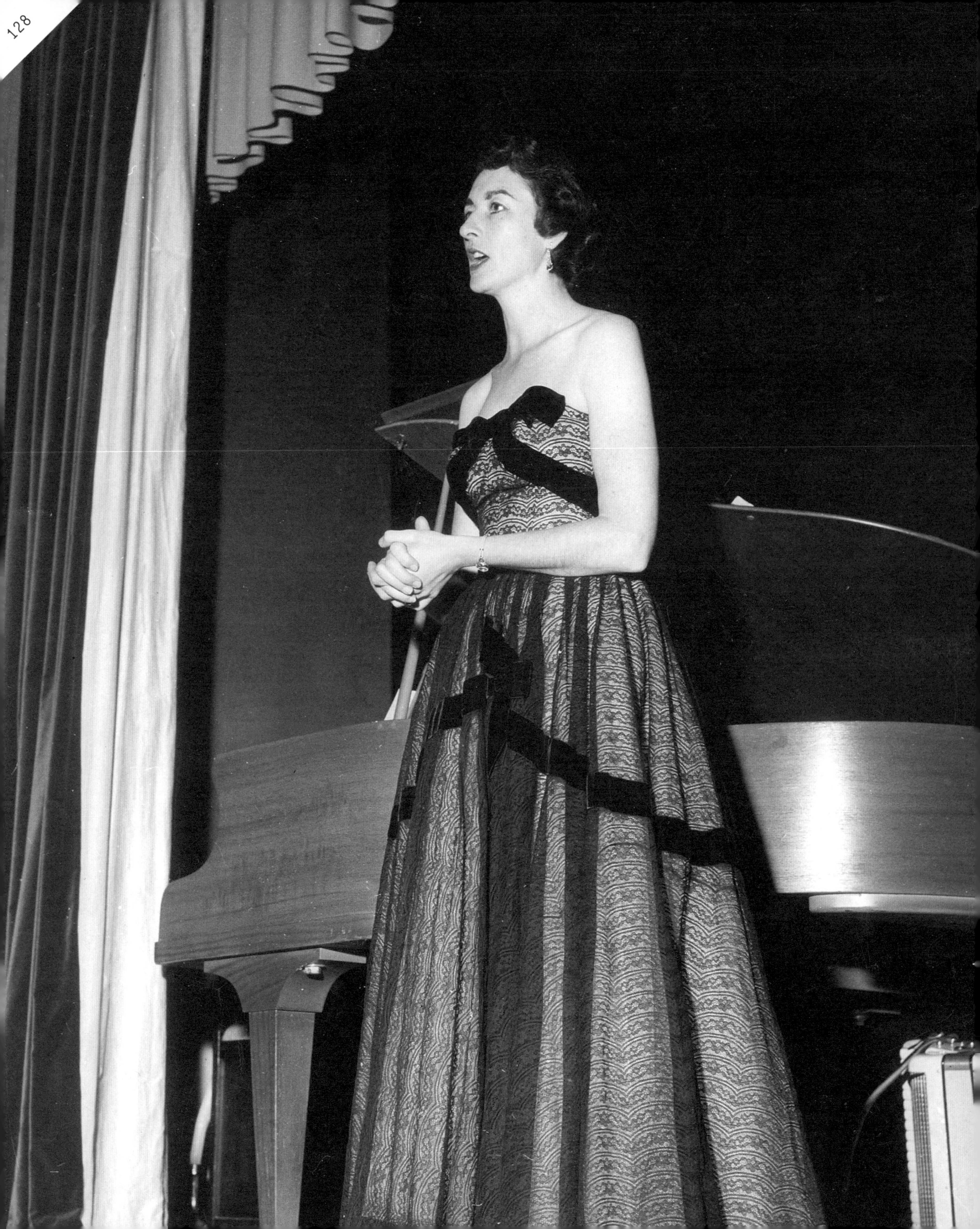

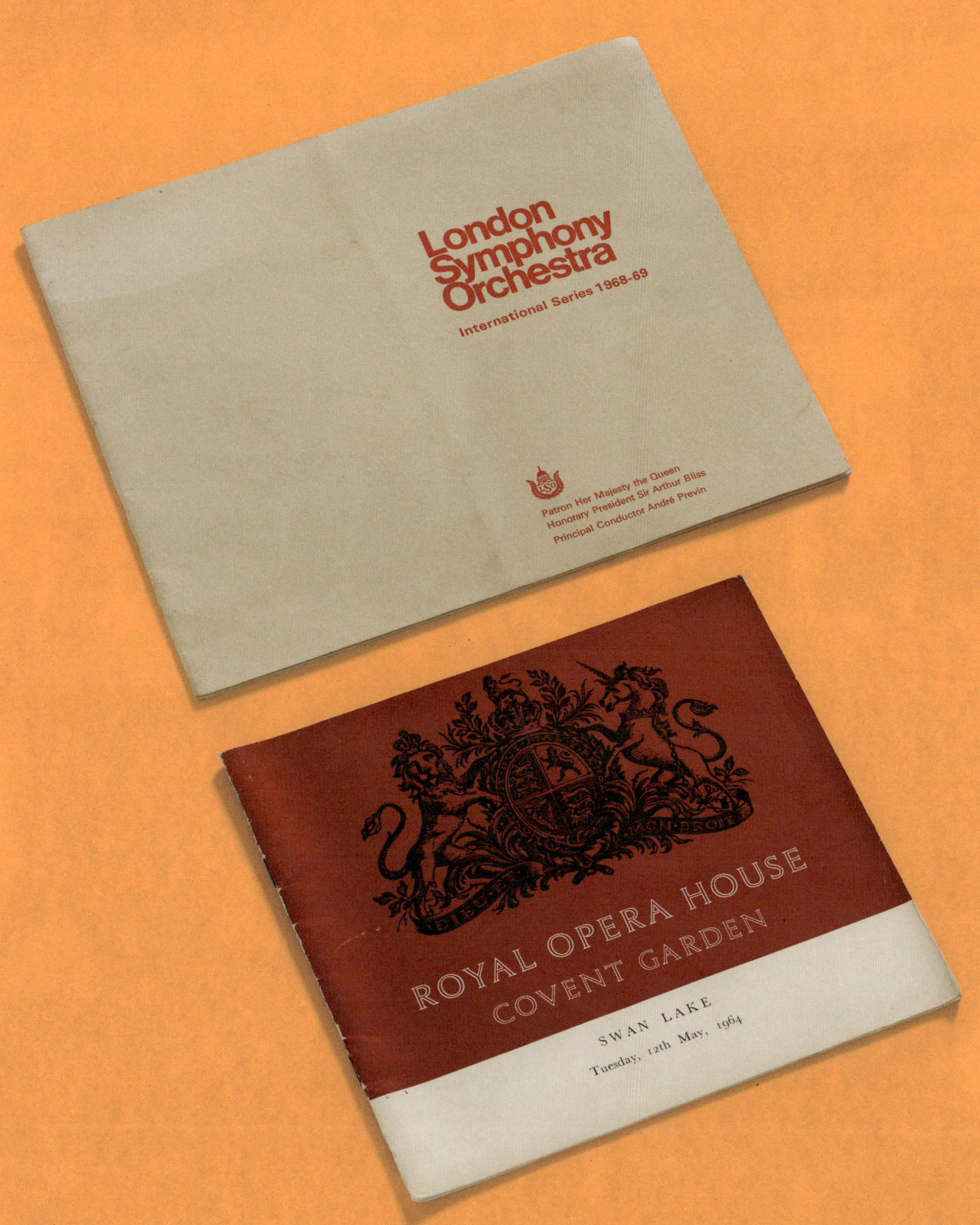
London
Symphony
Orchestra
International Series 1968-69
Patron Her Majesty the Queen
Honorary President Sir Arthur Bliss
Principal Conductor André Previn
ROYAL OPERA HOUSE
COVENT GARDEN
SWAN LAKE
Tuesday, 12th May, 1964

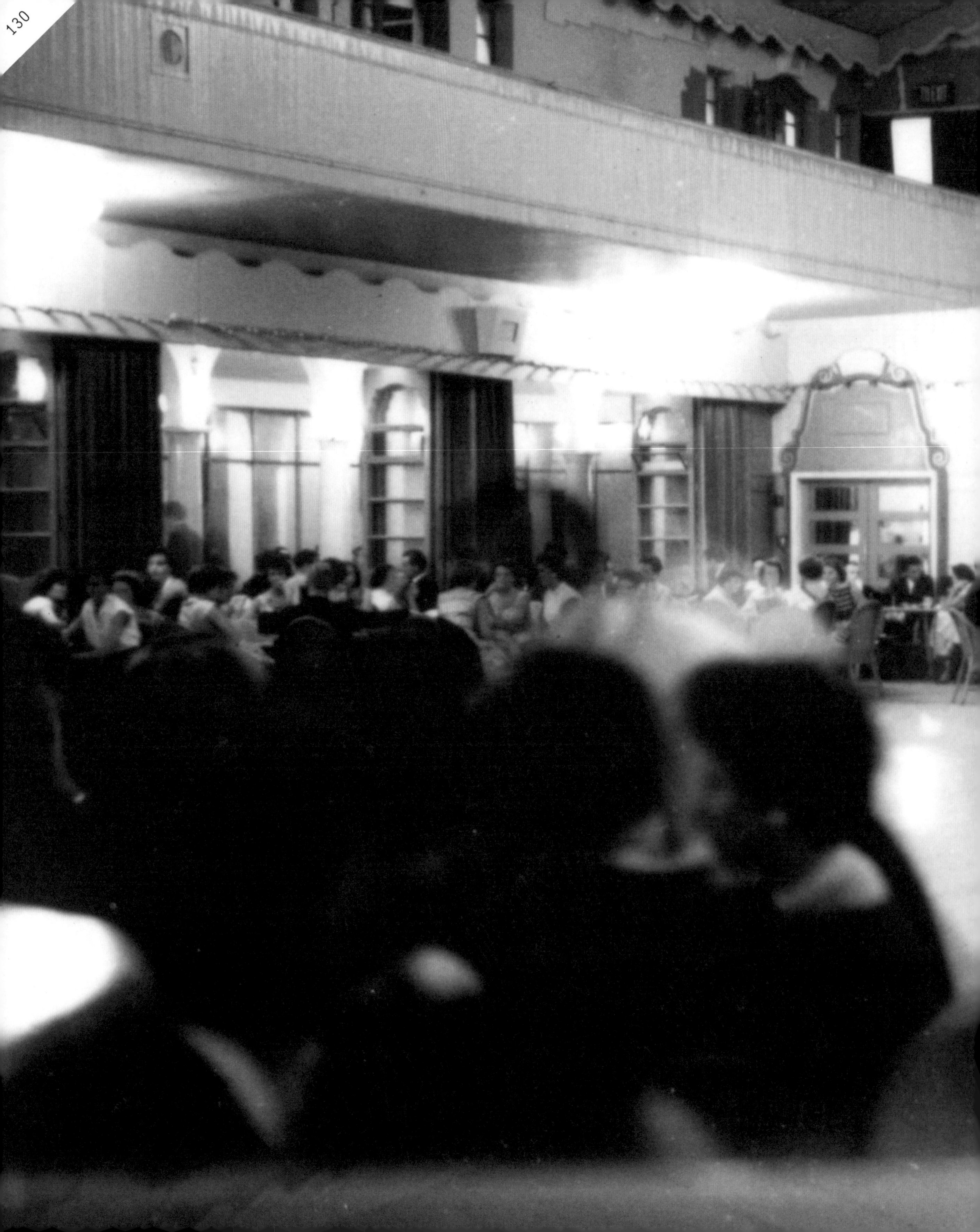

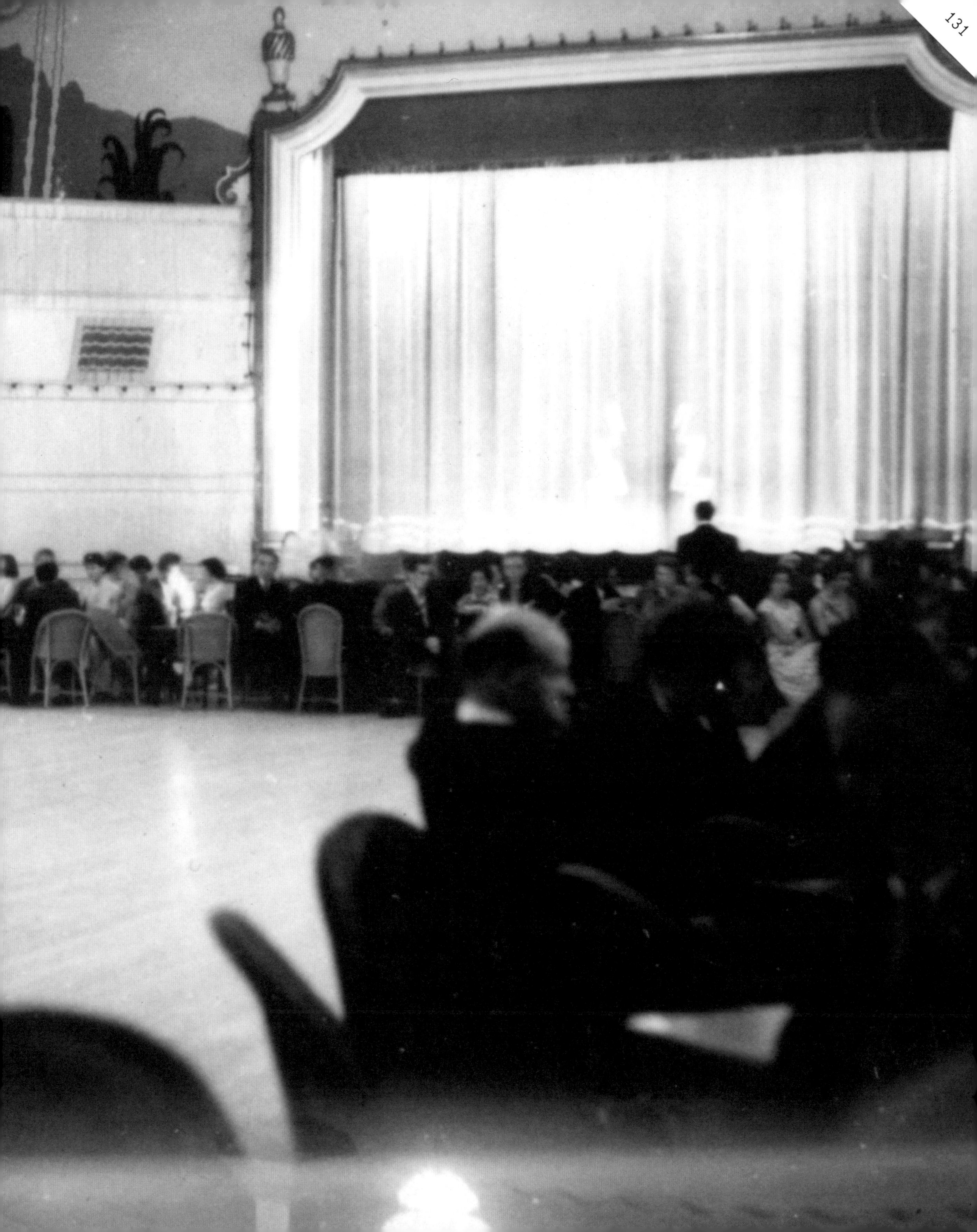

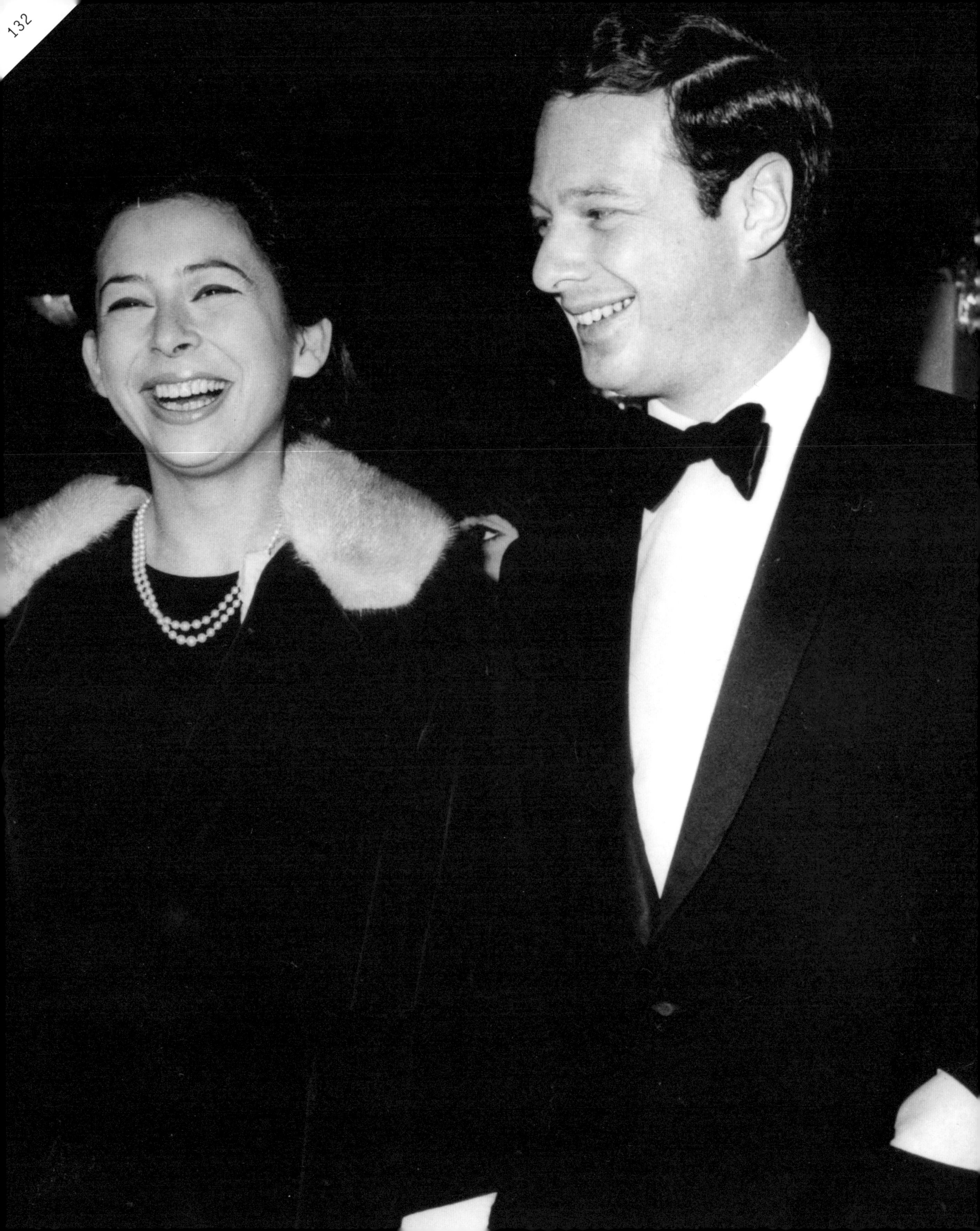

Brian Epstein

An iconic figure of the sixties who died tragically in the summer of 1967 far too young, the Liverpool-born Brian Epstein, pre-Beatles, was totally dedicated to building the finest record store in the North of England. It was only when the Liverpool youth came into the shop to ask about 'this unknown group' that he went to the Cavern Club. He was completely mesmerised by The Beatles' performance and became their manager within weeks. His conviction that they were extraordinary made him make repeated trips to London. He went to nearly every record company in order to get them signed up on a contract, but he did not get an encouraging response. One Friday night he came for dinner and the conversation turned to the Liverpool group. Brian explained that he was getting rejections nearly all the time and asked what he should do. My father wisely said: 'try one more time and if you have no success then give up'. The following week Brian went on this final mission to EMI and this led to George Martin, who agreed to a contract with the group. The rest is history: Brian catapulted The Beatles to stardom, together with various other Northern performers including Gerry and the Pacemakers, Cilla Black and Billy Kramer and the Dakotas.

As well as this public persona, however, he was my cousin and friend, who features in some of the photographs I took during the fifties and sixties. He valued all his family highly and had a very close relationship with his parents, who adored him, as well as with his brother Clive and all his cousins. Always well-groomed, Brian took great care with his immaculate appearance and had a showman's ability to get attention. It was probably quite unusual for a celebrity group to wear suits and ties on stage rather than the jeans they might have favoured, which was an innovation at the time.

I remember Brian with great affection. We had much in common, particularly our love of well-designed furniture, and used to browse in shops such as Heal's. Never in my wildest dreams did I believe he would become so revered in this field. He first played *Love Me Do*, the Beatles' very first single, for me and Doreen, my sister, on our Dansette record-player. I was such a bad judge of music that I thought it was doomed. I just did not get it, particularly as Brian's previous heroes had been the American Gospel group The Deep River Boys. A symbol of the 1950s and 1960s, Brian was central to the success of The Beatles and a part of their history. His association with them, as well as his untimely death, have made him into a legend, yet I remember him as totally calm and unfazed by all the fame and furore surrounding the group and can still picture him sitting on the carpet surrounded by records. Equally I remember him on the steps of an Anglesey boarding house teaching us to do a chorus line.

I miss him still.

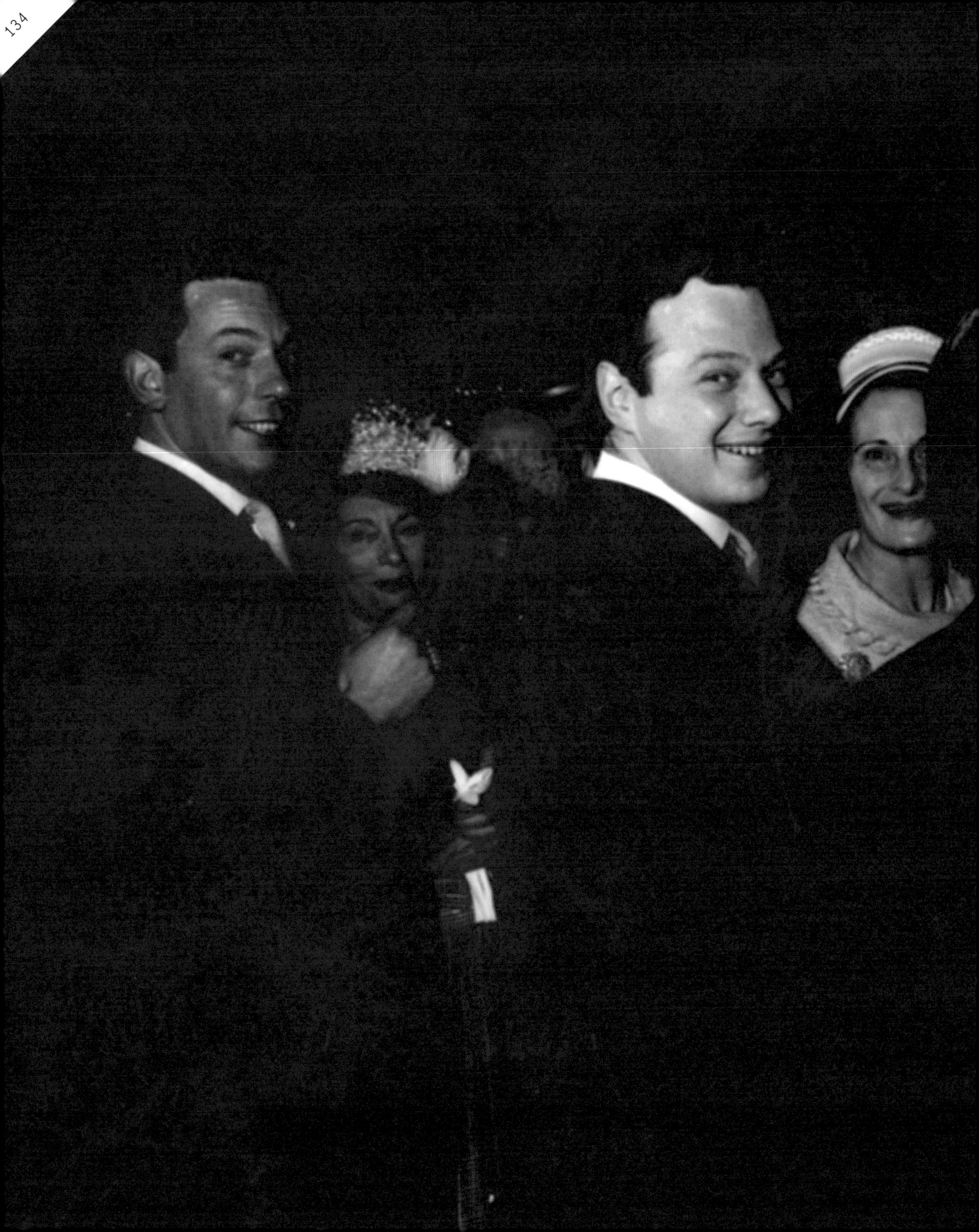

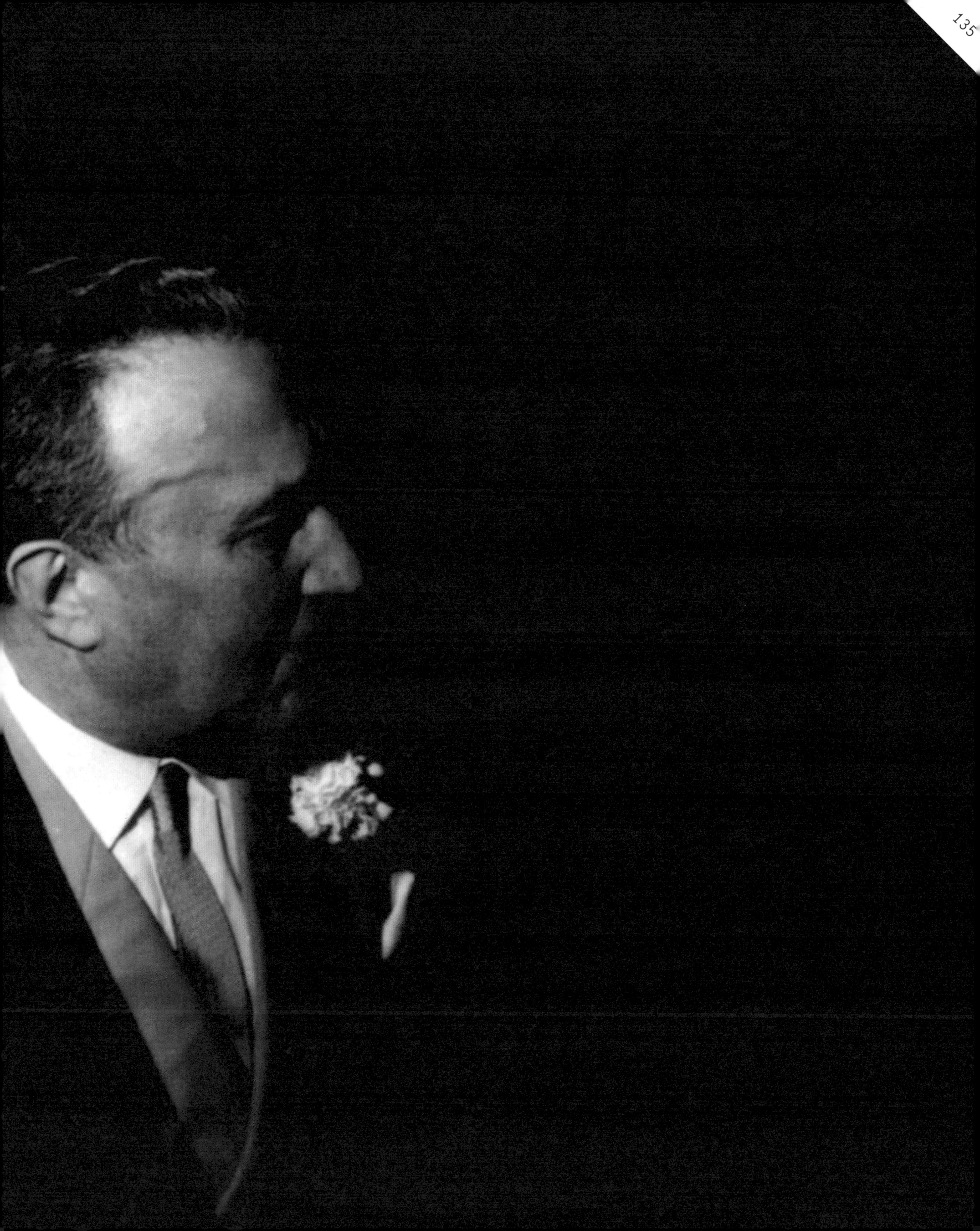

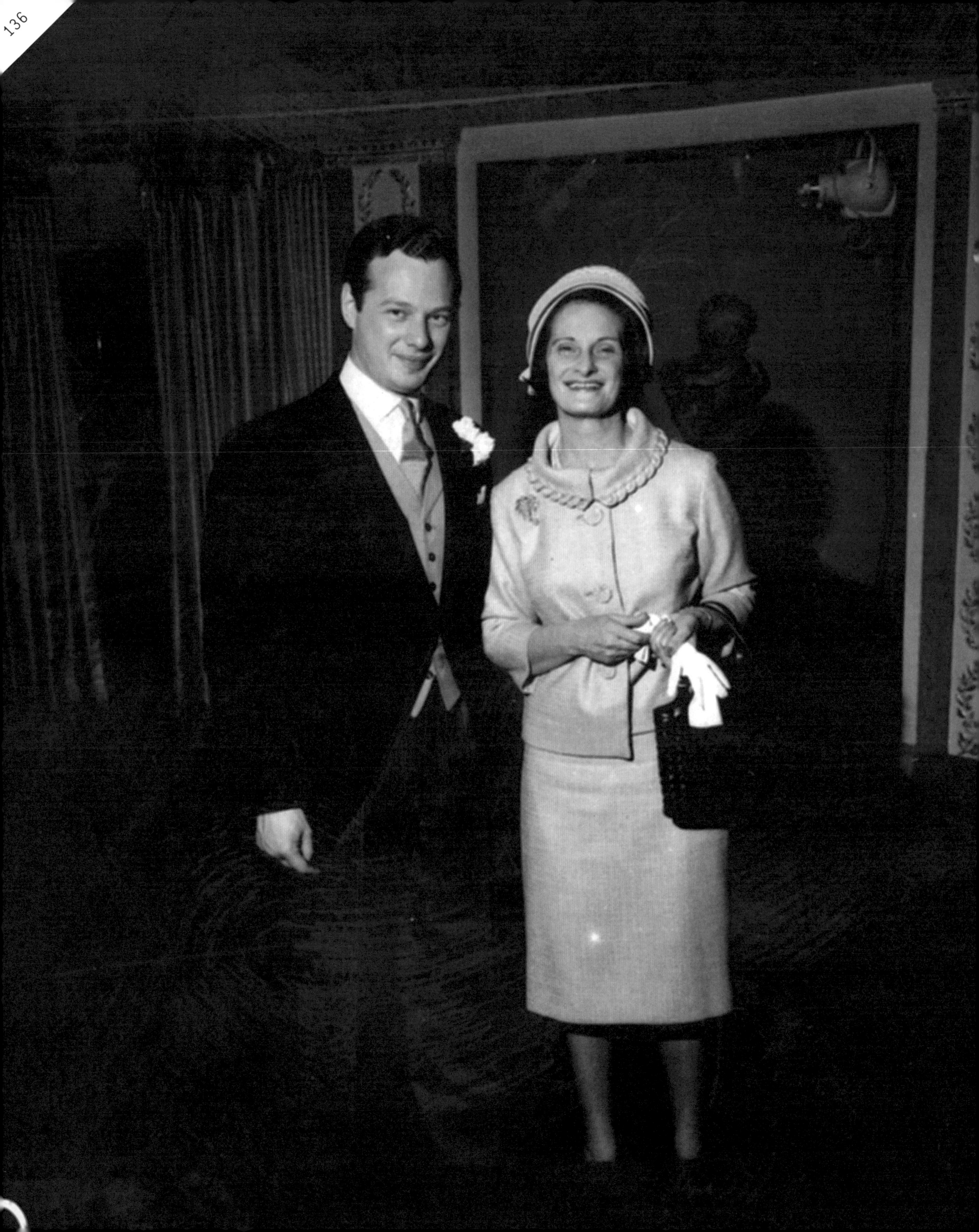

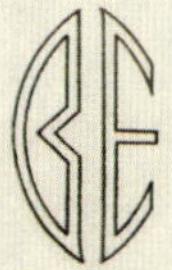

Mr. Brian Gutein wishes to thank
Mr. & Mrs. Perkin for their kind
invitation for May 14th which he has
much pleasure in accepting.

15 Whaddon House

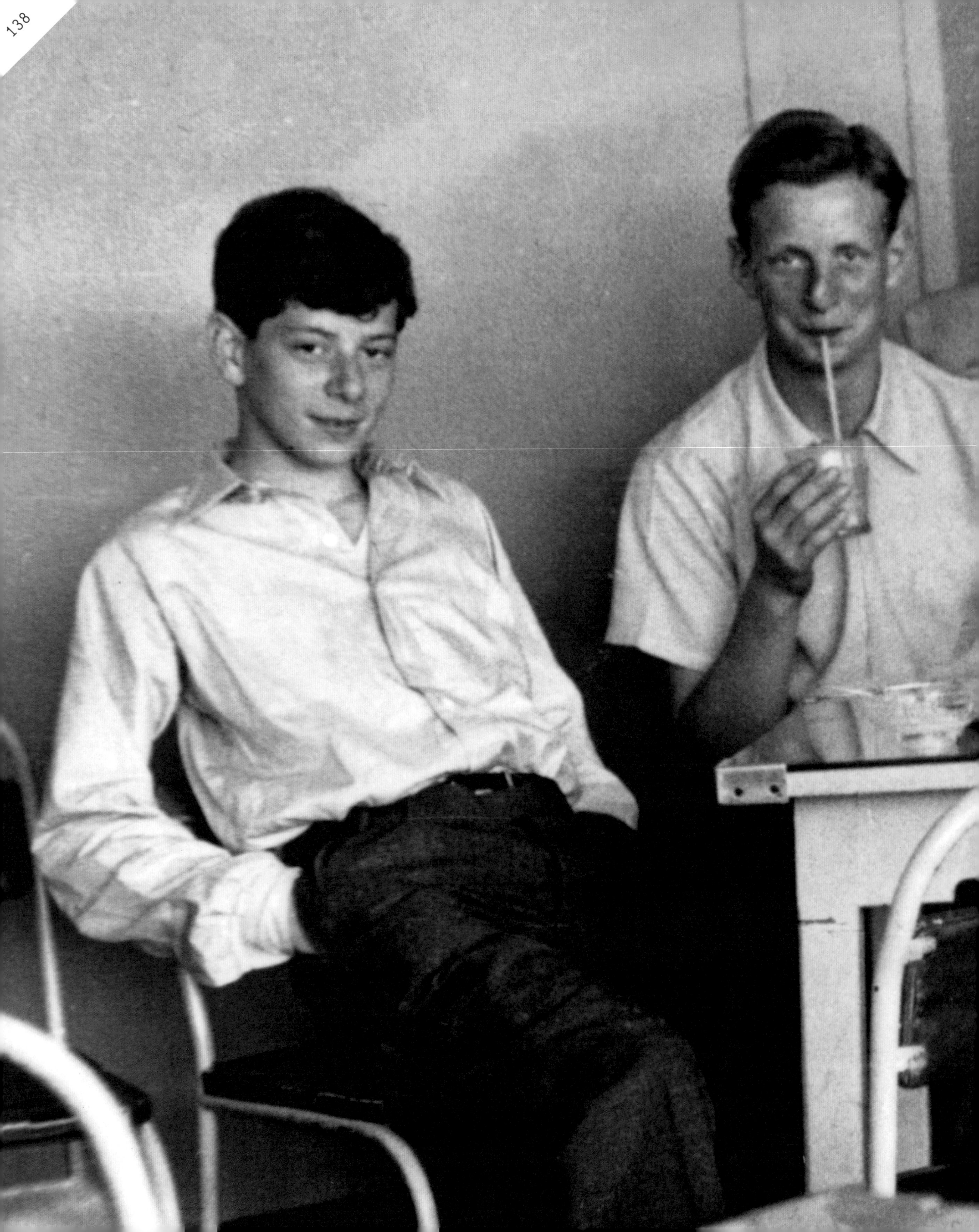

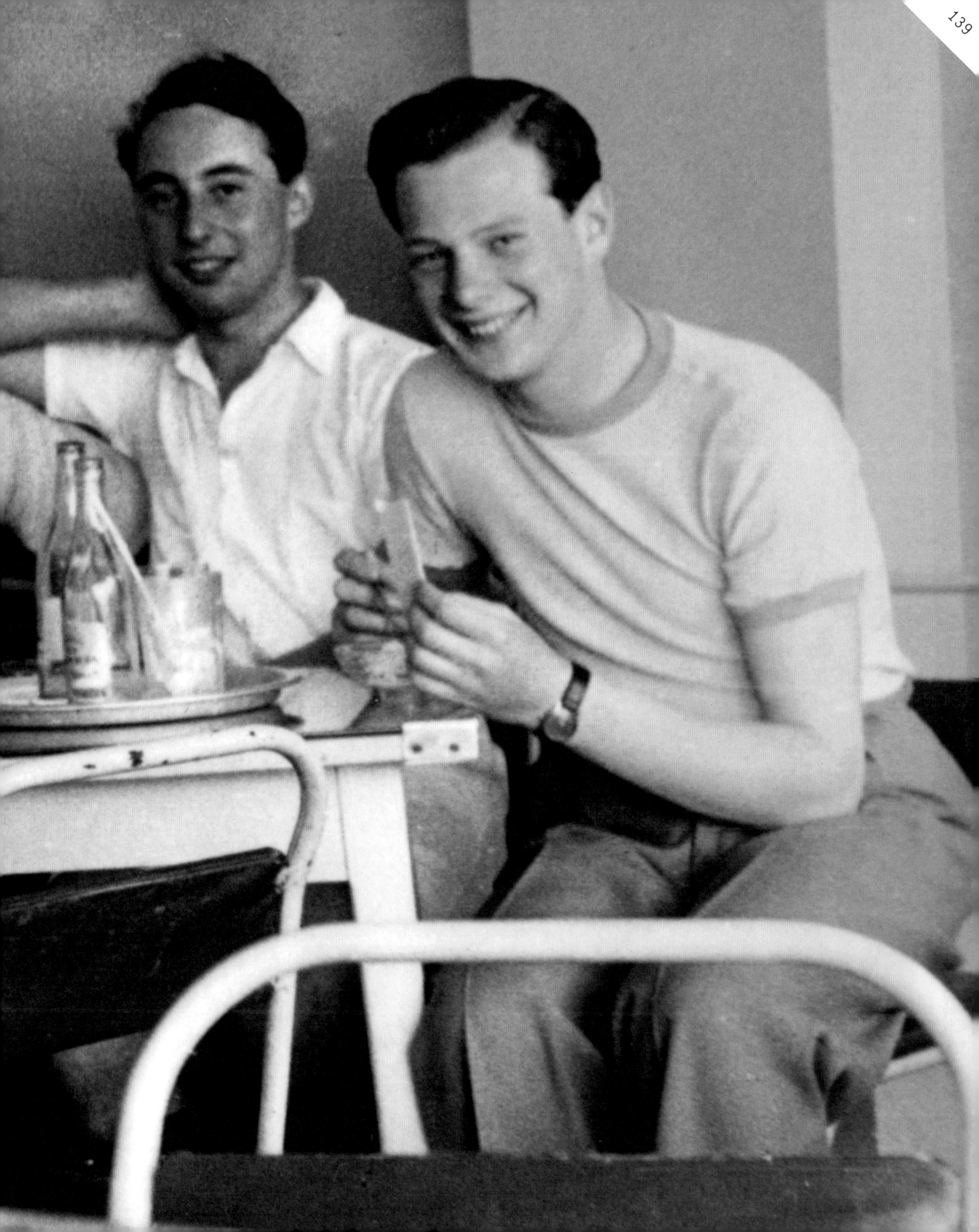

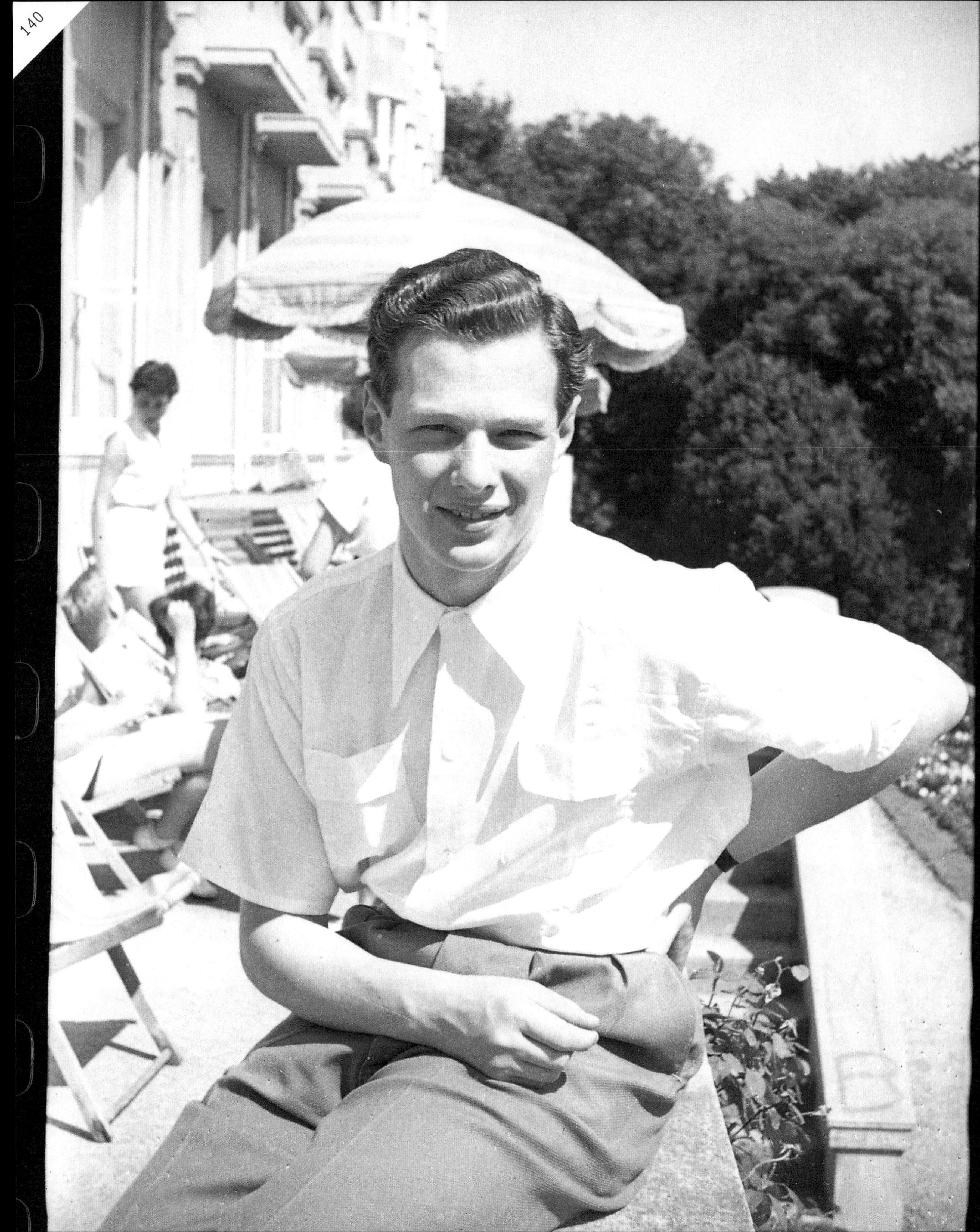

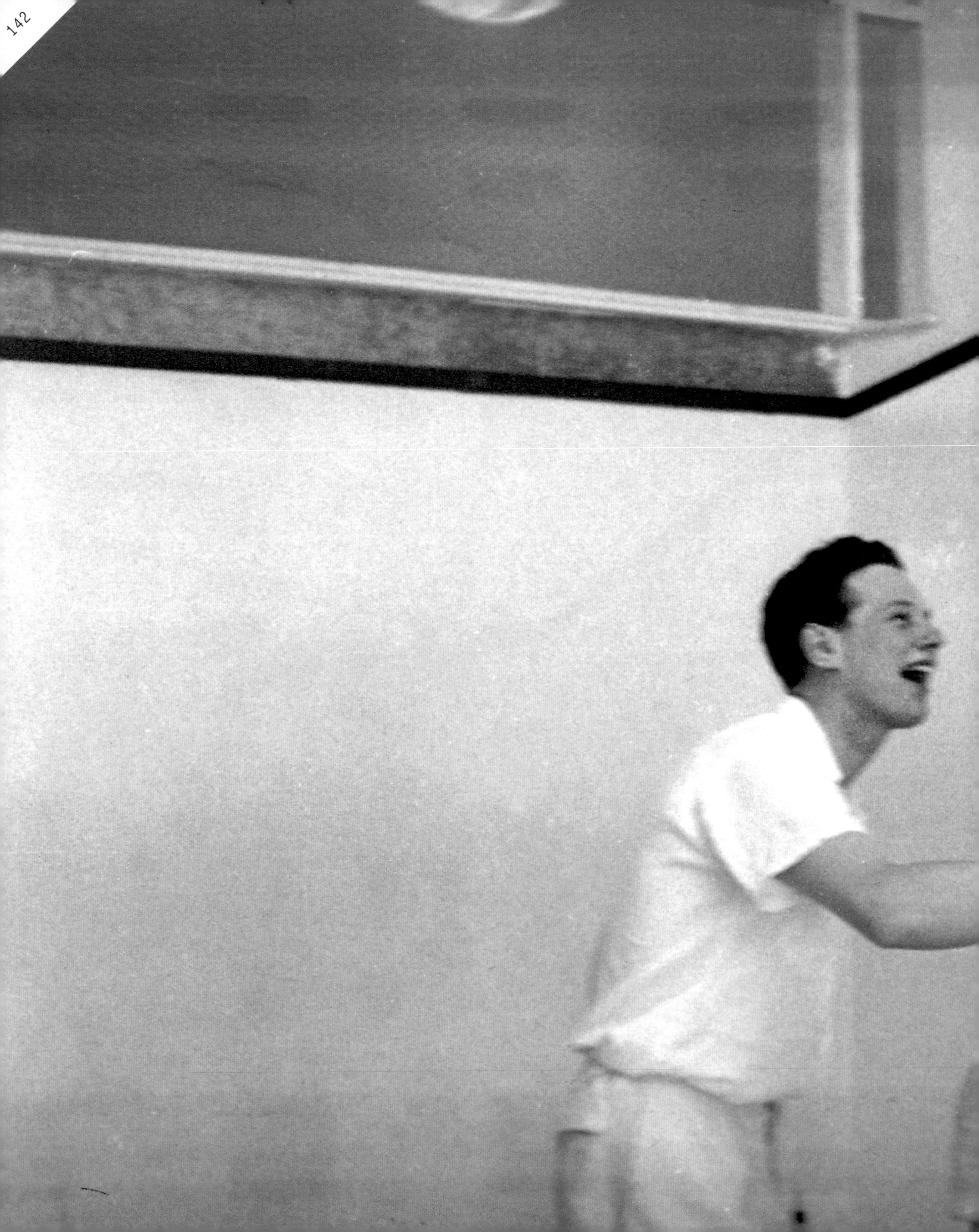

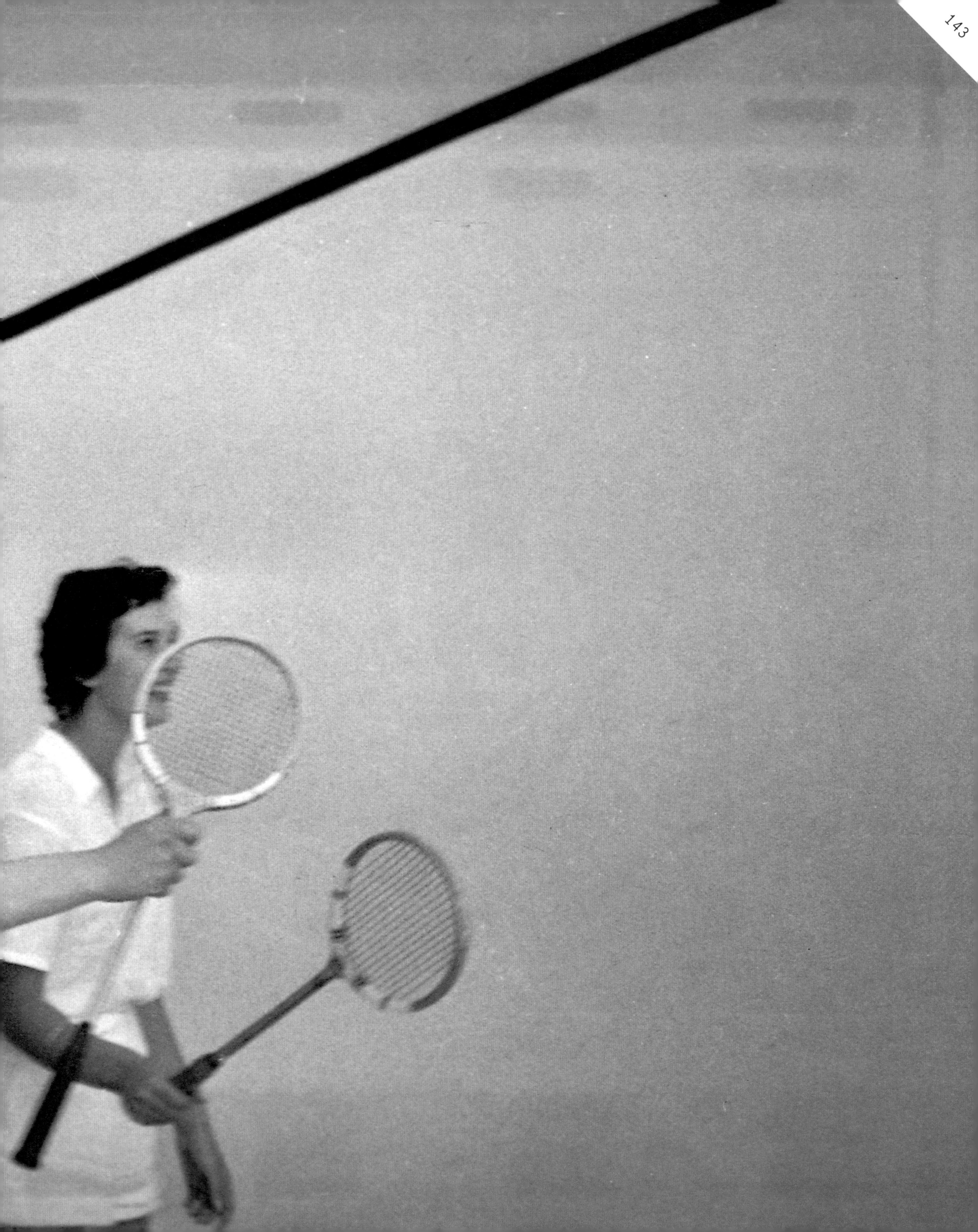

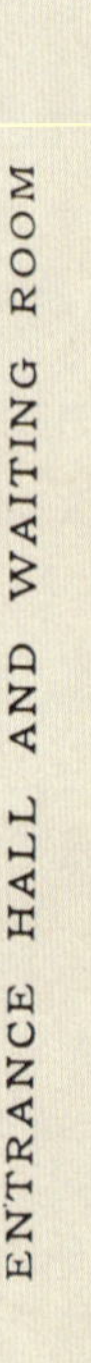

ENTRANCE HALL AND WAITING ROOM

The Origin an

The author of "
has, in no sense, atten
learned essay, or anythi
an interesting collectio
an account of its forn
went to its making :
readily understood by
of scientific idioms whi
to the average lay mind

The story of the
engrossing interest to a
the story is told, the m

The writer has lar
and scientific deductio
facts ; and some of t
receive due acknowledg

The Rev. J. MacEr
R. Hunt, F.G.S. ; A.
members of the Torqu
writers, specialists in
enumerate—to all of wh

The main purpose
hands of visitors the st
with a descriptive tour
actual one is made,
anticipation of pleasur
leisurely after its conclu
it to be made again,
wonders actually enjoy

In conclusion, a g
of the wonderful work
Messrs. W. F. & L. W

The superb syste
cost and masterly pla
wonders of the format
and the building of th
room, call for the grate

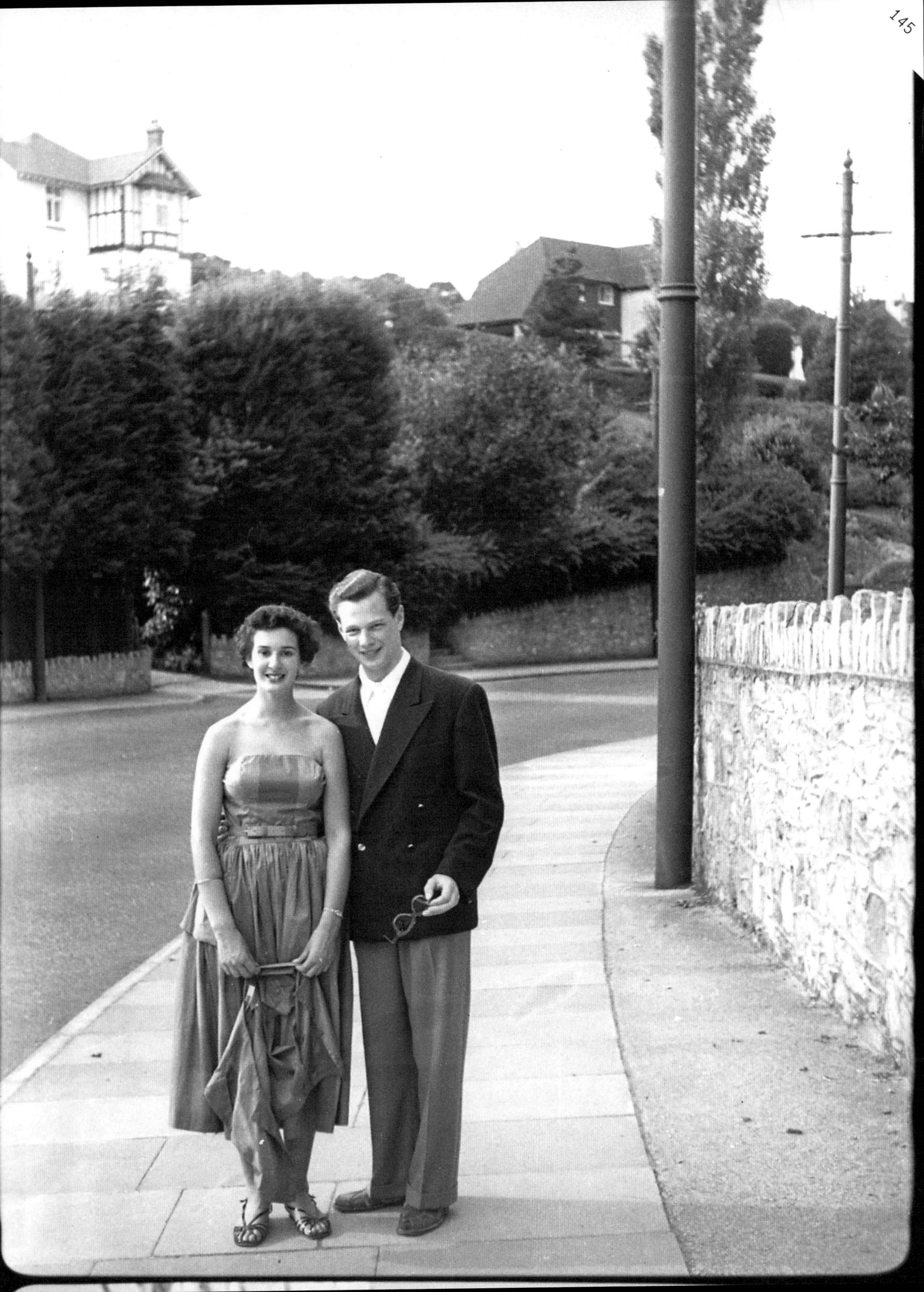

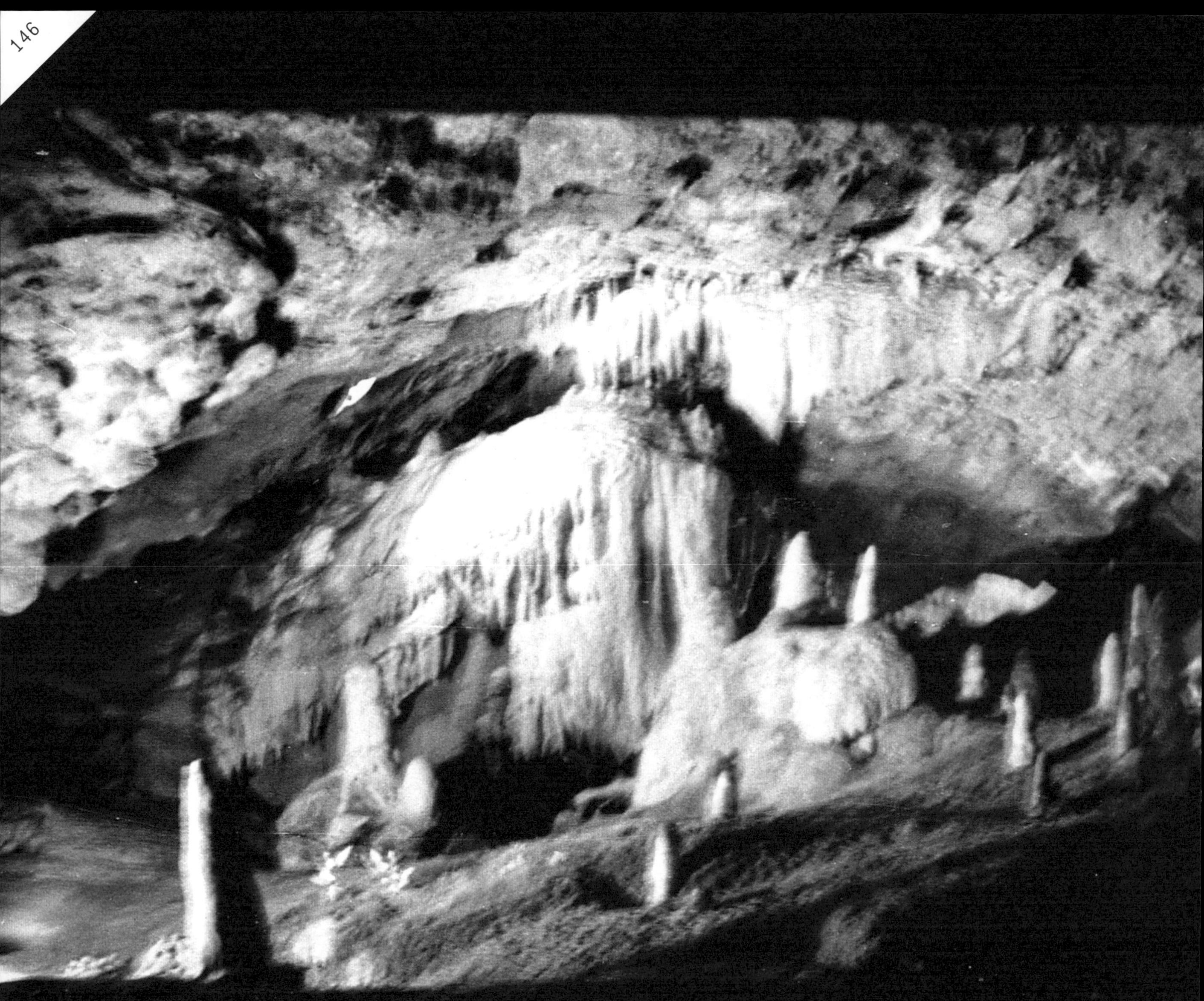

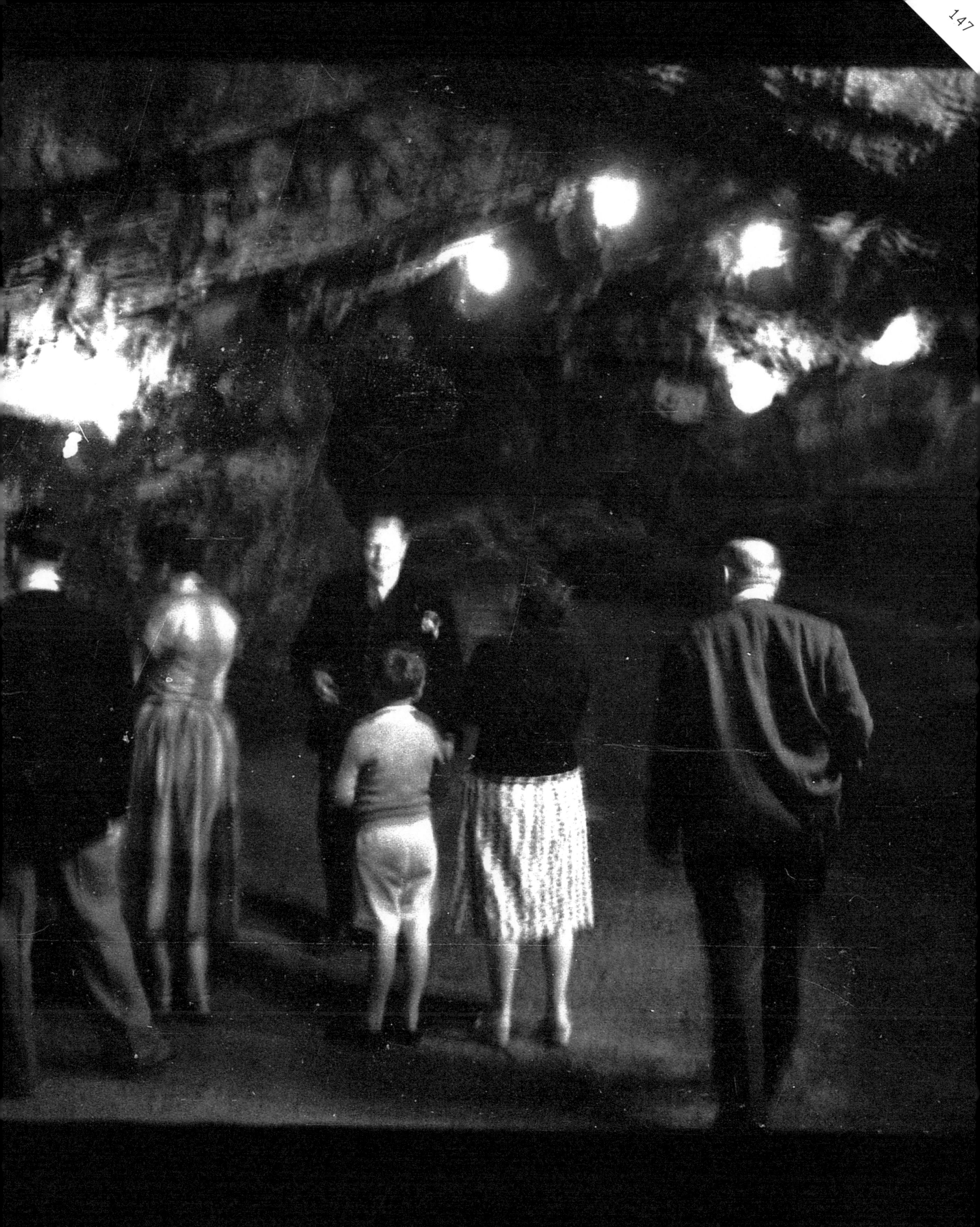

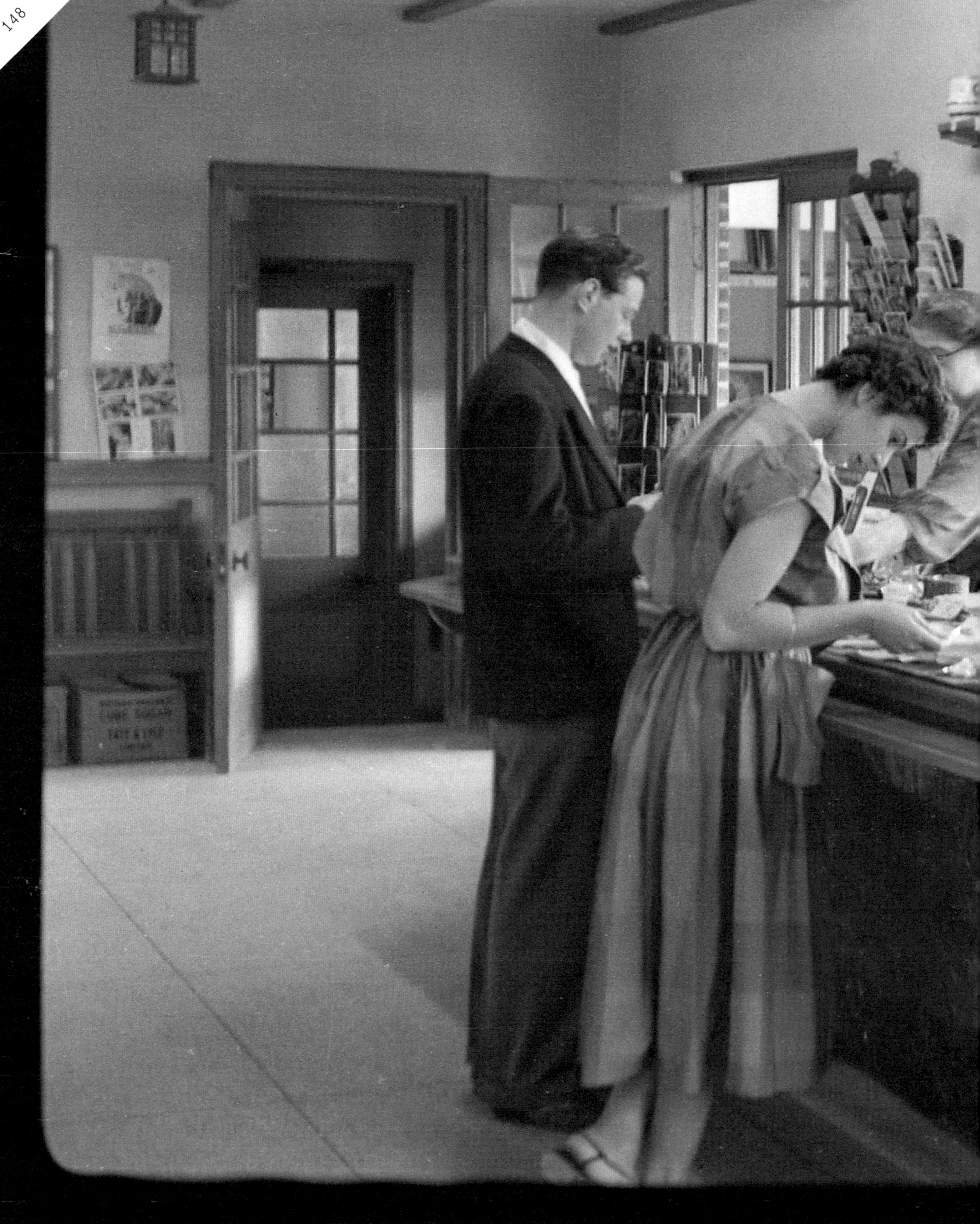

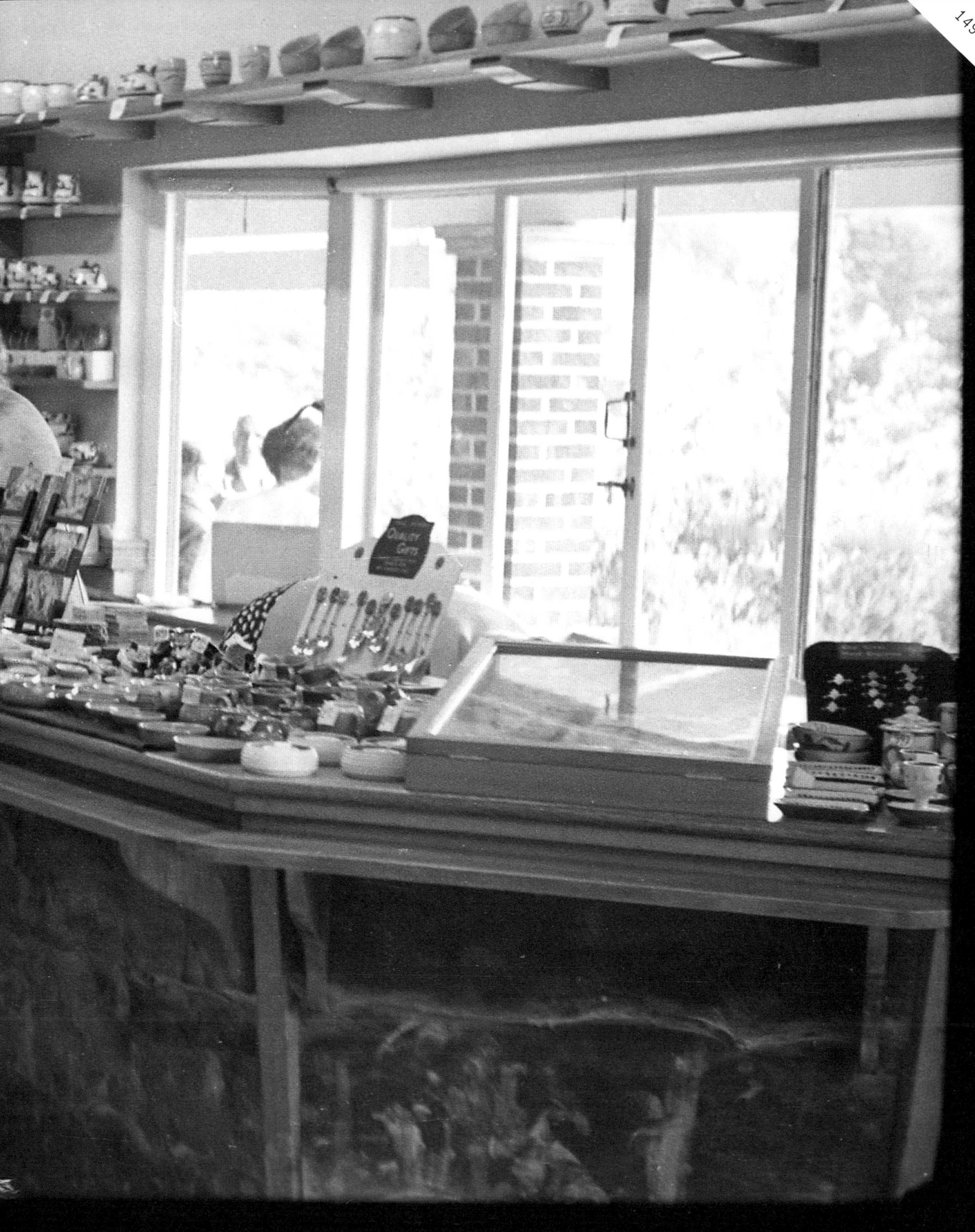

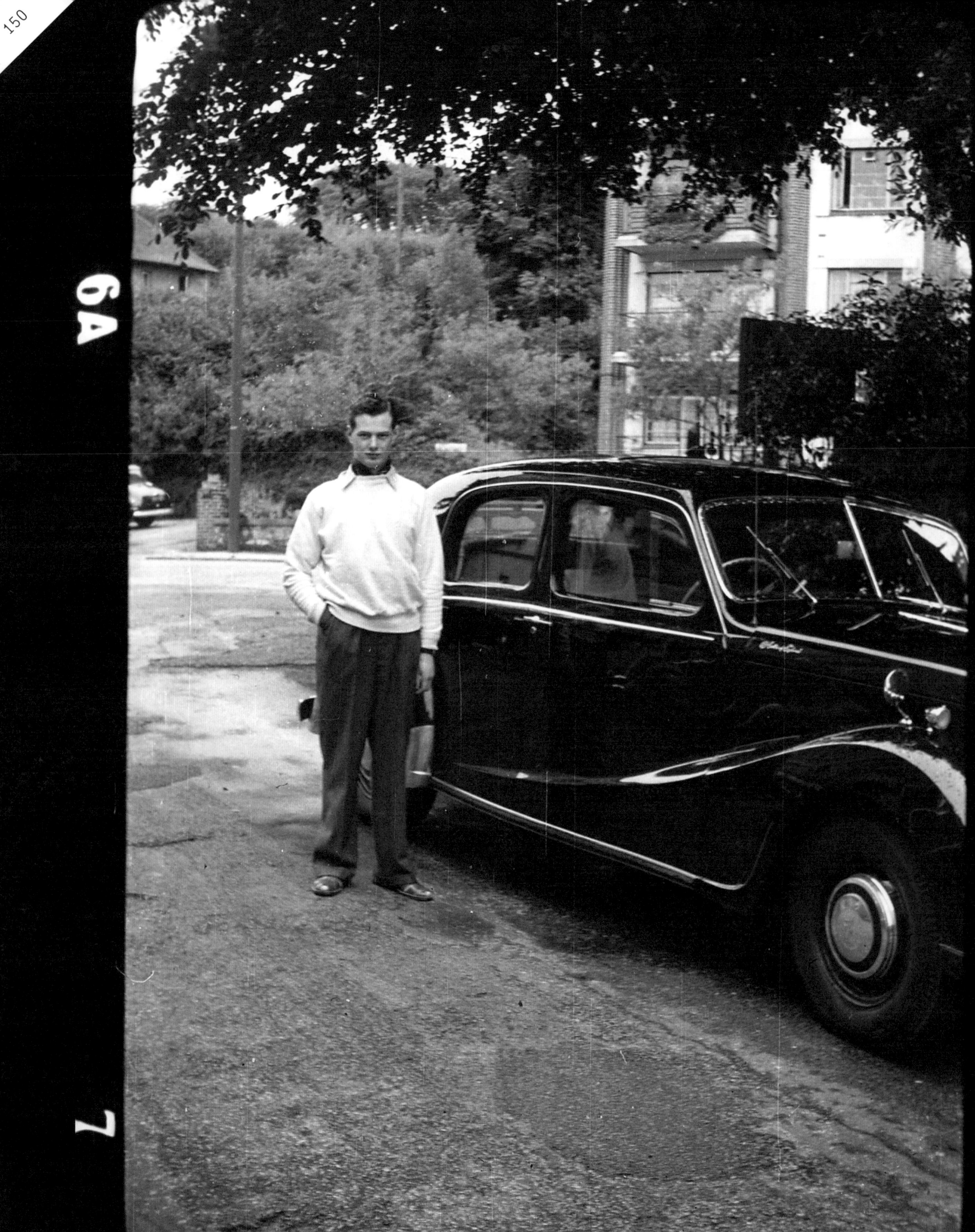

150
6A
7

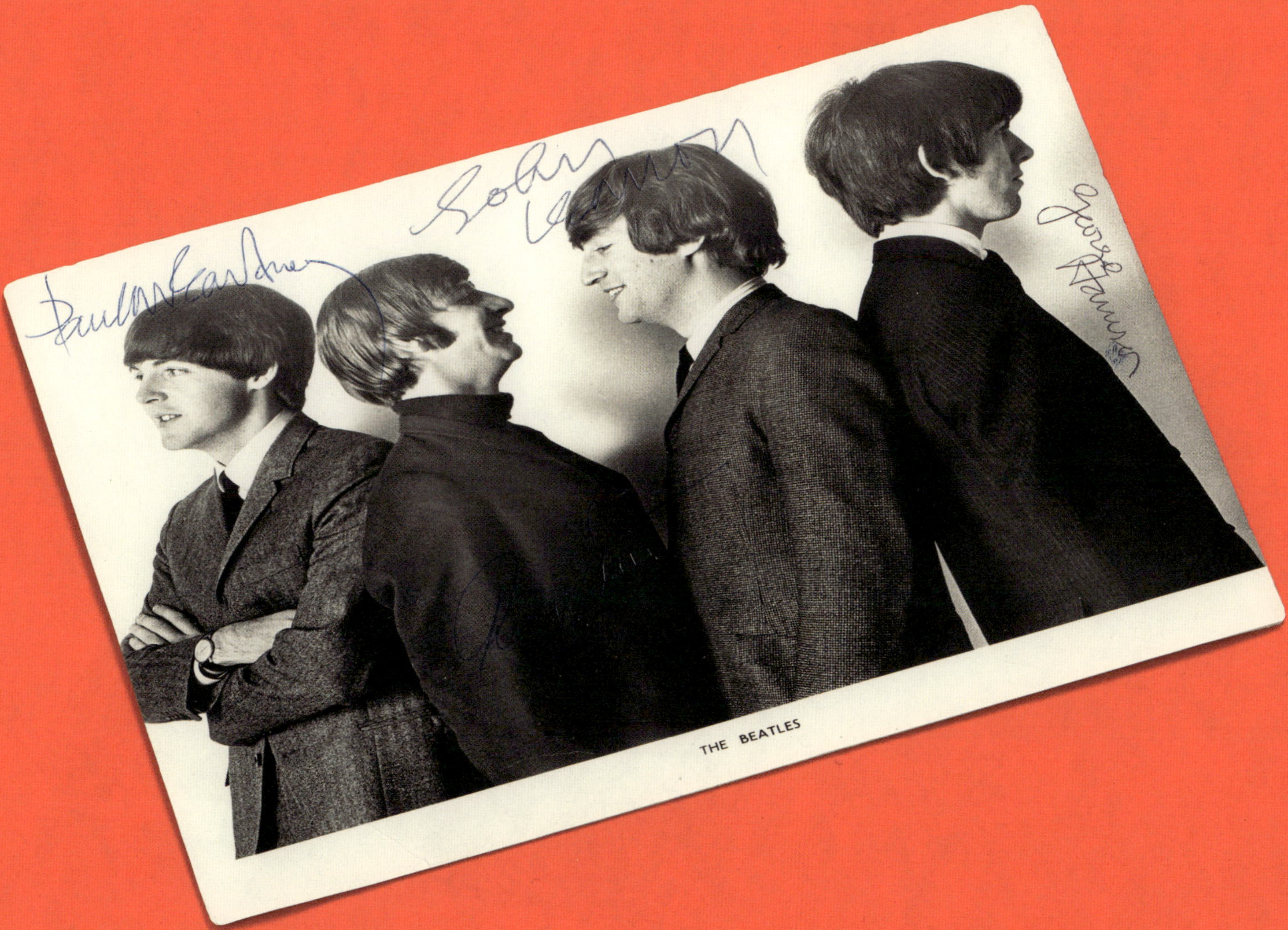

THE BEATLES

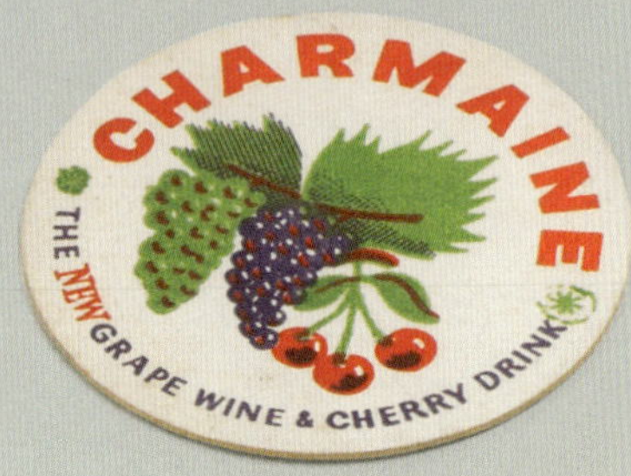
CHARMAINE
THE NEW GRAPE WINE & CHERRY DRINK

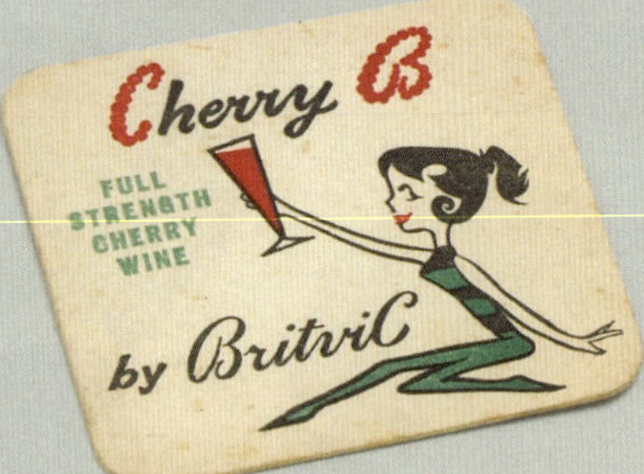
Cherry B
FULL
STRENGTH
CHERRY
WINE
by BritviC

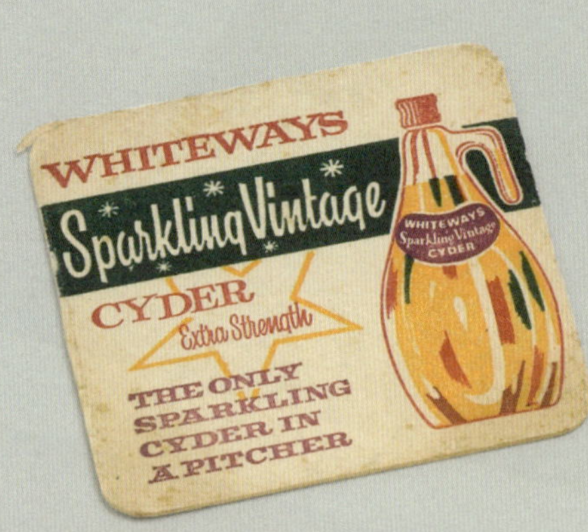
WHITEWAYS
Sparkling Vintage
CYDER
Extra Strength
WHITEWAYS
Sparkling Vintage
CYDER
THE ONLY
SPARKLING
CYDER IN
A PITCHER

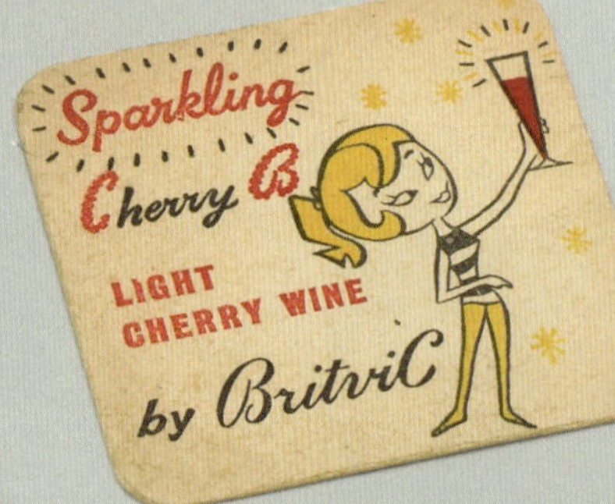
Sparkling
Cherry B
LIGHT
CHERRY WINE
by BritviC

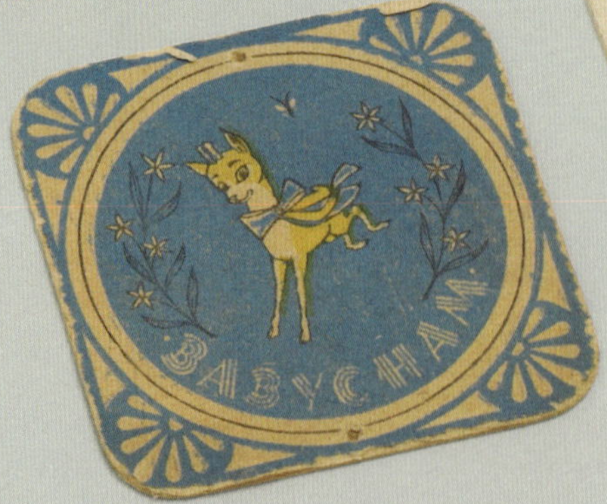
BABYCHAM

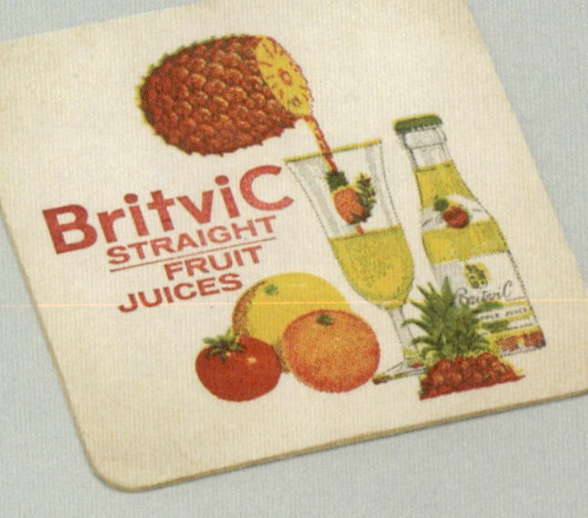
BritviC
STRAIGHT
FRUIT
JUICES

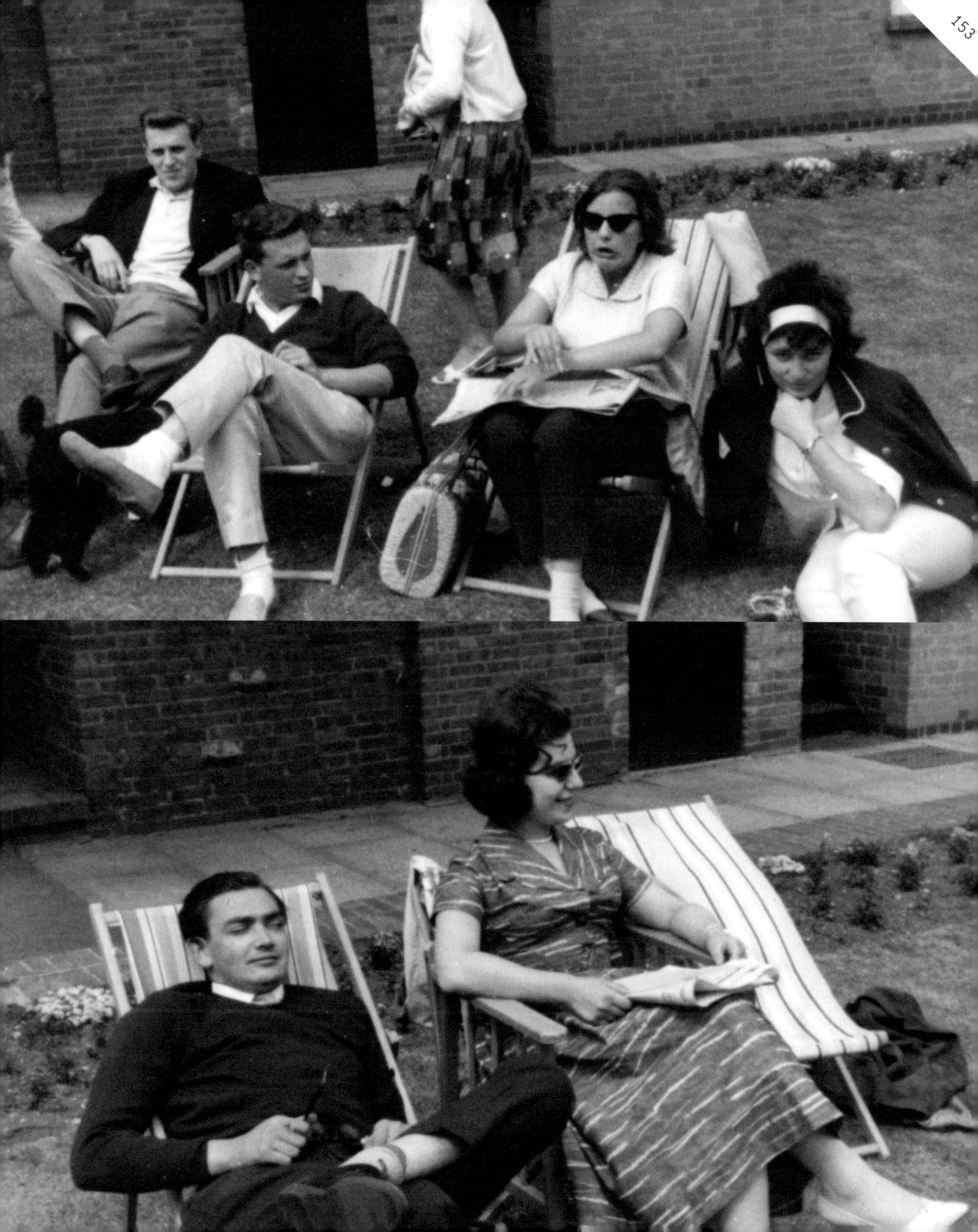

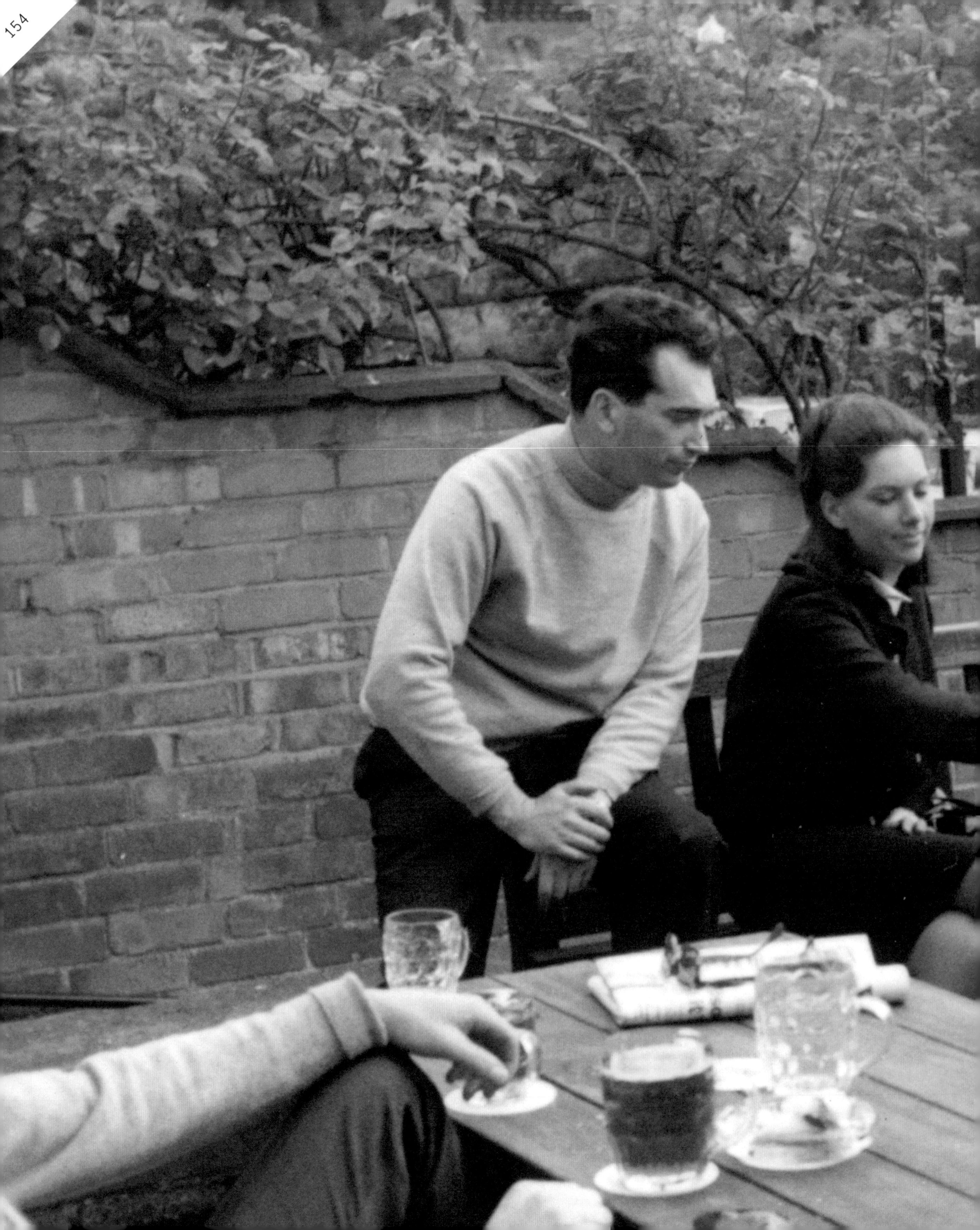

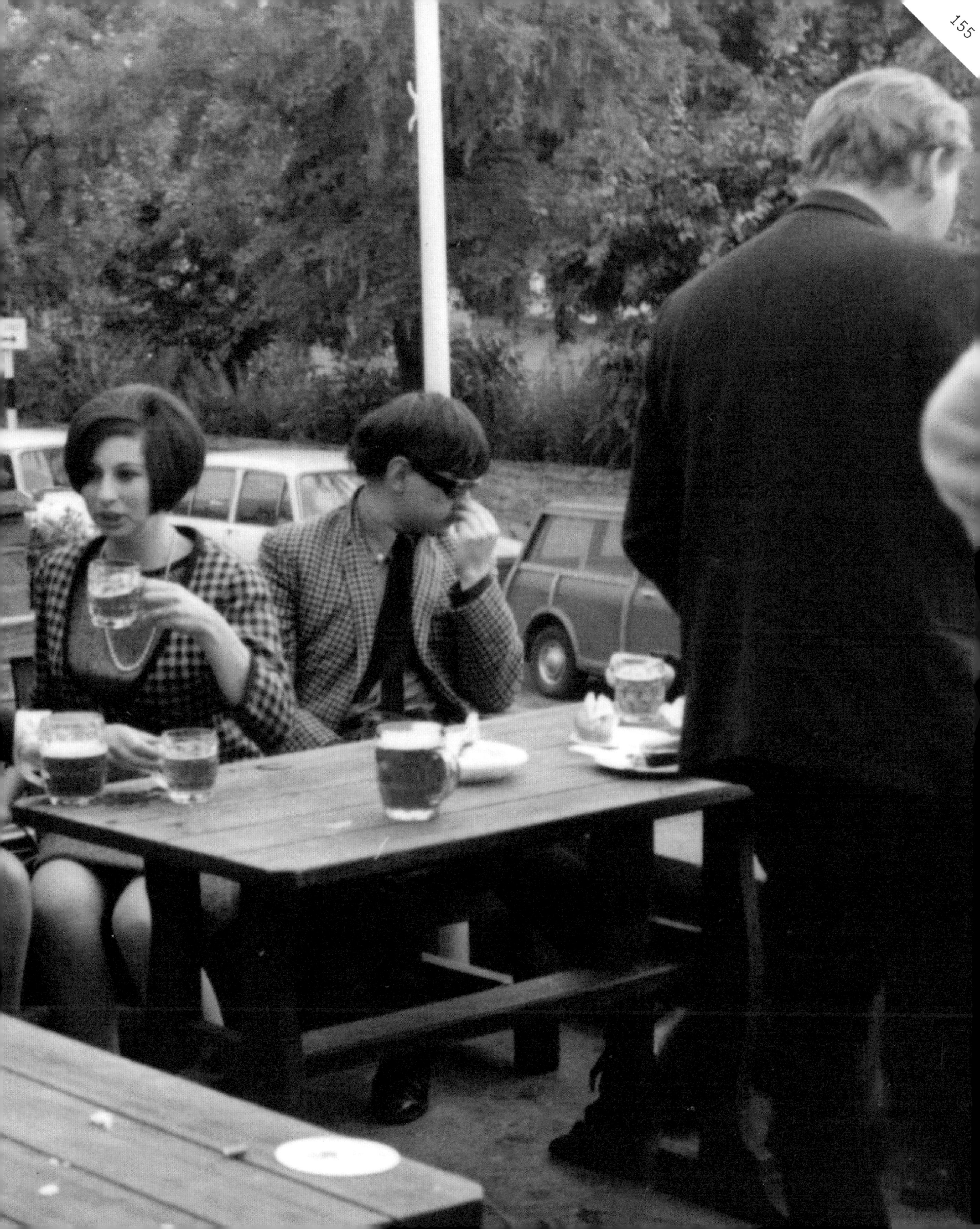

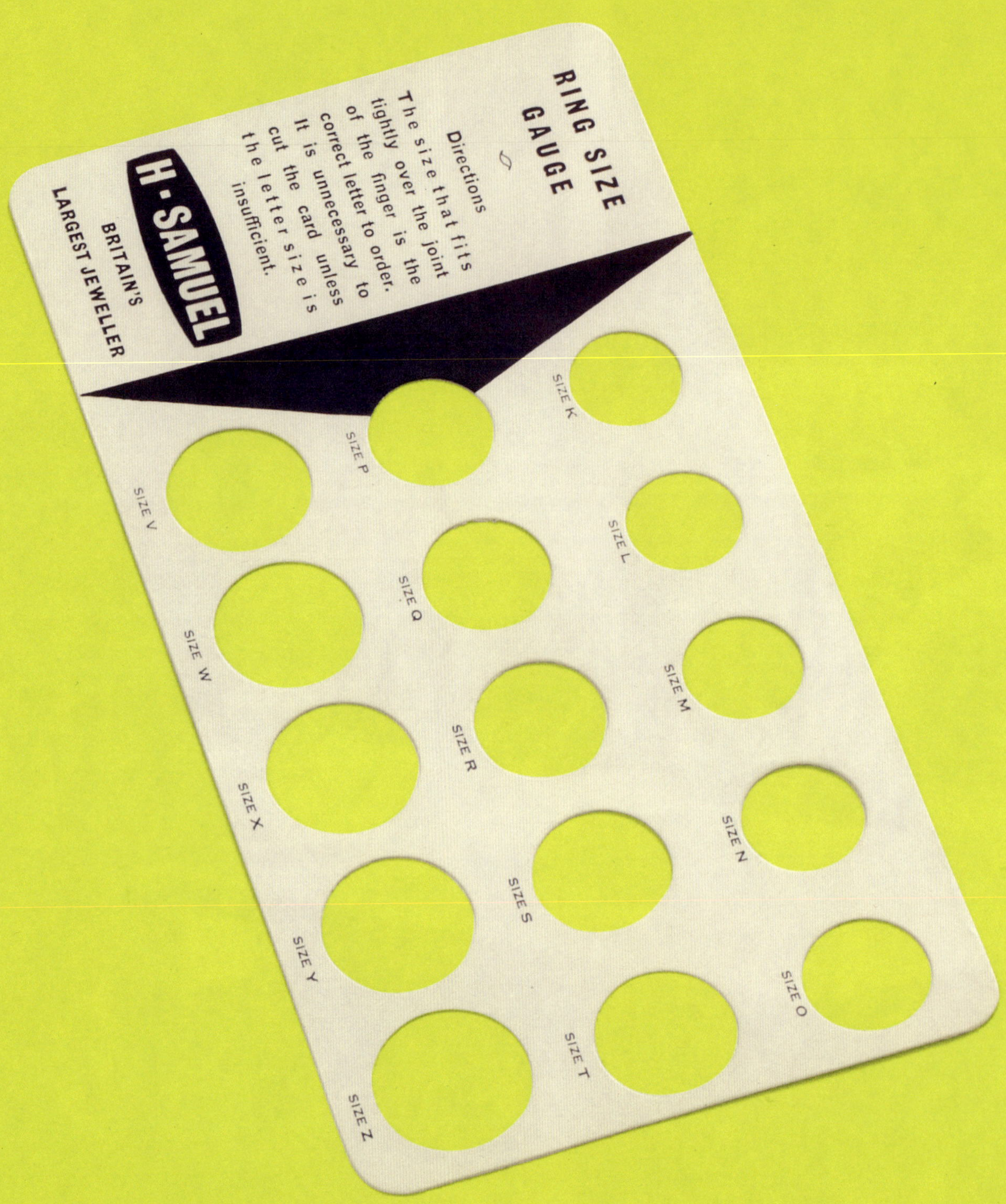

RING SIZE GAUGE
Directions
The size that fits
tightly over the joint
of the finger is the
correct letter to order.
It is unnecessary to
cut the card unless
the letter size is
insufficient.
H·SAMUEL
BRITAIN'S LARGEST JEWELLER
SIZE K
SIZE L
SIZE M
SIZE N
SIZE O
SIZE P
SIZE Q
SIZE R
SIZE S
SIZE T
SIZE V
SIZE W
SIZE X
SIZE Y
SIZE Z

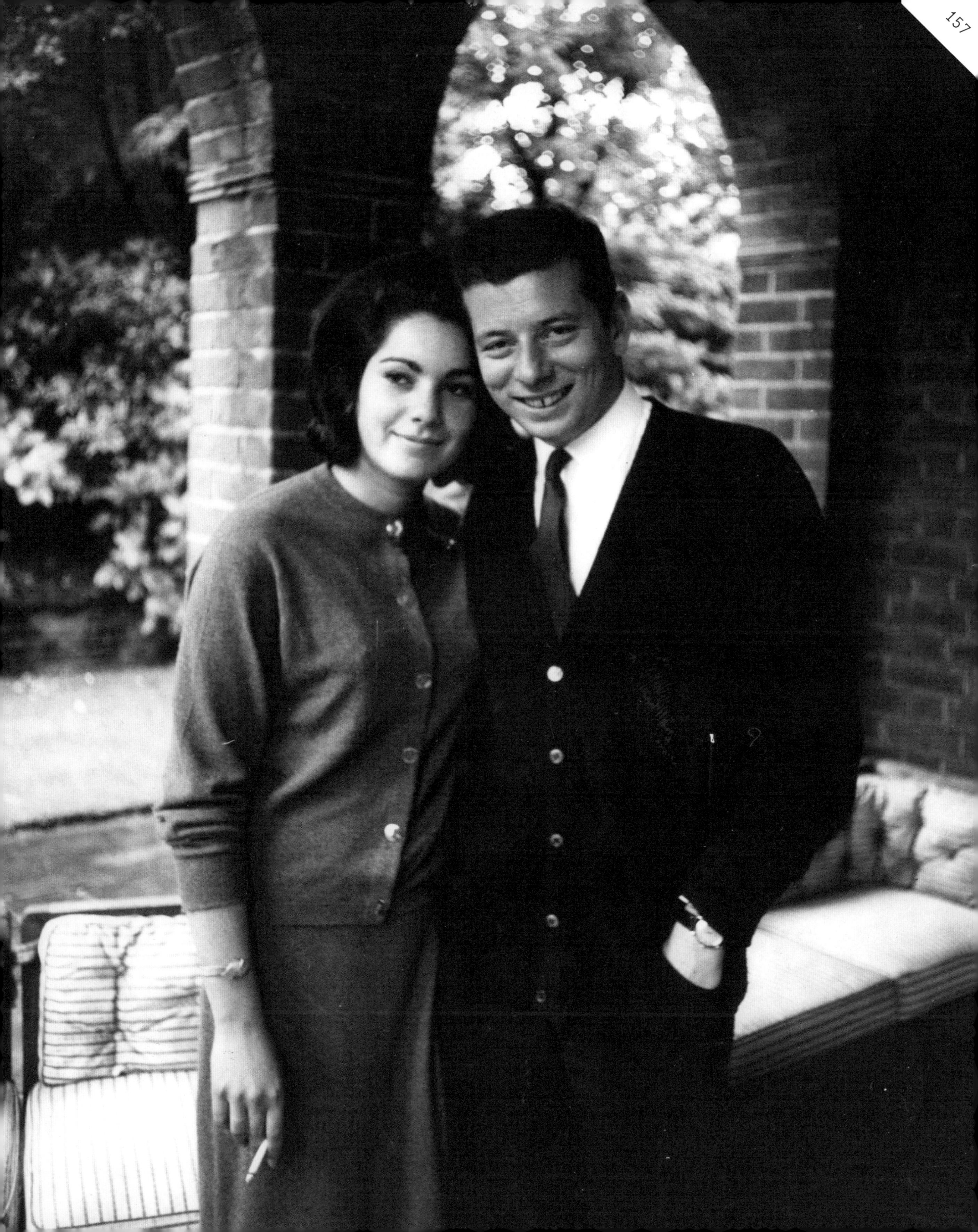

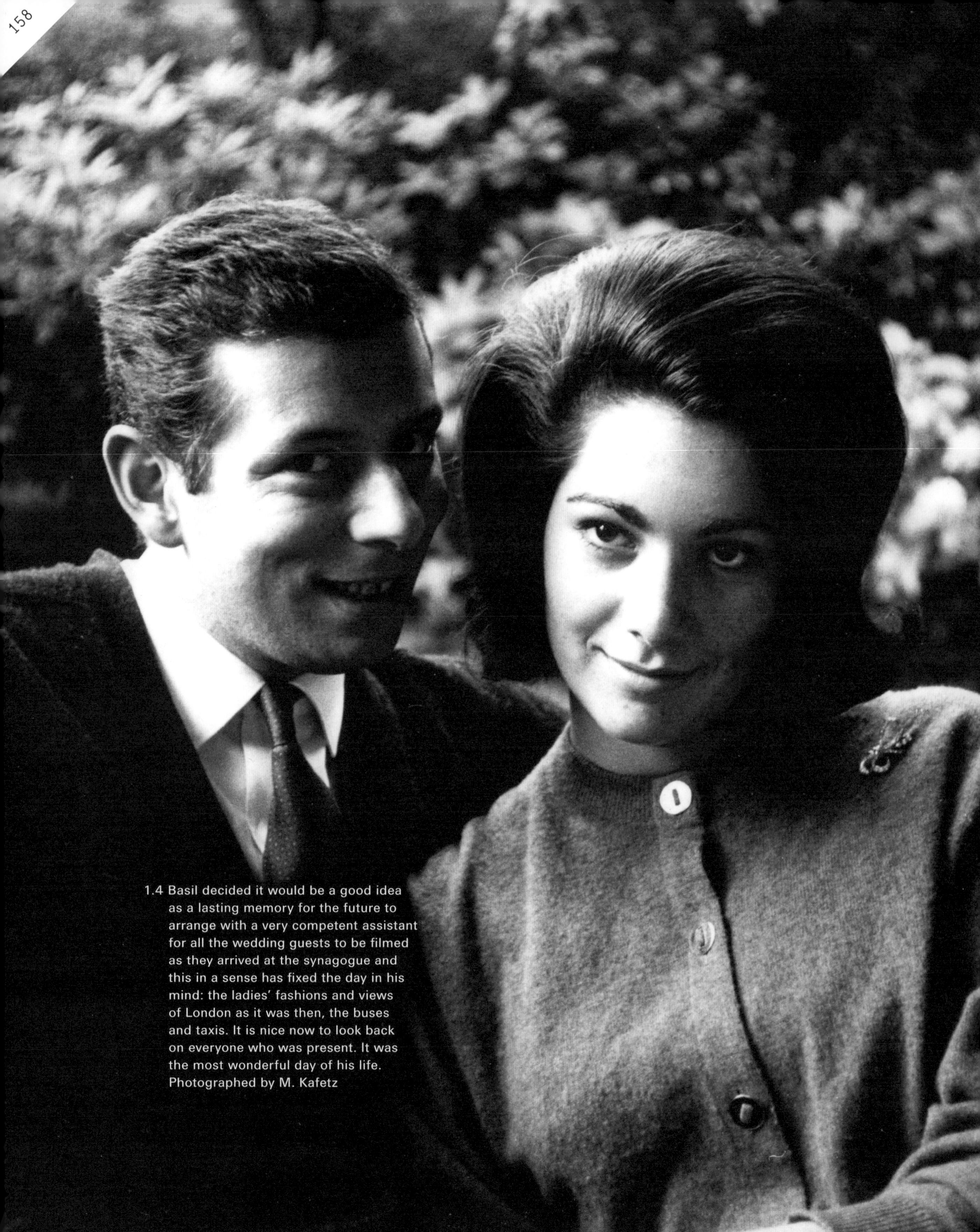

1.4 Basil decided it would be a good idea as a lasting memory for the future to arrange with a very competent assistant for all the wedding guests to be filmed as they arrived at the synagogue and this in a sense has fixed the day in his mind: the ladies' fashions and views of London as it was then, the buses and taxis. It is nice now to look back on everyone who was present. It was the most wonderful day of his life. Photographed by M. Kafetz

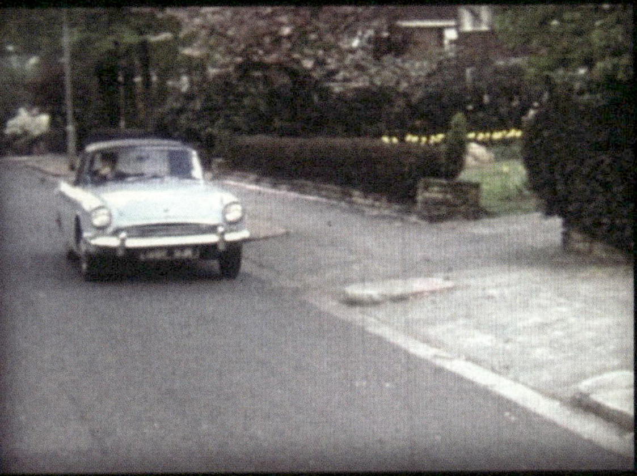

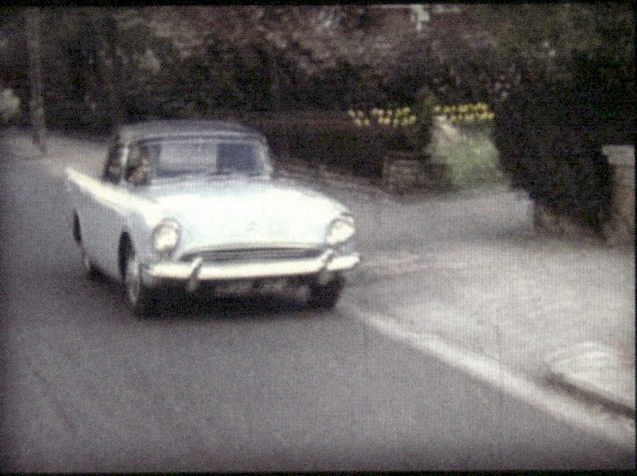

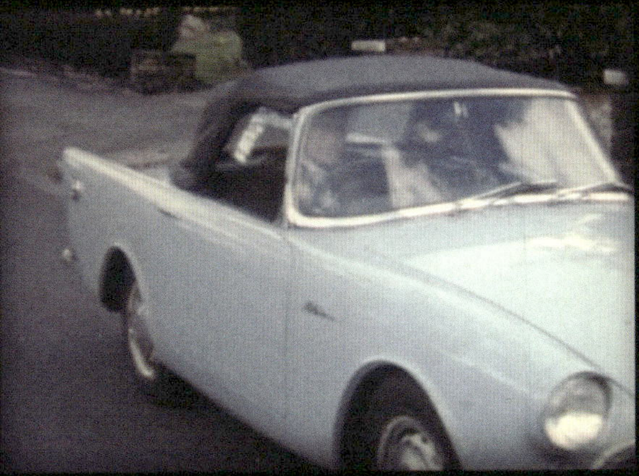

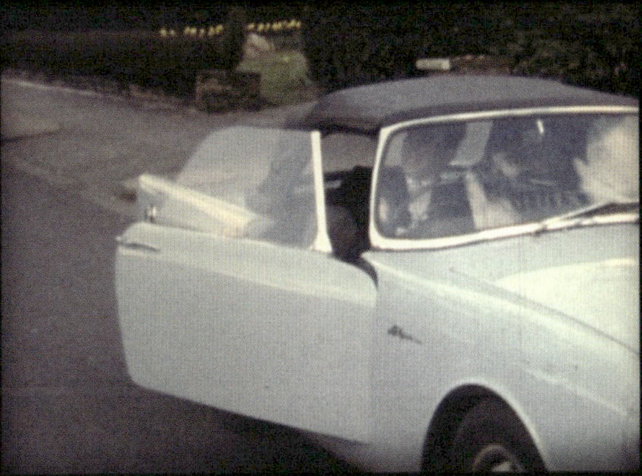

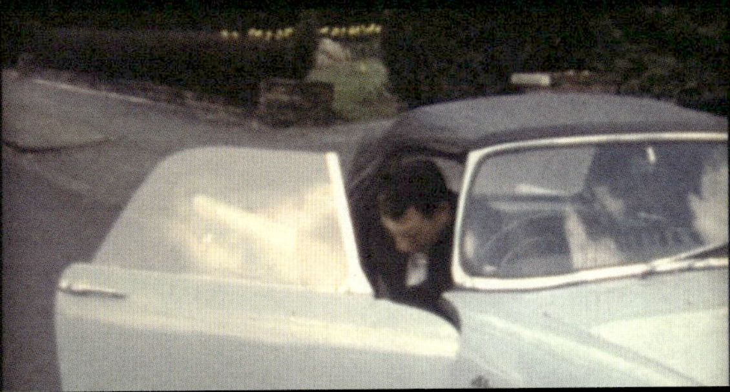

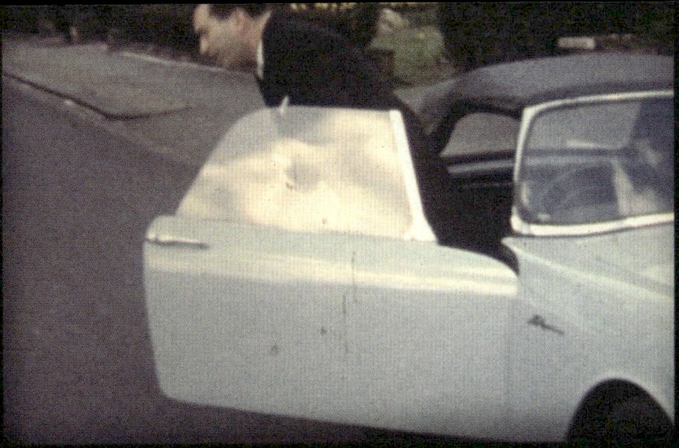

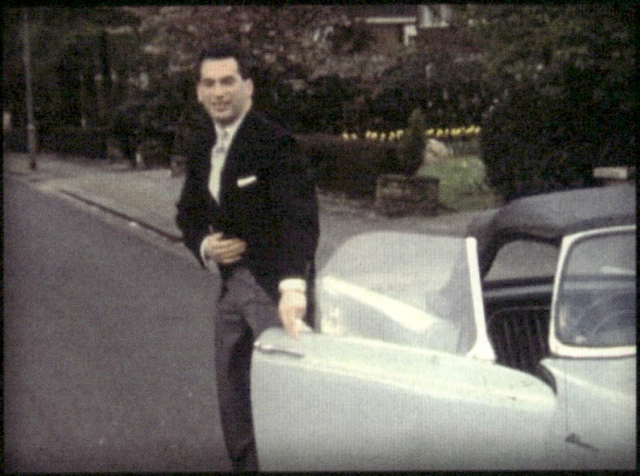

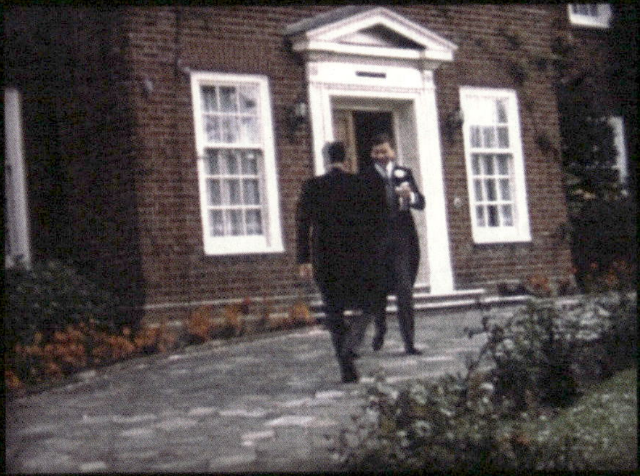

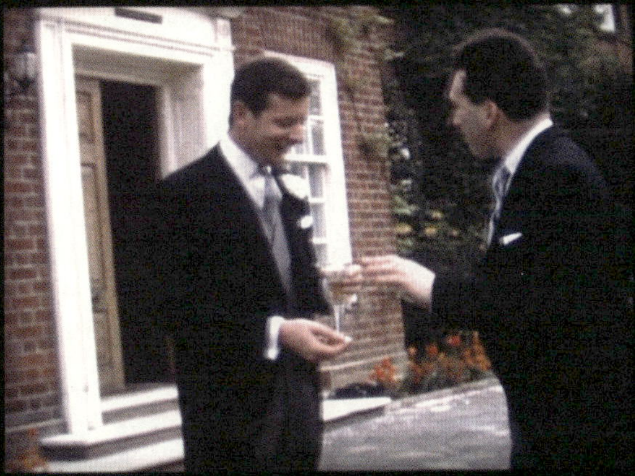

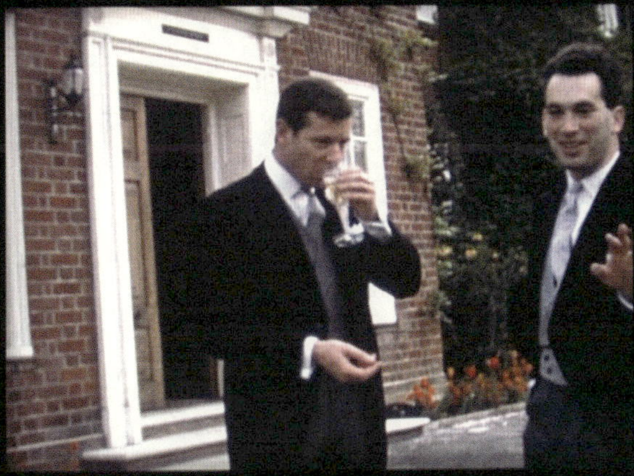

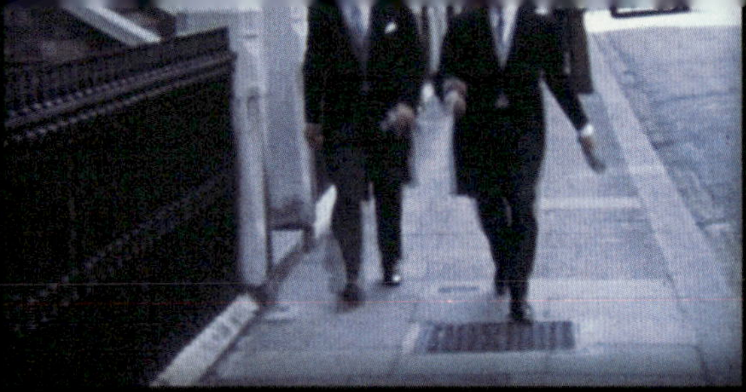

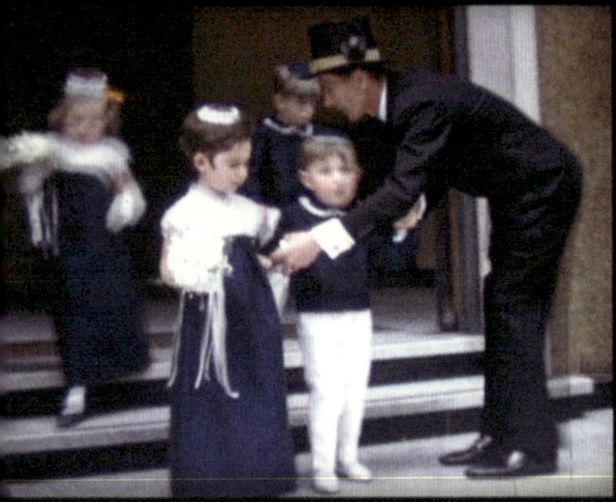

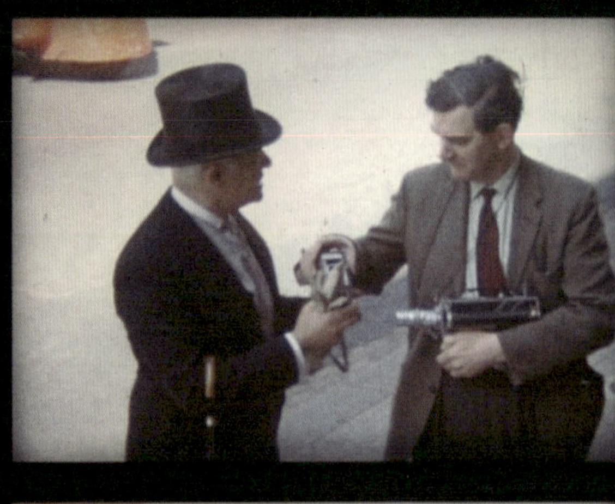

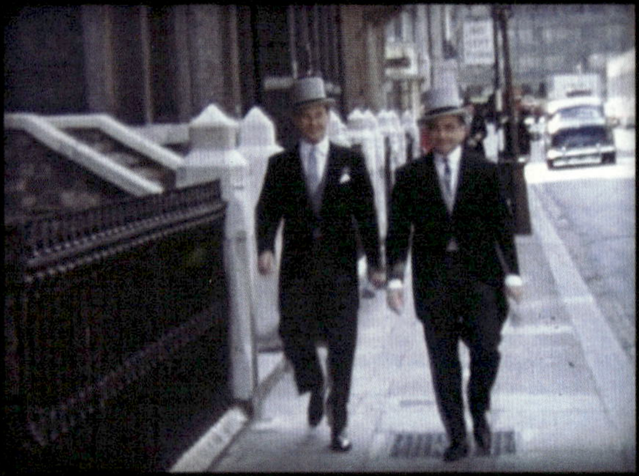

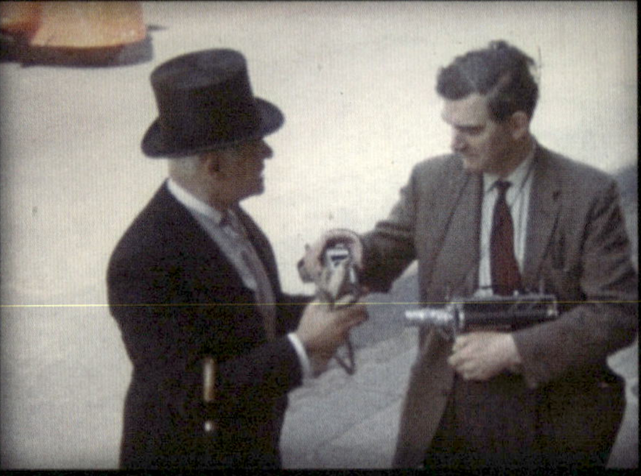

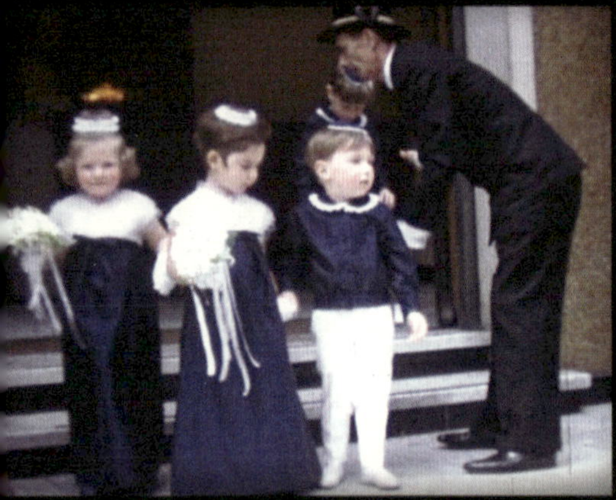

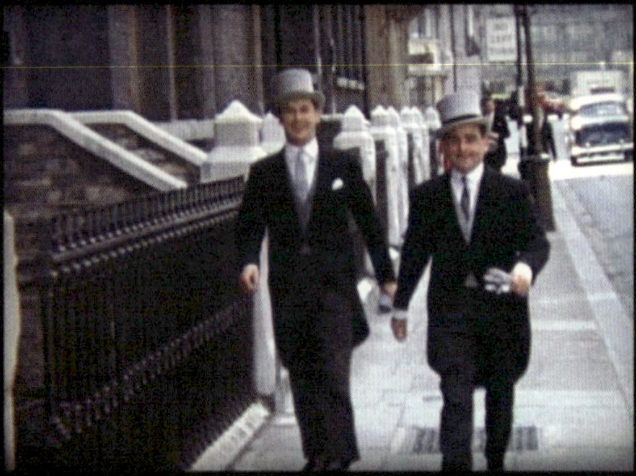

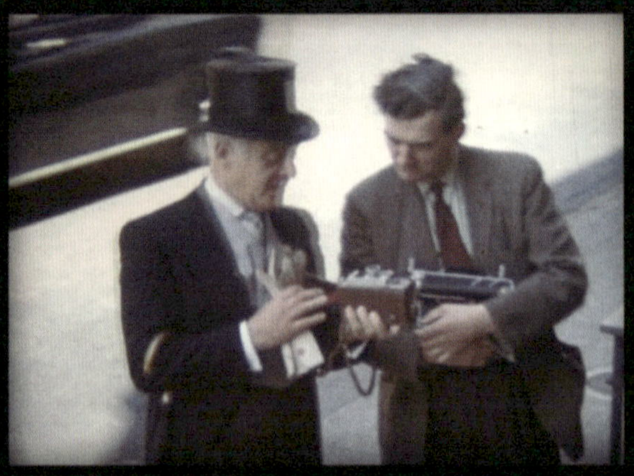

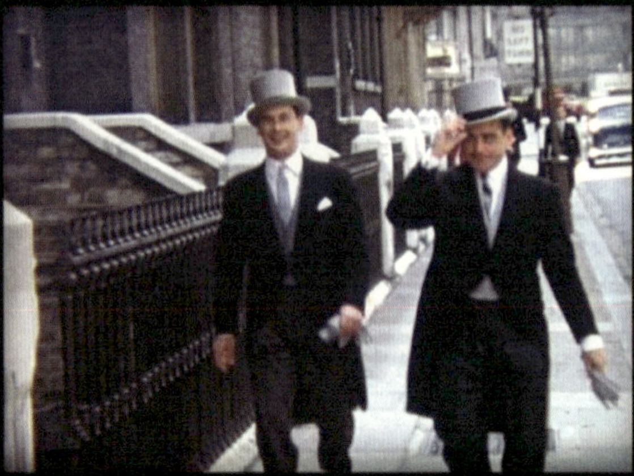

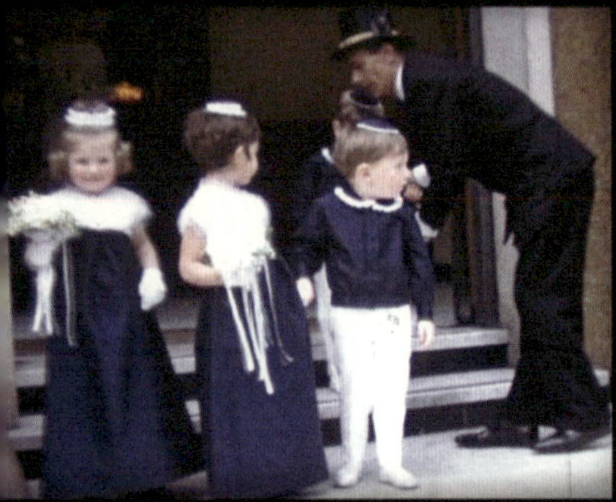

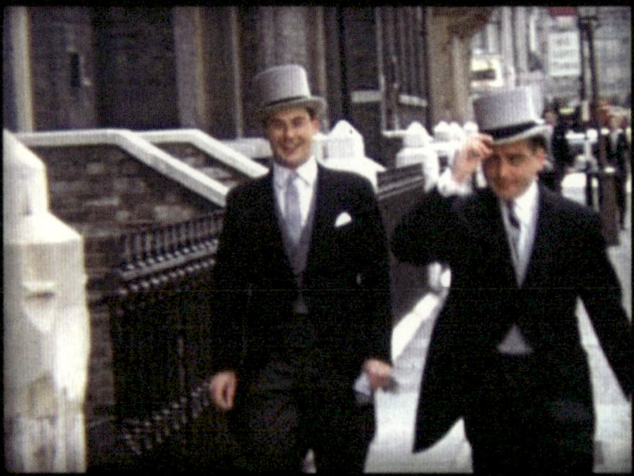

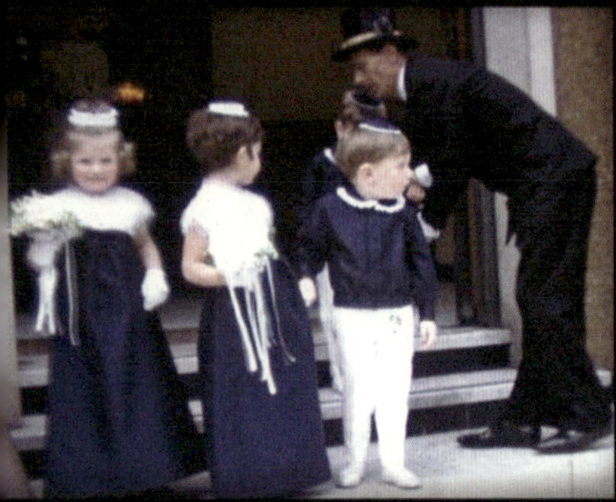

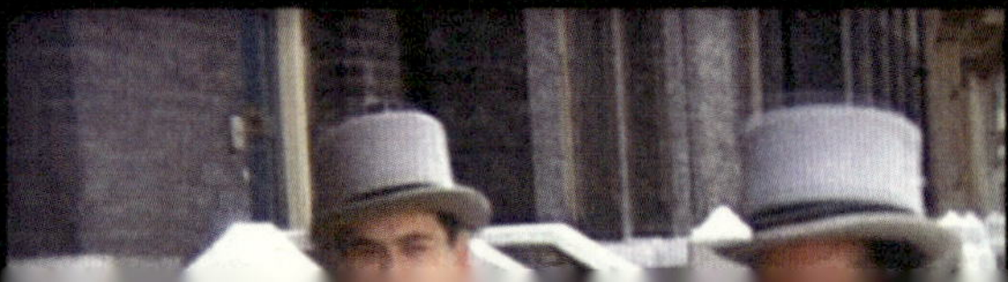

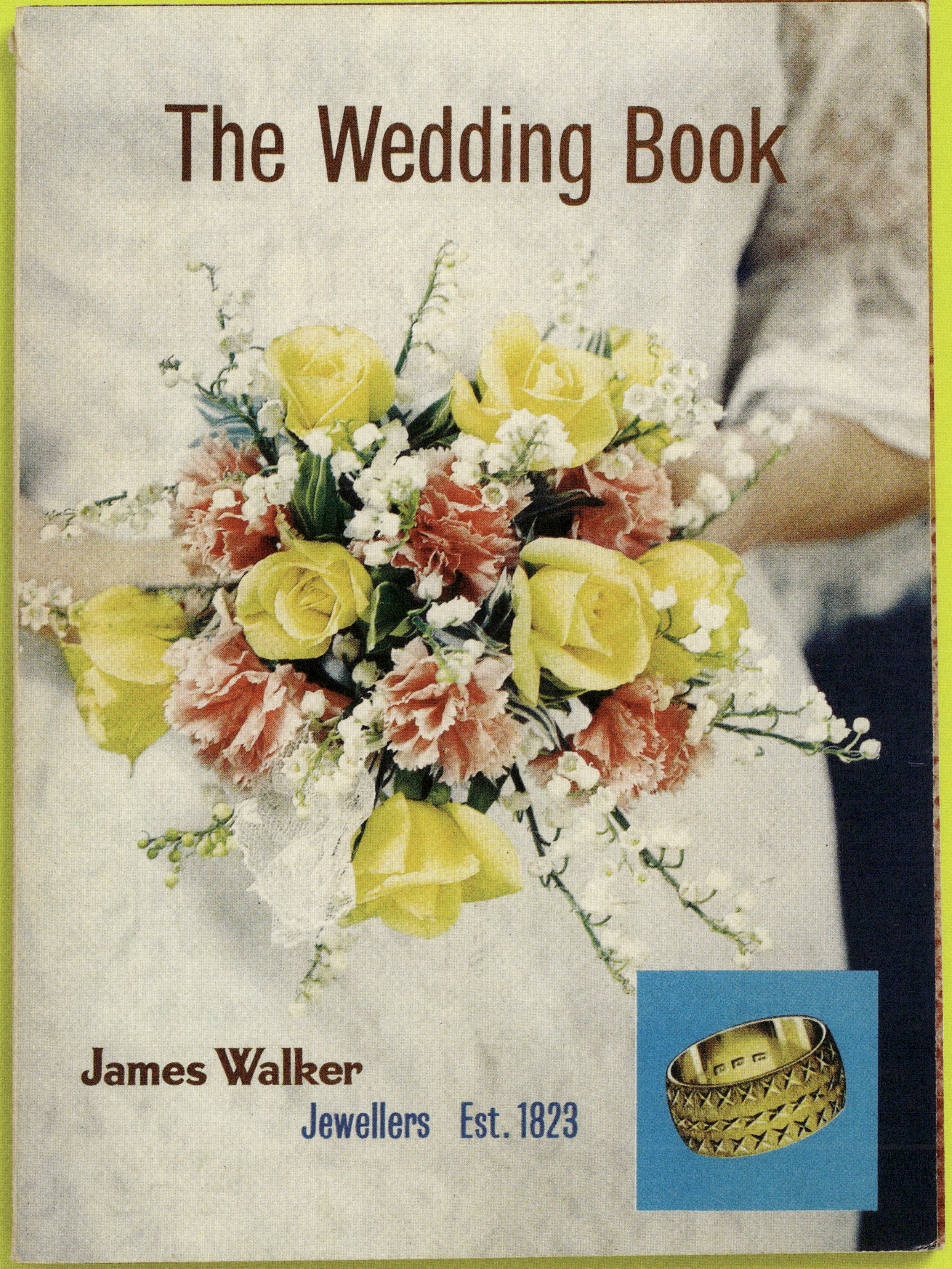

The Wedding Book
James Walker
Jewellers   Est. 1823

WHO DOES AND PAYS FOR WHAT

THE BRIDE

What She Does

Chooses church and type of service.
Decides date of wedding.
Chooses her own dress and advises bridesmaids on theirs.

What She Pays For

Wedding dress.
Bridesmaids' dresses (optional).

THE GROOM

What He Does

Arrives at the church on time.

What He Pays For

The wedding ring.
Church Fees:
  Licence.
  The wedding certificate.
  Marriage service.
  The verger.
  Organist.
  Choir.
  Altar servers.
Presents for:
  Bride.
  Bridesmaids.
  Best Man.
  Ushers.
Flowers for:
  Bride.
  Bridesmaids.
  Bride's mother.
  His own mother.
  Best man and himself (buttonholes).
Transport:
  To take him and best man to church.
  To take him and bride from reception.
Honeymoon (these days, cost is shared).

BRIDE-TO-BE AND GROOM TOGETHER

What They Do

Arrange to see Minister and/or Registrar three months before wedding, if possible, to discuss:
  Date of wedding. Reading of banns. Licence.
Discuss general wedding arrangements.
Arrange the honeymoon.
Decide where they will live.
Plan their new home.

What They Pay For

Honeymoon (unless groom is a millionaire!).
Things for new home.

THE BEST MAN

What He Does

Ensures arrival of groom at church.
Carries wedding ring before service.
Passes wedding ring to minister during service.
Stands to the right of groom during service.
After service pays any tips, fees, etc. as necessary (with the groom's money).
Ensures transportation of guests from church to reception.
At reception receives telegrams.
Makes short speech.
After reception ensures that transport, travel tickets, passports, etc., are in order for the couple's honeymoon.

THE CHIEF BRIDESMAID

What She Does

Generally assists the bride.
Helps choose wedding dress and trousseau.

Helps bride to dress before wedding.
At ceremony follows bride: holds bride's bouquet during service.
Looks after other bridesmaids and pages.
Helps bride to change after reception.

What She Pays For

Her dress.

THE BRIDE'S FATHER

What He Does

Takes bride to church.
Remains on bride's left during ceremony.
Gives bride away.
Receives guests at reception.
Proposes health of bride and groom.

What He Pays For

Press announcements.
Invitation cards.
Wedding photographs.
Cars (except the groom's).
Flowers.
The reception.

THE BRIDE'S MOTHER

What She Does

All arrangements for wedding.
Decides who is to be invited (in conjunction with the bride and with groom's mother).
Decides venue of reception.
Supervises catering arrangements.
Floral decorations at church and reception.
Any newspaper announcements concerning forthcoming wedding.
Arranges for wedding service cards and/or prayer books.
Arranges wedding cake—liaising with caterers.
Goes to reception immediately after bride and groom to greet guests who will be following.

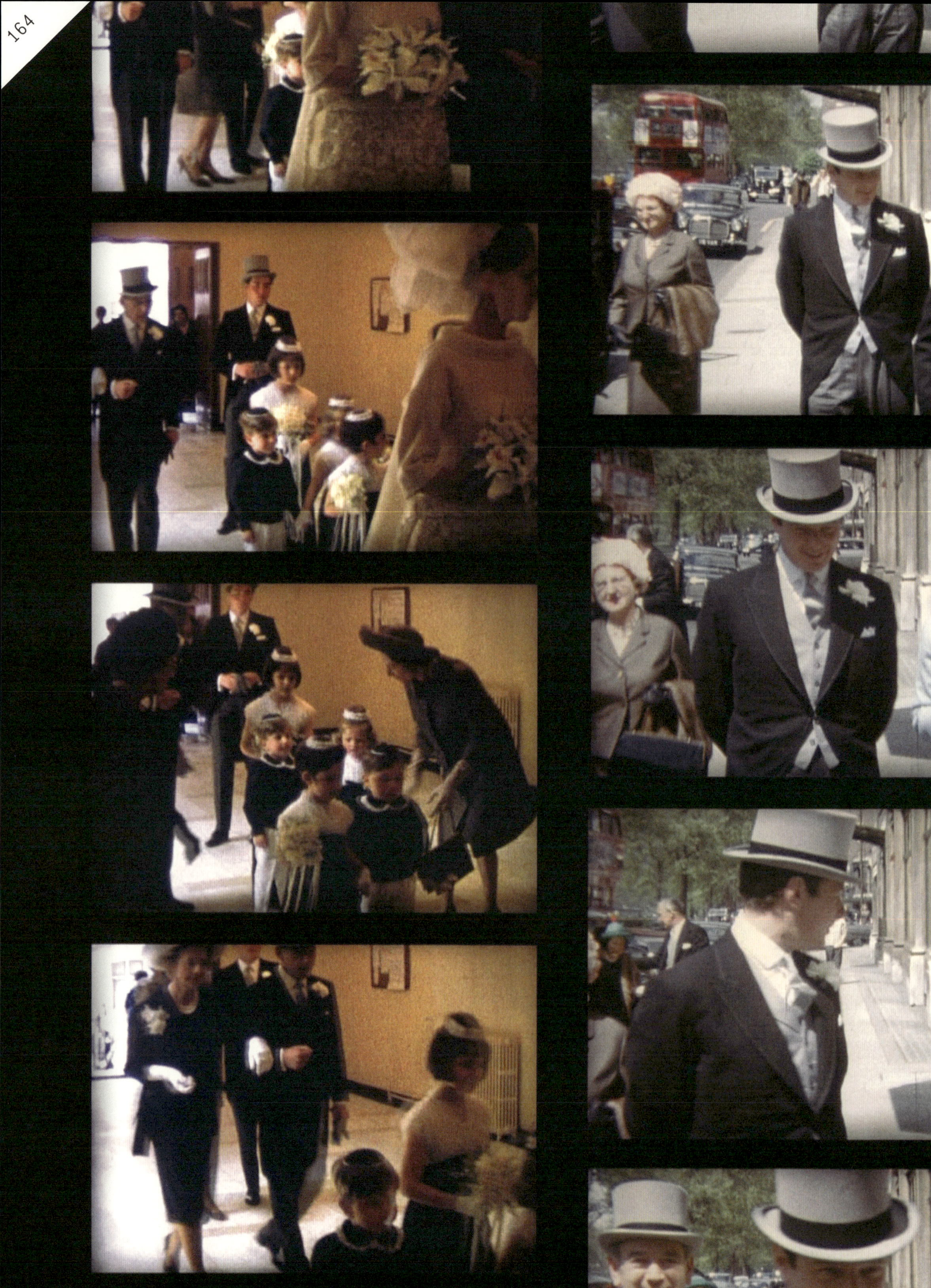

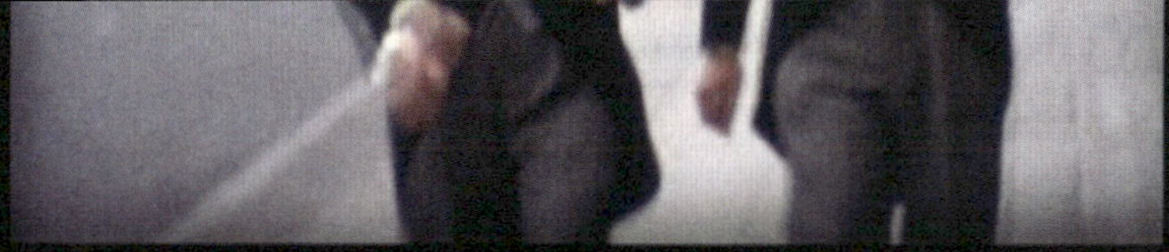

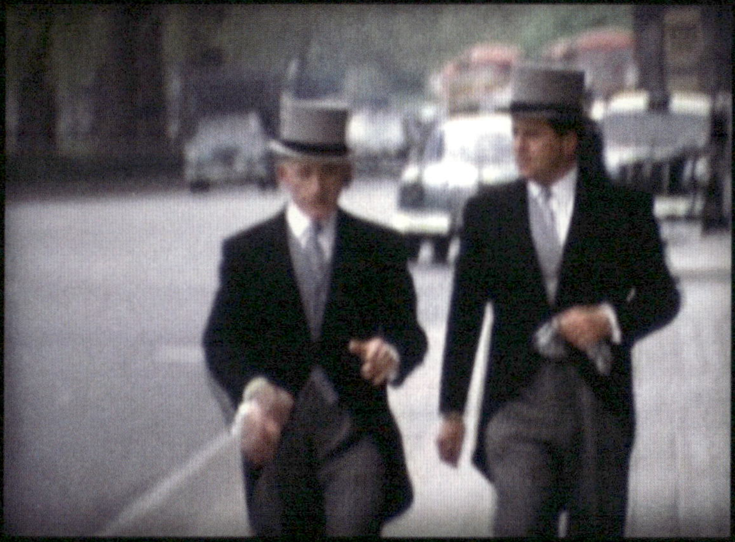

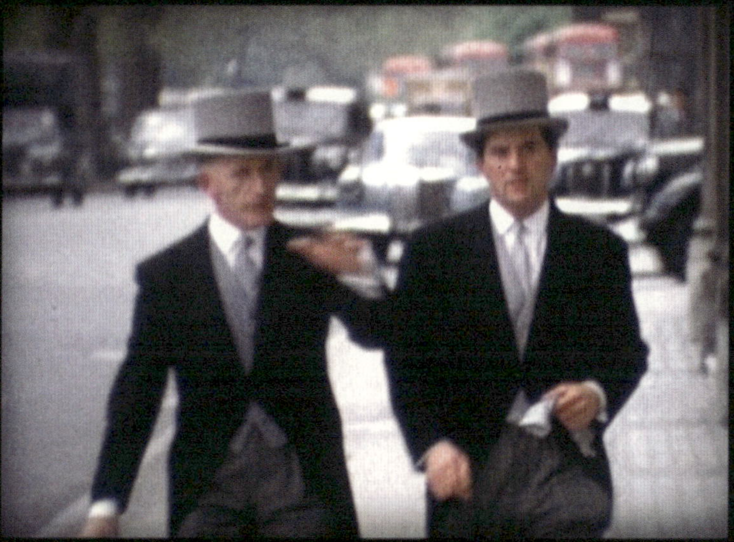

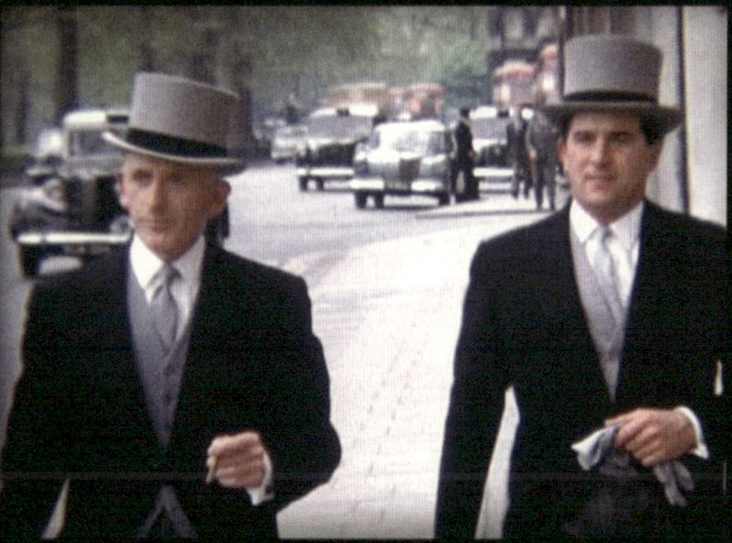

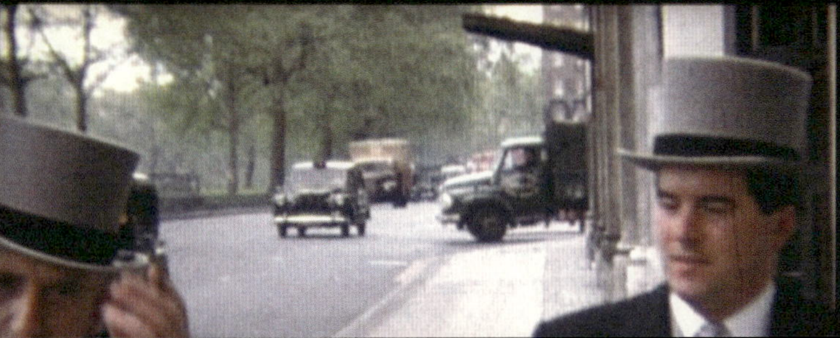

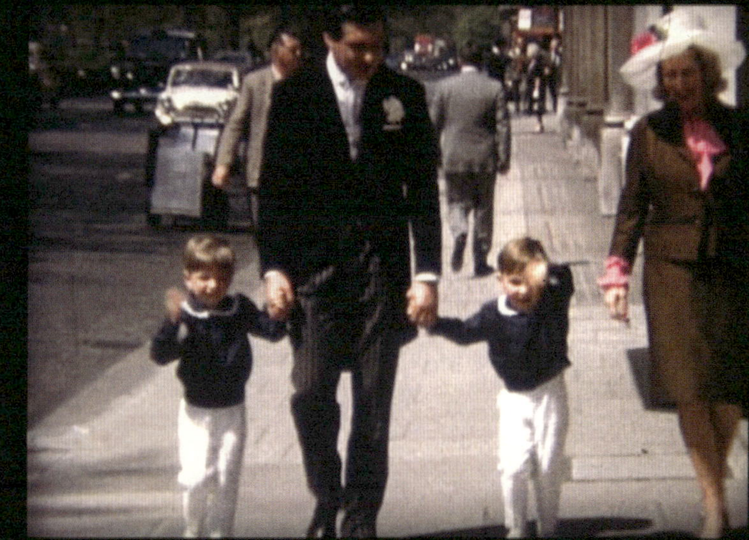

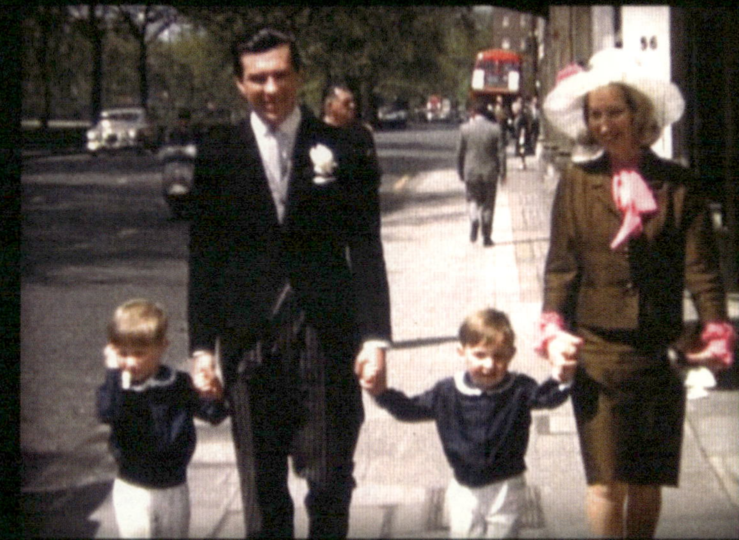

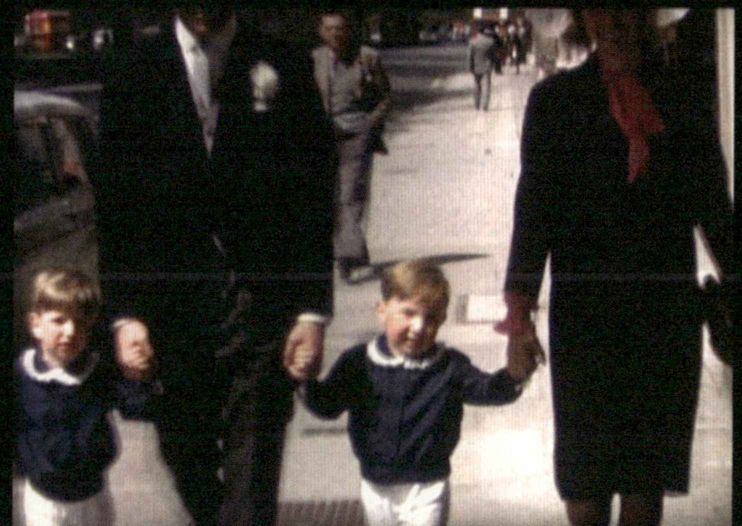

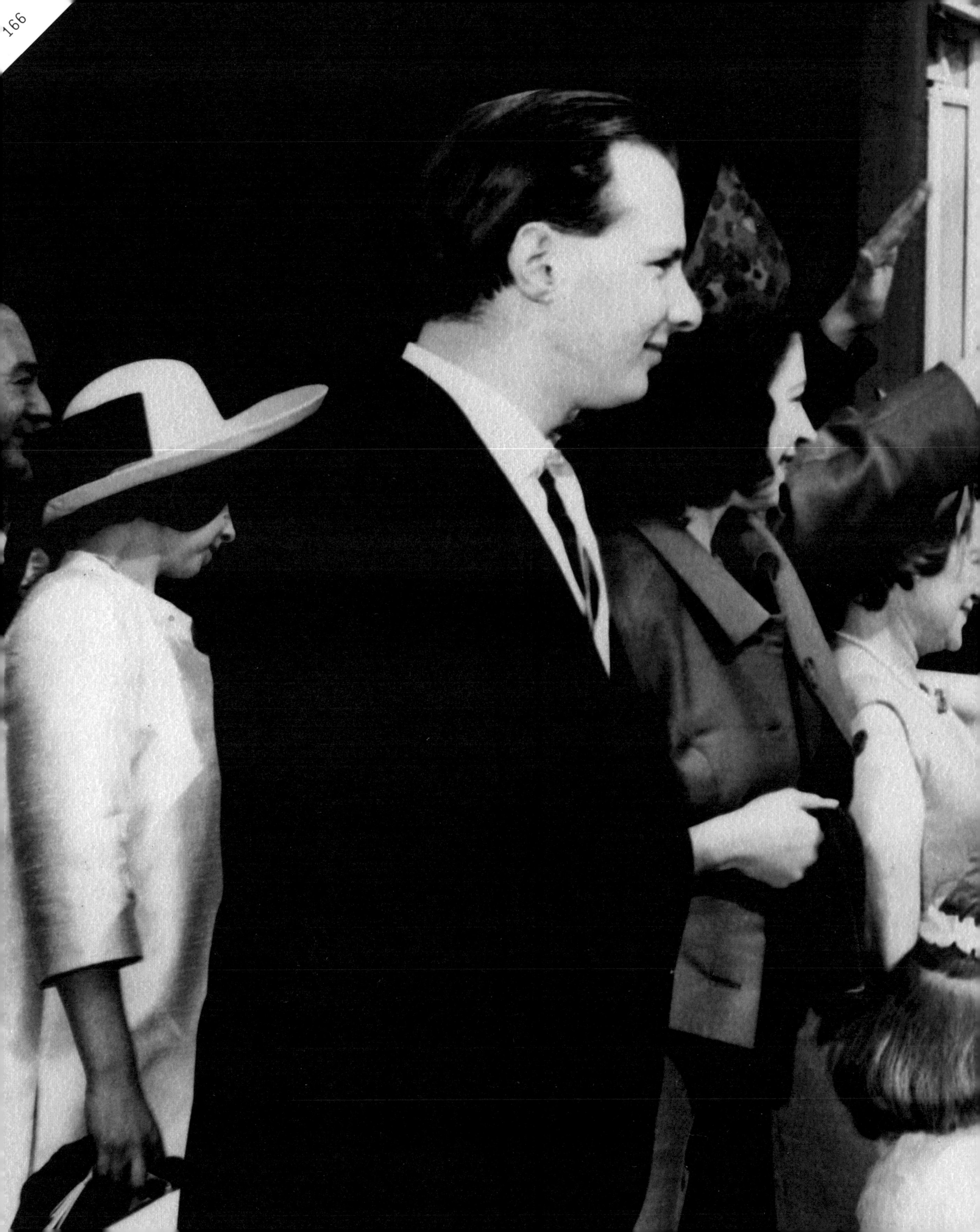

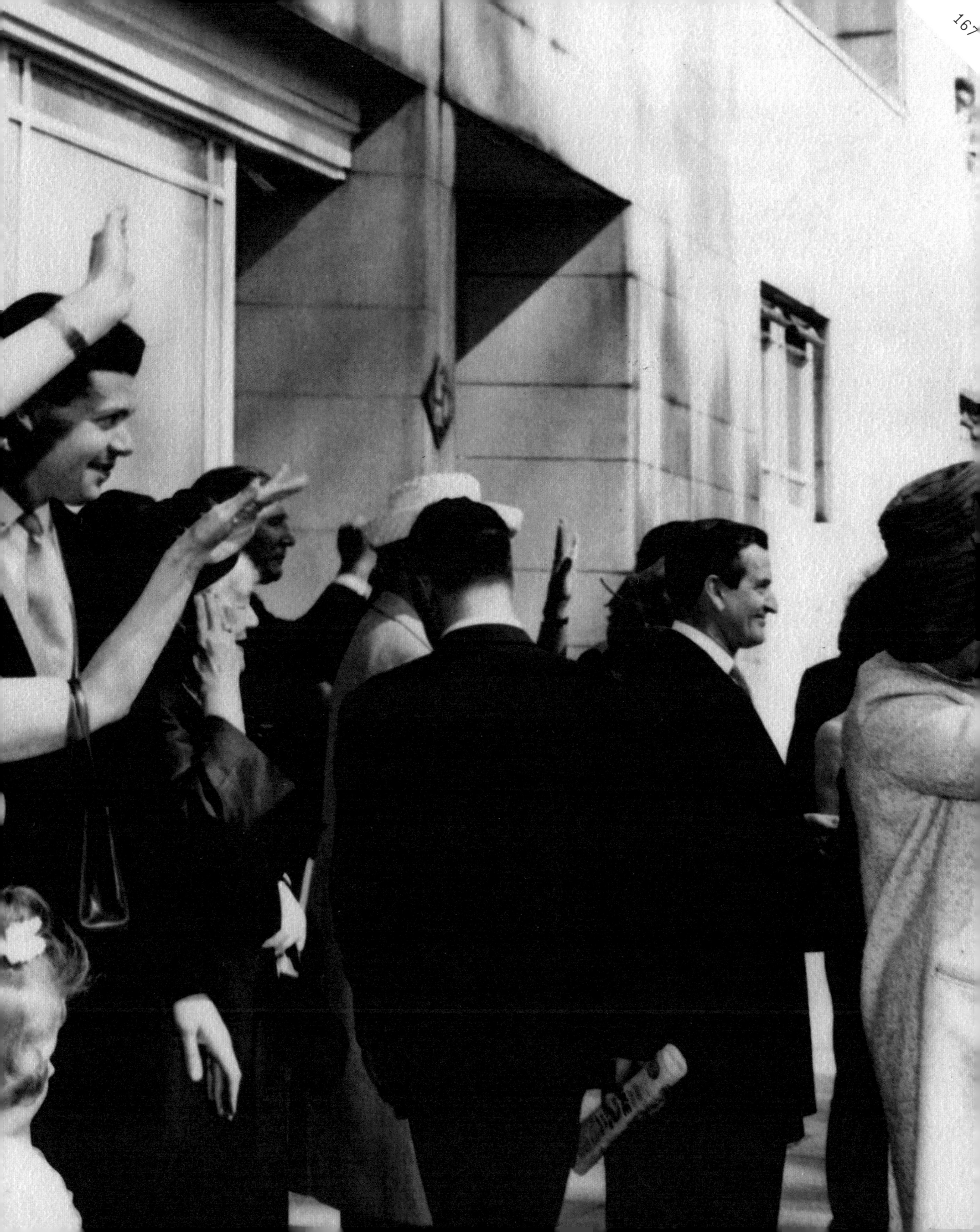

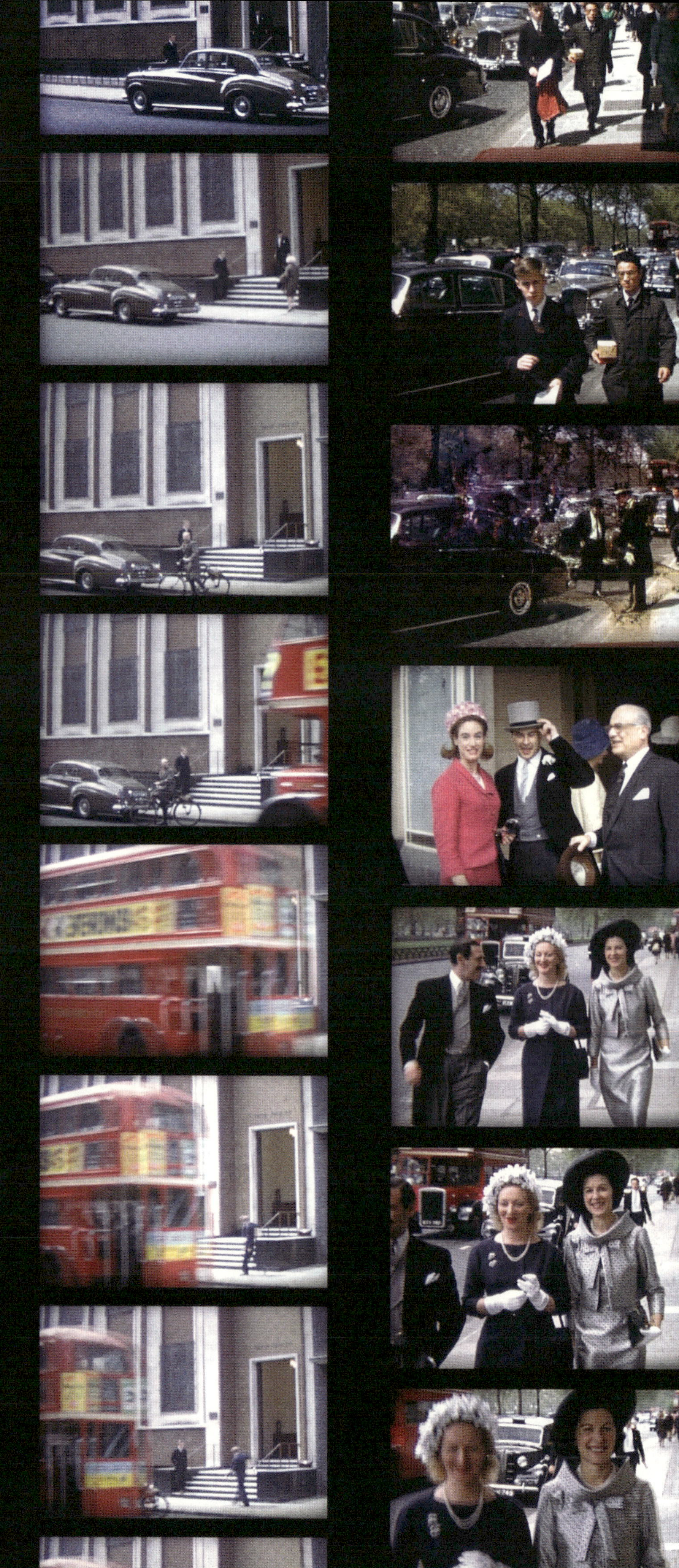

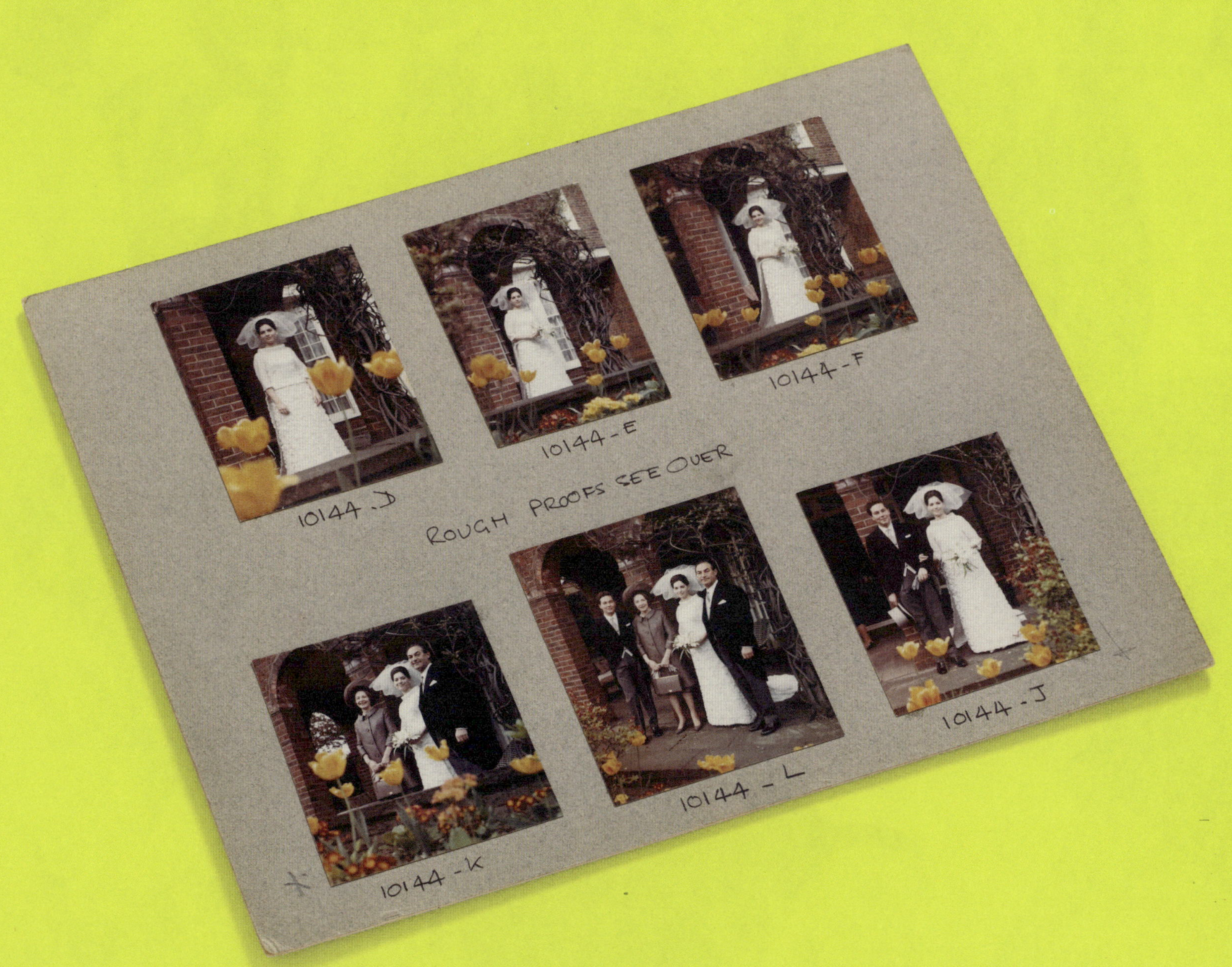
10144 - D
10144 - E
10144 - F
ROUGH PROOFS SEE OVER
10144 - K
10144 - L
10144 - J

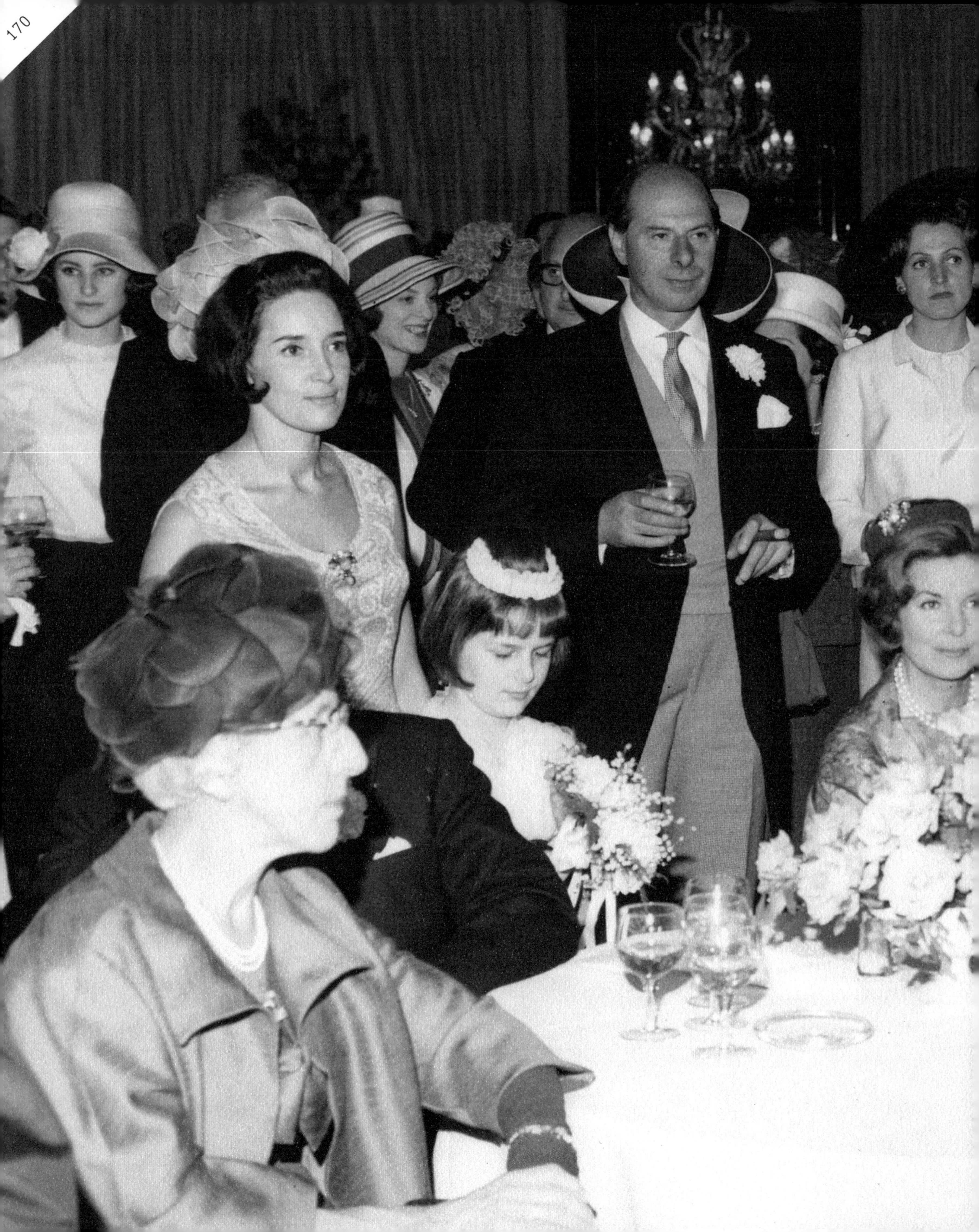

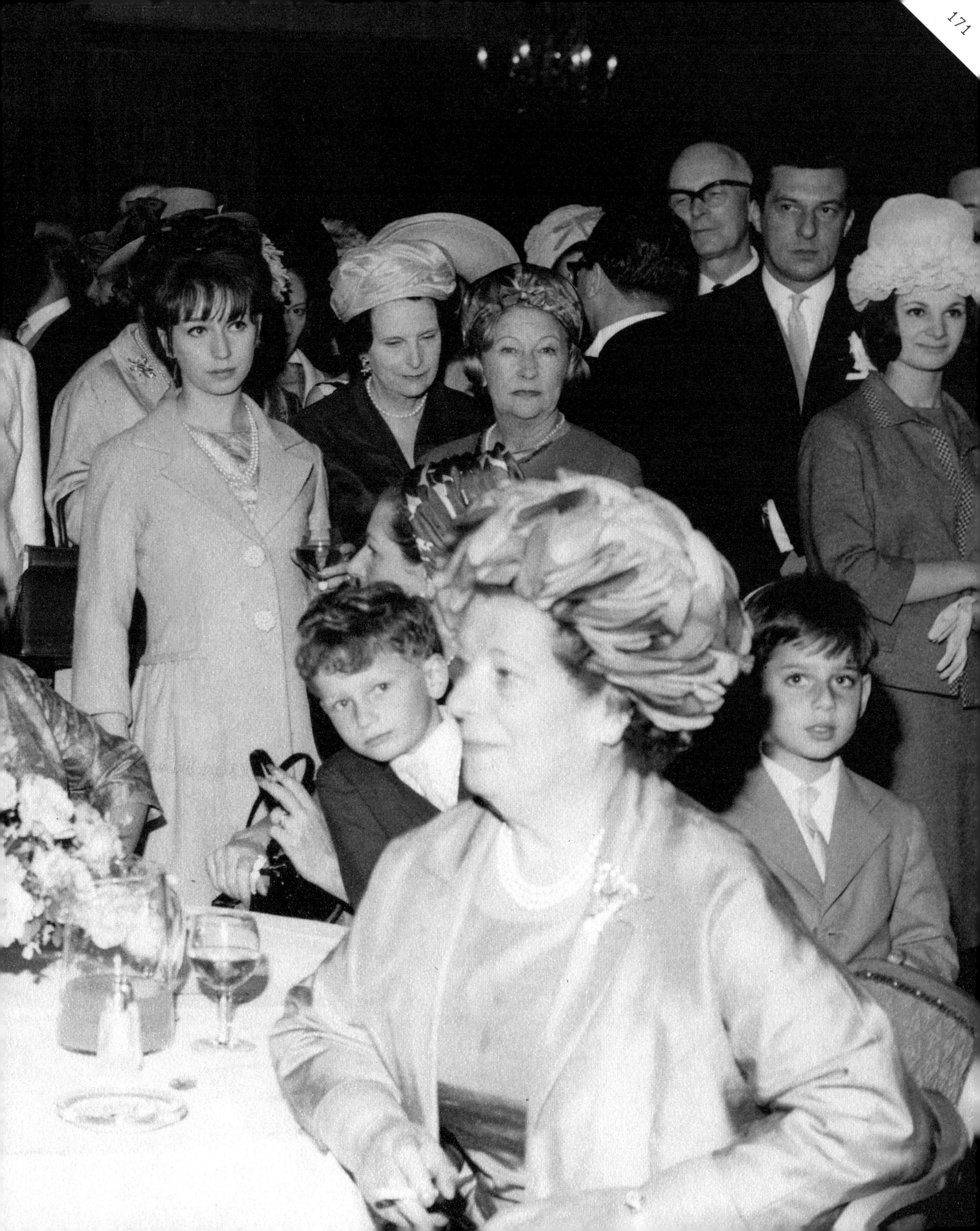

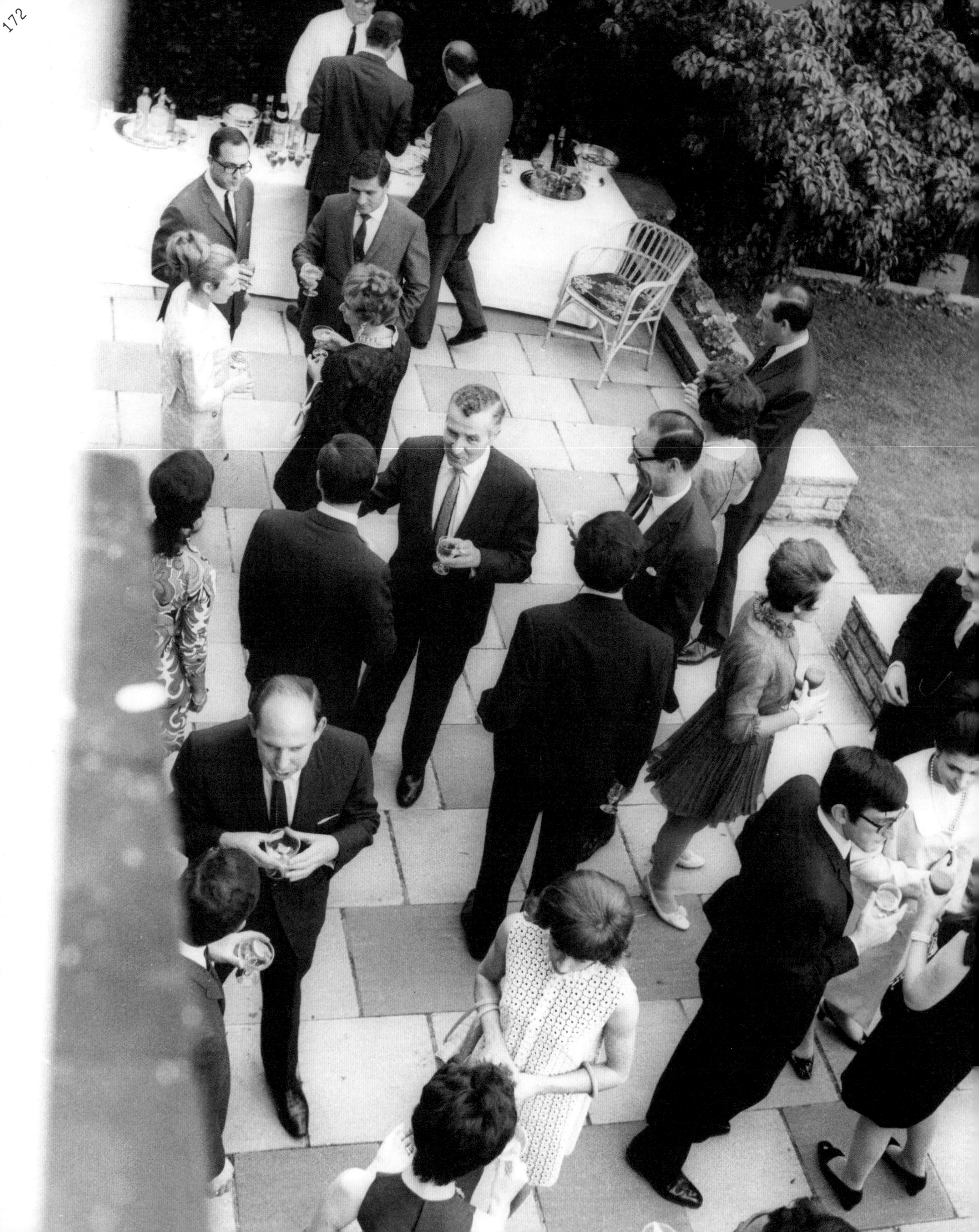

our experience,
n earlier stage.
ce evaporation.
apers while still
er suitable jam-
e covered with

tely it has been
f good lacquer
ds can be kept
d be put in the
ned fruit which
possible change

lk may be kept
eat 4 to 5 years
n tomato sauce
once.

ng bread fresh.
bread-bin (an
sy to keep free
t of a kitchen
a refrigerator if

lf or in a cup-
es and biscuits,
e attractive for
bake and not
aluminium foil.

ping vegetables
where air can
y dirt or debris.
acks that slide
vegetables, but
ot be kept in a

citrus and hard
f the refrigera-
a special plastic
gerator.
der is to use a
pple storage.

s are essentially
ge plate so that
other. Handle
e any mouldy
reme cold. A
an be covered
salad drawer.

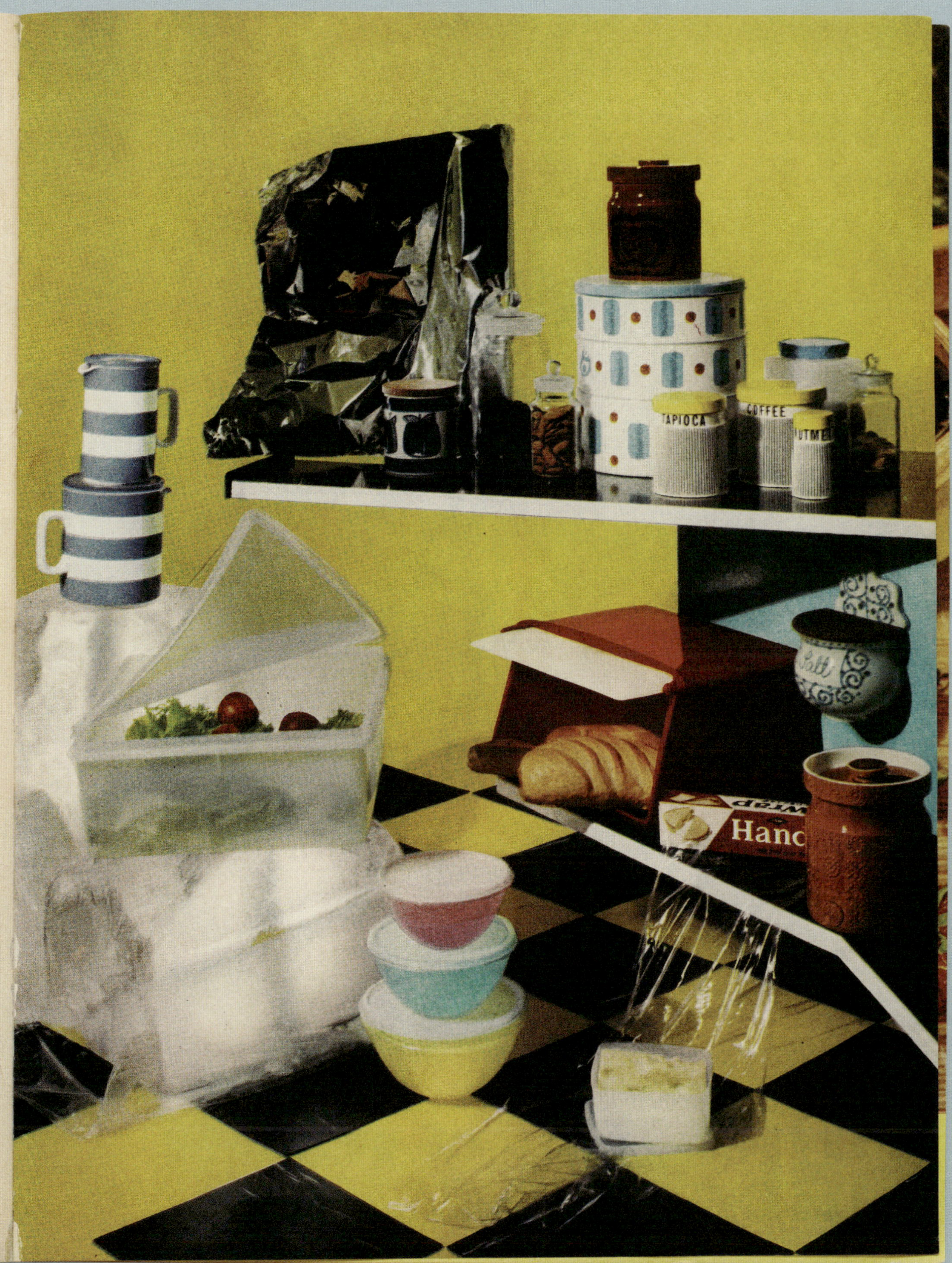

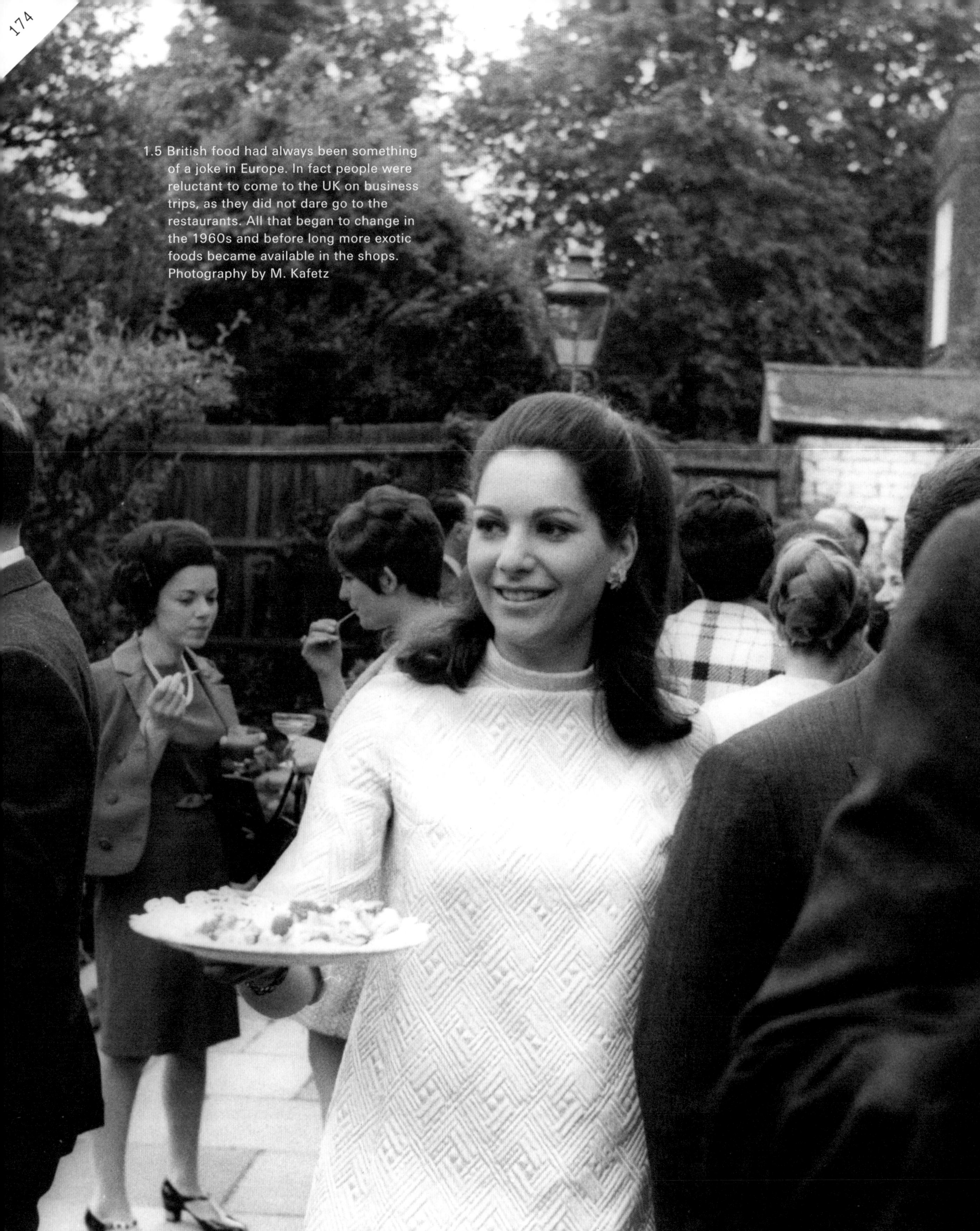

1.5 British food had always been something of a joke in Europe. In fact people were reluctant to come to the UK on business trips, as they did not dare go to the restaurants. All that began to change in the 1960s and before long more exotic foods became available in the shops. Photography by M. Kafetz

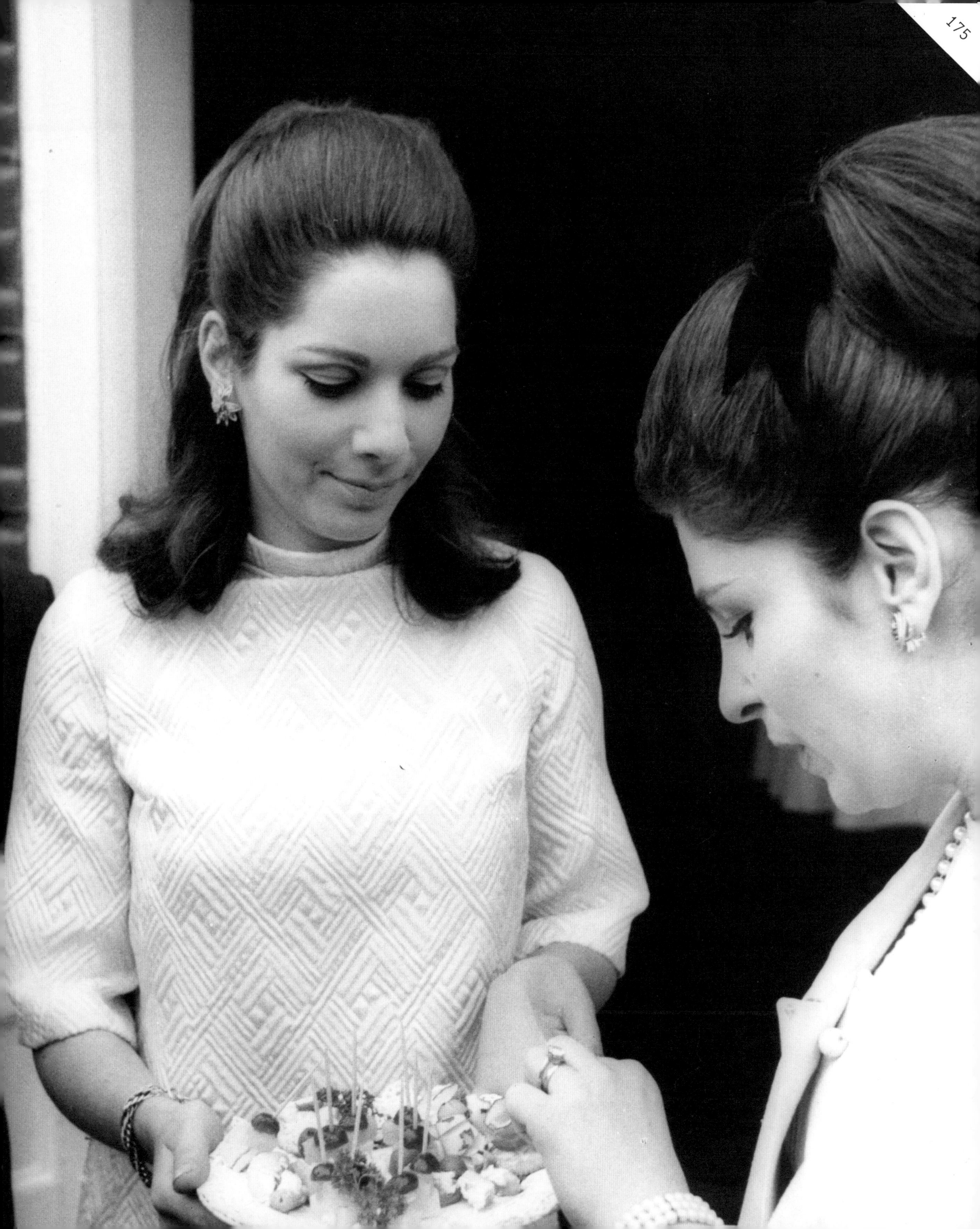

Try this BAR-B-Q for outdoor grills
BY W. A. G. BRADMAN

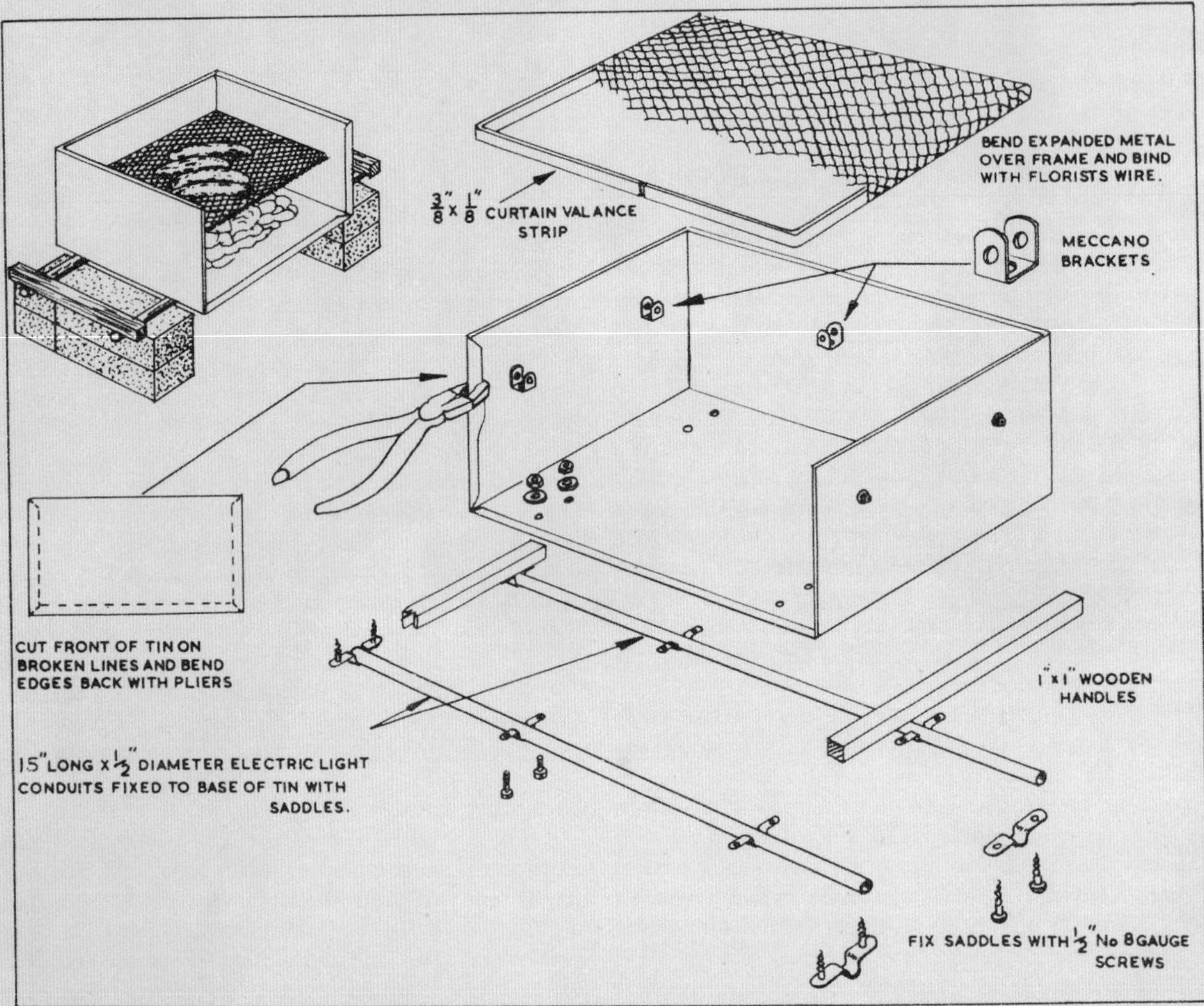

You can cook your own meals outdoors on this miniature barbecue, which is made from a half-size biscuit tin, bought cheaply from any grocer. Using a pair of tinman's snips, cut the front of the tin as shown, bend the "tabs" back and squeeze them flat with pliers to make a smooth edge. Drill small holes in the sides and fix five Meccano brackets with bolts and nuts, about 1½ ins. below the top of the tin to support the grill.

Make the grill frame from a 3 ft. length of aluminium or brass curtain rail valance strip, bending it to shape with pliers. From a builders merchant, buy a piece of expanded metal (like heavy wire mesh) – about 1 in. longer and wider than the grill frame. Bend it over the edges of the frame and bind it in place with florists wire. The completed grill should fit loosely in the Meccano brackets.

You will also need two 15 in. lengths of ½ in. diameter electric light conduit and eight saddles, all bought from an electricians store. Fix the lengths of conduit to the bottom of the tin, using four of the saddles secured with nuts and bolts. Use the other four saddles to fix the wooden lifting handles, cut from 1 in. by 1 in. batten, as shown.

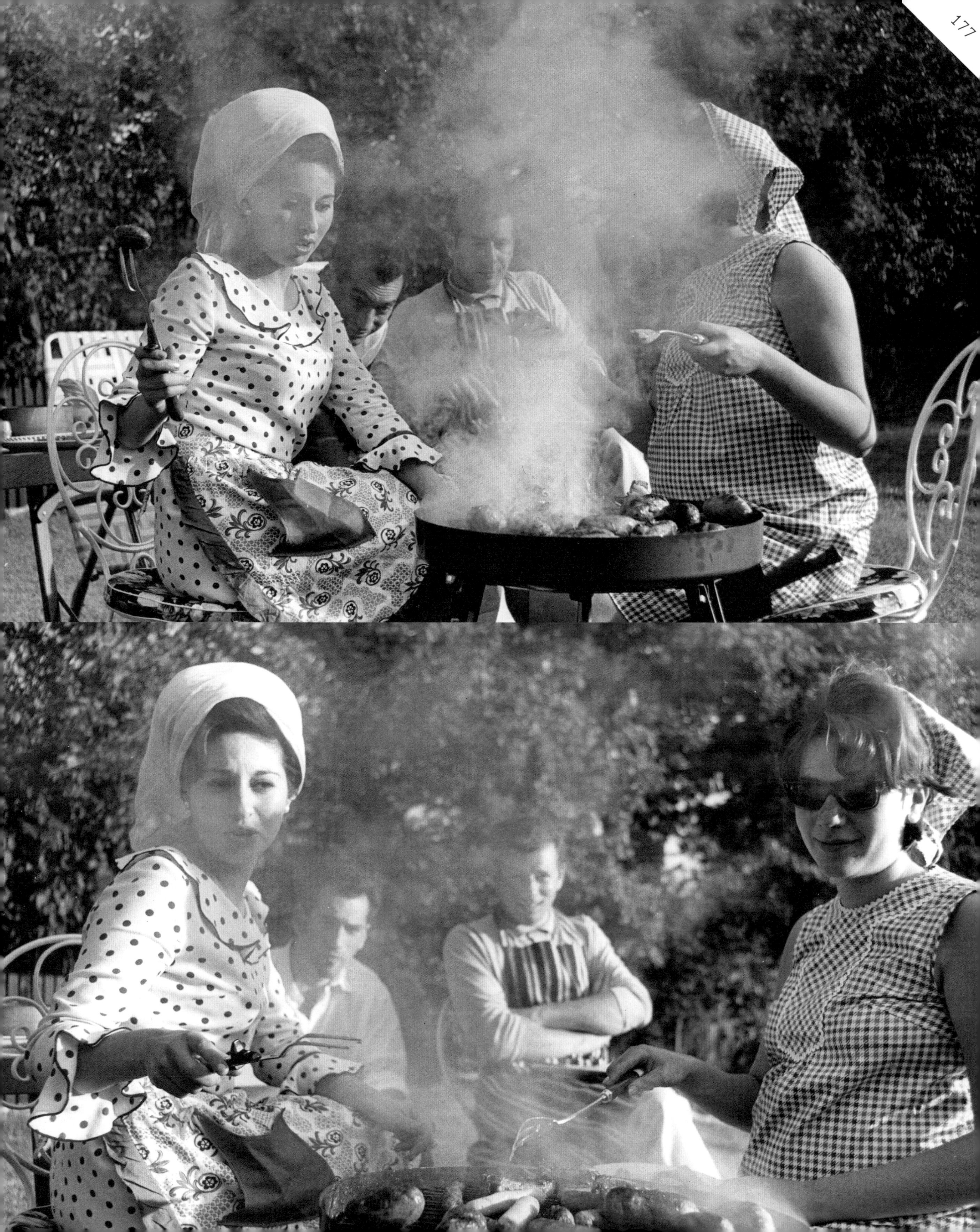

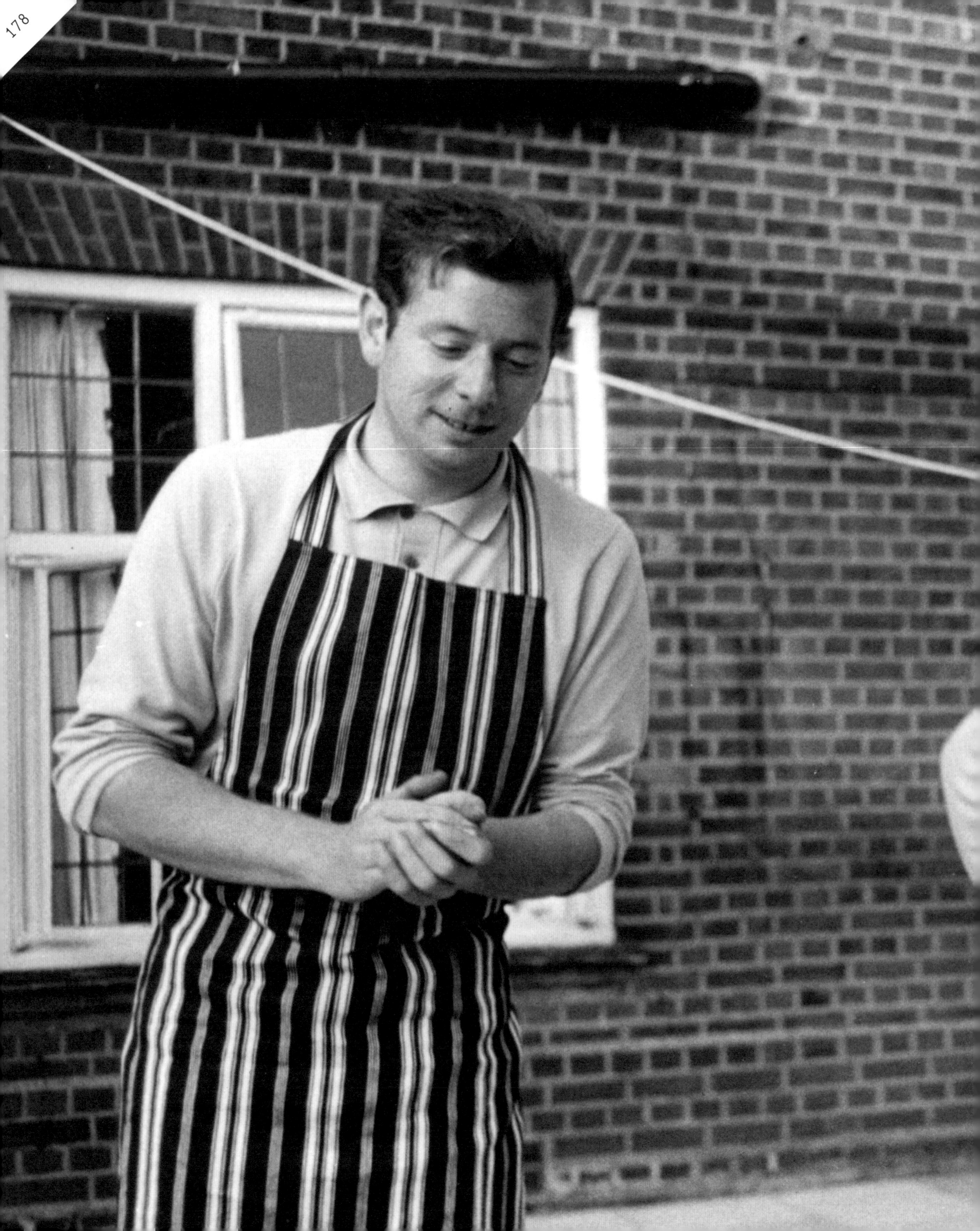

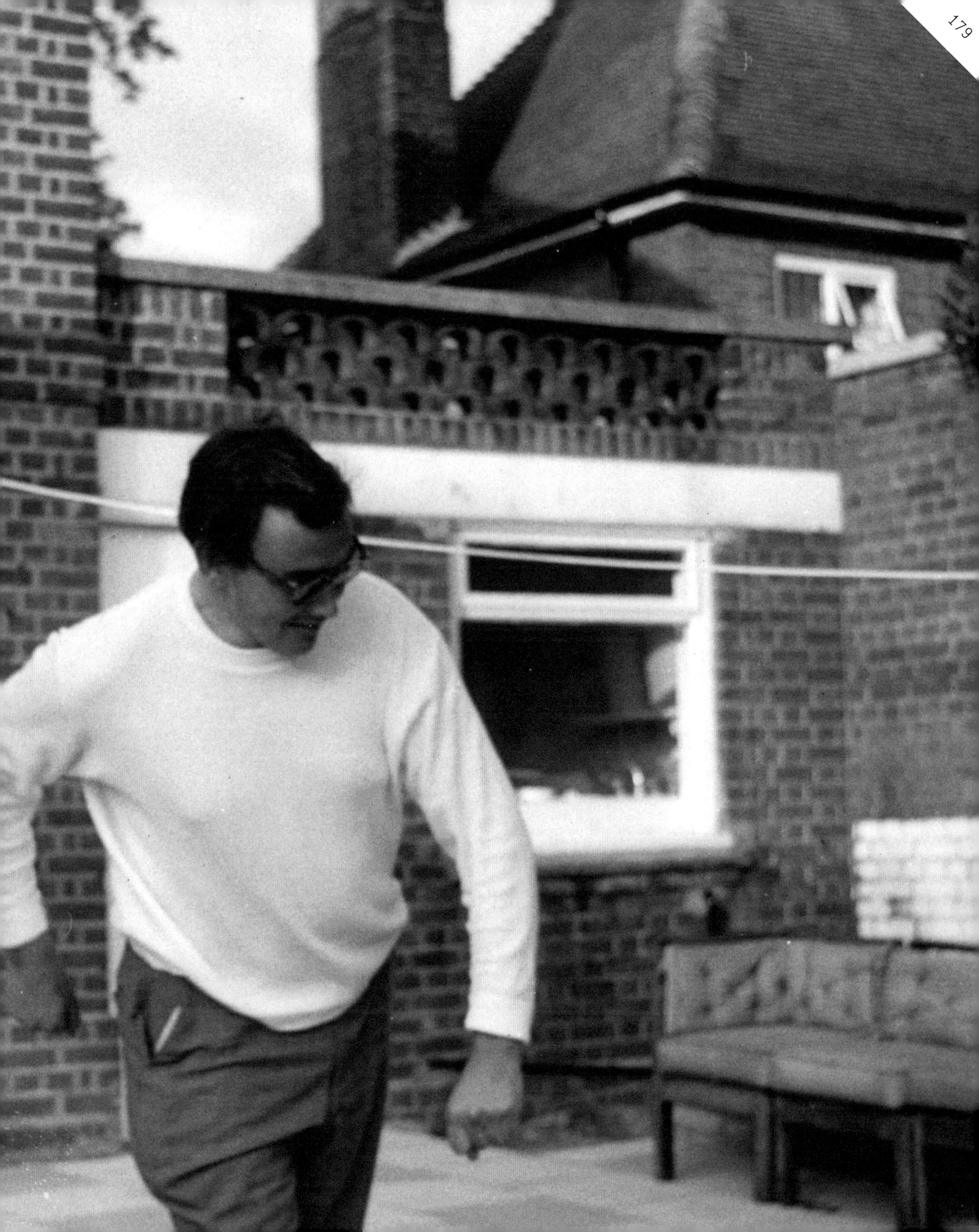

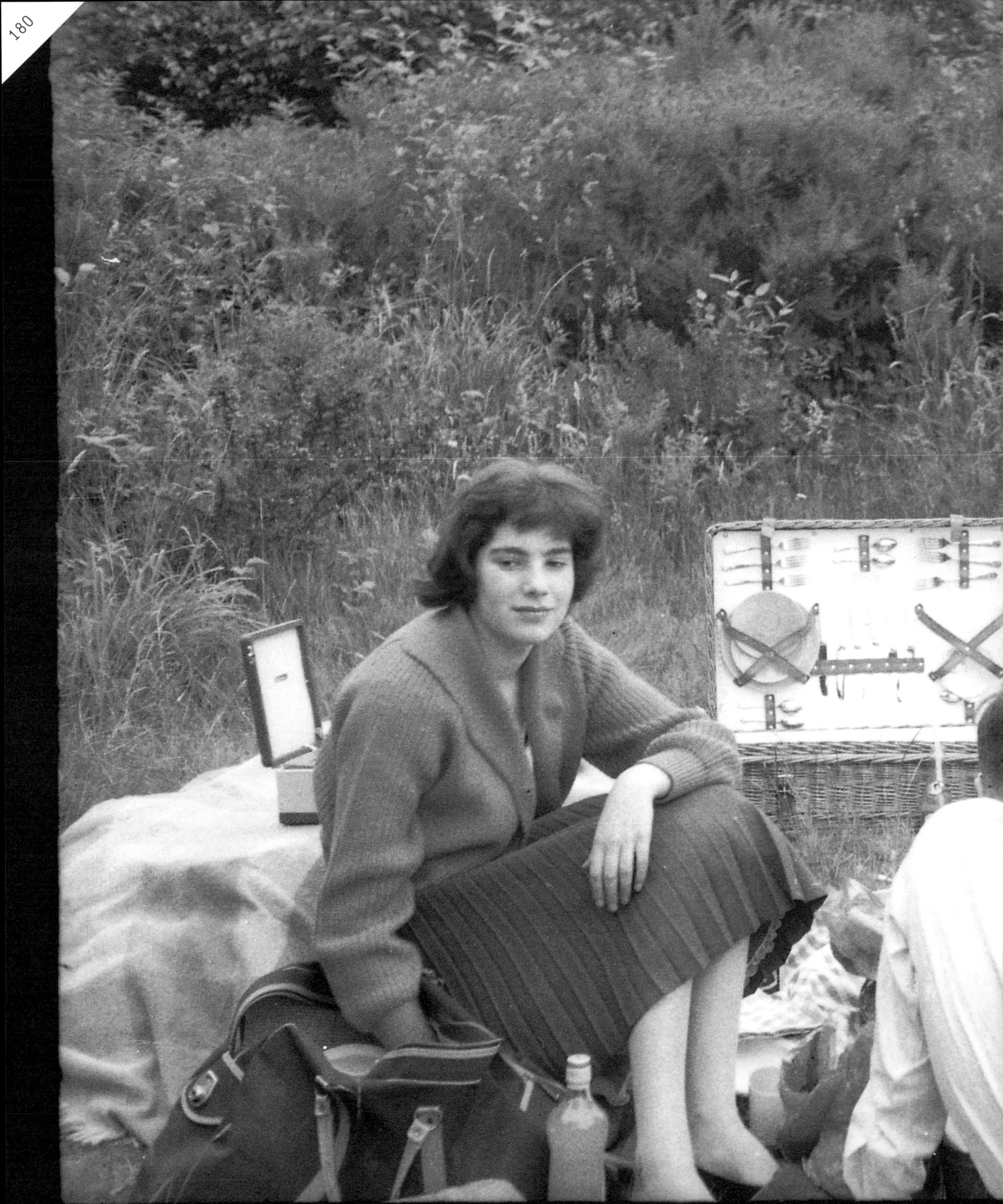

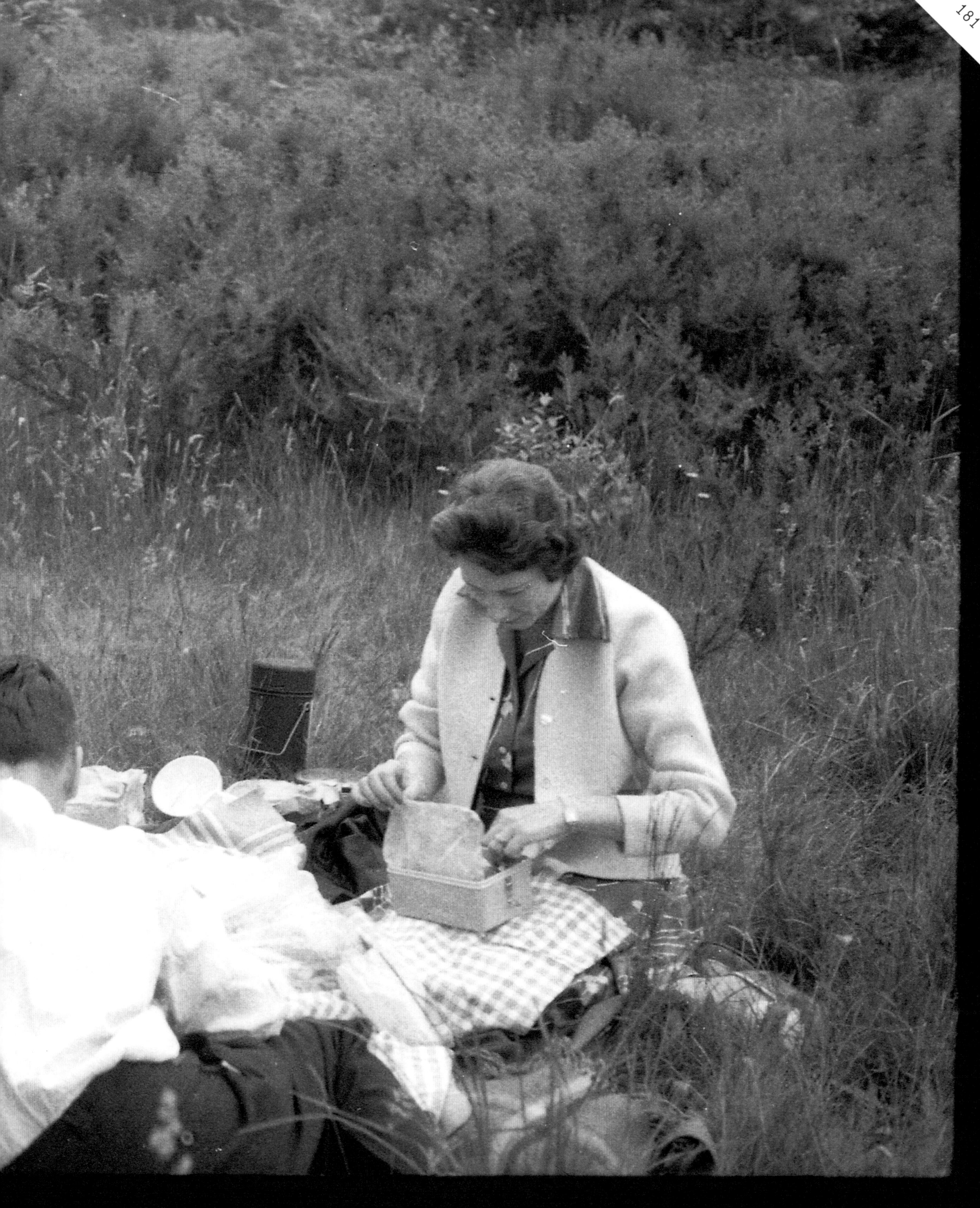

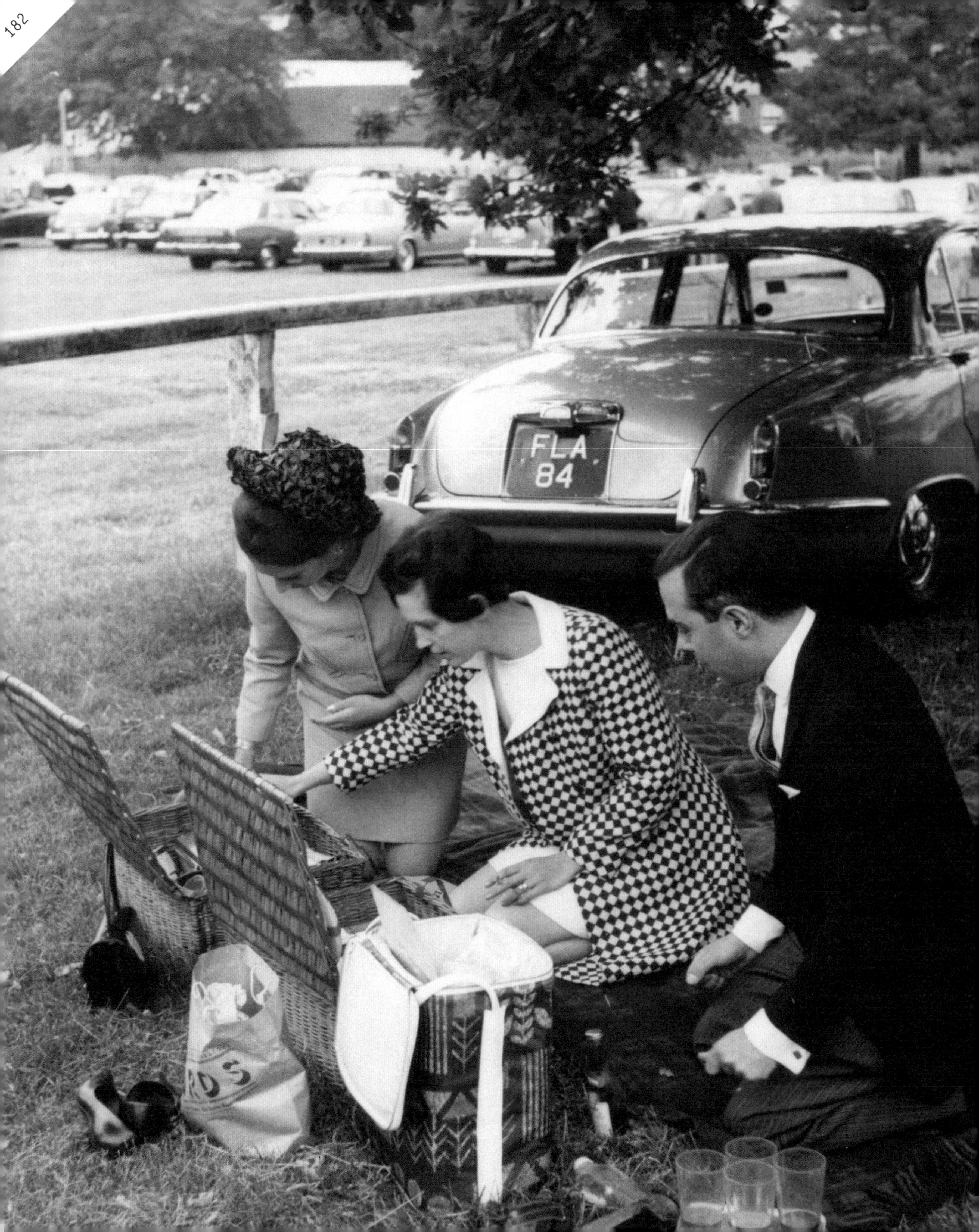

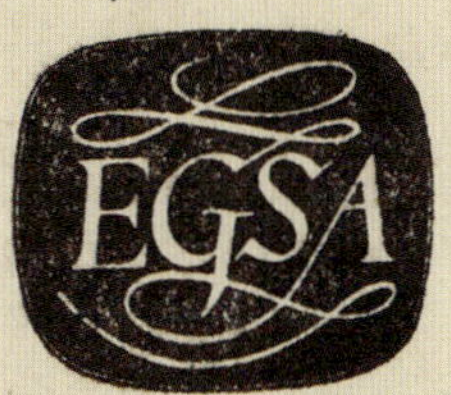

EPSOM
SPRING MEETING
(Under Rules of Racing)

City and Suburban Day

Wednesday, 24th April, 1963

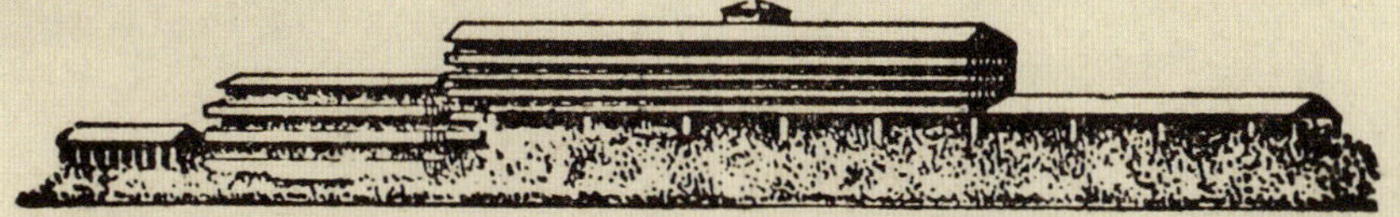

COPYRIGHT—racecards not bearing this signature are spurious

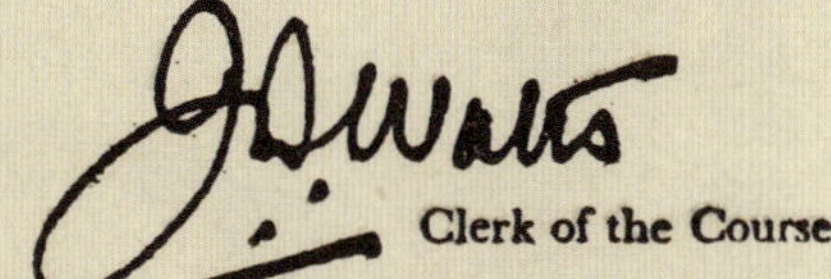

Clerk of the Course

PRICE ONE SHILLING

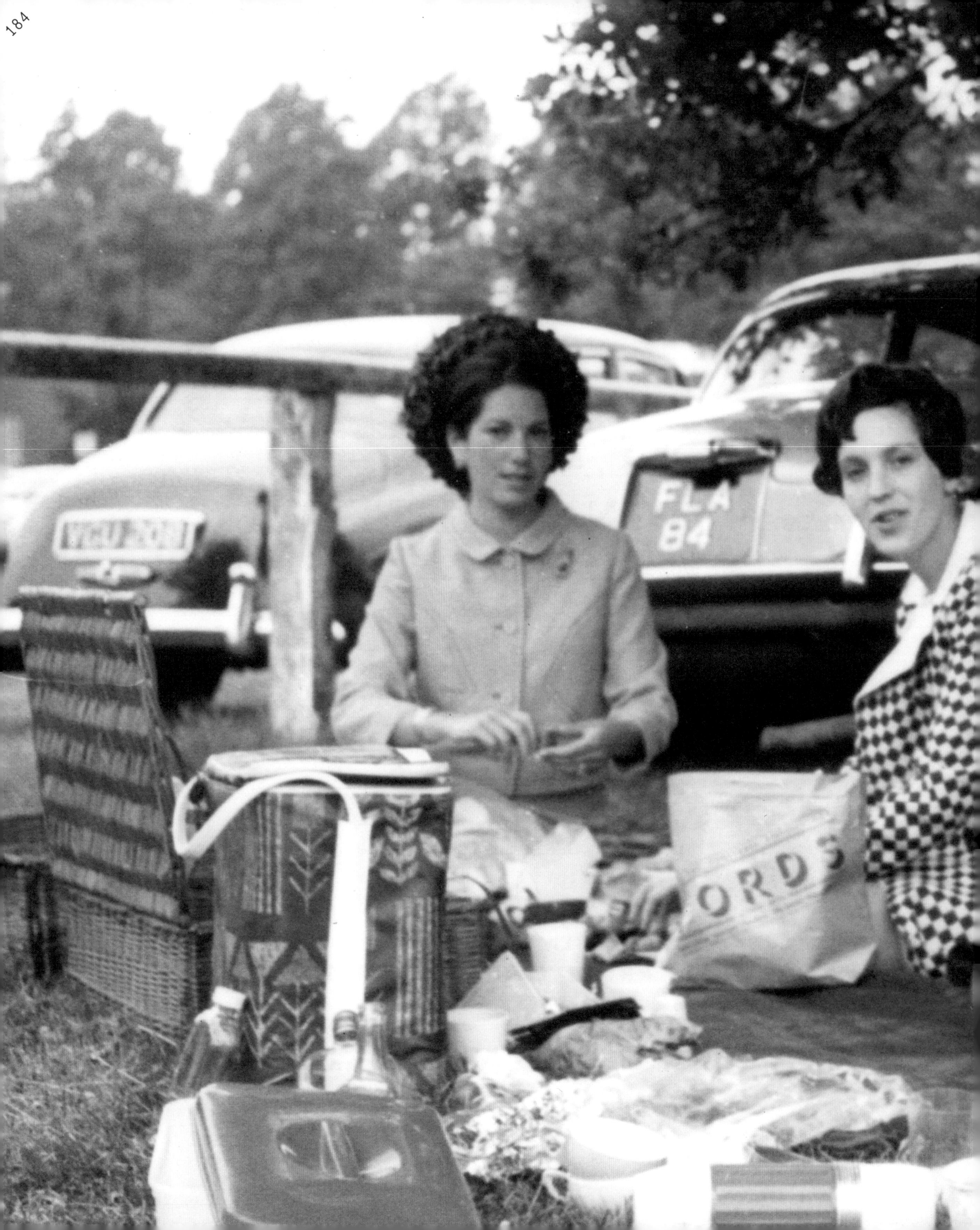

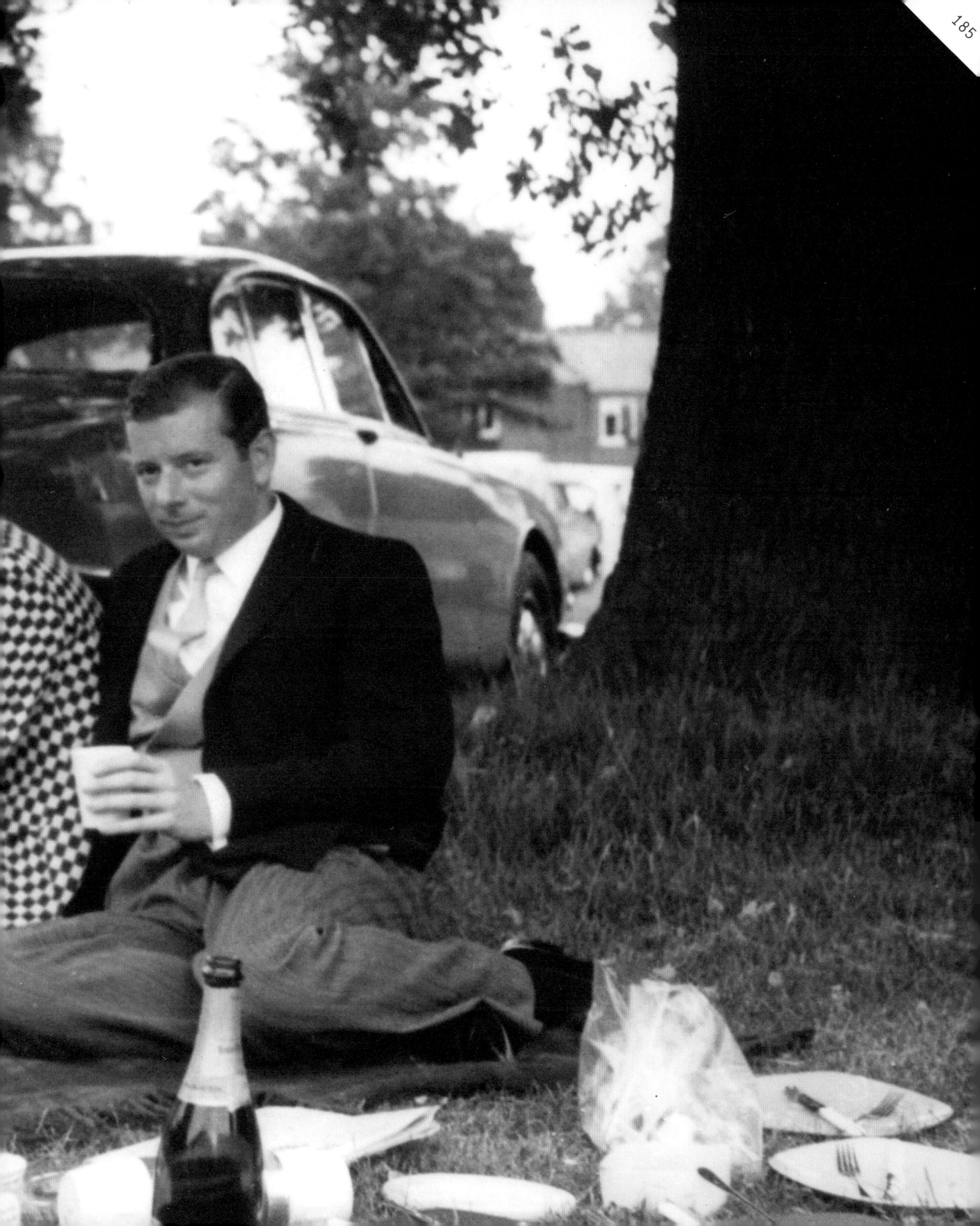

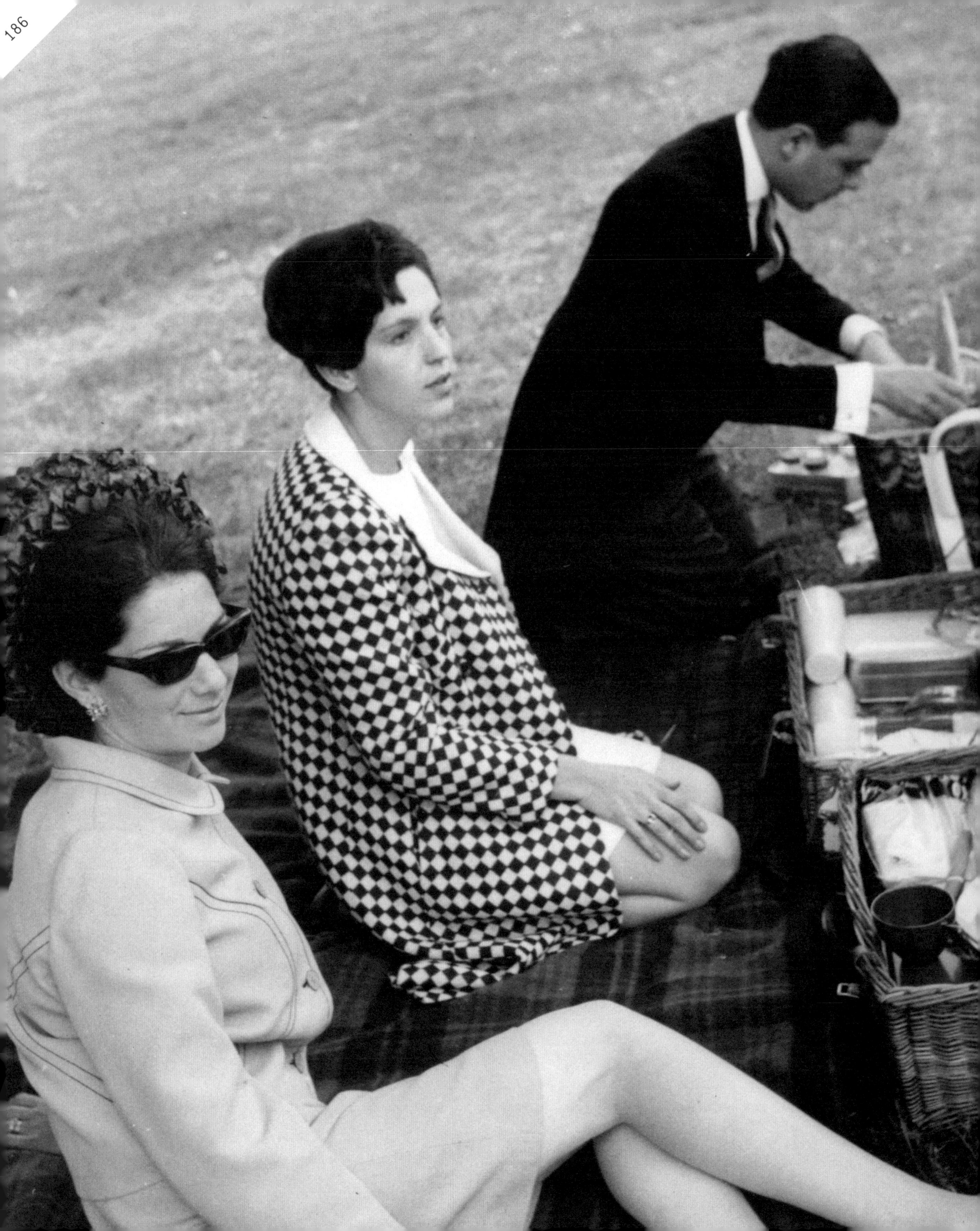

Armlet—YELLOW

THE 112th CITY AND SUBURBAN HANDICAP—Continued

Jockey	Form No.	Name	Age st	lb	Owner	Colours	Trainer
		11 PERSIAN CREST *Ch c Darius—Suncrest*	4 8	7	Mr C. R. Harper	**White, claret** sleeves & cap	*H. Wallington*
		12 TOUROY *B c Tourment—La Castigata*	4 8	4	Mr A. Kennedy	**Black, red & yellow** crossbelts & qrtd cap	*W. Nightingall*
		13 TAHIRI *B f Persian Gulf—Dickneos*	4 8	4	Sir Harold Wernher	**Green & yellow** (halved), slvs & cap reversed	*J. Gosden*
	20	**14 KALIMNOS** *B c Dionisia—Wild Girl*	4 8	4	Mr E. R. More O'Ferrall	**Emerald green, gold** braid, stars & tassel on cap	*R. Smyth*
	100	**15 MONAWIN** *B m Hyperbole—Whinmoor*	8 7	13	Mr R. E. Mason	**Royal blue & red** (qrtd), **red cap, blue** spots	*Owner*
		16 KING CHARMING *B h King of the Tudors—Windsor Charm*	5 7	12	Mr J. Kennedy	**Sea green, old gold** sash	*E. Cousins*
		17 APRIL 26th *B c Amber X—Dehesa*	4 7	9	Mr W. E. King	**White, scarlet** slvs & cap	*H. Geering*
	00	**18 SABLE SKINFLINT** *B h Arctic Star—Juanita*	5 7	6	Mrs S. Raber	**Violet, pink 'V'** & sleeves	*A. Smyth*

* Corrected under Rule 83.

SEVENTEEN DECLARED RUNNERS

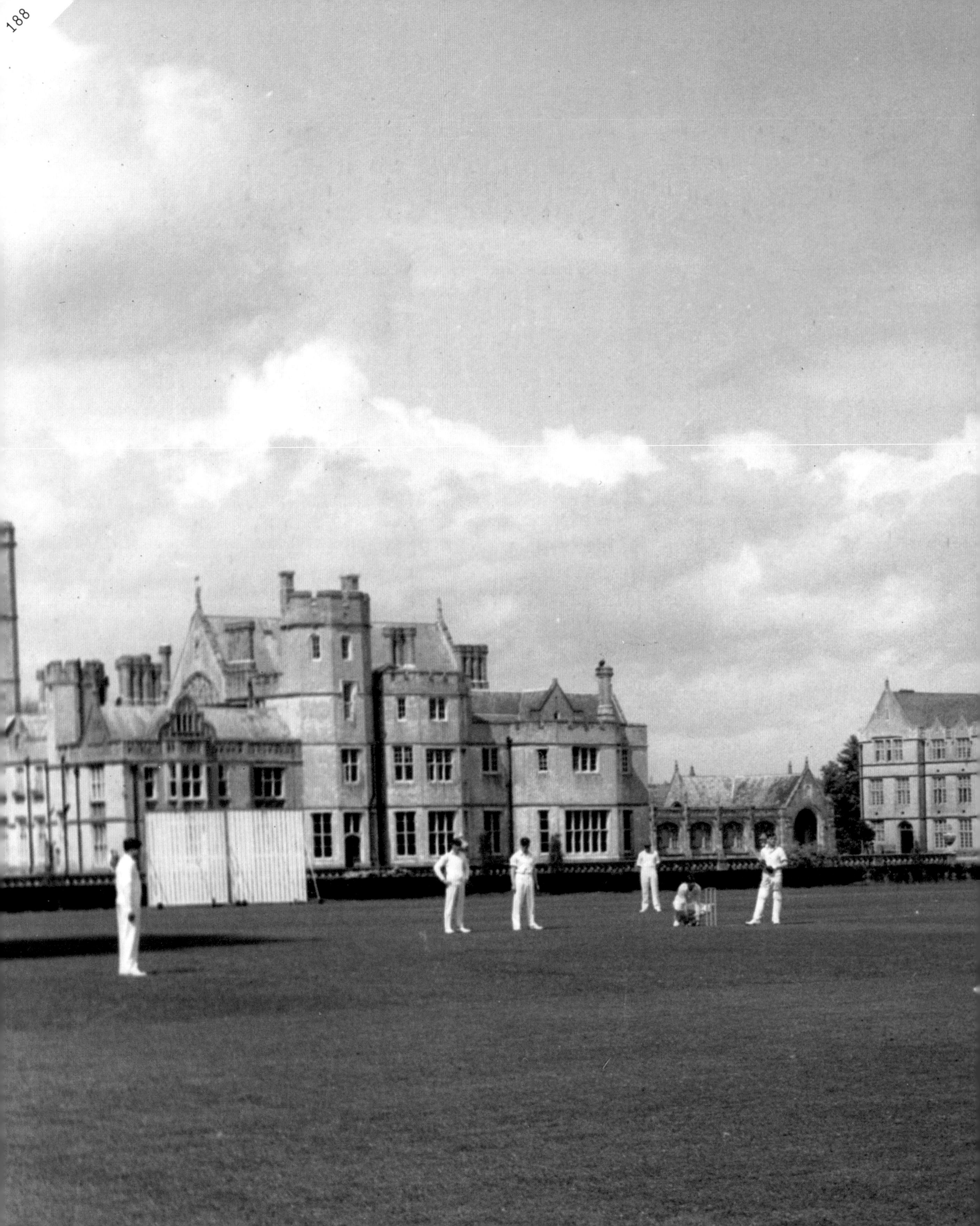

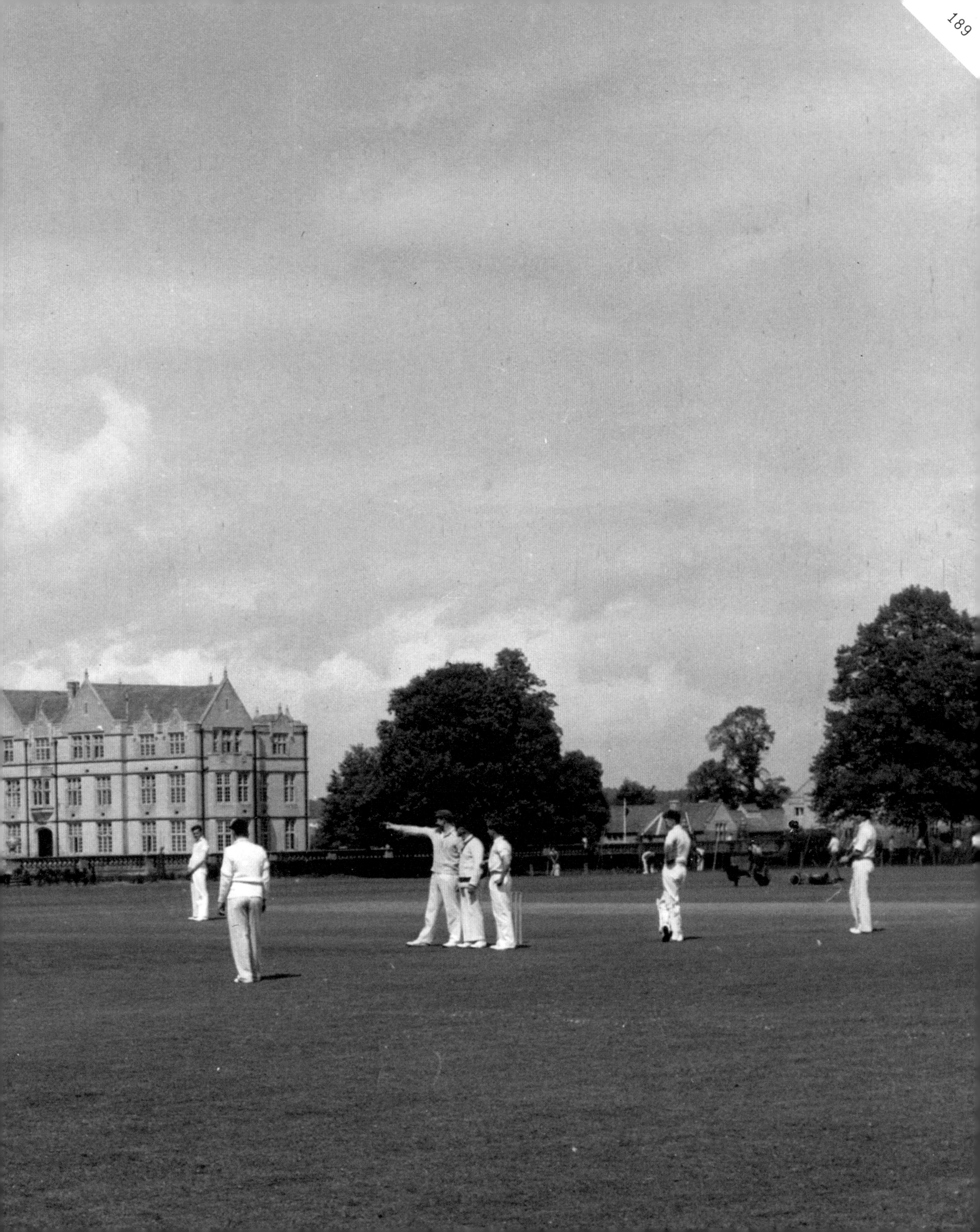

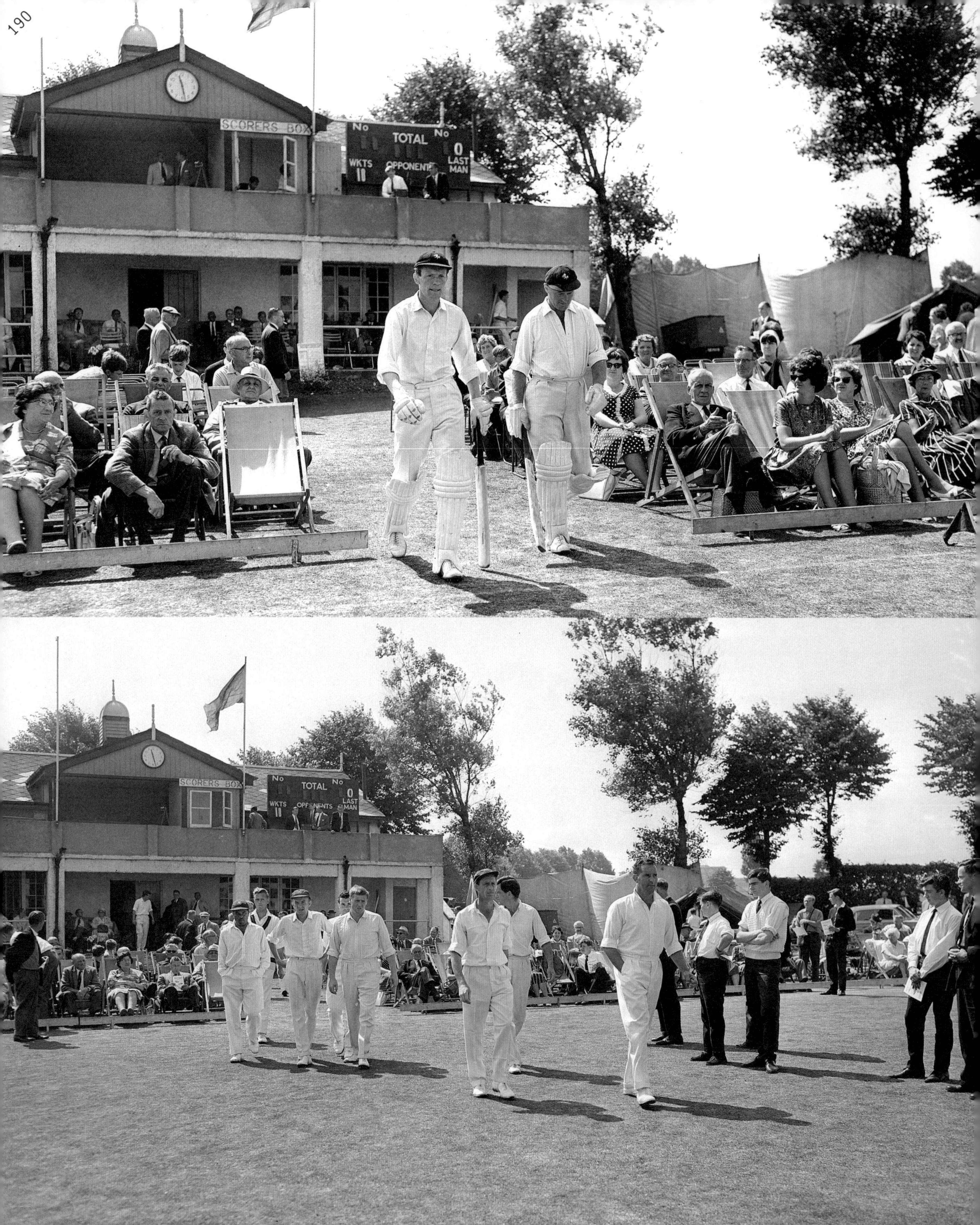

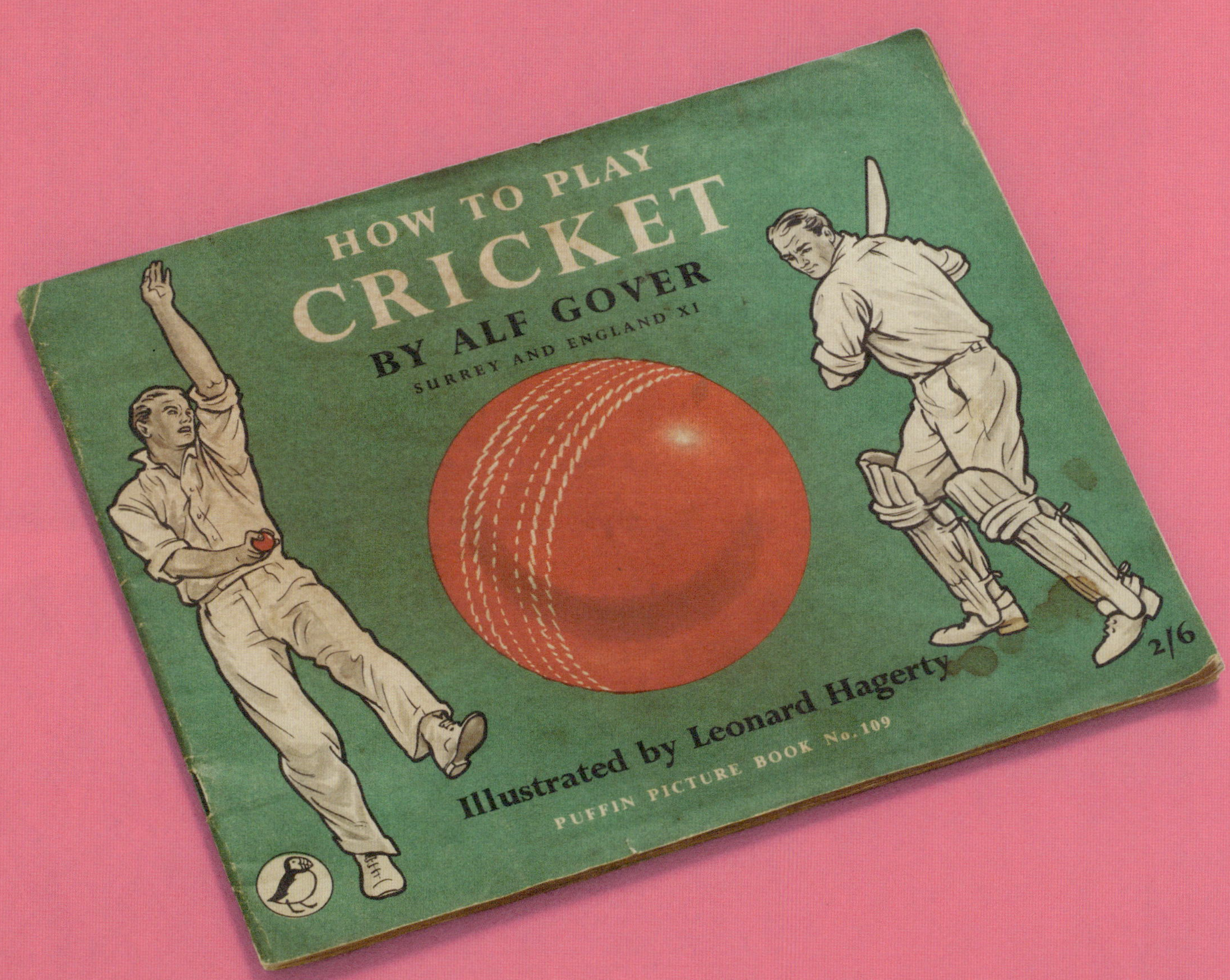

HOW TO PLAY
CRICKET
BY ALF GOVER
SURREY AND ENGLAND XI
Illustrated by Leonard Hagerty
PUFFIN PICTURE BOOK No. 109
2/6

The new Base Line, I

The Big Game thrives on the player's ability to get to the net quickly. Jack Kramer suggests a new base line three feet further back. On a deeper court, the serve would be weakened substantially, and the net game would be harder to play. Were a man to serve and then race forward to the net (above), the increased length of the court would enable the receiver to get a lob or a passing shot by him (two longest white lines). Then, too, should a man try to play it safe and stay in the backcourt, his opponent could fox him by putting a short drop shot over the net (short white line) into the forecourt. Such a ploy would have new effectiveness, since one would have to come further in from the backcourt to retrieve the ball. "As the court is laid out now," Kramer says, "the server automatically rushes in to take up a position at the net. But if the base line were moved back a little, he'd have to earn his way in"

8

The Single Serve

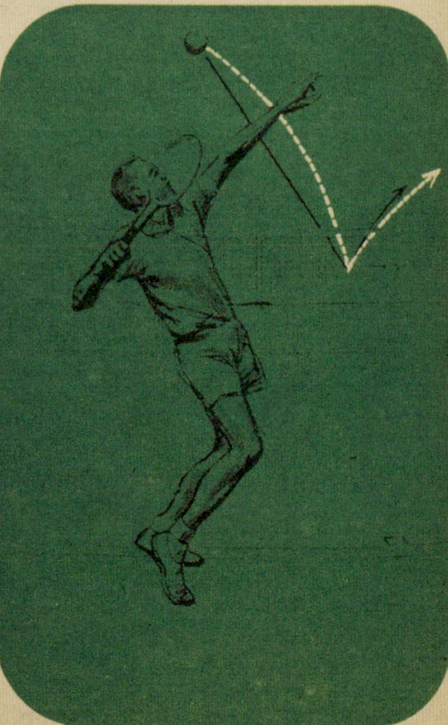

Chuck McKinley argues for restraining the Big Serve without adding a new base line. "I think you can get the same results by limiting the game to one serve. If a man has two chances, he'll slam the first (black line) and then use a slower twist for the second (dotted white line)." The character of the single serve would be closer to the present second serve: higher arch, slower speed with a better chance for a return and subsequent rally

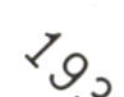
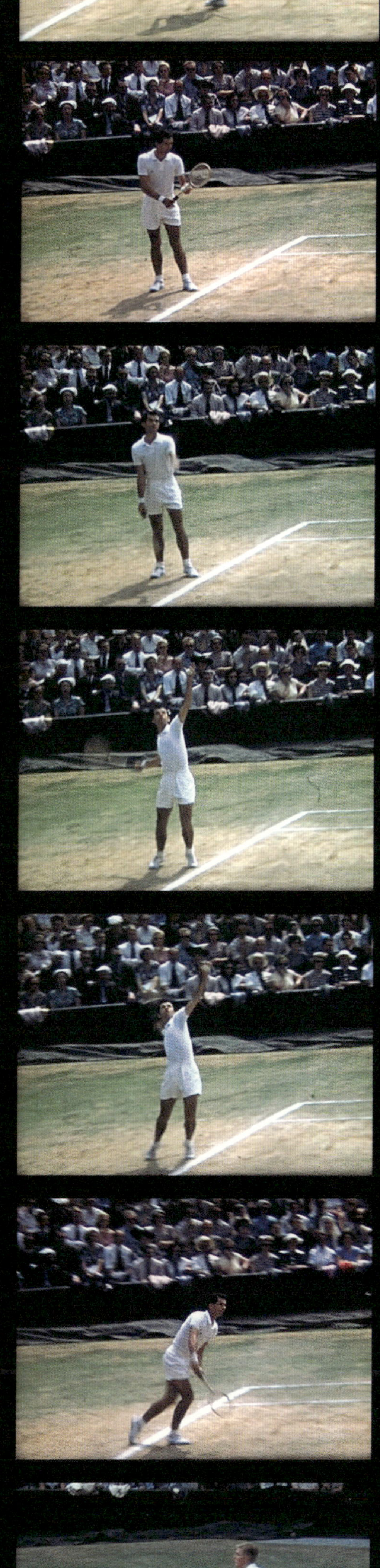
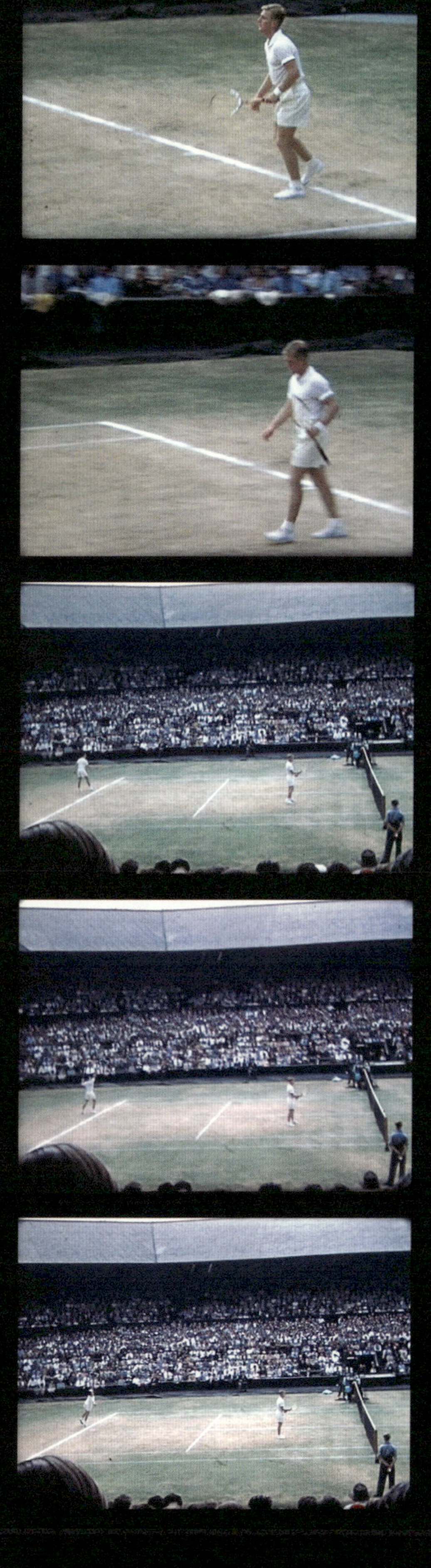
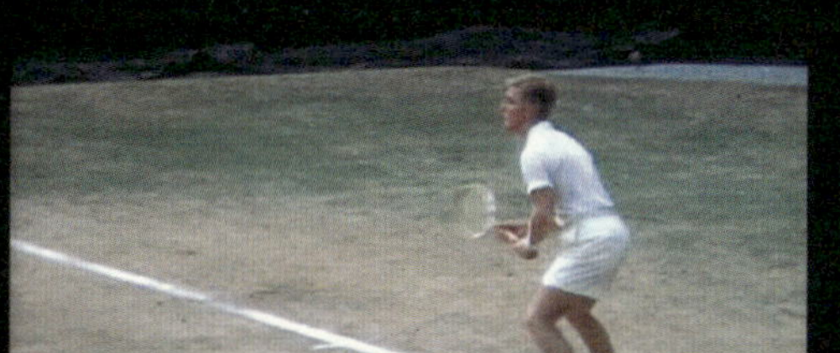

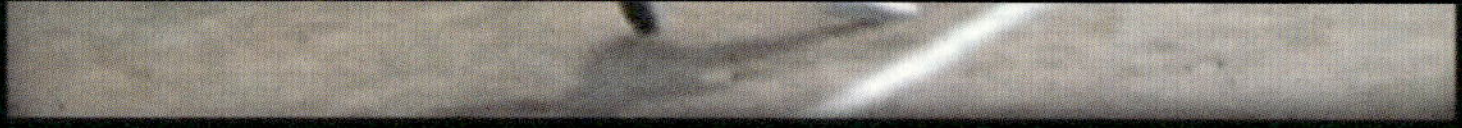

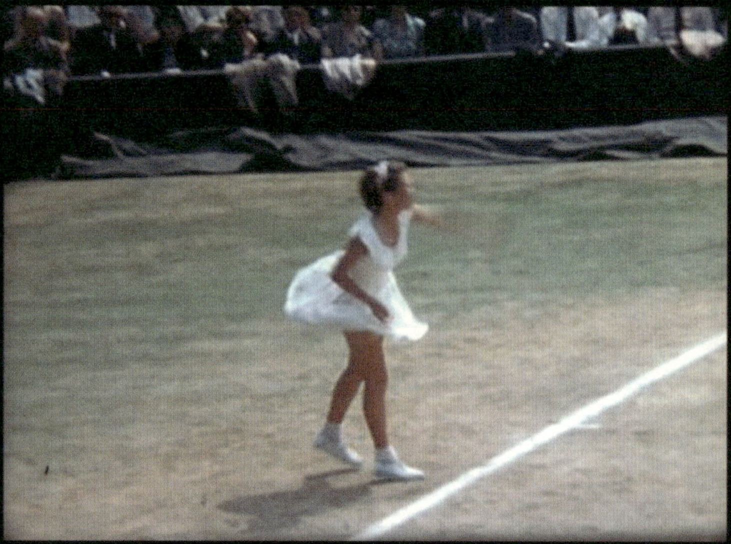

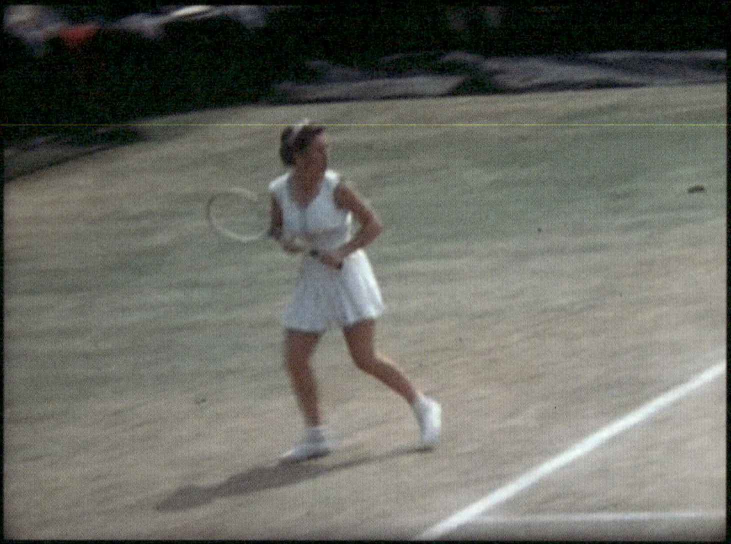

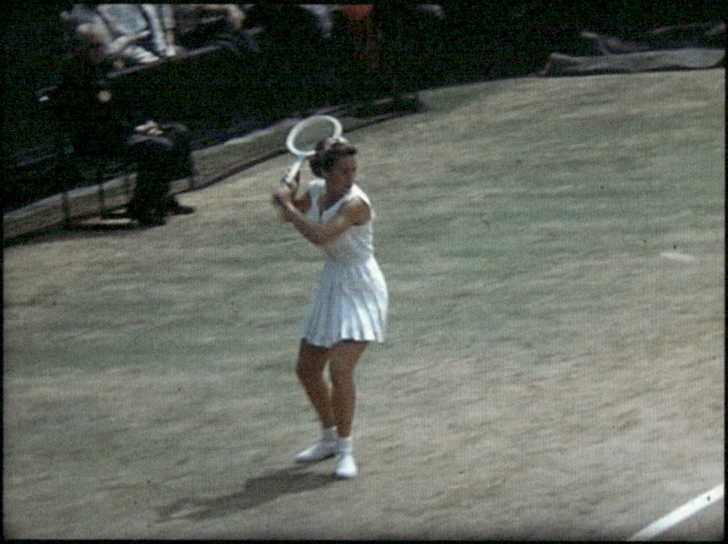

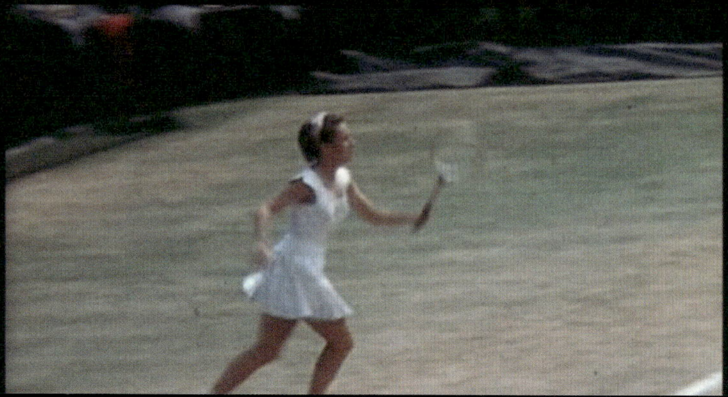

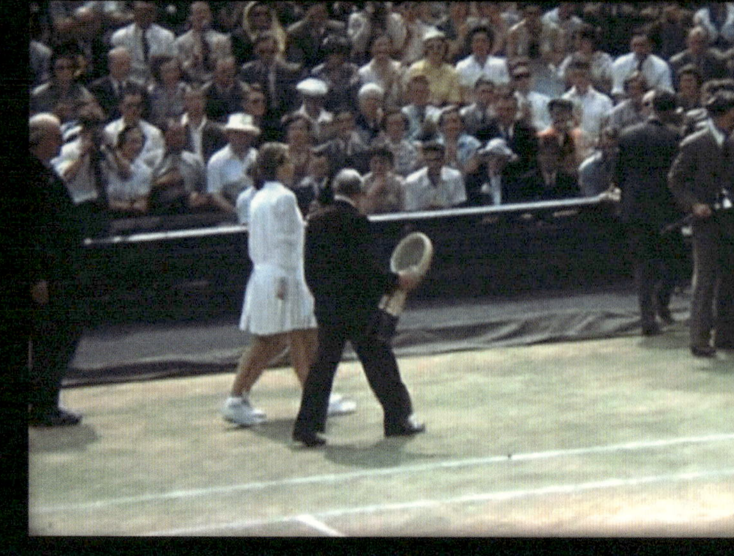

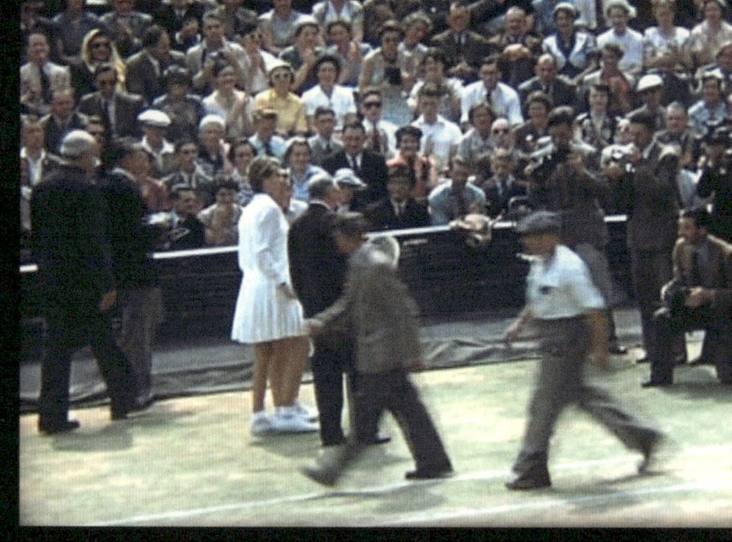

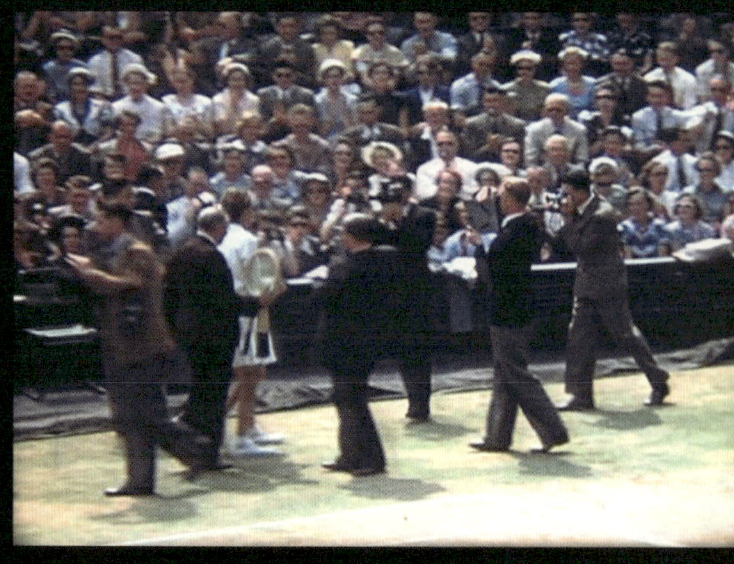

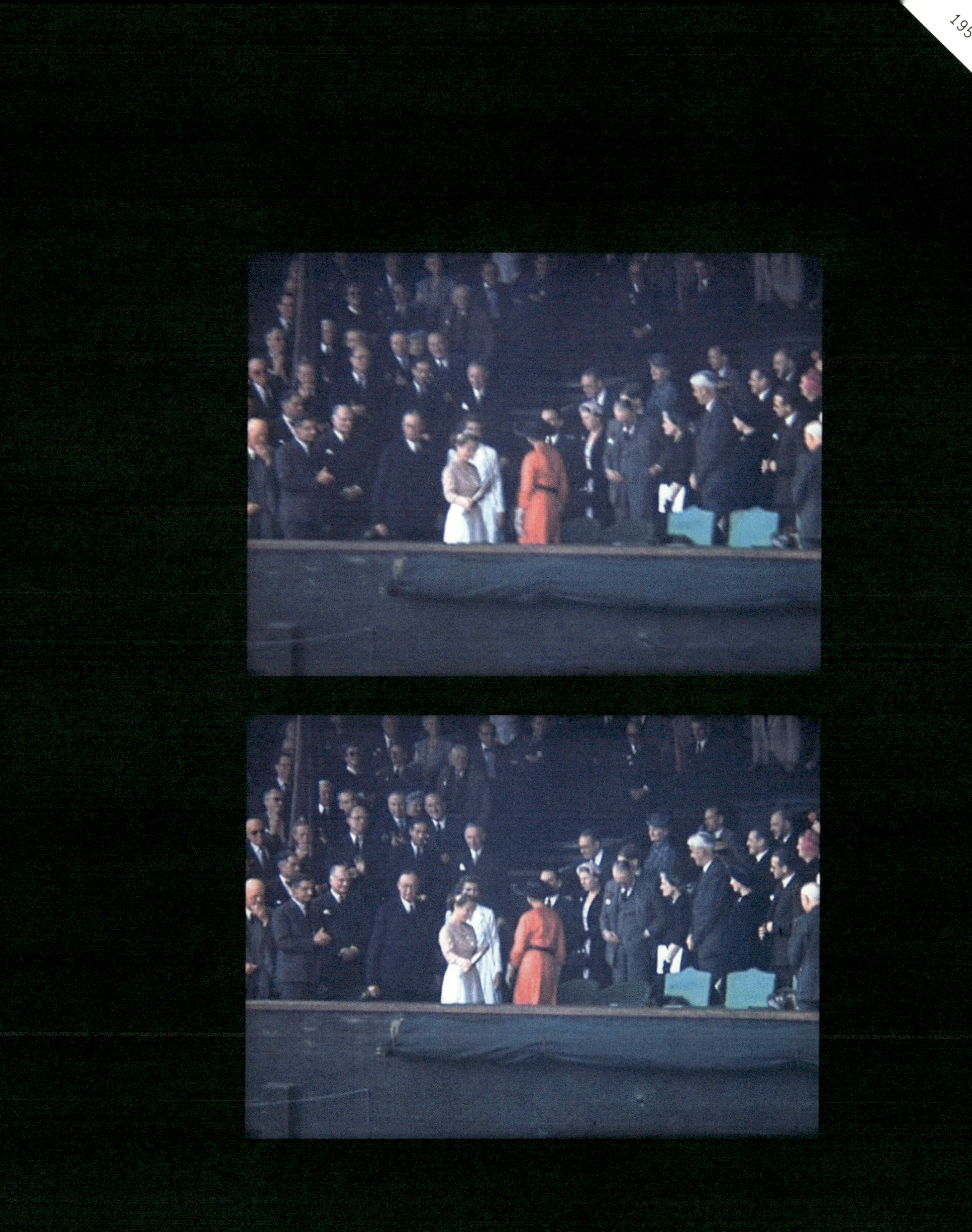

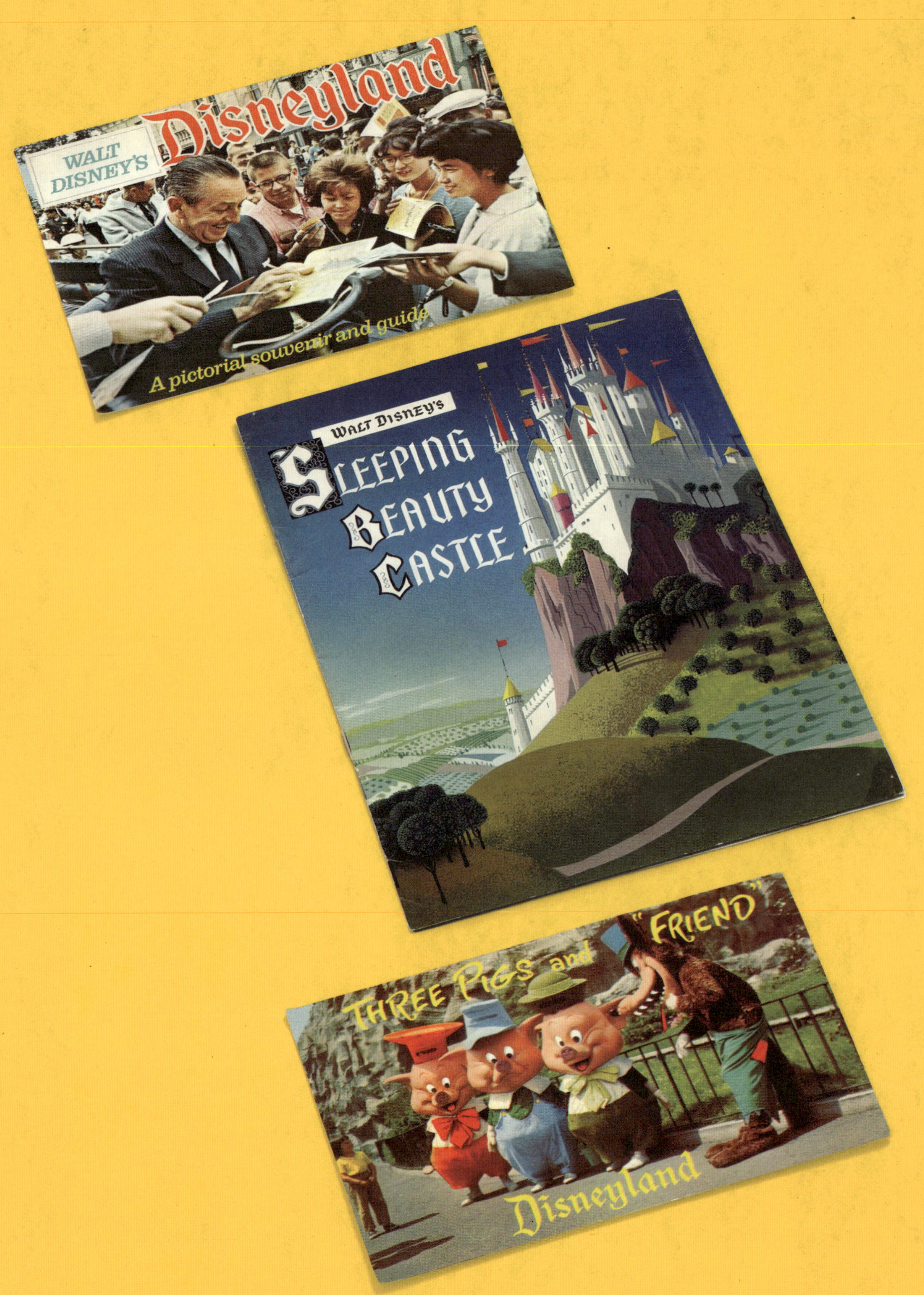
WALT DISNEY'S
Disneyland
A pictorial souvenir and guide
WALT DISNEY'S
SLEEPING
BEAUTY
CASTLE
THREE PIGS and "FRIEND"
Disneyland

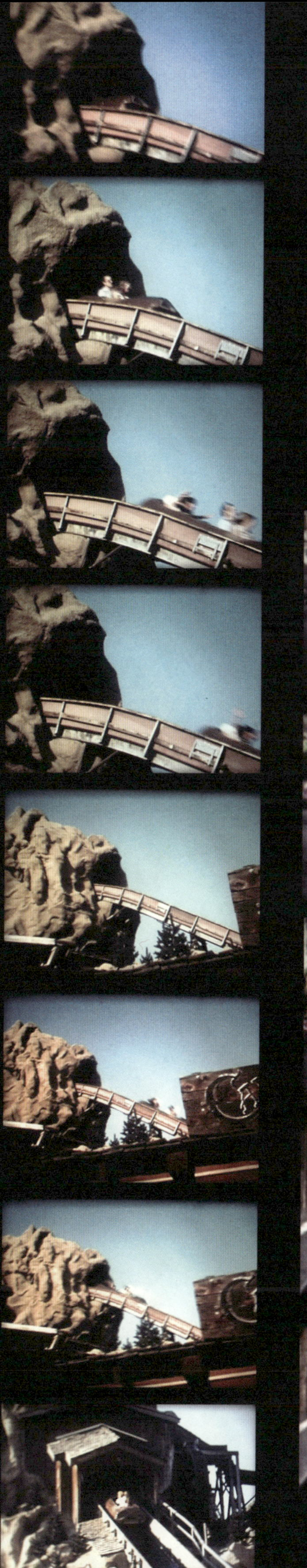
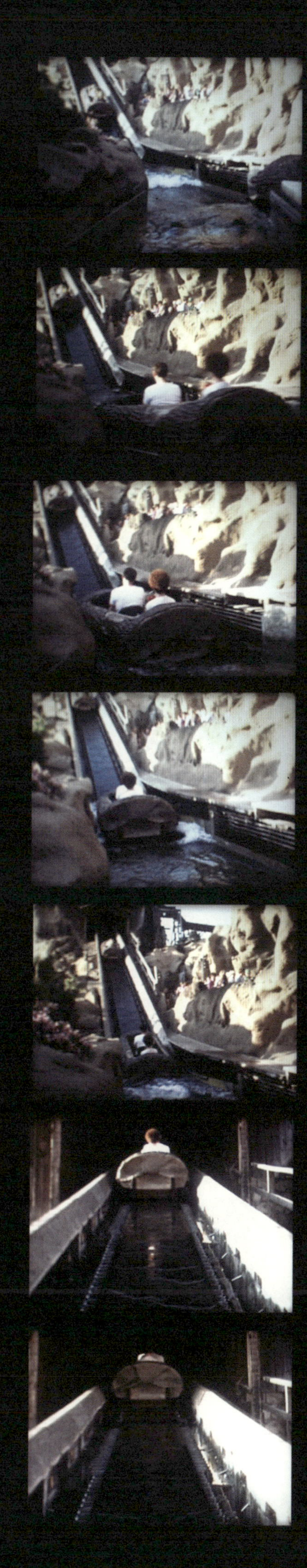
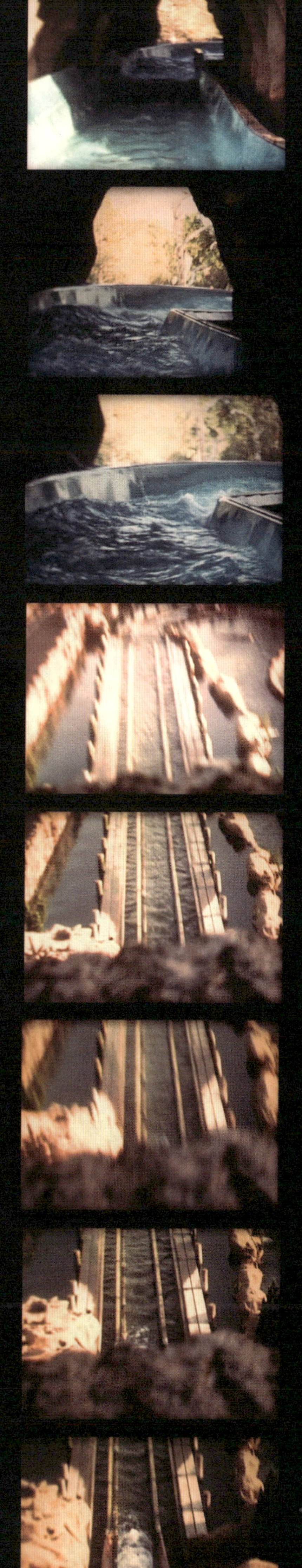

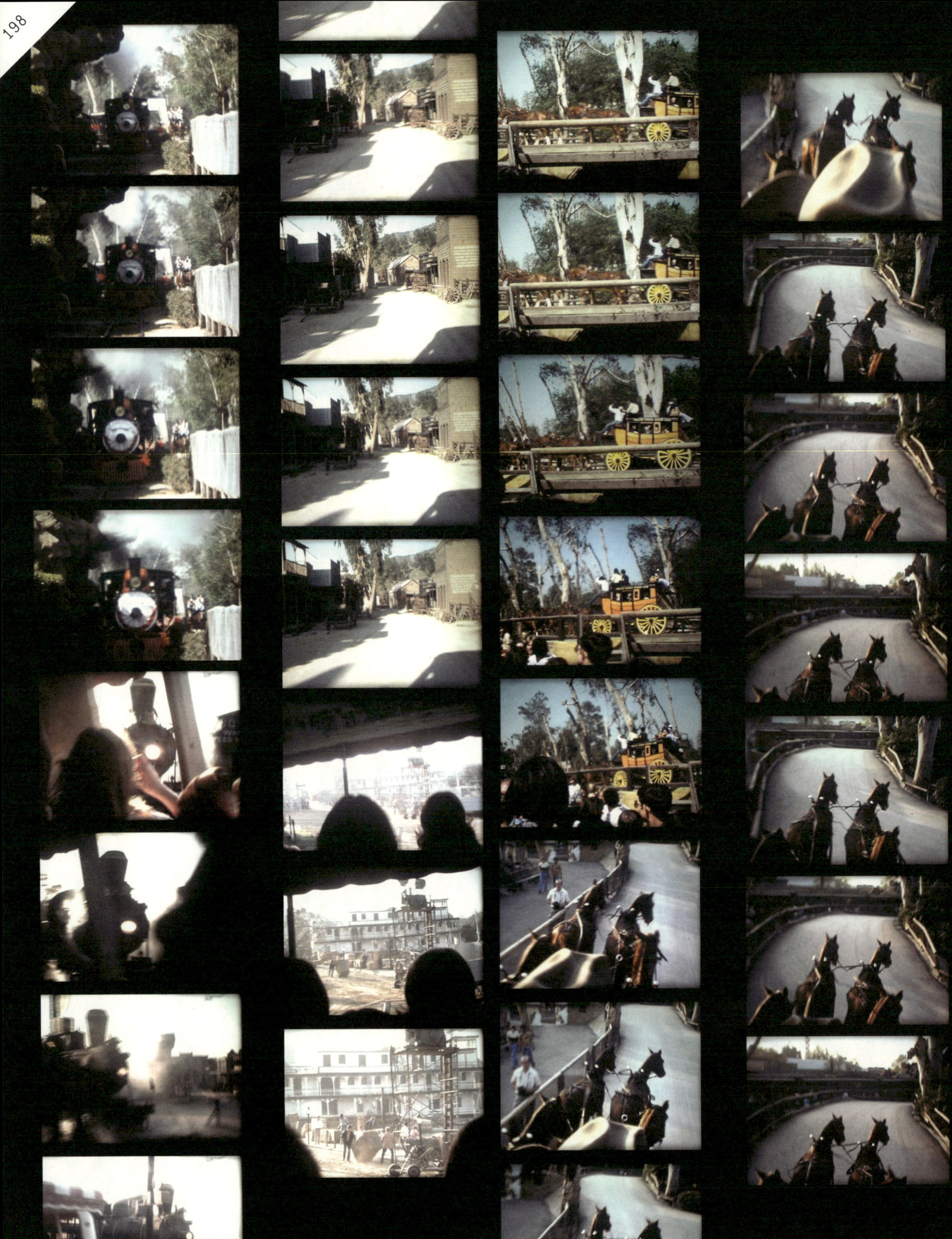

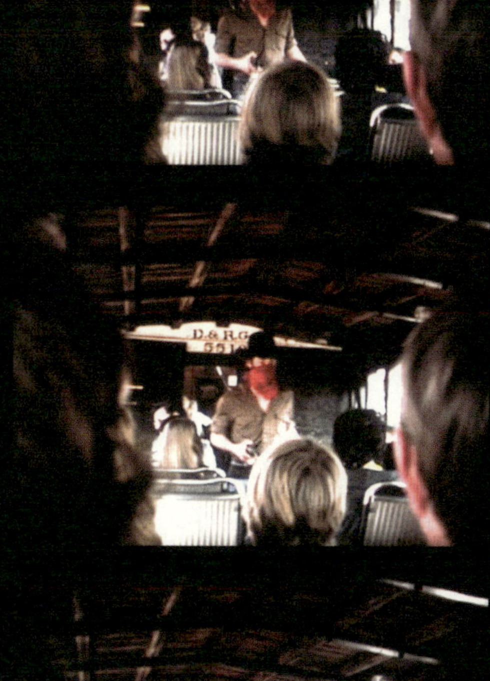
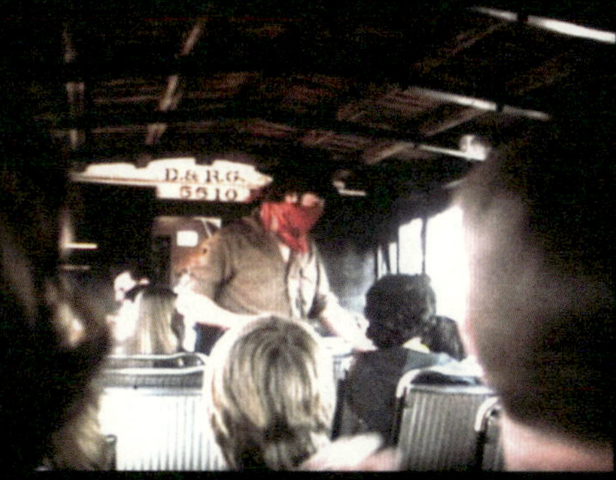
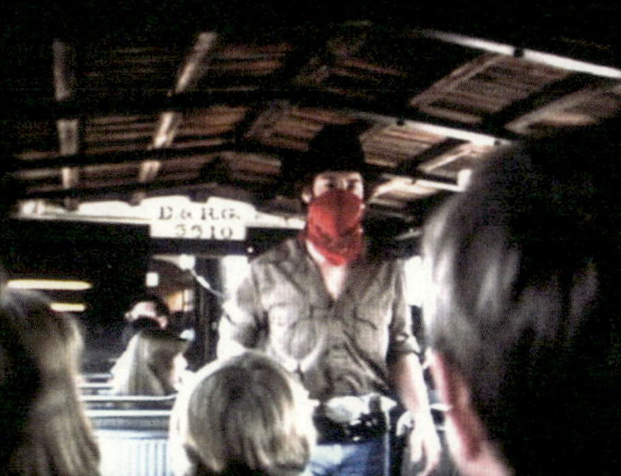
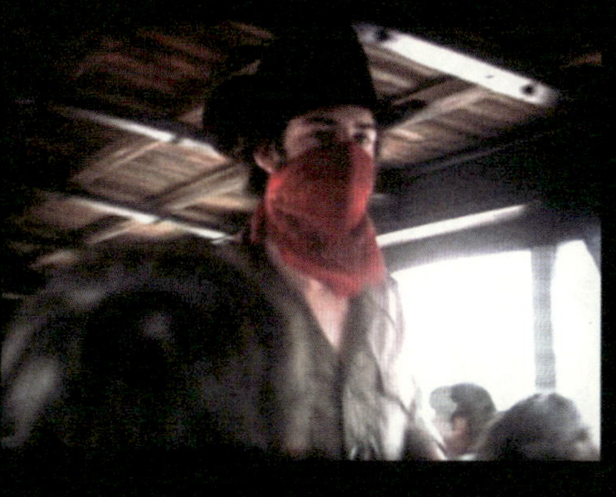
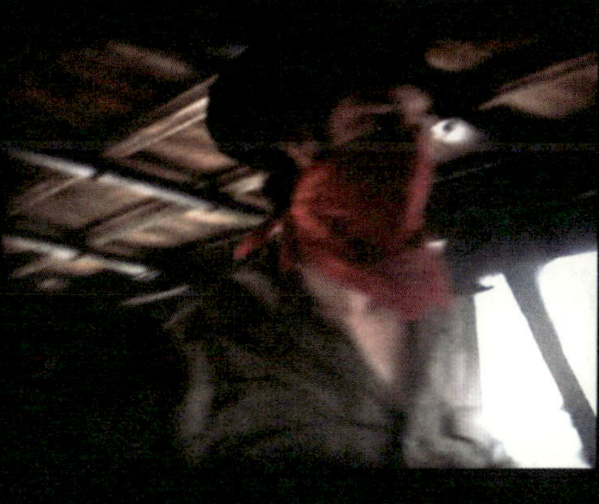
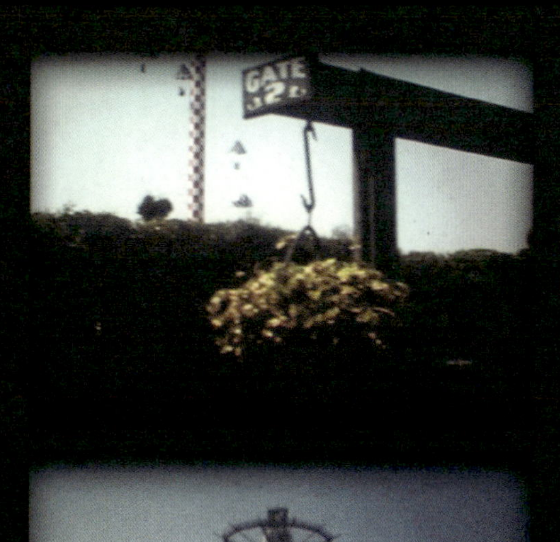
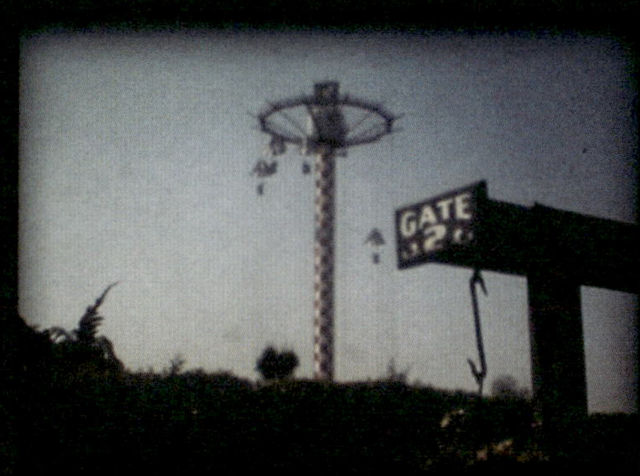
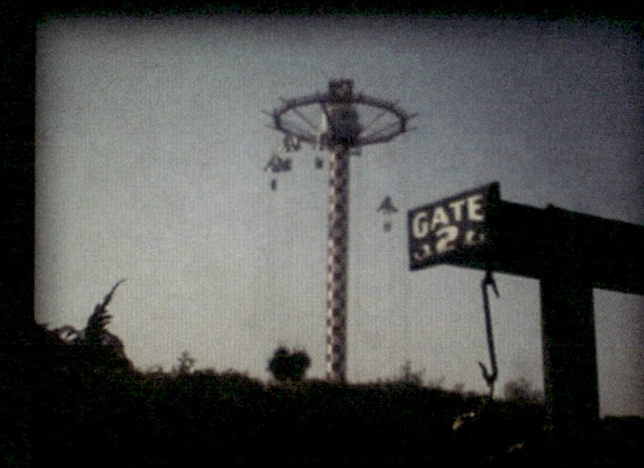
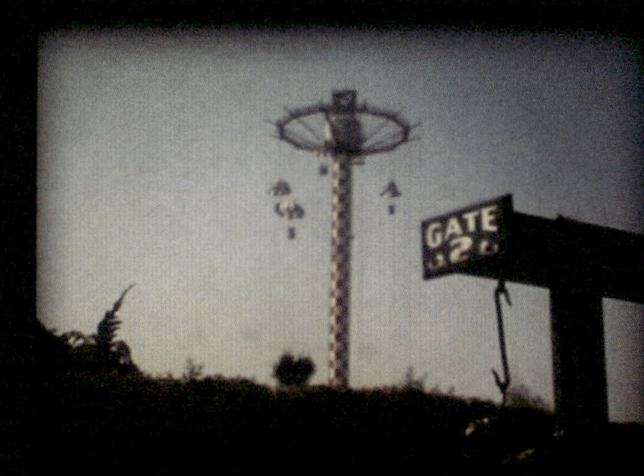
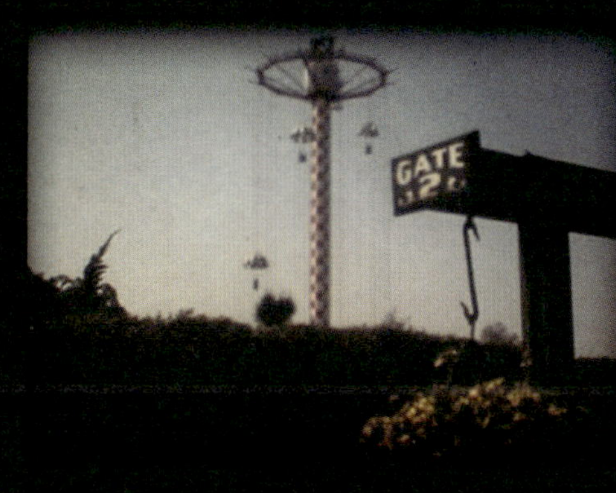
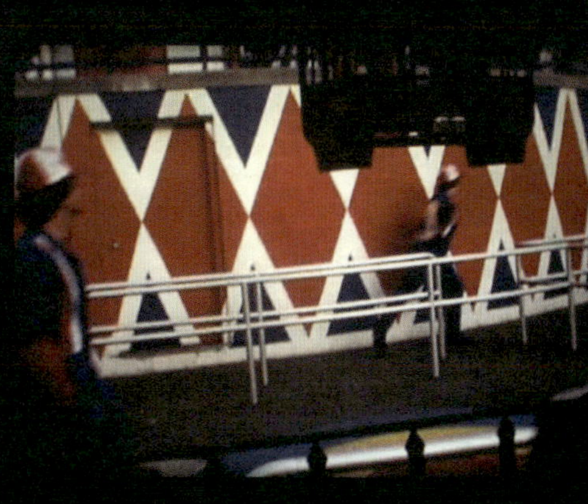
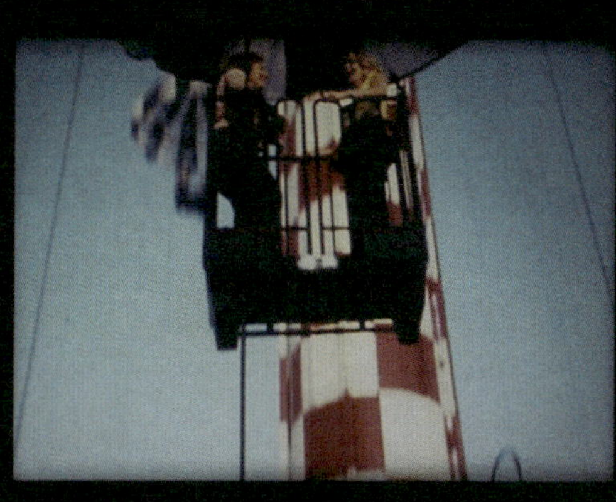
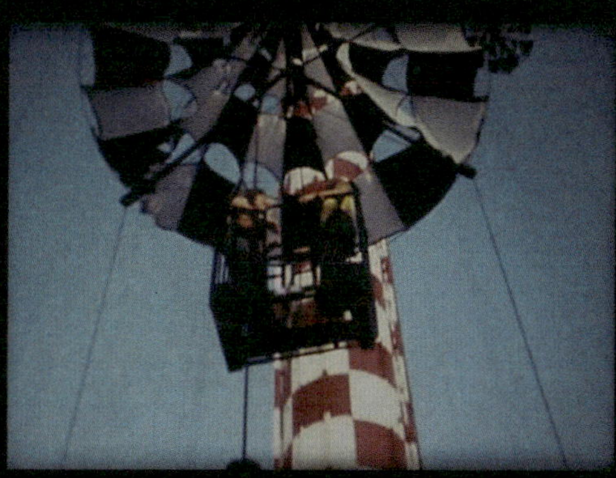
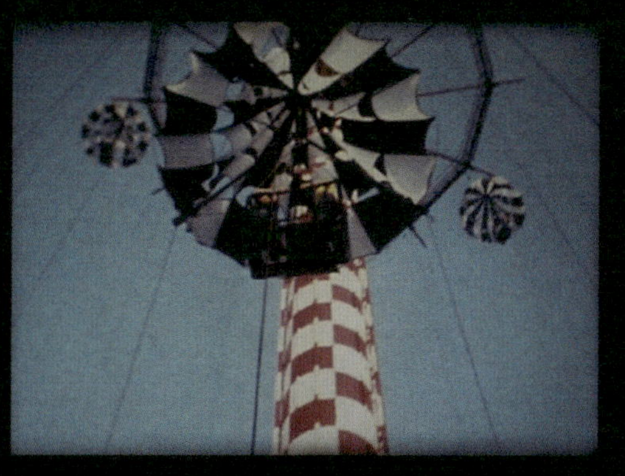
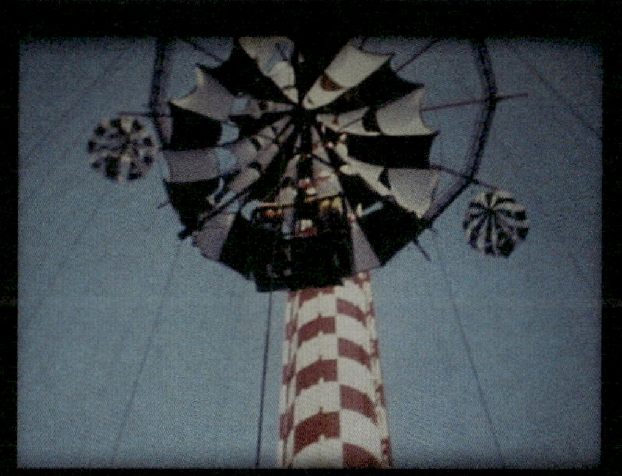
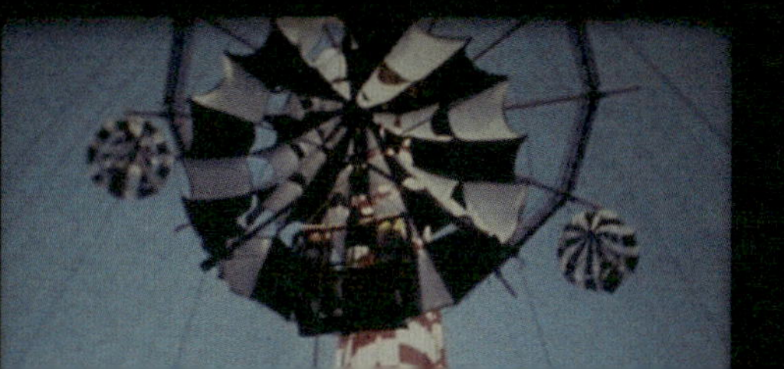

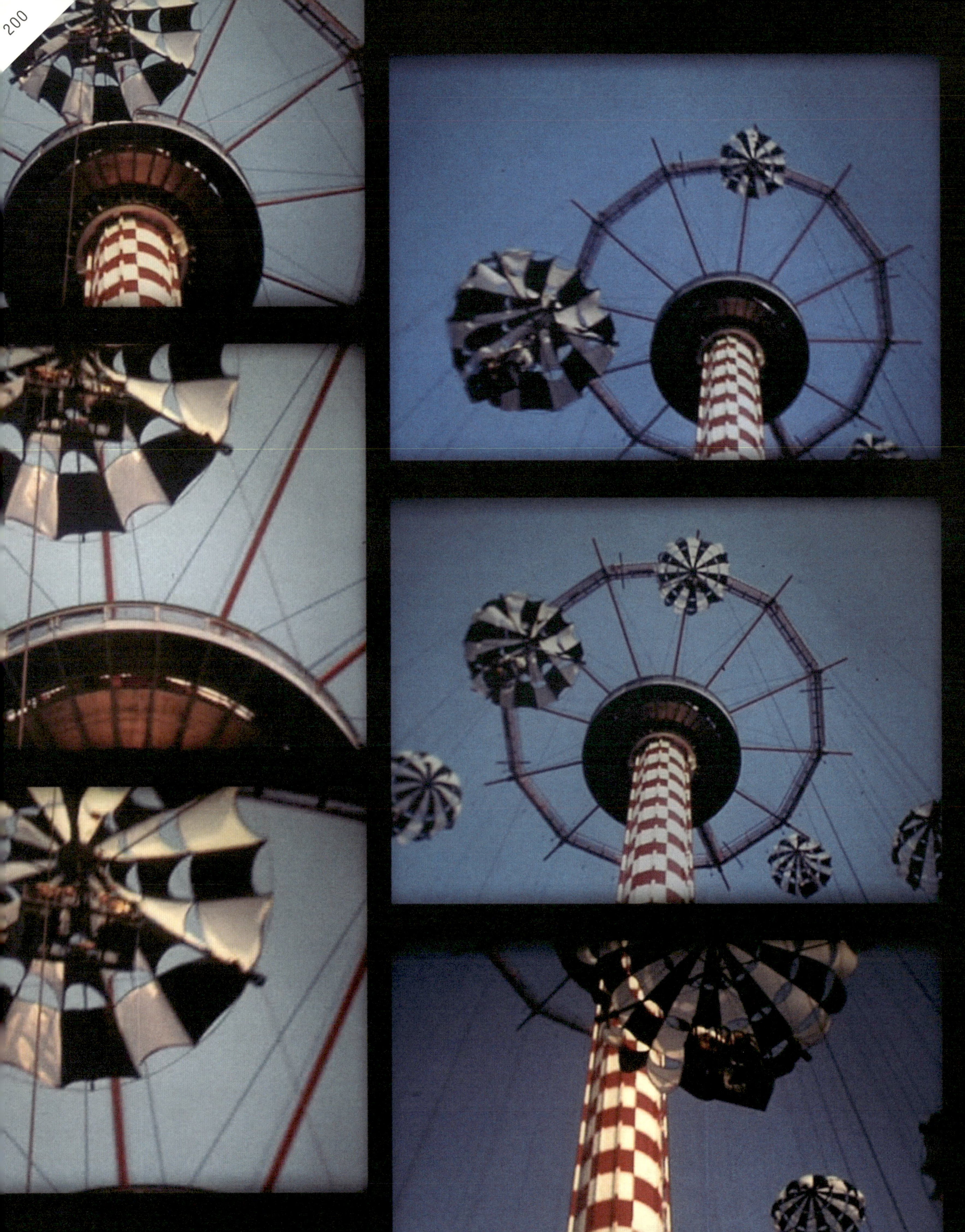

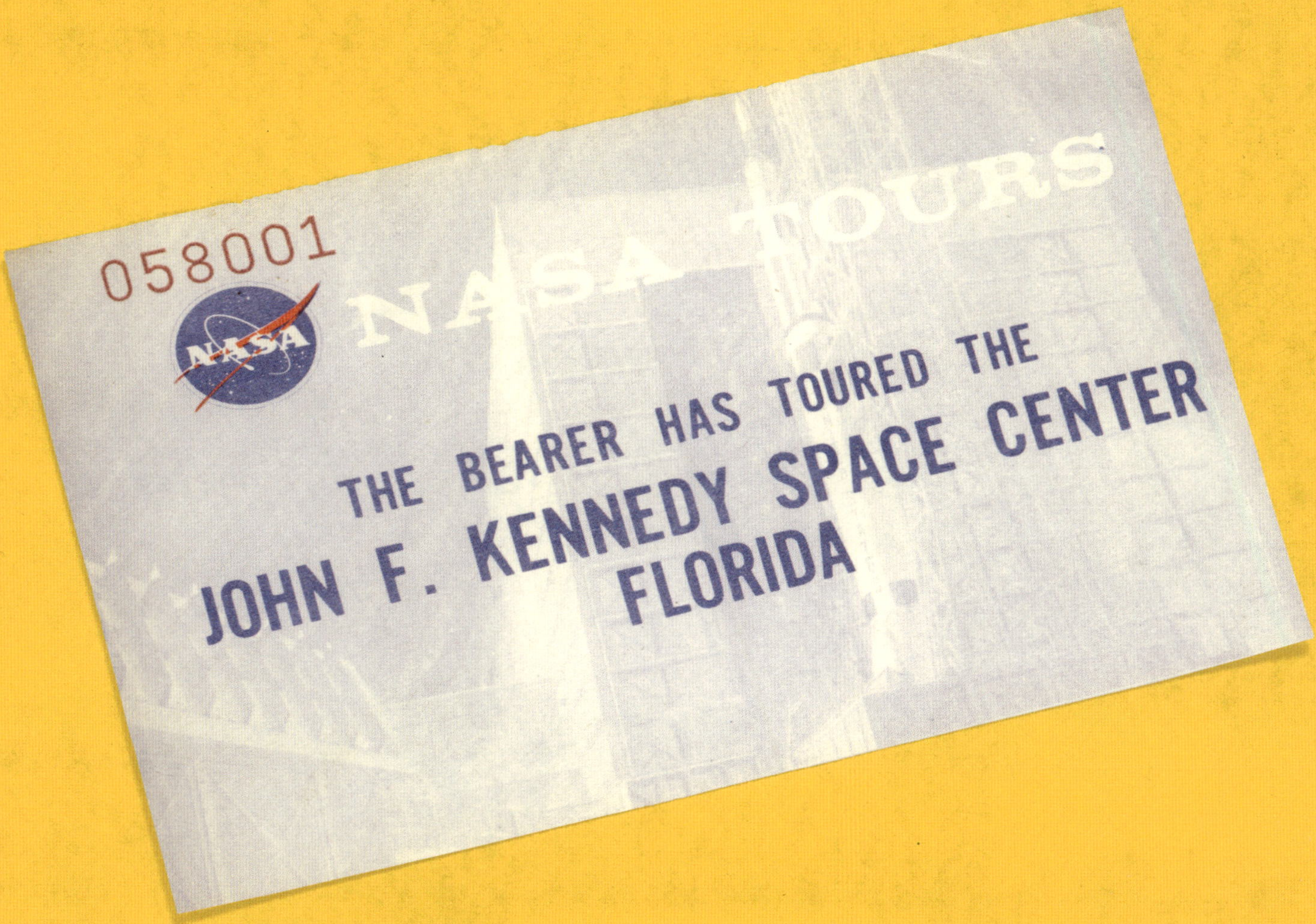

058001
NASA TOURS
THE BEARER HAS TOURED THE
JOHN F. KENNEDY SPACE CENTER
FLORIDA

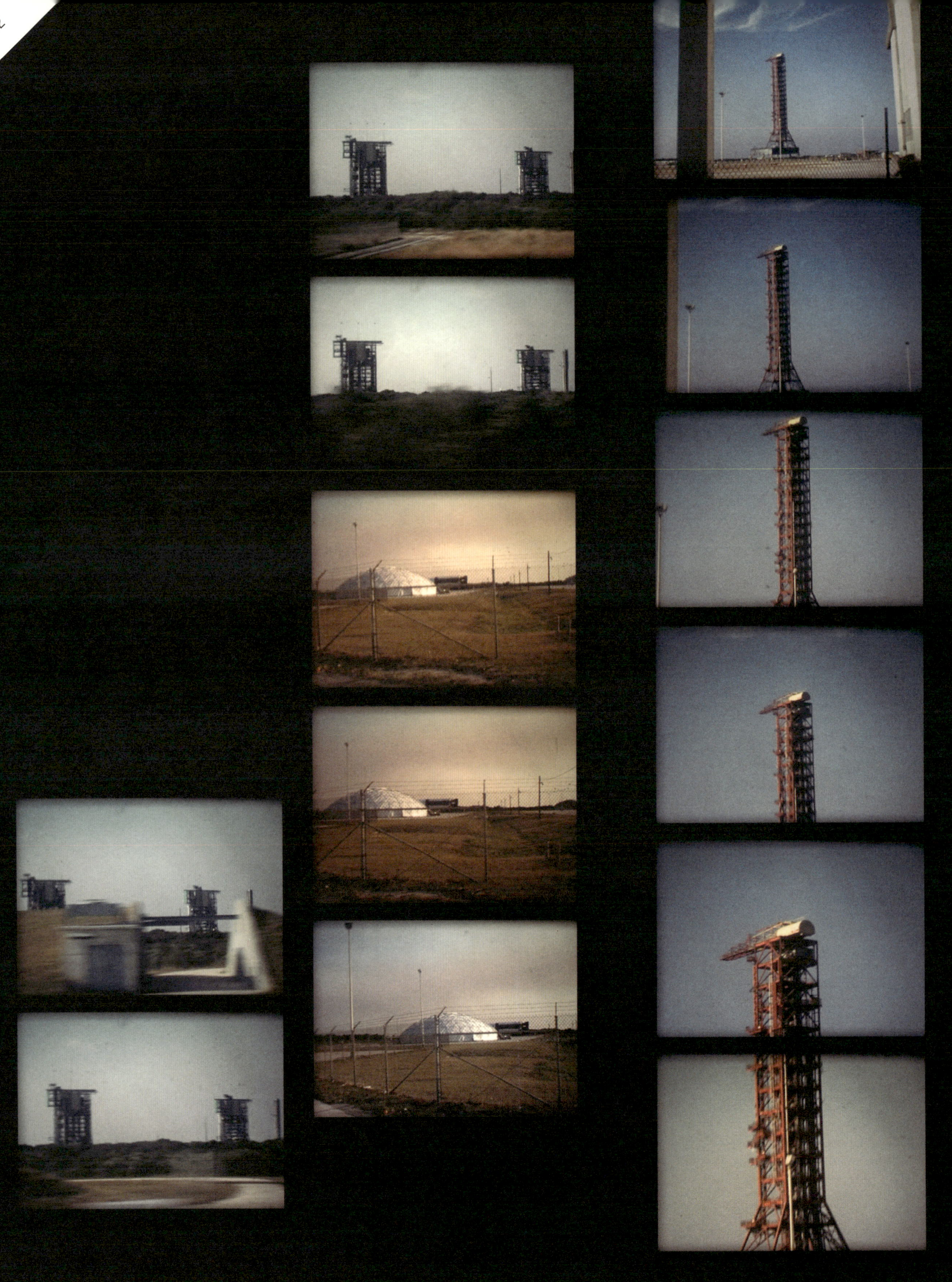

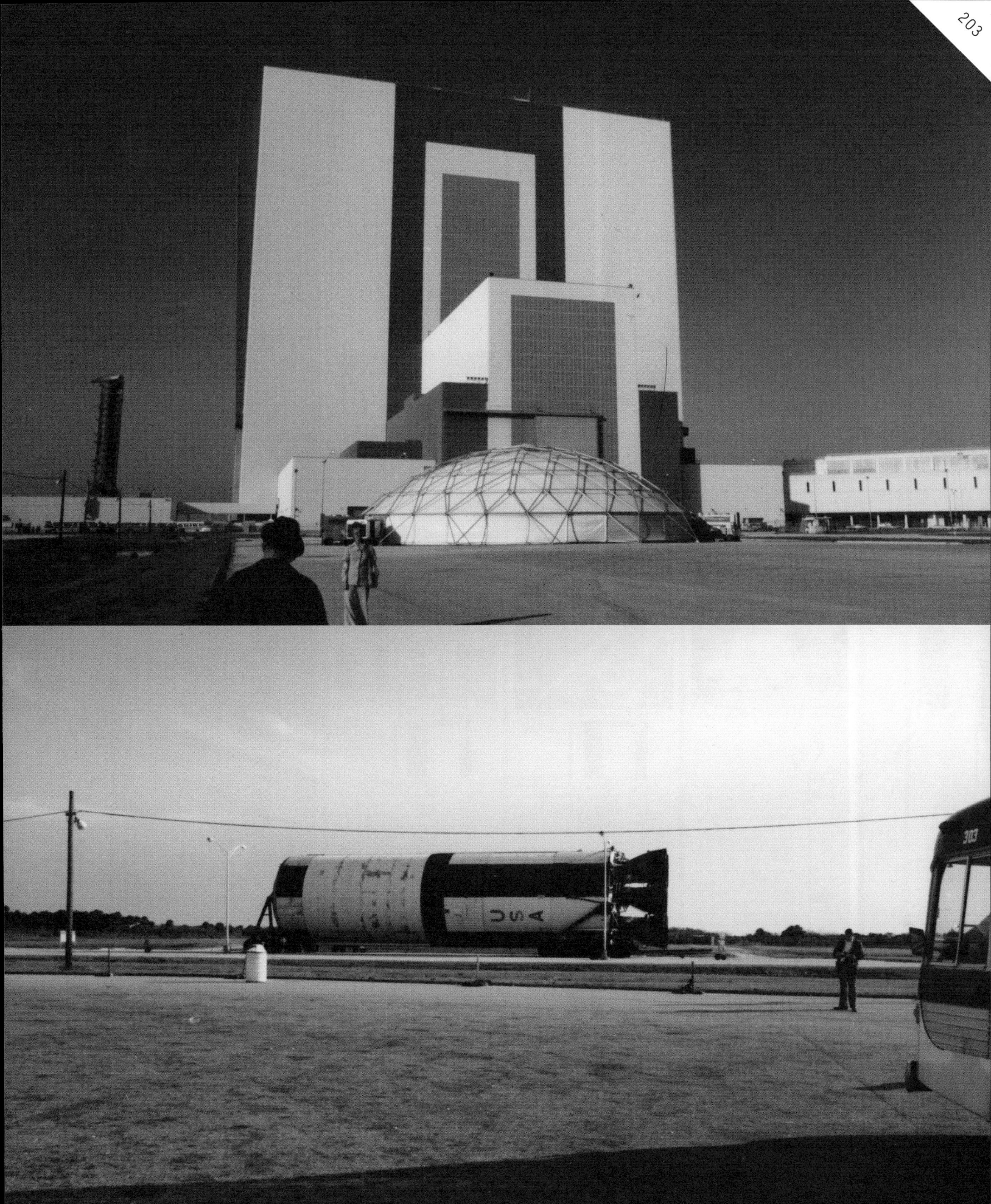

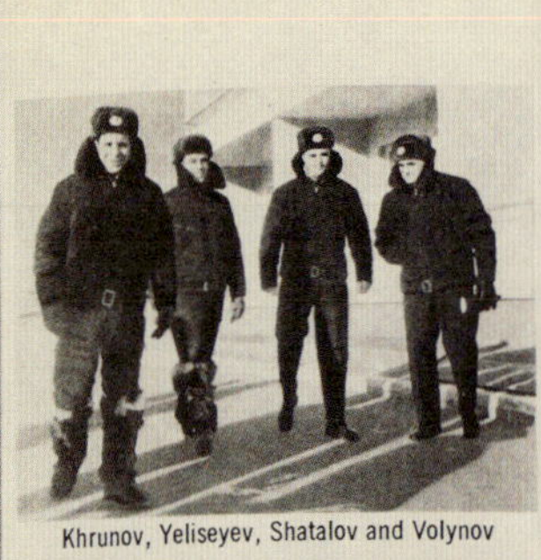

Khrunov, Yeliseyev, Shatalov and Volynov

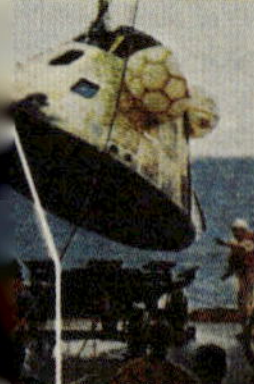

d from the moon

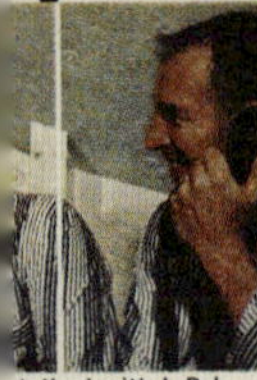

U.S.S. "Yorktown"

talked with L.B.J.

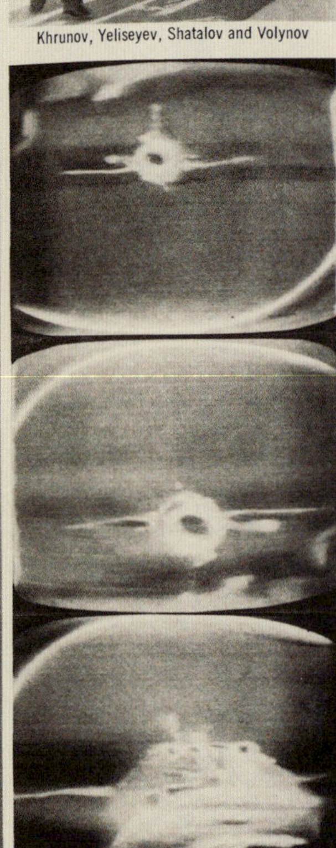

Soyuz 4 approached, then docked with Soyuz 5

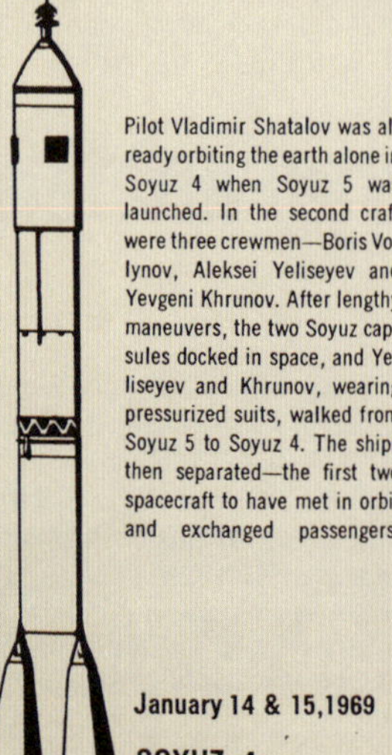

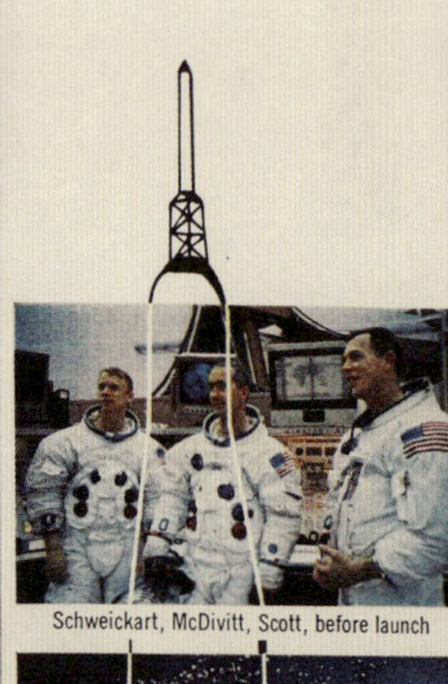

Schweickart, McDivitt, Scott, before launch

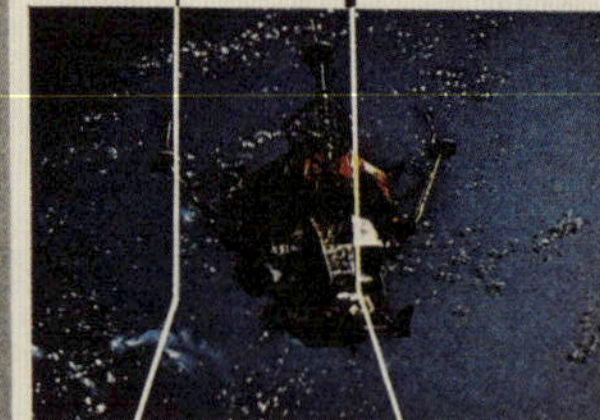

LM floated free 145 miles above Atlantic

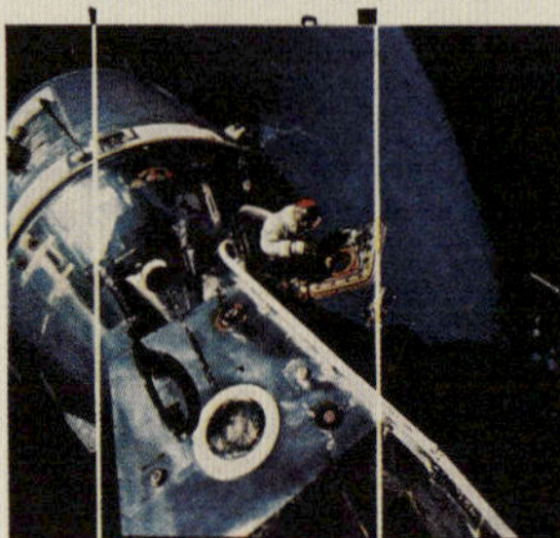

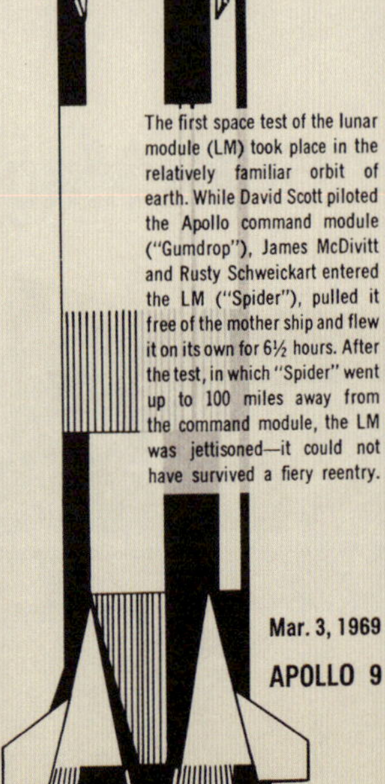

Scott in "Gumdrop" doorway, seen from LM

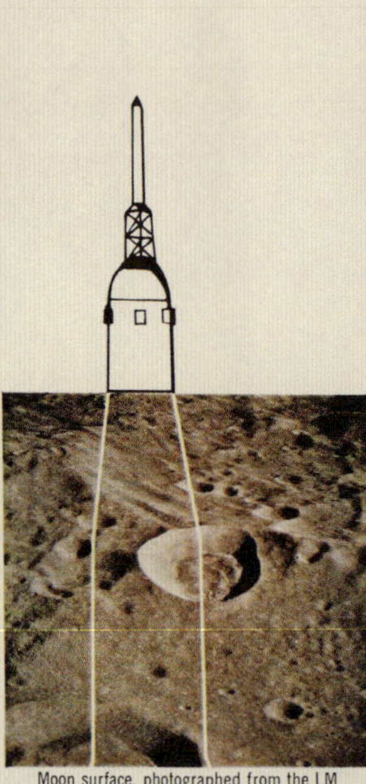

Moon surface, photographed from the LM

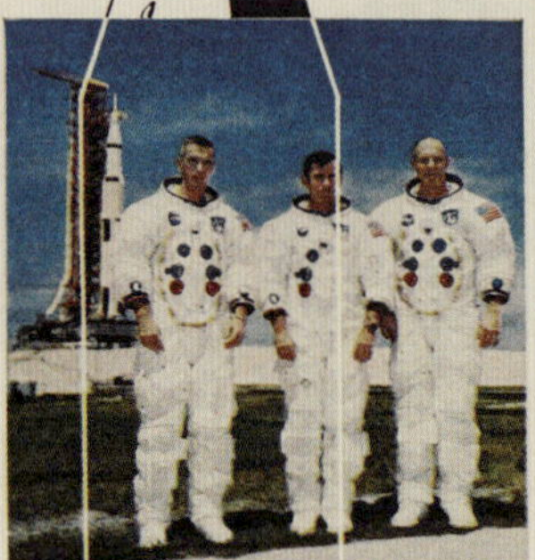

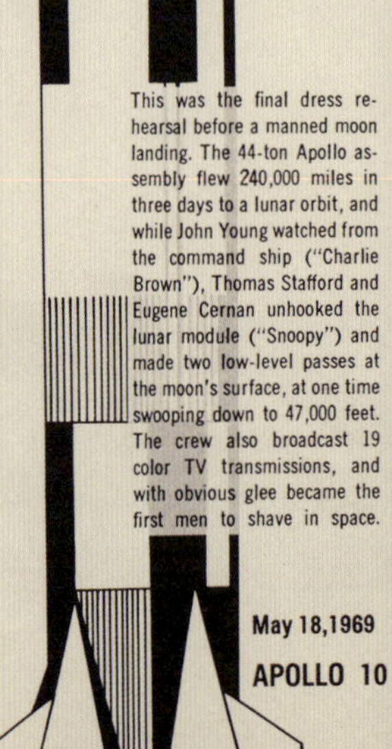

Cernan, Young, Stafford, of Apollo 10

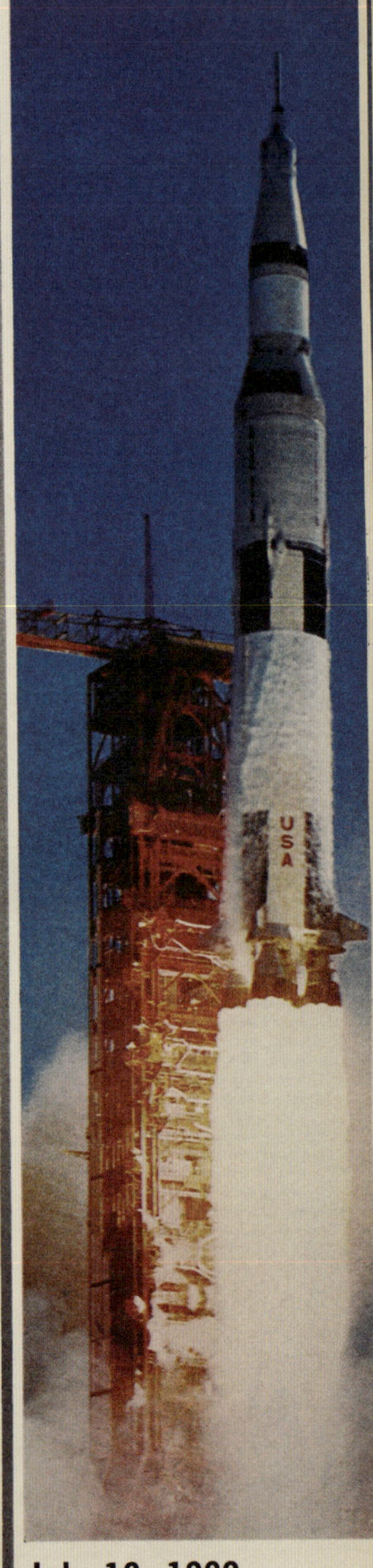

s was both a reconnais-
the moon and a test of
nology and equipment
y to get there. It was
first manned test of the
Saturn V rocket, with
illion pounds of lift-off
The spacecraft, with
Frank Borman, James
d William Anders, left
t shortly after lift-off
ched the moon three
r. They circled it ten
n returned to earth
e landing. While in the
bit, the crew looked for
sites and broadcast
s, including a Christ-
reading of Genesis.

Dec. 21, 1968

APOLLO 8

Pilot Vladimir Shatalov was already orbiting the earth alone in Soyuz 4 when Soyuz 5 was launched. In the second craft were three crewmen—Boris Volynov, Aleksei Yeliseyev and Yevgeni Khrunov. After lengthy maneuvers, the two Soyuz capsules docked in space, and Yeliseyev and Khrunov, wearing pressurized suits, walked from Soyuz 5 to Soyuz 4. The ships then separated—the first two spacecraft to have met in orbit and exchanged passengers.

January 14 & 15, 1969

SOYUZ 4
SOYUZ 5

The first space test of the lunar module (LM) took place in the relatively familiar orbit of earth. While David Scott piloted the Apollo command module ("Gumdrop"), James McDivitt and Rusty Schweickart entered the LM ("Spider"), pulled it free of the mother ship and flew it on its own for 6½ hours. After the test, in which "Spider" went up to 100 miles away from the command module, the LM was jettisoned—it could not have survived a fiery reentry.

Mar. 3, 1969

APOLLO 9

This was the final dress rehearsal before a manned moon landing. The 44-ton Apollo assembly flew 240,000 miles in three days to a lunar orbit, and while John Young watched from the command ship ("Charlie Brown"), Thomas Stafford and Eugene Cernan unhooked the lunar module ("Snoopy") and made two low-level passes at the moon's surface, at one time swooping down to 47,000 feet. The crew also broadcast 19 color TV transmissions, and with obvious glee became the first men to shave in space.

May 18, 1969

APOLLO 10

July 16, 1969
APOLLO 11

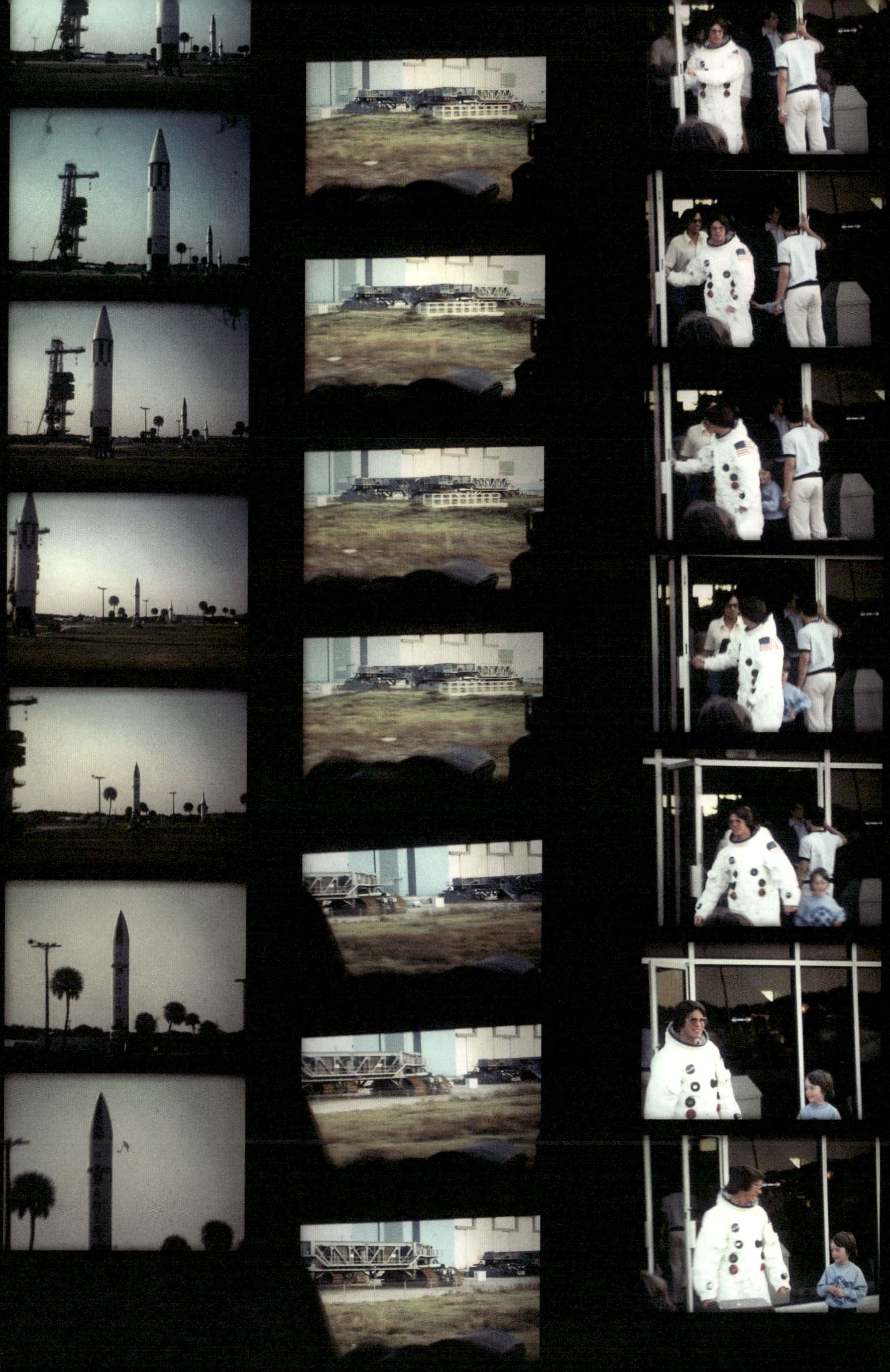

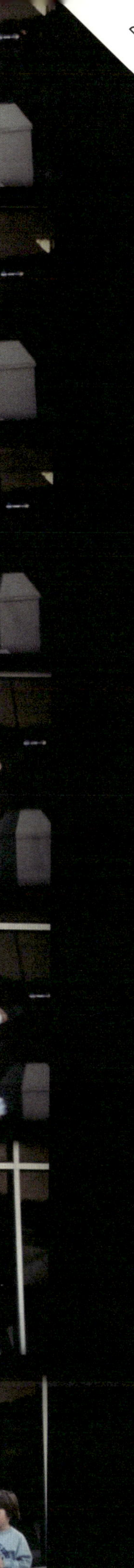

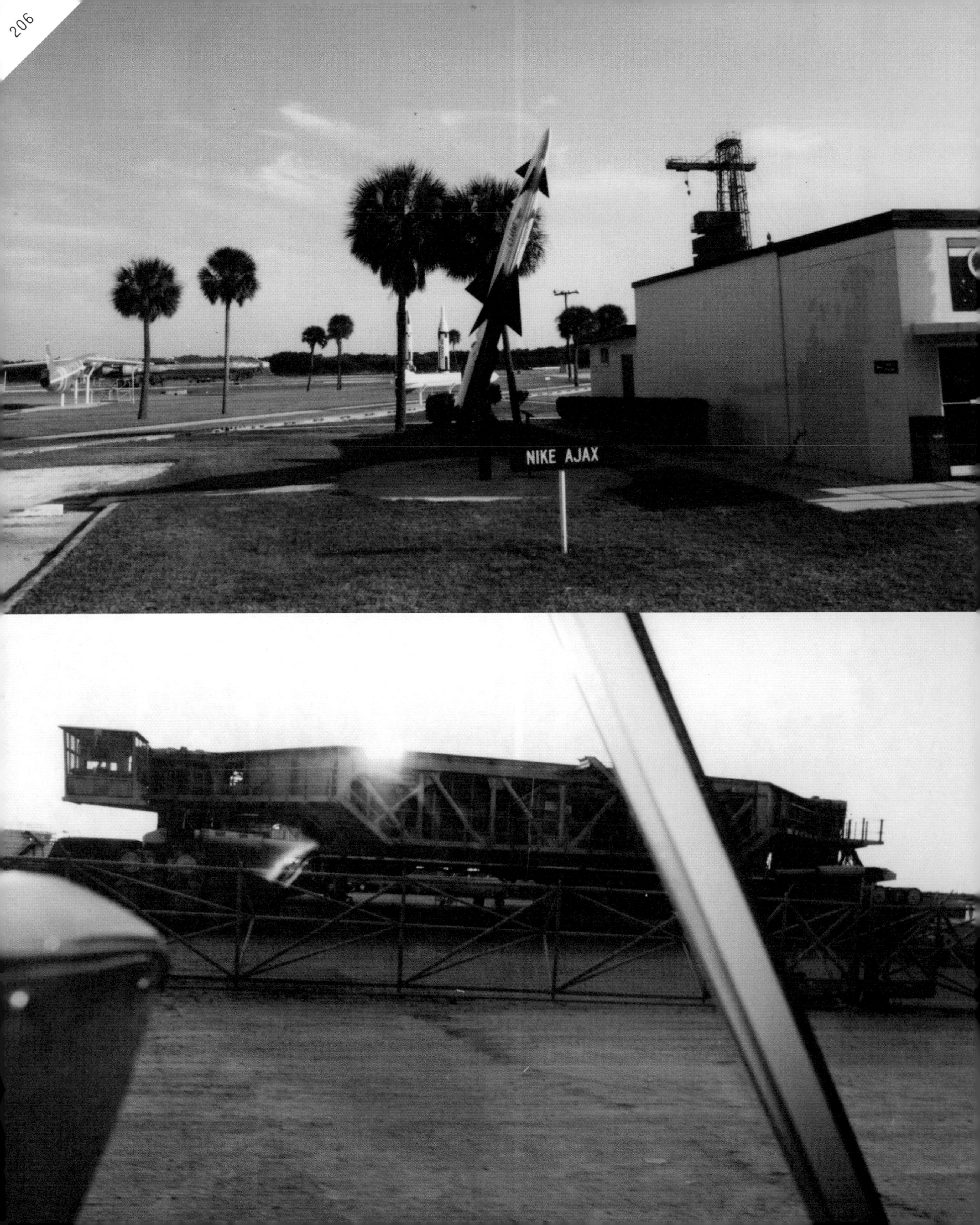
NIKE AJAX

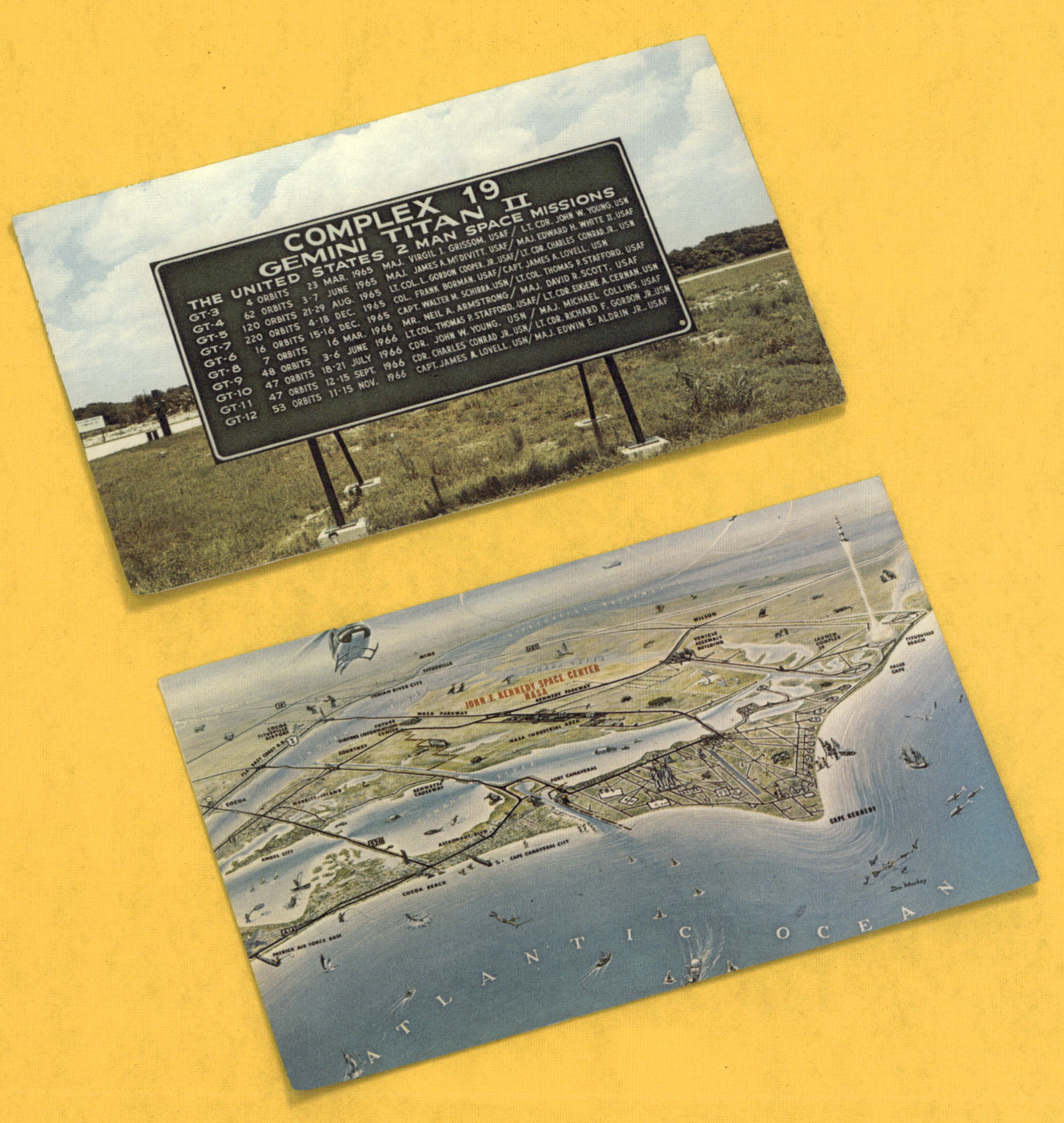
COMPLEX 19
GEMINI TITAN II
THE UNITED STATES 2 MAN SPACE MISSIONS
GT-3   4 ORBITS   23 MAR. 1965   MAJ. VIRGIL I. GRISSOM, USAF / LT. CDR. JOHN W. YOUNG, USN
GT-4   62 ORBITS   3-7 JUNE 1965   MAJ. JAMES A. McDIVITT, USAF / MAJ. EDWARD H. WHITE, II. USAF
GT-5   120 ORBITS   21-29 AUG. 1965   LT. COL. L. GORDON COOPER, JR. USAF / LT. CDR. CHARLES CONRAD, JR. USN
GT-7   220 ORBITS   4-18 DEC. 1965   LT. COL. FRANK BORMAN, USAF / CAPT. JAMES A. LOVELL, USN
GT-6   16 ORBITS   15-16 DEC. 1965   CAPT. WALTER M. SCHIRRA, USN / LT. COL. THOMAS P. STAFFORD, USAF
GT-8   7 ORBITS   16 MAR. 1966   MR. NEIL A. ARMSTRONG / LT. COL. DAVID R. SCOTT, USAF
GT-9   48 ORBITS   3-6 JUNE 1966   LT. COL. THOMAS P. STAFFORD, USAF / LT. CDR. EUGENE A. CERNAN, USN
GT-10   47 ORBITS   18-21 JULY 1966   CDR. JOHN W. YOUNG, USN / LT. COL. MICHAEL COLLINS, USAF
GT-11   47 ORBITS   12-15 SEPT. 1966   CDR. CHARLES CONRAD JR., USN / LT. CDR. RICHARD F. GORDON, JR. USN
GT-12   53 ORBITS   11-15 NOV. 1966   CAPT. JAMES A. LOVELL, USN / MAJ. EDWIN E. ALDRIN JR., USAF
JOHN F. KENNEDY SPACE CENTER
NASA
NASA PARKWAY
NASA INDUSTRIAL AREA
TITUSVILLE
MIMS
WILSON
COCOA
MERRITT ISLAND
PORT CANAVERAL
CAPE KENNEDY
COCOA BEACH
CAPE CANAVERAL CITY
PATRICK AIR FORCE BASE
ATLANTIC OCEAN

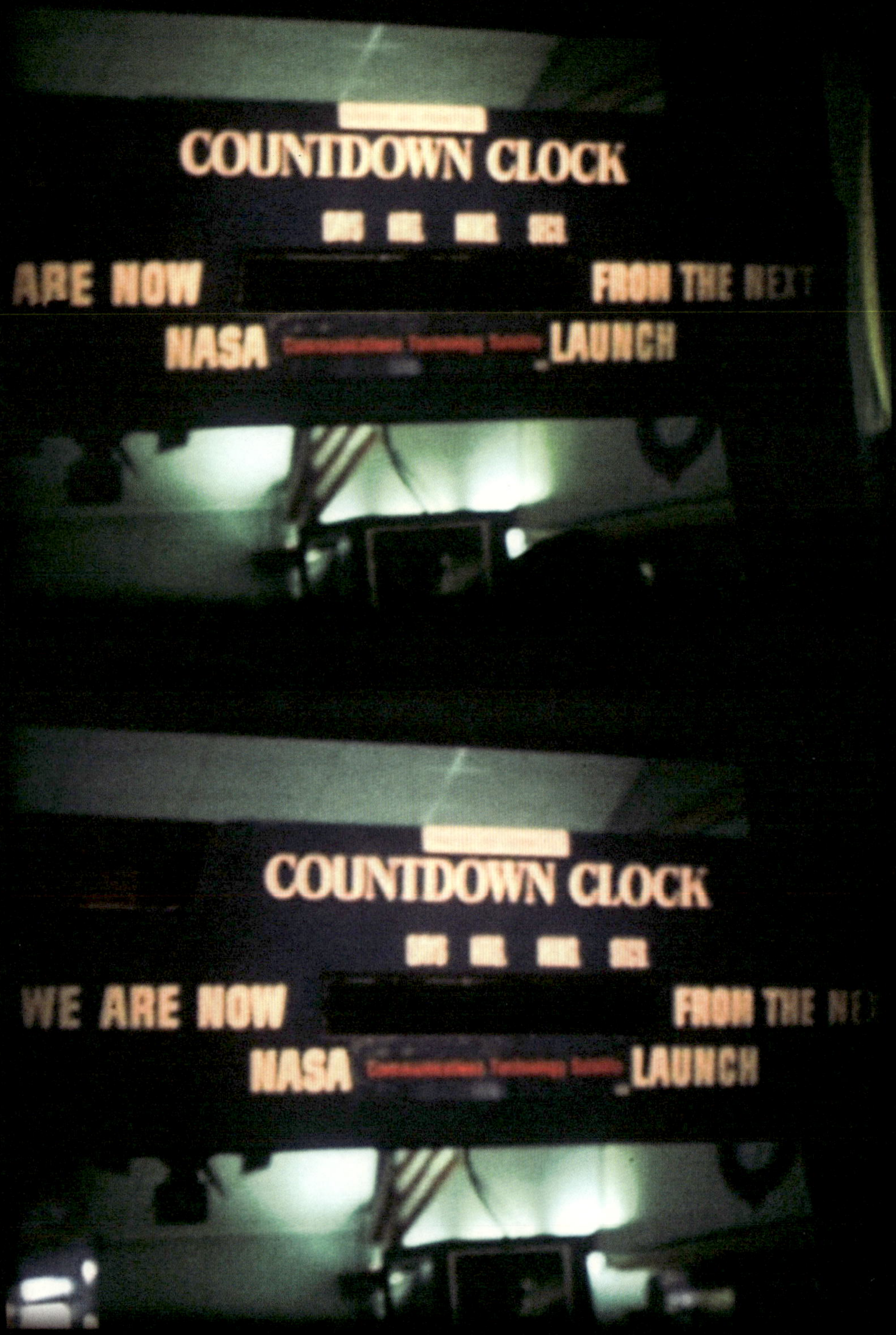

COUNTDOWN CLOCK
DAYS   HRS.   MINS.   SECS.
ARE NOW   FROM THE NEXT
NASA Communications Technology Satellite LAUNCH
COUNTDOWN CLOCK
DAYS   HRS.   MINS.   SECS.
WE ARE NOW   FROM THE NE
NASA Communications Technology Satellite LAUNCH

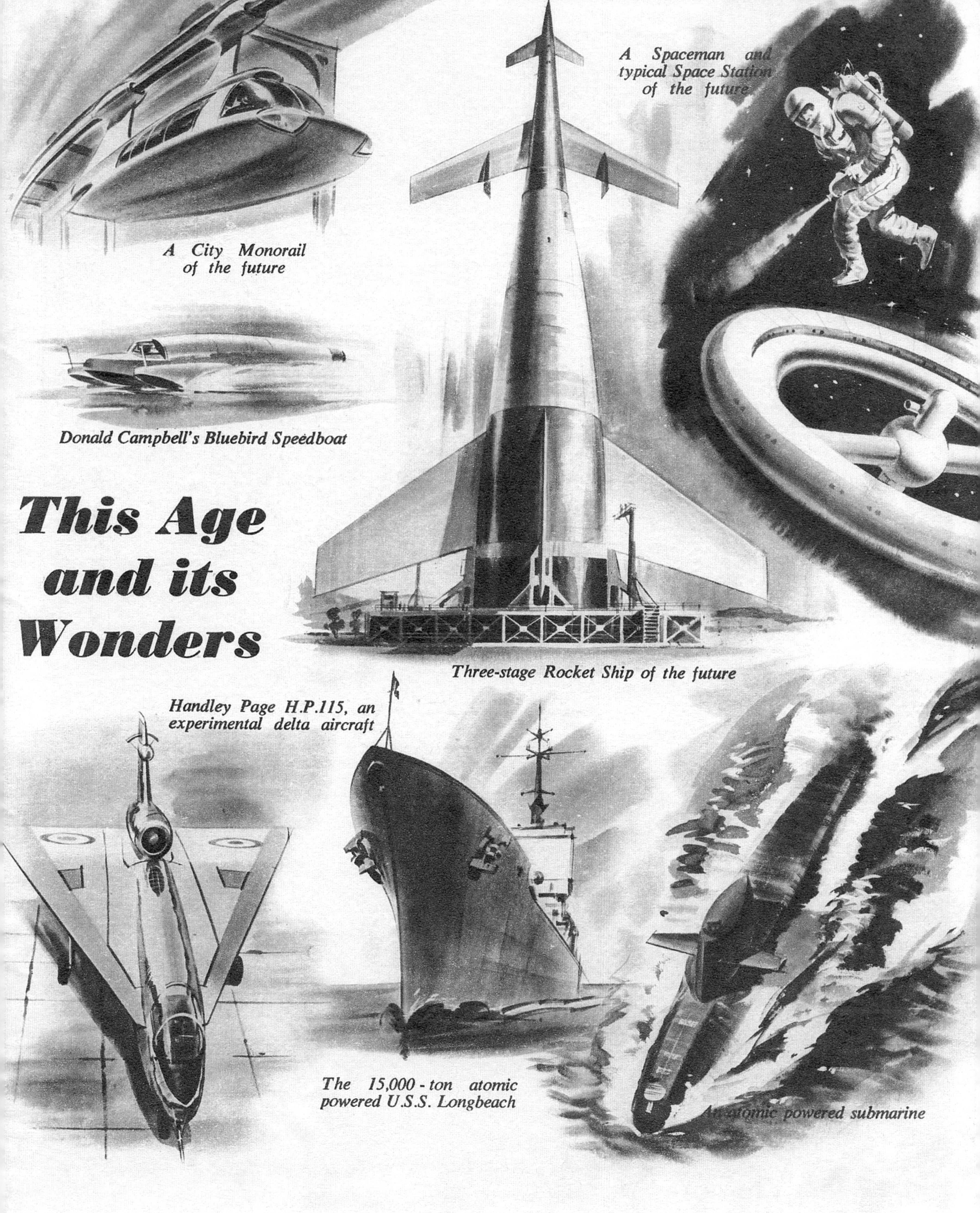

A City Monorail of the future

Donald Campbell's Bluebird Speedboat

This Age and its Wonders

A Spaceman and typical Space Station of the future

Three-stage Rocket Ship of the future

Handley Page H.P.115, an experimental delta aircraft

The 15,000 - ton atomic powered U.S.S. Longbeach

An atomic powered submarine

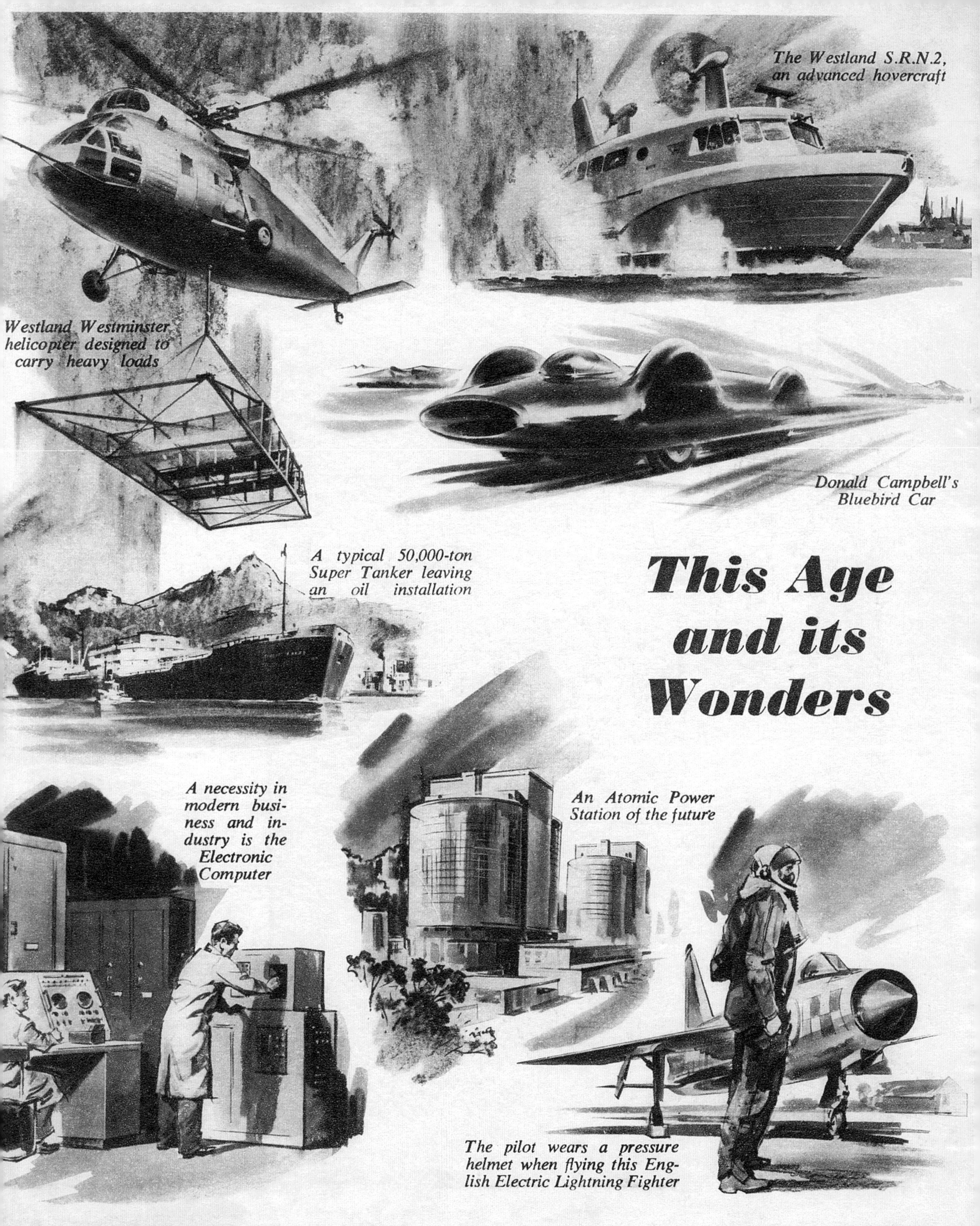

This Age and its Wonders

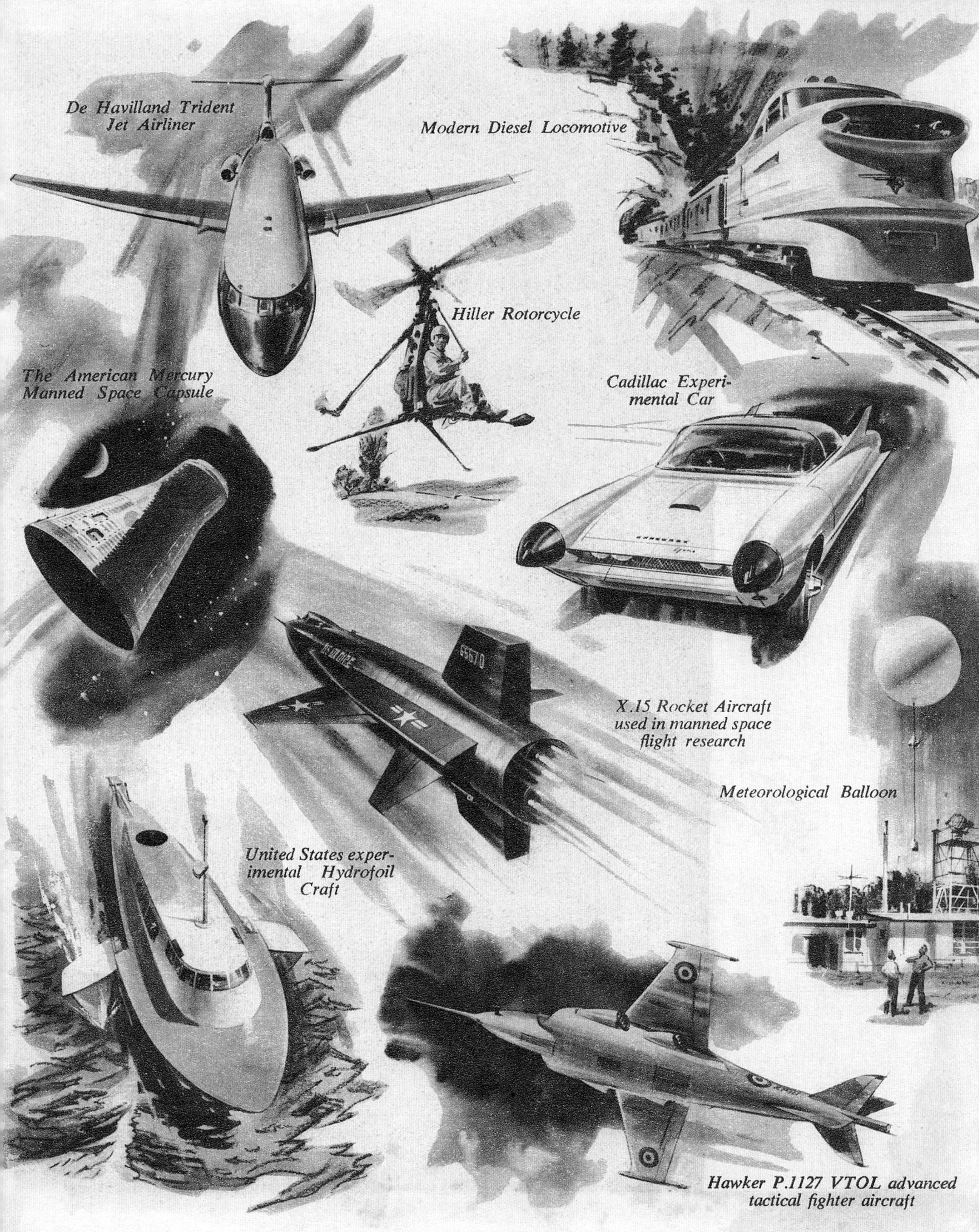

De Havilland Trident Jet Airliner
Modern Diesel Locomotive
Hiller Rotorcycle
The American Mercury Manned Space Capsule
Cadillac Experimental Car
X.15 Rocket Aircraft used in manned space flight research
Meteorological Balloon
United States experimental Hydrofoil Craft
Hawker P.1127 VTOL advanced tactical fighter aircraft

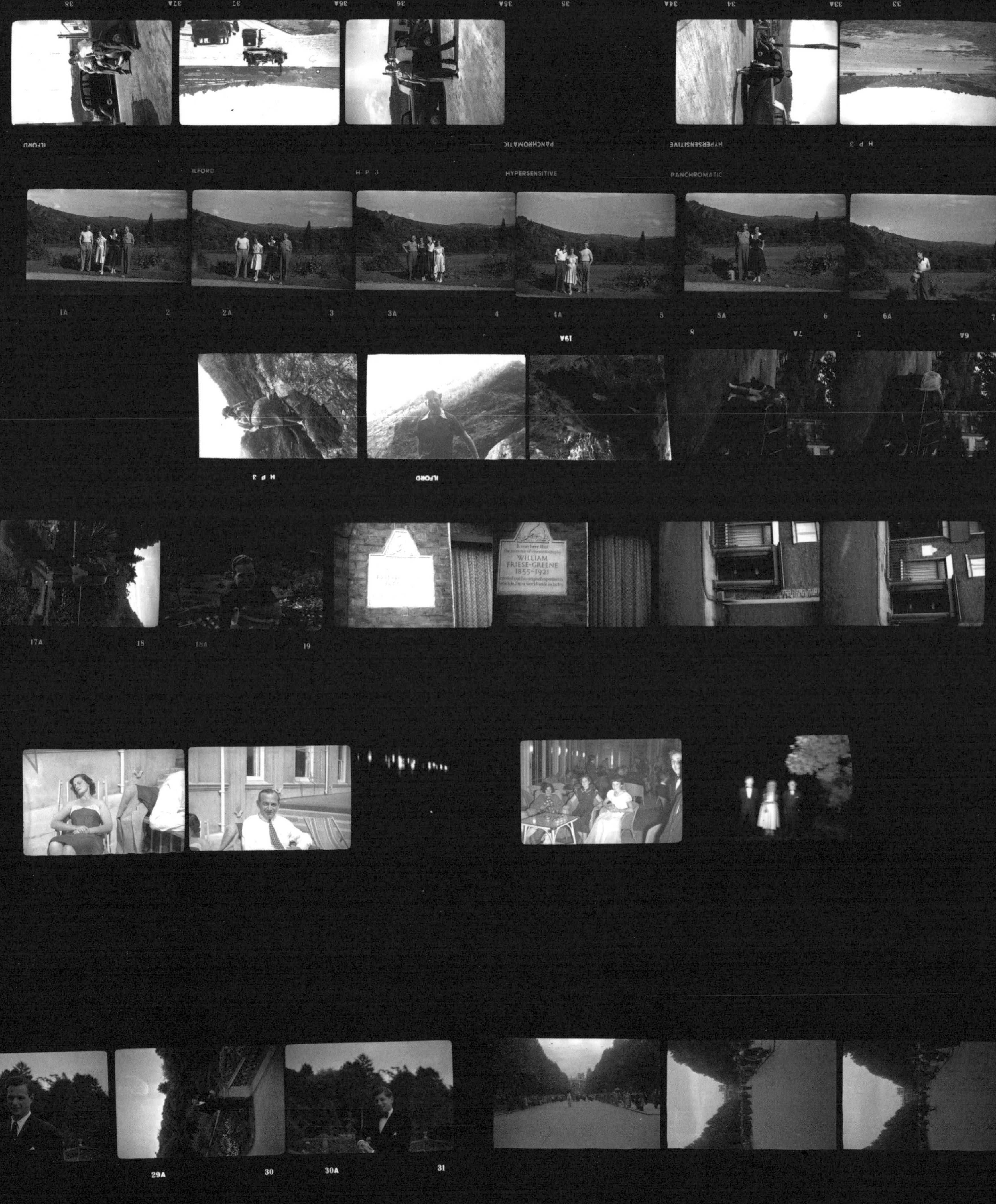